THE SACRED BOOKS OF THE EAST

F. MAX MULLER (ED.)

LIST OF THE 50 VOLUMES

1. Upanishads.
2. Sacred Laws of Aryas.
3. Texts of Confucianism.
4. Zend-Avesta.
5. Pahlavi Texts.
6. Qur'an.
7. Institutes of Vishnu.
8. Bhagavadgita, & c.
9. Qur'an.
10. (i) Dhammapada.
10. (ii) Sutta-Nipata.
11. Buddhist Suttas.
12. Satapatha-Brahmana.
13. Vinaya Texts.
14. Sacred Laws of Aryas.
15. Upanishads.
16. Texts of Confucianism.
17. Vinaya Texts.
18. Pahlavi Texts.
19. Fo-sho-hing-tsanking.
20. Vinaya Texts.
21. Saddharma Pundarika.
22. Gaina-Sutras.
23. Zend-Avesta.
24. Pahlavi Texts.
25. Laws of Manu.
26. Satapatha-Brahmana.
27. Texts of Confucianism (Li Ki).
28. Texts of Confucianism (Li Ki).
29. Grihya-Sutras.
30 Grihya-Sutras.
31. Zend-Avesta.
32. Vedic Hymns.
33. Minor Law-Books.
34. Vedanta-Sutras.
35. Milinda.
36. Milinda.
37. Pahlavi Texts.
38. Vedanta-Sutras.
39. Texts of Taoism
40. Texts of Taoism
41. Satapatha-Brahmana
42. Atharva-veda.
43. Satapatha-Brahmana.
44. Satapatha-Brahmana.
45. Gaina-Sutras.
46. Vedic Hymns.
47. Pahlavi Texts.
48. Vedanta-Sutras.
49. (i) Buddhakarita.
49. (ii) Mahayana Texts.
50. A General Index

The Sacred Books of the East, Vol. 21

THE SADDHARMA-PUNDARIKA

OR

THE LOTUS OF THE TRUE LAW

Edited by

F. MAX MULLER

Translated by

H. KERN

GYAN

Published by

GYAN

Gyan Publishing House
5, Ansari Road
Daryaganj, New Delhi-110002
Phone: 011-47034999, 9811692060
E-mail: books@gyanbooks.com

Distribution Network
gyanbooks.com
India, USA, Canada, UK, Australia, France

ISBN : 978-81-212-2937-1 (Set)
ISBN : 978-81-212-1346-2 (PB)
First Published, 1884

2nd Impression 2021

Printed at: Gyan Press, Delhi.

The Sacred Books of the East, Vol. 21

The Saddharma-Pundarika
Edited by: F. Max Muller, Translated by: H. Kern

THE

SADDHARMA-PUN*D*ARÎKA

OR

THE LOTUS OF THE TRUE LAW

TRANSLATED BY

H. KERN

Oxford

AT THE CLARENDON PRESS

1884

CONTENTS.

INTRODUCTION.

THE Saddharma-pu*nd*arîka is one of the nine Dharmas which are known by the titles of—1. Ash*t*asahasrikâ Pra*gñ*âpâramitâ; 2. Ga*nd*a-vyûha; 3. Da*s*abhûmî*s*vara; 4. Samâdhi-râ*g*a; 5. Laṅkâvatâra; 6. Saddharma-pu*nd*arîka; 7. Tathâgata-guhyaka; 8. Lalita-vistara; 9. Suvar*n*a-prabhâsa.

These nine works, to which divine worship is offered, embrace (to use the words of the first investigator of Nepalese Buddhism[1]) 'in the first, an abstract of the philosophy of Buddhism[2]; in the seventh, a treatise on the esoteric doctrines; and in the seven remaining ones, a full illustration of every point of the ordinary doctrine and discipline, taught in the easy and effective way of example and anecdote, interspersed with occasional instances of dogmatic instruction. With the exception of the first, these works are therefore of a narrative kind; but interwoven with much occasional speculative matter.'

As to the form, it would seem that all the Dharmas may rank as narrative works, which, however, does not exclude in some of them a total difference in style of composition and character. The Lalita-vistara e.g. has the movement of a real epic, the Saddharma-pu*nd*arîka has not. The latter bears the character of a dramatic performance, an undeveloped mystery play, in which the chief interlocutor, not the only

---

[1] B. H. Hodgson, Essays on the Language, Literature, and Religion of Nepál and Tibet, p. 13; cf. p. 49.

[2] As the Perfect Pra*gñ*â is she who has produced all Tathâgatas, the mother of all Bodhisattvas, Pratyekabuddhas, and Disciples (see Cowell and Eggeling, Catalogue of Buddhist Sanskrit Manuscripts, Journal of the Royal Asiatic Society, New Series, VIII, p. 3), we must infer that the work is chiefly intended to set forth the principia rerum. It begins with chaos (pradhâna or pra*gñ*â); and hence its place at the commencement of the list. We may, perhaps, best designate it as an abstract of mystic-natural or materialistic philosophy.

one, is *S*âkyamuni, the Lord. It consists of a series of dialogues, brightened by the magic effects of a would-be supernatural scenery. The phantasmagorical parts of the whole are as clearly intended to impress us with the idea of the might and glory of the Buddha, as his speeches are to set forth his all-surpassing wisdom. Some affinity of its technical arrangement with that of the regular Indian drama is visible in the prologue or Nidâna, where Ma*ñg*u*s*rî at the end prepares the spectators and auditors—both are the same—for the beginning of the grand drama, by telling them that the Lord is about to awake from his mystic slumber and to display his infinite wisdom and power.

In the book itself we find it termed a Sûtra or Sûtrânta of the class called Mahâvaipulya. In a highly instructive discussion on the peculiar characteristics and comparative age of the different kinds of Sûtras, Burnouf arrives at the conclusion that the Mahâvaipulya Sûtras are posterior to the simple Sûtras in general[1]. As there are two categories of simple Sûtras, 1. those in which the events narrated are placed contemporary with the Buddha, 2. those which refer to persons living a considerable time after his reputed period, e.g. A*s*oka[2], it follows that the composition of the Mahâvaipulya Sûtras must be held to fall in a later time than the production of even the second category of simple Sûtras. Now in one of the latter, the A*s*oka-Avadâna, we read of A*s*oka using the word dînâra[3], which leads us to the conclusion that the said Avadâna was composed, not only after the introduction of dînâra from the West, in the first century of our era or later, but at a still more modern time, when people had forgotten the foreign origin of the coin in question.

The results arrived at by Burnouf may be right so far as any Mahâvaipulya Sûtra, as a whole, is concerned; they cannot be applied to all the component parts of such a work. Not to go further than the Saddharma-pu*nd*arîka

[1] Introduction à l'histoire du Buddhisme indien, pp. 103–128.

[2] Burnouf, Introd. p. 218 seq.

[3] Burnouf, Introd. p. 423; cf. p. 431, where Pushyamitra is made to speak of Dînâras; Max Müller, History of Ancient Sanskrit Literature, p 245.

and the Lalita-vistara, it can hardly be questioned that these works contain parts of very different dates, and derived from various sources. The material discrepancies between the version in prose and that in verse are occasionally too great to allow us to suppose them to have been made simultaneously or even by different authors conjointly at work[1]. Further it can be shown that the Mahâvaipulya Sûtras are partially made up of such materials as must be referred to the oldest period of Buddhism. Let me adduce some examples to render more clear what I mean.

If we compare Lalita-vistara (Calc. ed.), p. 513, 13–p. 514, 2, with Mahâvagga (ed. Dr. Oldenberg) I, 5, 2, we perceive that the passages are to a great extent literally identical, and that the variations amount to little more than a varietas lectionis.

The passage adduced is in prose; now let us take some stanzas. In Mahâvagga I, 5, 3, the Lord utters the following *s*lokas:

> ki*kkh*ena me adhigata*m* hala*m* dâni pakâsitum,
> râgadosaparetehi nâya*m* dhammo susambudho.
> pa*t*isotagâmi nipu*n*a*m* gambhîra*m* duddasa*m* a*n*um
> râgarattâ na dakkhanti tamokhandhena âvutâ.

This does not materially differ from Lalita-vistara, p. 515, 16 seq.:

pratisrotagâmiko mârgo gambhîro durd*ri*s*o mama,
na ta*m* drakshya(n)ti[2] râgândhâ ala*m* tasmât prakâ*s*itum.
anusrota*m* pravâhyante kâmeshu patitâ*h* pra*g*â*h*;
k*rikkh*re*n*a me'ya*m* samprâptam(!) alam tasmât prakâ*s*itum.

Though there is some difference in the wording and arrangement of the verses, it is of such a kind as to exclude all idea of the compiler of the Lalita-vistara having composed the distichs himself. Even the words aya*m* dhammo susambudho and nipu*n*a*m* of the Pâli text were known to him, as appears from the passage in prose immediately preceding the *s*lokas quoted: gambhîra*h*

[1] See e.g. the foot-note, p. 413.

[2] An erroneous Sanskritisation of the present tense dakkhanti.

khalv ayam, Mahâbrahman, mayâ dharmo 'bhisambuddhah sûkshmo nipunah. What follows, api ka me, Brahman, ime gâthe abhîkshnam pratibhâsatah[1], is but a slight, not very felicitous modification of what we read in the Mahâvagga l. c.: api 'ssu bhagavantam imâ anakkhariyâ gâthâyo patibhamsu pubbe assutapubbâ.

Evidently from the same source are the verses in Trishtubh uttered by the god Brahma, Mahâvagga I, 5, 7, and those found in Lalita-vistara, p. 517, 3 seq. The former text has:

pâturahosi Magadhesu pubbe
dhammo asuddho samalehi kintito,
apâpur' etam amatassa dvâram
sunantu dhammam vimalenânubuddham[2].

The other runs thus:

vâdo babhûva samalair vikintito
dharmo hy[3] asuddho Magadheshu pûrvam;
amritam mune tad vivrinîshva dvâram
srinvanti[4] dharma vipulam[5] vimalena buddham.

On comparing the two texts we may infer that the Pâli version is purer, that vâdo babhûva is a corruption of pâdû babhûva or something like it, answering to a Sanskrit prâdur babhûva, but we cannot deny that the stanzas have the same origin.

In Mahâvagga I, 5, 12, the Lord addresses the god Brahma with the following Trishtubh:

apârutâ tesam amatassa dvârâ
ye sotavanto, pamuñkantu[6] saddham.

---

[1] Obviously an unhappy attempt to Sanskritise a Pâli or Prâkrit patibhamsu; it ought to have been pratyabhâsishtâm.

[2] The text is corrupt; we have either to read vimalânubuddham, a Tatpurusha compound expressing the same as what the text exhibits, or vimalena buddham.

[3] Hi is meaningless, and only a clumsy device to satisfy the exigency of Sanskrit phonetical rules, which are not applicable to Prâkrit.

[4] Read srinvantu.

[5] Read dharmam vimalena. Vipula probably owes its origin to a dittography.

[6] I do not understand this pamuñkantu, i. e. let them cast off, loose or emit. Perhaps we have to read payuñgantu, let them practise.

vihi*m*sasa*ññ*î pagu*n*a*m* na bhâsi
dhamma*m* pa*n*îta*m* manu*g*esu, Brahma; iti.

Then in prose: Atha kho Brahmâ Sahampati katâvakâso kho 'mhi bhagavatâ dhammadesanâyâ 'ti bhagavantam abhivâdetvâ padakkhi*n*a*m* katvâ tatth' ev' antaradhâyi.

The parallel passage in Lalita-vistara, p. 520, 19 seq., has:

apâv*ri*tâs teshâm [1] am*ri*tasya dvârâ
Brahmann iti [2] satata*m* ye *s*rotavanta*h*,
pravi*s*anti *s*raddhâ na vihe*th*asa*ṅ*g*ñ*â
*s*r*in*vanti dharma*m* Magadheshu sattvâ*h*.

Atha khalu *S*ikhî Mahâbrahmâ Tathâgatasyâdhivâsanâ*m* viditvâ tush*t*a udagra âttamanâ pramudita*h* prîtisaumanasya*g*âtas Tathâgatasya pâdau *s*irasâbhivanditvâ tatraivântaradhât.

At the meeting of the Â*g*îvaka monk Upaka and the Buddha, the latter is represented as having pronounced the following *s*lokas (Mahâvagga I, 6, 8 and 9):

na me â*k*ariyo atthi, sadiso me na vi*gg*ati,
sadevakasmi*m* lokasmi*m* n' atthi me pa*t*ipuggalo.
aha*m* hi arahâ loke, aha*m* satthâ anuttaro,
eko 'mhi sammâsambuddho, sîtibhûto 'smi nibbuto.
mâdisâ ve *G*inâ honti ye pattâ âsavakkhaya*m*,
*g*itâ me pâpakâ dhammâ tasmâham Upaka [3] *g*ino.

Materially the same *s*lokas, albeit in somewhat different arrangement, occur Lalita-vistara, p. 526, 22 seq., as being spoken at the same meeting:

â*k*âryo nahi me ka*sk*it, sad*ri*so me na vidyate,
eko 'ham asmi sambuddha*h*, *s*îtibhûto nirâsrava*h*.
aham evâha*m* [4] loke *s*âstâ hy aham anuttara*h*,
sadevâsuragandharve nâsti me pratipudgala*h* [5].

---

[1] Read tesham, if not tesam, because a contraction of am and a following vowel into one syllable is as common as one of âm is unheard of.

[2] These words do not suit the metre, and have undoubtedly been transposed from their original place, which they have kept in the Pâli text.

[3] Rather Upakâ, a common Prâkrit form of the vocative case. See Sukhâvatî-vyûha, p. xi, in Anecdota Oxoniensia, Aryan Series, vol. i, part ii.

[4] Read aham evâraha*m* (Sanskrit arhan).

[5] The Calc. ed. has wrongly °dharvo and °puṅgala*h*.

*G*inâ hi mâd*ri*s*â* *g*ñeyâ ye prâptâ âsravakshaya*m*,
*g*itâ me pâpakâ dharmâs tenopa(ka) *G*ino [hy] aham.

The following verses, taken from Mahâvagga and Lalita-vistara l. c., have likewise the same origin, notwithstanding some variations:

dhamma*k*akka*m* pavattetu*m* ga*kkh*âmi Kâsina*m* pura*m*,
andhabhûtasmi lokasmi*m* âha*ñ*hi amatadudrabhi*m*.

Compare:
Vârâ*n*asî*m* gamishyâmi gatvâ vai Kâ*s*ikâ*m* purîm,
andhabhûtasya lokasya kartâsmy asad*ri*sî*m*[1] prabhâm.
Vârâ*n*asî*m* gamishyâmi gatvâ vai Kâ*s*ikâ*m* purîm,
*s*abdahînasya lokasya tâ*d*ayishye[2] 'm*ri*tadundubhim.
Vârâ*n*asî*m* gamishyâmi gatvâ vai Kâ*s*ikâ*m* purîm,
dharma*k*akra*m* pravartishye lokeshv aprativartitam.

An important passage on the divine sight of the Buddha in Lalita-vistara, p. 439 seq., almost literally occurs in the Sâma*ññ*aphala-Sutta, as has been pointed out by Burnouf[3].

These few examples I have chosen will suffice to prove that the material of a Mahâvaipulya Sûtra is partly as old as that of any other sacred book of the Buddhists. The language of the prose part of those Sûtras does not differ from that used in the simple Sûtras of the Northern canon. Should the Sanskrit text prove to be younger than the Pâli text, then we may say that we do not possess the Northern tradition in its original shape. That result, however, affords no criterion for the distinction between the simple Sûtras and the Mahâvaipulya Sûtras, for both are written in the very same Sanskrit, if we except the Gâthâs.

It would lead me too far, were I to enter into the heart of the question which of the three idioms, Sanskrit, Pâli, and the so-called Gâthâ dialect, was the oldest scriptural language of the Buddhists, and I will therefore confine myself to a few remarks. In the first place it will be granted

---

[1] The reading aha*m* sad*ri*sî*m* of the Calc. ed. is clearly a corrupt reading.

[2] This word, which spoils the metre, has manifestly replaced an older expression, not unlikely âha*ñ*hi, or a similar form of the future tense of âhan (Sansk. âhanishye).

[3] Lotus de la bonne Loi, p. 864.

that the same person cannot have uttered any speech or stanza in two languages at the same time, and, further, that he is not likely to have spoken Sanskrit, when expressing himself in prose, and to have had recourse to a mere dialect, when speaking in poetry. One need not suppose that the common and every-day language of the god Brahma and the Buddha was Pâli or Prâkrit, in order to call it an absurdity that those persons would have spoken prose in Sanskrit and poetry in the Gâthâ dialect, such as we find in some passages already quoted and in many others. Nor is it absurd, even if we do not believe that Pâli is the original language of scripture, to contend that the Sanskrit text of the canonical works is at any rate a translation from some dialect. If the Sanskrit text of the Northern Sûtras, in general, were the original one, it would be impossible to account for occasional mistranslations and for the fact that the most palpable dialect forms have been left untouched, whenever the passage by being Sanskritised would have been spoilt. A striking instance is afforded in Lalita-vistara, p. 145. There we read that the pronouncing of the letter *th*a of the Indian alphabet is to be brought in connection with the word *th*apanîyaprasna, i.e. a question that should be avoided, set aside, Pâli *th*apanîyapañho. Here the context absolutely opposed itself to the Pâli or Prâkrit *th*apanîya being rendered by the Sanskrit sthâpanîya, because the initial syllable of this form could not be made to agree with the letter *th*a. On the same page of the Lalista-vistara we also meet with a word airapatha[1], the initial syllable of which must needs harmonise with the diphthong ai, so that airapatha did not admit of being Sanskritised into âryapatha. From the occurrence of this airapatha I infer that the original text was composed in some kind of Prâkrit, and not in regular Pâli, because the latter has lost both the primary and secondary diphthong ai, though it may be asked whether forms such as kayira (Sansk. kârya), payirupâsati

[1] Written âirapatha, for the V*ri*ddhi vowel denotes the sound of âi in Sanskrit, at least originally; from the same diphthong being used in the Asoka edicts in thaira (Sansk. sthavira), we must infer that the diphthong was, in the then Prâkrit, sounded ai, not âi.

(Sansk. paryupâsati), and the like are anything else but instances of inaccurate spelling[1]. This much is certain that thaira occurs in the inscriptions of Asoka, and in these the diphthong cannot but have the value of a short a followed by i.

If we eliminate the Sanskrit, there remain two dialects, Pâli and the Gâthâ idiom. Which of the two can lay claim to being the original language of the Buddhist scriptures or is the nearest approach to it? Pâli is intelligible in its phonetics, the Gâthâs are not. Under ordinary circumstances the comparatively greater regularity of Pâli would tend to favour its claims; the case before us is, however, so peculiar that it is not safe to draw inferences from the state in which the Gâthâs have come to us. It seems to me that the verses in the Northern books in general, as well as the prose of the Mahâvastu[2], have been Sanskritised to a large extent, so that they ought to be restored, as much as possible, to a more primitive form, before a comparison with Pâli can lead to satisfactory results. When we come across such words as heshthâd (Sansk. adhastâd), gunebhih, &c., we easily perceive that these forms are more primitive than Pâli hetthâ, gunehi; but what warrant have we of such forms being really in use at the time when the Gâthâs were composed, if we observe that in a verse, Lalita-vistara 53, the syllable bhih is reckoned as a short one in the words gunebhih pratipûrna? In short, in their present state the Gâthâs afford no conclusive evidence that the language in which they were composed is older than Pâli.

Whatever may have been the phonetic aspect of the oldest standard dialect of the Buddhists, its vocabulary is unmistakably closely related to that of the Satapatha-brâhmana. The coincidences are so striking that the

[1] That is, kayira was probably pronounced kăira, which cannot be exactly expressed by कैर, because those who were acquainted with the rules of Sanskrit grammar would pronounce this and similar words with the sound of âi.

[2] The able editor of this work, M. Senart, makes the following remarks on its language (p. xii): 'Nous sommes ici en présence d'une langue irrégulière et instable, mélange singulier de formes diverses d'âge et d'origine.'

interval separating the younger parts of the *S*atapatha and the beginnings of Buddhist literature can hardly be supposed to have been very great. Among those coincidences I cite sarvâvat, a word which as yet has not been discovered in the whole range of Sanskrit literature except *S*atap. XIV, 7, 1, 10, and in Northern Buddhist writings, as well as in Pâli (sabbâvâ). The ἅπαξ λεγόμενον ekoti *S*atap. XII, 2, 2, 4 recurs in ekoti-bhâva, Lalita-vistara, p. 147, 8[1]; p. 439, 6; Pâli ekodi-bhâva[2]. The expression samîrita in the sense of 'equipped, furnished with' occurs in *S*atapatha thrice[3], in Atharva-veda once, in Saddharma-pu*nd*arîka several times, e.g. in pa*tt*agha*nt*âsamîrita, chap. xxii. We may add the Prâkritism i*ñg* in sami*ñg*ayati, B*ri*had-âra*n*yaka VI, 4, 23, the usual form in Buddhist works in Sanskrit, Gâthâ dialect, and Pâli; further mañku, *S*atap. V, 5, 4, 11; ma*nd*a in the compound nauma*nd*a, *S*atap. II. 3, 3, 15; cf. bodhi-ma*nd*a. An archaic trait in the stanzas is the expletive use of the particle u, e.g. in teno, yeno, tasyo, adyo, for tena, yena, tasya, adya. Both in prose and poetry[4] we meet with no, sometimes in the sense of Sansk. no, which etymologically of course is identical with it, at other times in that of Sansk. na. An analogous case is Sansk. atho, almost imperceptibly differing from atha. Perhaps the most curious of similar forms in the Gâthâs is *k*o, in meaning exactly coinciding with *k*a; this *k*o I take to be the older form of the Mâgadhî *k*u in the A*s*oka edicts.

From the occurrence of peculiar old words and forms we may draw inferences as to the age of certain compositions in ordinary cases; but it is not safe to apply the same test, if there is sufficient reason to suppose that the work, the date

[1] Ekâbhibhâva of the Calc. text is a clerical blunder.

[2] See Childers' Pâli Dict. p. 134, where the Thero Subhûti's etymology eko udeti proves that he does not know the origin of the word; nor is it likely that the writer of the Pâli passage cited by Childers knew more, for had he recognised the word, he would have written ekoti, because a Prâkrit d between two vowels, if answering to a Sanskrit t, usually requires a t in Pâli.

[3] III, 5, 1, 31; VIII, 2, 6; XIV, 1, 3, 31.

[4] Also in the inscriptions of Asoka.

of which we wish to determine, has been carefully moulded upon time-honoured models. In such a case new words prove a good deal[1], old ones next to nothing. Therefore it would be an abuse of the argument ex silentio to infer from the total absence of such new words in our Saddharma-pu*nd*arîka that the bulk of the Sûtra must date from the earlier period of Buddhism.

I had already occasion to notice that the two versions, the prose and the metrical one, in our Sûtra show here and there material discrepancies. The question arises to which of the two we must award the palm of priority. Repeatedly, both in prose and poetry, the Sûtra is spoken of as consisting of stanzas; e. g. chap. vii, st. 82; chapters x and xxii in the prose portion, several times. As the term of stanza (gâthâ), for aught I know, is never used to denote a certain number of syllables, there is a strong presumption that the ancient text consisted of verses, with an admixture of short prose passages serving as introduction or to connect the more solemn poetical pieces. The idea to expand such passages into a regular prose version would especially recommend itself at a period when the poetical dialect began to become obsolete and obscure. Without being a formal commentary, the prose version would yet tend to elucidate the older holy text.

It will not be objected that, because not all chapters in the Saddharma-pu*nd*arîka have a poetical version added, the original cannot have been a poem. For the chapters containing but one version, viz. xxi, xxii, xxiii, xxv, and xxvi, show decided traces of being later additions; and as to the final chapter, it may be held to be a moderate amplification of a short prose epilogue.

In contending that the original text of our Sûtra was probably, in the main, a work in metrical form, I do not mean to say that the poetical version in all the chapters must be

[1] As e.g. the word dînâra in the Asoka Avadâna; the passage on the Greeks Yonâs, in Assalâyana Sutta (ed. Pischel), p. 10; cf. the editor's remark, p. 6; the word karama for kalama, calamus to write with, in Kâra*nd*a-vyûha (Calc. ed.), p. 69.

considered to be prior to the prose[1]. The Gâthâs of the Saddharma-pu*nd*arîka are nowhere very brilliant, but in some chapters they are so excessively clumsy and mechanically put together that involuntarily we are led to the assumption of their having been made by persons to whom the old dialect was no longer familiar. The stanzas, e.g. in chapters xi and xiv, are abominable in form, and unusually silly; those in chap. xxiv are a pattern of mechanical verse-making, and give the impression as if they were intended rather to stultify than to edify the credulous reader. Now it is a curious fact that in a Chinese preface to the translation of our Sûtra by *G*ñânagupta and Dharmagupta, A.D. 601[2], we meet with the following notice: 'The omission of the Gâthâs in No. 134, chaps. 12 and 25[3], have since been filled in by some wise men, whose example I wish to follow[4].'

Here we have a direct proof that the Gâthâs of some chapters have been added in later times. Had we similar notices concerning all the chapters in which the Gâthâs are of a comparatively modern date, and could we prove that the prose of such chapters belongs to a later period, then the supposition of the ancient text of the Saddharma-pu*nd*arîka having been in the main a metrical one would seem to lose in strength. For, reasoning by analogy, one might say that just as some later chapters have notoriously been enriched with a metrical version in later times, so the ancient parts also will have gradually received their Gâthâs. Still the fact remains that those chapters in which the metrical portion is wanting clearly belong to a later period, so that it is questionable whether their case is entirely analogous to that of the more ancient part of the whole work.

---

[1] Isolated stanzas, as in chapters xxii, xxv, and elsewhere, are wholly left out of question.

[2] Catalogue of the Tripi*t*aka (Oxford), by Mr. Bunyiu Nanjio; Sûtra Pi*t*aka, col. 45.

[3] In the English translation chapters xi and xxiv.

[4] Another notice in the above-mentioned Catalogue, col. 44, runs thus: 'The portion of prose' (of chap. xxiv) 'was translated by Kumâra*g*îva, of the latter Tshin dynasty, A.D. 384–417; and that of Gâthâs by *G*ñânagupta, of the Northern *K*eu dynasty, A.D. 557–589.' So it seems that the Gâthâs have been added, and, not unlikely, been composed, between 417 and 557 A.D.

At present we are far from the ultimate end which critical research has to reach; we are not able to assign to each part of our Sûtra its proper place in the development of Buddhist literature. We may feel that compositions from different times have been collected into a not very harmonious whole; we may even be able to prove that some passages are as decidedly ancient as others are modern, but any attempt to analyse the compound and lay bare its component parts would seem to be premature. Under these circumstances the inquiry after the date of the work resolves itself into the question at what time the book received its present shape.

There exist, as it is well known, various Chinese translations of the Saddharma-pu*nd*arîka, or parts of it, the dates of which are well ascertained. The above-mentioned Catalogue by Mr. Bunyiu Nanjio affords some valuable information about the subject, from which I borrow the following particulars[1]:

The oldest Chinese translation, known by the title of *K*an-fâ-hwâ-*k*iṅ, is from *K*u Fâ-hu (Dharmaraksha), of the Western Tsin dynasty, A.D. 265–316; in 28 chapters[2].

Equally old is an incomplete translation entitled Sâ-thân-fan-tho-li-*k*iṅ, of an unknown author.

Next in time comes the Miâo-fâ-lien-hwâ-*k*iṅ, by Kumâra*g*îva, of the latter Tshin dynasty, A.D. 384–417[3]. It agrees with the Tibetan version, and contains 28 chapters. Of one chapter (xxiv in the Nepalese MSS. and the English translation) Kumâra*g*îva translated the prose only; the Gâthâs were rendered by *G*ñânagupta, of the Northern *K*eu dynasty, A.D. 557–589.

The last translation in order of time, entitled Thien-phin-miâo-fâ-lien-hwâ-*k*iṅ, is from *G*ñânagupta and Dharmagupta, A.D. 601, of the Sui dynasty; in 27 chapters.

We see that the older translations—and, consequently, their originals—counted one chapter more than our MSS.

---

[1] Sûtra Pi*t*aka, col. 44 seqq.

[2] In S. Beal, The Buddhist Tripi*t*aka, p. 14, the name of the author *K*u Fâ-hu (Chu-fa-hu) is identified with Dharmagupta.

[3] Cf. Beal, Buddhist Tripi*t*aka, p. 15.

The difference, however, does not affect the contents of the whole, because the matter divided over chapters 11 and 12 of the older translations is contained in chap. xi of our texts and the latest Chinese version. The order of the chapters is the same in all the texts, both original and translated, up to chap. xx (=21 older division); the discrepancies first begin at chap. xxi, on Dhâra*n*îs. The subjoined comparative table, to begin with the chapter on Dhâra*n*îs, exhibits the order of the last seven chapters in the various texts. The first column refers to the Nepalese MSS. and the Chinese translation by *G*ñânagupta and Dharmagupta; the second to the oldest Chinese translation; the third to that of Kumâra*g*îva.

1	4	5
2	1	2
3	2	3
4	3	4
5	5	6
6	6	7
7	7	1

A glance at this table will suffice to convince us that chapters xxi–xxvi (1–6) are of later growth, if we bear in mind that the order of the chapters down to the Dhâra*n*îs is the same in all sources. This result is quite in harmony with what we would have guessed upon internal grounds. The last chapter, entitled Dharmaparyâya, must, from its very nature, have been the close, the epilogue of the whole. In the Chinese translation of Kumâra*g*îva it occurs, as the table shows, immediately after chap. xx, by itself a clear indication that xxi–xxvi are later additions. It is somewhat strange that in the older translation of *K*u Fâ-hu the Dharmaparyâya has already taken its place after the additional matter, but this may be explained on the supposition that Kumâra*g*îva, though living in a later time, made use of ancient manuscripts[1]. However that

[1] The preface to the Chinese translation of *G*ñânagupta and Dharmagupta says: 'The translations of *K*u Fâ-hu and Kumâra*g*îva are most probably made from two different texts.'

may be, I think that the following facts may be held to be established, both from internal and external evidence: 1. The more ancient text of the Saddharma-pu*nd*arîka contained 21 chapters and an epilogue, i.e. the matter of chaps. i–xx and of chap. xxvii; 2. The later additions, excepting probably some verses, had been connected with the work, in the way of Pari*s*ish*t*as or Addenda, about 250 A.D. or earlier. As the book, along with the Pari*s*ish*t*as, already existed some time before 250 A.D., we may safely conclude that the more ancient text in 21 chapters, the epilogue included, dates some centuries earlier. Greater precision is for the present impossible.

We know that a commentary on the Saddharma-pu*nd*arîka was composed by Vasubandhu[1]. The date of that work, not yet recovered, it seems, must fall between 550 and 600 A.D., or at least not much earlier, for Vasubandhu's pupil Gu*n*aprabha became the Guru of the famous *S*rî-Harsha, alias *S*îlâditya, king of Kanauj, the friend of Hiouen Thsang[2]. The latter often mentions Vasubandhu and some of that great doctor's writings, as well as Gu*n*aprabha[3]. As both worthies at the time of Hiouen Thsang's visiting India had already departed this life, and Vasubandhu must have been at least one generation older than Gu*n*aprabha, we cannot be far amiss in assigning to Vasubandhu's commentary the date above specified.

It appears from the above-mentioned preface to the Chinese translation of A.D. 601, that the text-differences in the MSS. current in those days were more important than such as we observe in the Nepalese MSS. from 1000 A.D. downward, with which the Tibetan closely agree. The Chinese preface is so interesting that it is worth while to

---

[1] Wassiljew, Buddhismus, p. 222. This was written before the publication of my Cambridge Lectures, 'India, what can it teach us?' and affords valuable, because independent, confirmation of the chronological system contained in Note G, 'Renaissance of Sanskrit Literature,' pp. 281–366.—The Editor, F. M. M.

[2] Wassiljew, Buddhismus, p. 78; cf. pp. 64 and 219; Târanâtha, Geschichte des Buddhismus (transl. Schiefner), p. 126.

[3] See especially Histoire de la vie de Hiouen Thsang, pp. 83, 93, 97, 114; 106.

copy a passage from it as quoted in the Catalogue of the Tripiṭaka[1]:

'The translations of *K*u Fâ-hu, No. 138, and Kumâra*g*îva, No. 134, are most probably made from two different texts. In the repository of the Canon, I (the author of the preface) have seen two texts (or copies of the text, of the Saddharma-pu*nd*arîka); one is written on the palm leaves, and the other in the letters of Kwei-tsz', or Khara*k*ar, Kumâra*g*îva's maternal country. The former text exactly agrees with No. 138, and the latter with No. 134. No. 138 omits only the Gâthâs of the Samantamukha-parivarta, chap. 24. But No. 134 omits half of the Ôshadhi-parivarta, chap. 5, the beginning of the Pa*ñk*abhikshu*s*ata-vyâkara*n*a-parivarta, chap. 8, and that of the Ŝaddharmabhâ*n*aka-parivarta, chap. 10, and the Gâthâs of the Devadatta-parivarta, chap. 12[2], and those of the Samantamukha-parivarta, chap. 25. Moreover, No. 134 puts the Dharmaparyâya-parivarta (the last chapter of the Sûtra) before the Bhaisha*g*yarâ*g*a-parivarta, chap. 23. Nos. 138 and 134 both place the Dhâra*n*î-parivarta next to the Samantamukha-parivarta, chaps. 24 and 25 respectively. Beside these, there are minor differences between the text and translation. The omission of the Gâthâs in No. 134, chaps. 12 and 25, have since been filled in by some wise men, whose example I wish to follow. In the first year of the *Z*an-sheu period, A.D. 601, I, together with *G*ñâna-gupta and Dharmagupta, have examined the palm-leaf text, at the request of a *S*rama*n*a, *S*hâṅ-hhiṅ, and found that the beginning of two chapters, 8th and 10th, are also wanting in the text (though No. 138 contains them). Nevertheless we have increased a half of the 5th chapter, and put the 12th chapter into the 11th, and restored the Dhâra*n*î-parivarta and Dharmaparyâya-parivarta to their proper order, as chaps. 21 and 27. There are also some words and passages which have been altered (while the greater

[1] Sûtra Piṭaka, col. 45.

[2] In the Nepalese MSS. and the European translations the latter part of chap. xi.

part of No. 134 is retained). The reader is requested not to have any suspicion about these differences.'

According to the opinion of an eminent Chinese scholar, the late Stanislas Julien, the translation of Kumâra*g*îva widely differs from Burnouf's. He gives utterance to that opinion in a letter dated June 12, 1866, and addressed to Professor Max Müller, to whose obliging kindness it is due that I am able to publish a specimen of Kumâra*g*îva's version rendered into French by Stanislas Julien. The fragment answers to the stanzas 1–22 of chap. iii. As it is too long to be inserted here, I give it hereafter on page xl.

On comparing the fragment with the corresponding passages in Burnouf's French translation and the English version in this volume, the reader cannot fail to perceive that the discrepancies between the two European versions are fewer and of less consequence than between each of them and Kumâra*g*îva's work. It is hardly to be supposed that the text used by Kumâra*g*îva can have differed so much from ours, and it seems far more probable that he has taken the liberty, for clearness sake, to modify the construction of the verses, a literal rendering whereof, it must be owned, is impossible in any language. It is a pity that Stanislas Julien has chosen for his specimen a fragment exclusively consisting of Gâthâs. A page in prose would have been far more useful as a test of the accuracy of the Chinese version.

Proceeding to treat of the contents of our Sûtra, I begin by quoting the passage where Burnouf, in his usual masterly way, describes the general character of the book and the prominent features of the central figure in it. The illustrious French scholar writes[1]:

'Là, comme dans les Sûtras simples, c'est Çâkya qui est le plus important, le premier des êtres; et quoique l'imagination du compilateur l'ait doué de toutes les perfections de science et de vertu admises chez les Buddhistes; quoique Çâkya revête déjà un caractère mythologique, quand il

[1] Introduction, p. 119.

déclare qu'il y a longtemps qu'il remplit les devoirs d'un Buddha, et qu'il doit les remplir longtemps encore, malgré sa mort prochaine, laquelle ne détruit pas son éternité; quoiqu'enfin on le représente créant de son corps des Buddhas qui sont comme les images et les reproductions idéales de sa personne mortelle, nulle part Çâkyamuni n'est nommé Dieu; nulle part il ne reçoit le titre d'Âdibuddha.'

To this I have nothing to object, only something to add. It is perfectly true that *S*âkya does not receive the simple title of Deva; why? Because that title is far too poor for so exalted a personage who is the Devâtideva, the paramount god of gods. So he is called in the Lotus, chap. vii, st. 31[1], and innumerable times in the whole range of Buddhist literature, both in Pâli and Sanskrit[2]. It is further undeniable that the title of Âdibuddha does not occur in the Lotus, but it is intimated that *S*âkya is identical with Âdibuddha in the words: 'From the very beginning (âdita eva) have I roused, brought to maturity, fully developed them (the innumerable Bodhisattvas) to be fit for their Bodhisattva position[3].' It is only by accommodation that he is called Âdibuddha, he properly being anâdi, i.e. existing from eternity, having no beginning. The Buddha most solemnly declares (chap. xv) that he reached Bodhi an immense time ago, not as people fancy, first at Gayâ. From the whole manner in which *S*âkya speaks of his existence in former times, it is perfectly clear that the author wished to convey the meaning that the Lord had existed from eternity, or, what comes to the same, from the very beginning, from time immemorial, &c.

*S*âkya has not only lived an infinite number of Æons in the past, he is to live for ever. Common people fancy that he enters Nirvâ*n*a, but in reality he only makes a show of Nirvâ*n*a out of regard for the weakness of men. He, the

[1] Burnouf's rendering is 'Déva supérieur aux Dévas.'

[2] Less frequent than devâtideva is the synonymous devâdhideva, e.g. Lalita-vistara, p. 131; essentially the same is the term sarvadevottama, the highest of all gods, ib. p. 144.

[3] See chap. xiv, p. 295.

Father of the world[1], the Self-born One, the Chief and Saviour[2] of creatures, produces a semblance of Nirvâna, whenever he sees them given to error and folly[3]. In reality his being is not subject to complete Nirvâna; it is only by a skilful device that he makes a show of it; and repeatedly he appears in the world of the living, though his real abode is on the summit of the Gridhrakûta[4]. All this is, in other words, the teaching of Nârâyana in Bhagavad-gîtâ IV, 6 seqq.:

> Ago 'pi sann avyayâtmâ bhûtânâm îsvaro 'pi san,
> prakritim svâm adhishthâya sambhavâmy âtmamâyayâ.
> yadâ-yadâ hi dharmasya glânir bhavati, Bhârata,
> abhyutthânam adharmasya tadâtmânam srigâmy aham.
> paritrânâya sâdhûnâm vinâsâya ka dushkritâm,
> dharmasamsthâpanârthâya sambhavâmi yuge-yuge.

The Buddha is anthropomorphic, of course; what god is not? The Lotus, far from giving prominence to the unavoidable human traits, endeavours as much as possible to represent the Lord and his audience as superhuman beings. In chap. xiv there is a great pause, as in a drama, of no less than fifty intermediate kalpas, during which Sâkyamuni and all his hearers keep silence[5]. A second pause of 1000, or according to a various reading, 100,000 years is held in chap. xx. Now it is difficult to conceive that any author, wilfully and ostentatiously, would mention such traits if he wished to impress the reader with the notion that the narrative refers to human beings.

It will not be necessary to multiply examples. There is, to my comprehension, not the slightest doubt that the

---

[1] Cf. Krishna declaring of himself in Bhagavad-gîtâ IX, 17: Pitâham gagato mâtâ dhâtâ pitâmahah. Cf. XI, 43. The significant title of Pitâmaha is given to Buddha in an inscription found at Dooriya (Bithâ); Cunningham, Archæol. Survey, vol. iii, pl. xviii; cf. p. 48.

[2] Like Nârâyana in Bhagavad-gîtâ XII, 7: Teshâm aham samuddhartâ-mrityusamsârasâgarât.

[3] Chap. xv, st. 21.

[4] Chap. xv, st. 6, 10.

[5] One intermediate kalpa is, in the system, equal to 8 yugas. As 4 yugas number 4,320,000 years, it follows that the pause lasted 432 millions of years. Esoterically, kalpa has certainly denoted a short interval of time, but even if we take the 'intermediate kalpa' to mean, in reality, a lapse of time equal to a few hours, the pause would not refer to an historical event.

Saddharma-pu*nd*arîka intends to represent *S*âkya as the supreme being, as the god of gods, almighty and all-wise. But what have we to understand by the words 'god' and 'god of gods?' that is the question. To find the answer let us recall to memory the theosophic notions prevailing in ancient India at certain periods.

In general it may be said that the Upanishads recognise two supreme beings, which in a mystical way are somehow identified; one is the great illuminator of the macrocosm, and is sometimes called the Sun, at other times Ether; the other, the enlightener of the microcosm, is Mind or Reason [1]. As soon as the Sun ceased to be considered an animate being or to be represented as such, he might continue, for worship's sake, honoris causâ, to be called the highest god; the really remaining deity was Reason, poetically termed the inward light. This idea is expressed by Nîlaka*nth*a in his commentary on Bhagavad-gîtâ V, 14, in the following terms: Prabhu*s k*idâtmâ sûrya ivâsmadâdînâm prakâ*s*aka*h*, the Lord (is) the intelligent Self that like a sun is the illuminator of ourselves and others [2]. Now the same author, in his notes on Bhagavad-gîtâ VI, 30, distinctly states that our inward consciousness, or as he puts it, the pratyagâtman, the individual Self, otherwise called *g*îva, is Nârâya*n*a, i.e. the supreme being. At IX, 28 he paraphrases Nârâya*n*a by sarveshâm pratyagâtman, the individual consciousness of all (sentient beings); at XII, 14 he identifies Nârâya*n*a with nirgu*n*am brahma. Just as here and there Nârâya*n*a is represented as clad in all the glory and majesty of a sovereign, as the illuminator, the vivifier of the world, in one word as the sun, so we find *S*âkyamuni invested with all the grandeur and all the resources of a ruler of nature. Philosophically, both Nârâya*n*a and his counterpart *S*âkyamuni are purushottama, paramâtman, the highest brahman, Mind. *S*âkyamuni

[1] See e.g. *Kh*ândogya-upanishad III, 18 and 19; cf. Bhagavad-gîtâ XV, 12.

[2] Cf. Bhagavad-gîtâ XIII, 33: yathâ prakâ*s*ayaty eka*h* k*ri*tsna*m* lokam ima*m* ravi*h*, kshetra*m* kshetrî tathâ k*ri*tsnam prakâ*s*ayati, Bhârata. The kshetra here is the body, the kshetrin is Mind, Reason, âtman. Cf. *S*a*n*kara on *Kh*ândogya-upanishad, l. c.

is, esoterically, the very same muni, the beholder of good and evil, the punyapâpekshitâ muni that is spoken of in Manu VIII, 91. It is acknowledged in Bhagavad-gîtâ IX, 14 seqq. that the supreme being may be conceived and respected in different ways according to the degree of intelligence of creatures. Some pay their worship by leading a virtuous life, others by pious devotion, others by contemplation, others by confessing a strictly monistic philosophy[1], others by acknowledging a personal god[2]. The Lord in the Saddharma-pundarîka admits of being viewed in all these various aspects. Whether the Buddha-theory, such as we find it developed in the Sûtra, not in plain words, indeed, but by circumlocutions and ambiguities, should be called atheistic or not, is a matter of comparatively slight importance, about which opinions may differ. This much, however, may be asserted, that the Lotus and the Bhagavad-gîtâ are, in this respect, exactly on a par.

The conclusion arrived at is that the *S*âkyamuni of the Lotus is an ideal, a personification, and not a person. Traits borrowed, or rather surviving, from an older cosmological mythology, and traces of ancient nature-worship abound both in the Lotus and the Bhagavad-gîtâ, but in the highest sense of the word, paramârthatas, the Purushottama in both is the centre of mental life. It is just possible that the ancient doctors of the Mahâyâna have believed that such an ideal once walked in the flesh here on earth, but the impression left by the spirit and the letter of the whole work does not favour that supposition. In later times fervent adherents of the Mahâyâna really held that belief, as we know from the example of the pious Hiouen Thsang, who was evidently as earnest in his belief that the Lord once trod the soil of India as he was convinced of Mañgusrî, Maitreya, and Avalokitesvara existing as animated beings. Whether the system of the Lotus can be said to agree with what is supposed to be 'genuine' Bud-

[1] The followers of the Upanishads, Aupanishadas, who say, 'Myself am God,' or as Nîlakantha puts it, 'Myself am the Lord Vâsudeva.'

[2] According to Nîlakantha the common people, who think, 'He, the Lord, is my Master.'

dhism, it is not here the place to discuss. So far as the Northern Church is concerned, the book must be acknowledged as the very cream of orthodoxy; it is the last, the supreme, the most sublime of the Sûtras exposed by the Lord; it is, so to say, the *siromani*, the crown jewel, of all Sûtras[1].

The contents of the separate chapters into which the Sûtra is divided may be described, summarily, as follows:

1. Prologue.

2. Awakening of the Lord from his mystic trance; display of his transcendent skilfulness, proved by the apparent trinity of vehicles, whereas in reality there is but one vehicle.

3. Prophecy of the Lord regarding the future destiny of *S*âriputra, his eldest son. Second turn of the wheel of the law on that occasion, with incidental commemoration of the first turn near Benares. Parable of the burning house, to exemplify the skill of the good father in saving his children from the burning pains of mundane existence.

4. Another parable, exemplifying the skill of the wise father in leading a child that has gone astray and lost all self-respect back to a feeling of his innate nobility and to happiness.

5. Parable of the plants and the rain, to exemplify the impartiality and equal care of the Lord for all creatures[2]. Parable of the blind man, to intimate that the phenomena have but an apparent reality, and that the ultimate goal of all endeavours must be to reach all-knowingness, which in fact is identical with complete nescience.

6. Sundry predictions as proofs of the power of the Sugata to look into the future.

7. He has an equal knowledge of the remotest past; his remembrance of the turning of the wheel by the Tathâgata Mahâbhi*gñ*â*gñ*ânâbhibhû. Edifying history of the sixteen sons of the said Tathâgata.

---

[1] Chap. xiii, st. 53 seq.

[2] Cf. Bhagavad-gîtâ IX, 29, where Nârâya*n*a declares: 'I am equal towards all creatures, none is hateful to me, none beloved;' samo 'ha*m* sarvabhûteshu, na me dveshyo 'sti na priya*h*.

8. Prophecy regarding five hundred Arhats.

9. Prophecy concerning Ânanda, Râhula, and the two thousand monks.

10. The Lord teaches how pious preachers of the law, who will come in after-times, ought to be duly honoured, and promises that he will always protect the ministers of religion.

11. Display of the miraculous power of Sâkyamuni shown in the appearance of a Stûpa, which, being opened by him, discloses to sight the frame of the expired Tathâgata Prabhûtaratna, who is desirous of hearing the exposition of the Lotus of the True Law. How Sâkyamuni in a former birth strove to acquire the Lotus. His great obligations to Devadatta. Episode of the wise daughter of the Ocean and her change of sex.

12. Prediction to Gautamî, Yasodharâ, and the nuns in their train. Promise of the host of disciples and Bodhisattvas to take up the difficult task of preaching the holy word in days to come, after the Lord's Nirvâna.

13. Vocation of the ministers of religion, and practical rules for their conduct in and out of society. Parable of the king who rewards his valiant warriors; in the same manner the Buddha will reward those who struggle for his sake, by bestowing upon them all kinds of favours, at last the most valuable of his boons—eternal rest.

14. Splendid phantasmagory of innumerable Bodhisattvas evoked by the creative power of the Lord. Long pause, during which the Tathâgata and the four classes of hearers are silent. Perplexity of Maitreya on hearing that the innumerable Bodhisattvas have all been the pupils of the Lord.

15. The Buddha explains the fact by revealing the immense duration of his lifetime, in the past and the future.

16. Meritoriousness of the belief in the immense duration of the Tathâgatas and all those who have once become Buddhas.

17. The Lord details the great merit attending a ready acceptance of the preaching of the law.

18. Exposition of the advantages, worldly and spiritual, enjoyed by the ministers of religion.

19. Story of Sadâparibhûta, exemplifying the superiority of simple-mindedness and pure-heartedness to worldly wisdom and scepticism.

20. Grand show exhibited by the two Tathâgatas *S*âkyamuni and Prabhûtaratna conjointly[1]. Pause after the performance. After the pause a great stir amongst gods, celestial and infernal beings, men, &c.[2] The Tathâgata extols the Sûtra of the Lotus in which 'all Buddha-laws are succinctly taught,' as well as the keepers of this most eminent of Sûtras.

Immediately after this chapter may have followed, in the oldest version, the epilogue entitled 'Period of the Law;' the reasons for this opinion have been already stated above. The supposed additional chapters contain the following topics, briefly indicated:

21. Efficacy of talismanic spells (Dhâra*n*îs).

22. Self-sacrifice of the Bodhisattva Sarvasattvapriyadar*s*ana, otherwise called Bhaisha*g*yarâ*g*a. Glorification of the Lotus as the most eminent of Sûtras.

23. Visit of the Bodhisattva Gadgadasvara to the Saha-world. Extraordinary qualities and achievements of this worthy, incidentally narrated by the Tathâgata. Return of the Bodhisattva to whence he came.

24. Grandeur and ubiquitousness of Avalokite*s*vara.

25. Wonderful and edifying story of the conversion of the king *S*ubhavyûha through the instrumentality of his two sons Vimalagarbha and Vimalanetra, al. Bhaisha*g*yarâ*g*a and Bhaisha*g*yasamudgata.

26. The Bodhisattva Samantabhadra charges himself with the task of being a protector to the preachers of religion in after-times after the Lord's Nirvâ*n*a[3].

---

[1] Both stretch their flaming tongues as far as the Brahma-world. In the Bhagavad-gîtâ XI, 30 it is said of Nârâya*n*a, when at the request of Ar*g*una he shows himself in his full grandeur: lelihyase grasamâna*h* samantâl lokân samagrân vadanair *g*valadbhi*h*, te*g*obhir âpûrya *g*agat samagram bhâsas tavogrâ*h* prapatanti, Vish*n*o!

[2] Cf. Bhagavad-gîtâ XI, 15.

[3] There is some incongruity between this chapter and chapter x, because

This summary, however meagre, will be sufficient to show that there is no lack of variety in our Sûtra. We may, indeed, be satisfied that the compilers of it intended giving an exposition of the principal truths of their religion in general, and of the peculiar tenets of their own system[1] in particular, the whole with anxious care arranged in such a form that the Sûtra admitted of an exoterical and esoterical interpretation. It contains a revelation of the state of things in the present, as well as in the past and the future, a revelation derived from a virtually eternal source, so that the doctrine taught in it must be deemed valid not only for a certain spiritual brotherhood or church, but for the human race at large. The highest authority to whom the doctrine is referred, is not a certain individual having lived a short span of time somewhere in India, but the sublime being who has his constant abode on the G*ri*dhrakû*t*a, i.e. he who is the terminology of other Indian creeds is called Kû*t*astha.

As a general rule it may be said that in such works of ancient Indian literature as are anonymous, we must distinguish between the authority and the author. In the Lotus we meet after the invocation in some MSS. the following distich:

Vaipulyasûtrarâ*g*am paramârthanayâvatâranirde*s*am ।
Saddharmapu*nd*arîka*m* sattvâya mahâpatha*m* vakshye ॥

I.e. 'I shall proclaim the king of the Vaipulya-sûtras, that teacheth how one arrives at the (right) method of attaining the highest truth; the Saddharma-pu*nd*arîka, the great road (leading) to substantiality (being in abstracto).' The person here speaking is not the Buddha, who is neither the author nor the writer of the work. Have we then to ascribe the distich to one of the ancient copyists? Burnouf[2] decidedly thinks so, and his opinion is corroborated by the fact that the verses do not occur in all MSS. I must con-

in the latter it is the Lord himself who promises to be in future the protector of the preachers.

[1] I.e. of the Mahâyâna, which according to Târanâtha, Geschichte des Buddhismus, p. 274, stands above the division of the Bauddhas into various schools.

[2] Lotus, p. 285.

fess that I am not so sure of it. As the Sûtra, like other compositions of the kind, begins with the solemn 'Thus have I heard, &c.,' it is at least possible that the distich belongs to the compiler. I am not aware that the scribes were in the habit of using such expressions as va*k* or synonymous terms instead of likh, to write; and as we find in the Mahâvastu similar futures as vakshye, viz. udîrayishya*m̃* and upavar*n*ayishyâmi[1], where they can hardly be imputed to the scribe, it is safer to leave the question, whether the opening distich of the Lotus is the work of a compiler or of a copyist, undecided, the more so because the parallel phrase athâto—vyâkhyâsyâma*h*, frequently found immediately after the invocation, in non-Buddhistic writings, must be held to refer to the author or authors, compilers.

The Lotus being one of the standard works of the Mahâyâna, the study of it cannot but be useful for the right appreciation of that remarkable system. A perusal of the book will convince the reader that a statement of Professor Wassiljew's[2] can only be accepted with some restrictions, when this scholar, so profoundly versed in the history and development of Northern Buddhism, says that the Buddha of the Mahâyâna is 'neither the creator nor the ruler of the world; he remains the same cold, indifferent egoist, absorbed in Nothingness.' The Tathâgata of the Lotus is passionless, indeed, but that does not involve his being an egoist. In general it may be said that the spirit of the Mahâyâna is more universal, its ideal less monastical than the Hînayâna's. According to Professor Rhys Davids we must not seek the superior vital power which enabled the Great Vehicle to outlive the earlier teaching in certain metaphysical subtleties, but in the idea of a desire to save all living creatures; 'the idea,' to quote his own words[3], 'as summarised in the theory of Bodisatship, is the key-note of the later school, just as Arahatship is the key-note of

[1] Mahâvastu (ed. Senart), p. 1, with the remarks of the editor, and p. 9.
[2] In his Buddhismus, p. 126.
[3] In Lectures on the Origin and Growth of Religion, p. 254.

early Buddhism.' The Mahâyâna doctors said in effect: 'We grant you all you say about the bliss of attaining Nirvâna in this life[1]. But it produces advantage only to yourselves; and according to your own theory there will be a necessity for Buddhas in the future as much as there has been for Buddhas in the past. Greater, better, nobler then, than the attainment of Arahatship must be the attainment of Bodisatship from a desire to save all living creatures in the ages that will come.' The teaching of the Lotus, however, is different, and comes to this, that every one should try to become a Buddha. It admits that from a practical point of view one may distinguish three means, so-called Vehicles, yânas, to attain the summum bonum, Nirvâna, although in a higher sense there is only one Vehicle. These means are, in plain language, piety, philosophy or rather Yogism, and striving for the enlightenment and weal of our fellow-creatures; these means are designated by the terms of Vehicle of (obedient) hearers or disciples, of Pratyekabuddhas, and of Bodhisattvas. Higher than piety is true and self-acquired knowledge of the eternal laws; higher than knowledge is devoting oneself to the spiritual weal of others[2]. The higher unity embracing the three separate Vehicles is the Buddha-vehicle.

The title of Bodhisattva is not always used in the same acceptation. Apart from a broad distinction we can draw

[1] It may be observed that there is nothing peculiarly Buddhistic in the searching for Nirvâna in this life, except in the sound of the word. It is exactly the same as what other Indian enthusiasts or mystics called *G*îvanmukti, the aim of Yogins in the fourth degree (answering to the Arhats of the Buddhists) and of the Brâhmans or Dvi*g*as in the fourth Âsrama.

[2] See chap. iii, p. 80. Something similar in Bhagavad-gîtâ XII, 12: sreyo hi *gñ*ânam abhyâsâ*g* *gñ*ânâd dhyâna*m* visishyate, dhyânât karmaphalatyâgas tyâgâ*k* *kh*ântir anantaram; and IV, 5: labhante brahmanirvâ*n*am *r*ishaya*h* kshî*n*akalmashâ*h*, *kh*innadvaidhâ yatâtmâna*h* sarvabhûtahite ratâ*h*. Neither in these passages of the Bhagavad-gîtâ nor in the three Vehicles is there anything new; abhyâsa, study, denotes the period of one's studying under a master, the Brahma*k*âriship, which the Lotus calls the Vehicle of Disciples; the period of dhyâna, alias the Vehicle of Pratyekabuddhas, coincides with the third Âsrama, that of Vânaprastha; the tyâga, alias Bodhisattvaship, is virtually the same with the life of a Sannyâsin, Yati, or Mukta. *Gñ*âna characterises the second Âsrama; in the Lotus it is merged in or combined with dhyâna.

between human and superhuman Bodhisattvas[1]—the latter are here left out of account—we find sometimes the word applied to those persons who in the passage of our Sûtra alluded to are styled *S*râvakas, hearers, learners. This appears to be the case at least in Nepâl, as we know from the following passage[2]: 'The Buddha is the adept in the wisdom of Buddhism (Bodhijnána), whose first duty, so long as he remains on earth, is to communicate his wisdom to those who are willing to receive it. These willing learners are the "Bodhisattvas," so called from their hearts being inclined to the wisdom of Buddhism, and "Sanghas," from their companionship with one another, and with their Buddha or teacher, in the viháras or cœnobitical establishments. The Bodhisattva or Sangha continues to be such until he has surmounted the very last grade of that vast and laborious ascent by which he is instructed that he can "scale the heavens," and pluck immortal wisdom from its resplendent source: which achievement performed, he becomes a Buddha, that is, an Omniscient Being.'

Here the Bodhisattvas are plainly distinguished from the cœnobitical monks; they are so likewise in the Lotus[3], in which we find them also in the function of learned or wise men (Pa*nd*itas), of preachers or ministers of religion. Wassiljew l.c. remarks about the Bodhisattva—the terrestrial one of course—that 'from one side, he seems to be the substitute of the ancient Bhikshu;' from which we ought not to infer that the mendicant monks, as such, ceased to exist, for that is notoriously not the case, but that the Bodhisattvas were charged with the office of preaching. They are persons who deserve to be honoured both by mendicant monks and lay devotees[4], and formed, it would seem, a kind of learned clergy, not to be confounded, however, with the modern Va*g*ra-Â*k*âryas or married clergymen in Nepâl. There is reason to suppose that one of the

---

[1] Cf. Wassiljew, Buddhismus, p. 124.

[2] B. H. Hodgson, Essays, p. 62. Cf. Stanislas Julien, Voyages des Pèlerins bouddhistes, II, p. 436 note.

[3] See especially the whole of chapter x.

[4] Lotus, chap. x, st. 27 seq.

honorific titles given to the preachers or interpreters of the law was 'wise' or 'learned man,' Pandita, for the word is so often applied to them that it looks more like a title than a common epithet[1]. Târanâtha knows Pandita to be a title[2], and considers it to be the equivalent of the older Mahâbhadanta; he distinguishes 'Bodhisattvas' from 'common Panditas' and 'Arhats.' How does this agree with the data in the Lotus? As it has been intimated in a foregoing note, the three Vehicles are imitations of three Âsramas or stages in the model life of an Ârya, in the first place of a Brâhman. The stages are that of a student, of a hermit living in the forest, and of a Sannyâsin, Yati, or Mukta, who has wholly given up the world. The second stage, that of a householder, does not exist, of course, for those who vow themselves to a monastic life. Our Sûtra does not prescribe that the three stages must be gone through by the same persons, no more than the Bhagavadgîtâ l.c. requires that one should pass the stages of study, knowledge, and meditation before resolving upon complete renunciation (tyâga); what follows from the context is only this, that the Vehicle of Bodhisattvas, alias those who strive for the weal of all creatures, is superior to the two preceding Vehicles. The Vehicle of the Bodhisattvas being the loftiest of the three, they themselves must be considered as occupying the highest rank. Now Târanâtha places the Arhats above them, and with the Nepalese also the first class of the monastic order is that of Arhat[3]. The question is, how are we to judge of the relation between Arhats and Bodhisattvas in the Lotus? As far as I am able to see, the compiler[4] of the Sûtra describes facts, or supposed facts, which he knew from oral or literary tradition, as having occurred in the past, whereas the actual state of things in his own time and shortly before is represented as that of the future. His Arhats are sages of the past, canonized saints; his human Bodhisattvas are sages,

[1] E.g. Lotus, chap. x, st. 4, cf. 6; 23, 33; xiii, 13, 16, 24, 26, 30, 32, 39, 44.
[2] Geschichte des Buddhismus, p. 60.
[3] Hodgson, Essays, p. 52; cf. p. 30.
[4] The reader should not lay stress upon this singular.

wise men of the present, most reverend worthies who should live a saintly life and generally do so, but who, however sanctimonious, are not acknowledged saints. Of an antagonism between Arhats and Bodhisattvas there is no trace in the book; the Arhats being dead, they cannot be active; the Bodhisattvas as living persons, can[1]. In a certain respect, then, the remark of Professor Rhys Davids holds good; the Bodhisattvas represent the ideal of spiritual activity, the Arhats of inactivity. It must be admitted that the Lotus, as a whole, breathes a less monastic and ascetic[2] spirit; it does not go the length to speak of ascetism and mortification in such scornful terms as the Bhagavad-gîtâ[3] does, but at the same time it never extols it. There are in the book many indications that the art of preaching was made much of and highly developed, and it may be supposed that a greater proficiency in hermeneutics combined with superior mental activity has enabled the Mahâyâna to supplant its rival, the Hînayâna, and to extend its spiritual conquests once from the snows of Siberia to the luxuriant islands of the Indian Archipelago.

After having touched upon such points in the text of the Saddharma-pu*nd*arîka as seemed to require more special notice, it behoves me to say a few words about the translation and its resources. In the first place, I must declare that I cannot speak in too warm terms of the benefit I have derived from the French translation by the illustrious Burnouf. I have taken that work throughout for my model, without having been able to reach its excellency. The material discrepancies between his translation are partly due to my having followed other MSS., partly to another interpretation, especially of frequently corrupt and difficult Gâthâs. If some reader not acquainted

[1] Something of contempt for the Arhats is shown in the story communicated by Hiouen Thsang in Voyages des Pèlerins bouddhistes, II, p. 176, where the editor inadvertently writes Vasubandhu instead of Vasumitra; his index affords the means of correcting the mistake; cf. Wassiljew in Târanâtha, p. 298.

[2] See chap. xiii, 28, where the eighth commandment of the Dasasîla, forbidding the use of ointment, is slighted.

[3] See there xvii, 5 seqq., and cf. 14 seqq., where we are taught what the true tapas should be.

with the peculiar difficulties of those Gâthâs should wonder at the occurrence of numerous discrepancies, I would repeat the words of the preface to the Chinese version from A.D. 601, and request him 'not to have any suspicion about these differences.' Let him compare the fragment from Kumâragîva's rendering on page xl with the corresponding passages in the French and English translations, and he will observe that the difference between the work of the learned Buddhist of the fourth century and the two European versions is far more considerable than between the latter.

The base of my translation has been an old manuscript on palm leaves, belonging to Dr. D. Wright's collection, in the University Library of Cambridge. The manuscript is dated Newar, era 159 (=A.D. 1039), and was written in the reign of the king Kâmadeva (?), in the bright half of the month Vaisâkha, on a Thursday[1]. It is one of the most ancient Sanskrit MSS. existing in Europe, and therefore I thought that it was advisable to follow its readings as much as possible, except in such passages as were evidently corrupt. A second MS., unfortunately incomplete, from the same collection, is of unknown date, since the latter part of the codex is lost; from the form of the characters it may be inferred that it is not much more modern than the other codex[2]. The difference between both is not very great; yet there can be no doubt that the second MS. belongs to another family. The varietas lectionis is strikingly similar in kind to what we find in the different texts of the Vagrakkhedikâ, edited by Professor Max Müller.

The former manuscript has much in common with the London codices, from which Burnouf in the notes on his translation has derived numerous various readings; it stands farther off from the Paris MS. that has formed the base of Burnouf's version, but not so far as the second

[1] Samvat 159 Vaisâkhasukle (illegible the Tithi) Gurudine, Kâmadevasya vigayarâgye likhitam iti. There seem to be wanting two syllables before kâma.

[2] The two Cambridge MSS. are marked Add. 1682 and 1683.

Cambridge MS., which shows the greatest number of peculiar readings. The text of chapter iv in Professor Foucaux's edition of the Parabole de l'enfant égaré is comparatively modern and bad. In general it may be said that all the known copies of the Saddharma-pu*nd*arîka are written with a want of care little in harmony with the holy character of the book.

Before closing this preface I beg to offer my sincere thanks to Professors William Wright and E. B. Cowell, at Cambridge, for the generous way in which they have enabled me to use the MSS. I wanted for my translation. My thanks are due also to the Council of Cambridge University and Mr. H. Bradshaw, for their readily complying with my wishes. To Professor Max Müller I owe a debt of gratitude for his kindly assisting me in my task in more than one respect, a debt which I am glad here openly to acknowledge.

H. KERN.

LEIDEN.

KUMÂRAGÎVA'S TRANSLATION OF SADDHARMA-PUNDARÎKA III, STANZAS 1–22, RENDERED INTO FRENCH BY STANISLAS JULIEN.

J'ai entendu le son de cette loi
J'ai obtenu ce que je n'avais pas encore eu
Dans mon cœur, j'en ai conçu une grande joie.
Les filets des doutes ont tous disparu
Jadis, j'ai reçu les instructions du Buddha
Je n'ai pas perdu le grand véhicule.
Le son (la voix) du Buddha existe (s'entend) très rarement.—
Elle peut détruire les tourments d'esprit de tous les mortels.—
Moi, j'ai obtenu l'épuisement (la délivrance complète) de mes fautes.
L'ayant entendue, j'ai été délivré des chagrins et des tourments d'esprit
Moi, lorsque je demeure sur les montagnes (ou dans) les vallées,
Ou bien au bas des arbres des forêts
Soit que je sois assis ou que je marche
Constamment, je pense à cette chose
Hélas, je m'adresse de sevères reproches
Je dis : pourquoi me trompé-je moi-même ?
Nous autres, nous sommes aussi les fils du Bouddha
Nous sommes entrés ensemble dans la loi exempts d'imperfections.
Nous ne pourrons dans l'avenir
Expliquer cette loi sans supérieure (anuttaradharma).
Les trente deux couleur d'or (signes qui ont la couleur de l'or),
Les dix forces, les moyens de délivrance,
Se trouvent ensemble au sein de la loi unique
Et cependant je n'ai pu obtenir ces choses ;
Les quatre vingt signes de beauté,
Les dix huit lois non-communes (à tous),
Les mérites et les vertus de cette sorte
Moi, je les ai tous perdus.
Moi, lorsque je me promenais seul
J'ai vu le Bouddha au milieu de la grande multitude
Son nom, sa réputation remplissaient les dix contrées
Il comblait d'avantages toutes les créatures

Je pense en moi-même que j'ai perdu ce profit
Moi, parce que je me suis trompé moi-même,
Constamment, jour et nuit
Chaque fois, je songe à cette chose
J'ai voulu demander à l'honorable du siècle
Louant et glorifiant les bôdhisattvas
C'est pourquoi jour et nuit
J'examine mûrement une telle chose
Exempte d'imperfections et difficile à concevoir
Qui fait arriver la multitude à l'estrade de l'Intelligence (Bôdhimanda)
Moi, dans l'origine, j'étais attaché aux vues perverses (à l'hérésie)
J'étais un maître de Brahmatcharis
L'honorable du siècle connaissait mon cœur
Me tira de l'hérésie et me parla du Nirvâna
Je me débarrassai complétement des vues perverses (de l'hérésie);
Dans la loi du vide, j'obtins des témoignages, des preuves (J'obtins la preuve que je comprenais la loi du vide)
Alors, je me dis à moi-même
Que j'avais obtenu d'arriver au Nirvâna.
Mais maintenant je m'aperçois
Que ce n'est pas le vrai Nirvâna
Si, un jour, j'obtiens de devenir Bouddha
Et que je sois pourvu des trente deux signes de beauté
Les Dêvas, les Yakchas
Les dragons, les esprits etc.
M'honoreront et me vénéreront
Dans ce temps là, je pourrai dire
Que pour toujours j'ai obtenu le Nirvâna complet.
Le Bouddha, dans la grande assemblée
M'a dit que je devais devenir Bouddha
Quand j'eus entendu le son de cette loi
Mes doutes, mes regrets, complétement disparurent.
Au commencement, lorsque j'eus entendu ce que disait le Bouddha,
Au fond de mon cœur, je fus remplis d'étonnement et de doutes.
(Je me dis) Le démon n'aurait pas pris la figure du Bouddha
Pour troubler mon cœur?
Le Bouddha ayant employé toute sorte de moyens
De comparaisons, de paroles et de discours habiles
Mon cœur devint calme comme la mer.
Quand je l'eus entendu, le filet de mes doutes se déchira
Le Bouddha dit que dans les siècles passés

Des bouddhas sans nombre, qui ont obtenu le Nirvâ*n*a
Reposaient en paix au milieu des moyens habiles
Et que tous avaient expliqué cette loi
Que des bouddhas présents et futurs
Dont le nombre est infini
A l'aide de toute sorte de moyens habiles
Avaient expliqué et développé une telle loi
Maintenant, Honorable du siècle
Depuis que tu es né et que tu es sorti de la famille
Tu as obtenu de tourner la roue de la loi
Et de l'expliquer par des moyens habiles
L'Honorable du siècle a exposé la vraie voie.
Le Mâra n'a pas fait cette chose (n'a pas pris la figure du Bouddha)
C'est pourquoi je sais fermement
Que le Mâra ne s'est pas déguisé en Bouddha (litt. ne s'est pas fait Bouddha).
Moi, à cause du filet des doutes auxquels je m'étais abandonné
Je m'étais dit que c'était une chose faite par le Mâra (c. à. d. que le Mâra avait pris la figure du Bouddha)
Mais quand j'eus entendu sa voix douce et souple
Profonde, éloignée, extrêmement déliée
Expliquant la loi pure
Mon cœur a été grandement rejoui.
Mes doutes ont pour toujours disparu
Je réside en paix au sein de la vraie science
Décidément, je dois devenir Bouddha.
Je serai respecté des Dêvas
Je tournerai la roue de la loi sans-supérieure
J'instruirai et je convertirai les Bôdhisattvas.

SADDHARMA-PU*N*D*A*RÎKA

OR

THE LOTUS OF THE TRUE LAW.

HOMAGE TO
ALL THE BUDDHAS AND BODHISATTVAS.

CHAPTER I.

INTRODUCTORY.

Thus have I heard. Once upon a time the Lord was staying at Râ*g*agr*i*ha, on the Gr*i*dhrakû*t*a[1] mountain, with a numerous assemblage of monks, twelve hundred monks, all of them Arhats, stainless, free from depravity, self-controlled[2], thoroughly emancipated in thought and knowledge, of noble breed, (like unto) great elephants, having done their task, done their duty, acquitted their charge, reached the goal; in whom the ties which bound them to existence were wholly destroyed, whose minds were thoroughly emancipated by perfect knowledge, who had reached the utmost perfection in subduing all their thoughts; who were possessed of the transcendent faculties[3];

[1] I. e. Vulture Peak.

[2] Va*s*îbhûta. Like va*s*in, it likewise means, 'having subdued others or the world.'

[3] The five Abhi*gñ*âs, viz. the magical powers, the divine ear,

eminent disciples, such as the venerable Âgñâta-Kaundinya, the venerable Asvagit, the venerable Vâshpa, the venerable Mahânâman, the venerable Bhadrika[1], the venerable Mahâ-Kâsyapa, the venerable Kâsyapa of Uruvilvâ, the venerable Kâsyapa of Nadî, the venerable Kâsyapa of Gayâ[2], the venerable Sâriputra, the venerable Mahâ-Maudgalyâyana[3], the venerable Mahâ-Kâtyâyana[4], the venerable Aniruddha[5], the venerable Revata, the venerable Kapphina[6], the venerable Gavâmpati, the venerable Pilindavatsa, the venerable Vakula, the venerable Bhâradvâga[7], the venerable Mahâ-Kaushthila[8], the venerable Nanda (alias Mahânanda), the venerable

---

knowledge of the thoughts of others, knowledge of former existences, the divine eye. Sometimes a sixth Abhigñâ is added, viz. the knowledge which causes the destruction of human passion; Burnouf, Lotus, p. 820 sqq.; Spence Hardy, Eastern Monachism, p. 284.

[1] These are known as the Five Bhadravargîyas, or, in Pâli, Pañkavaggîyas; they were the first five disciples.

[2] The conversion of Kâsyapa of Uruvilvâ and the two following is told in Buddhist Birth Stories (translated by Rhys Davids), I, 114; Mahâvagga (ed. Oldenberg) I, 15.

[3] Sâriputra and Maudgalyâyana are termed the foremost or chief disciples (agrasrâvaka) of the Lord. About their conversion, see Birth Stories, I, 118; Mahâvagga I, 23.

[4] About him, see Mahâvagga V, 13.

[5] In Pâli, Anuruddha; the story of his conversion is told Kullavagga (ed. Oldenberg) I, 8.

[6] The name is variously spelt Kapphina, Kasphina, Kashphina, Kapphilla, Kamphilla. The Tibetan form Kapina (in Lotus, p. 294) agrees with Mahâ-Kappina in Pâli writings; Mahâvagga II, 5; X, 5. I cannot help guessing that the name is identical with Σφίνης, the proper name of Kalanos, in Plutarch's Alexander, chap. 65; one would expect Κασφίνης.

[7] The same with Pindola-Bhâradvâga, Kullavagga V, 8.

[8] In Pâli Mahâ-Kotthita; Mahâvagga X, 5.

Upananda[1], the venerable Sundara-Nanda[2], the venerable Pûr*n*a Maitrâya*n*îputra, the venerable Subhûti, the venerable Râhula; with them yet other great disciples, as the venerable Ânanda, still under training, and two thousand other monks, some of whom still under training, the others masters; with six thousand nuns having at their head Mahâpra*g*âpatî[3], and the nun Ya*s*odharâ, the mother of Râhula, along with her train; (further) with eighty thousand Bodhisattvas, all unable to slide back[4], endowed with the spells of supreme, perfect enlightenment, firmly standing in wisdom; who moved onward the never deviating[5] wheel of the law; who had propitiated many hundred thousands of Buddhas; who under many hundred thousands of Buddhas had planted the roots of goodness, had been intimate with many hundred thousands of Buddhas, were in body and mind fully penetrated with the feeling of charity; able in communicating the wisdom of the Tathâgatas; very wise, having reached the perfection of wisdom; renowned in many hundred thousands of worlds; having saved many hundred thousand myriads[6] of ko*t*is[7] of beings; such as the Bodhisattva Mahâ-

[1] Surnamed *S*âkyaputra; Mahâvagga I, 52.

[2] Known from Lalita-vistara, p. 164; Burnouf has Sunanda.

[3] Gautamî, the aunt of Gautama Buddha.

[4] Or, to swerve from their course.

[5] Or, never rolling back.

[6] I have followed Burnouf in translating nayuta by ten thousand; this being the value of the Sanskrit term ayuta. According to the Petersburg Dictionary the Northern Buddhists attach to nayuta the value of 100,000 millions. The Pâli nahuta is said to be a vast number, one followed by twenty-eight ciphers; but in Spence Hardy's Manual of Buddhism, p. 193, its worth is put down at a myriad.

[7] I. e. ten millions.

sattva[1] Ma*ñg*u*s*rî, as prince royal[2]; the Bodhisattvas Mahâsattvas Avalokite*s*vara, Mahâsthâmaprâpta, Sarvârthanâman, Nityodyukta, Anikshiptadhura, Ratnapâ*n*i, Bhaisha*g*yarâ*g*a, Pradâna*s*ûra, Ratna*k*andra, Ratnaprabha, Pûr*n*a*k*andra, Mahâvikrâmin, Trailokavikrâmin, Anantavikrâmin, Mahâpratibhâna, Satatasamitâbhiyukta, Dhara*n*îdhara[3], Akshayamati, Padma*s*rî, Nakshatrarâ*g*a, the Bodhisattva Mahâsattva Maitreya, the Bodhisattva Mahâsattva Si*m*ha.

With them were also the sixteen virtuous men to begin with Bhadrapâla, to wit, Bhadrapâla, Ratnâkara, Susârthavâha, Naradatta[4], Guhagupta, Varu*n*adatta, Indradatta, Uttaramati, Vi*s*eshamati, Vardhamânamati, Amoghadar*s*in, Susa*m*sthita, Suvikrântavikrâmin, Anupamamati, Sûryagarbha, and Dhara*n*îdhara; besides eighty thousand Bodhisattvas, among whom the fore-mentioned were the chiefs; further *S*akra, the ruler of the celestials, with twenty thousand gods, his followers, such as the god *K*andra (the Moon), the god Sûrya (the Sun), the god Samantagandha (the Wind), the god Ratnaprabha, the god Avabhâsaprabha, and others; further, the four great rulers of the cardinal points with thirty thousand gods in their train, viz. the great ruler Virû*dh*aka, the great ruler Virûpâksha, the great ruler Dh*ri*tarâsh*t*ra, and the great ruler Vai*s*rava*n*a; the god Î*s*vara and the god Mahe*s*vara[5], each followed by thirty thousand gods; further,

---

[1] I.e. a great being.

[2] Or, 'still a youth,' kumârabhûta.

[3] In chap. XXIV he occurs as Bodhisattva Mahâsattva Dhara*n*îndhara.

[4] Burnouf has Ratnadatta.

[5] The distinction between Î*s*vara and Mahe*s*vara, both mere

Brahma Sahâmpati[1] and his twelve thousand followers, the Brahmakâyika gods, amongst whom Brahma *S*ikhin[2] and Brahma *G*yotishprabha, with the other twelve thousand Brahmakâyika gods[3]; together with the eight Nâga kings and many hundred thousand myriads of ko*t*is of Nâgas in their train, viz. the Nâga king Nanda, the Nâga king Upananda, Sâgara, Vâsuki, Takshaka, Manasvin, Anavatapta, and Utpalaka; further, the four Kinnara kings with many hundred thousand myriads of ko*t*is of followers, viz. the Kinnara king Druma, the Kinnara king Mahâdharma, the Kinnara king Sudharma, and the Kinnara king Dharmadhara; besides, the four divine beings (called) Gandharvakâyikas with many hundred thousand Gandharvas in their suite, viz. the Gandharva Mano*gñ*a, the Gandharva Mano*gñ*asvara, the Gandharva Madhura, and the Gandharva Madhurasvara; further, the four chiefs of the demons

---

epithets of *S*iva, has its counterpart in the equally fanciful difference between Tishya and Pushya, Meru and Sumeru, which occurs in Buddhist writings. In Mahâvastu, p. 355 (ed. Senart), we even find Mâyâ distinguished from Mahâmâyâ.

[1] On comparing Lalita-vistara, p. 515, l. 3, with the parallel passage Mahâvagga I, 5, 4, it appears that Sahâmpati and *S*ikhin are synonymous terms. As *S*ikhin is a common term for Agni and as to the latter in Rig-veda I, 97, 5; 127, 10; III, 14, 2, is applied the epithet of sahasvat, it may be inferred that Sahâmpati and the collateral form Sahapati answer to a Sanskrit sahasâmpati or sahaspati.

[2] Another instance of a fanciful distinction.

[3] It may be remarked that in the enumeration of gods, between *S*iva and Brahma, Vish*n*u is wanting. Those who adopt the view that *S*âkyamuni is an Avatâra of Vish*n*u, consequently a mythical being, will readily account for that omission by saying that Vish*n*u and the Lord Buddha are identical, so that Vish*n*u is present in the gathering, under the disguise of Buddha.

followed by many hundred thousand myriads of ko*t*is of demons, viz. the chief of the demons Bali, Kharaskandha [1], Vema*k*itri [2], and Râhu; along with the four Garu*d*a chiefs followed by many hundred thousand myriads of ko*t*is of Garu*d*as, viz. the Garu*d*a chiefs Mahâte*g*as, Mahâkâya, Mahâpûr*n*a, and Maharddhiprâpta, and with A*g*âta*s*atru, king of Magadha, the son of Vaidehî.

Now at that time it was that the Lord surrounded, attended, honoured, revered, venerated, worshipped by the four classes of hearers, after expounding the Dharmaparyâya [3] called 'the Great Exposition,' a text of great development, serving to instruct Bodhisattvas and proper to all Buddhas, sat cross-legged on the seat of the law and entered upon the meditation termed 'the station of the exposition of Infinity;' his body was motionless and his mind had reached perfect tranquillity. And as soon as the Lord had entered upon his meditation, there fell a great rain of divine flowers, Mandâravas [4] and great Mandâravas, Ma*ñg*ûshakas and great Ma*ñg*ûshakas [4], covering the Lord and the four classes of hearers, while the whole Buddha field shook in six ways: it moved,

[1] Burnouf has Suraskandha.

[2] This is a wrong Sanskritisation of a Prâkrit Vema*k*itti, Pâli Vepa*k*itti; the proper Sanskrit equivalent is Vipra*k*itti.

[3] I. e. turn, period, or roll of the law; it may often be rendered by 'a discourse on the law.' In the sense of period, term, end, it is used as the title of the closing chapter of the whole work.

[4] Mandârava, or rather Mândârava, derived from mandâru = mandâra, Erythrina, is here a heavenly flower, or, as the Indians say, 'a cloud-flower,' meghapushpa, i. e. raindrop and hailstone. Ma*ñg*ûsha is a name of the Rubia Manjista; the word is also said to mean, 'a stone;' in this case perhaps a hailstone or dewdrop.

removed, trembled, trembled from one end to the other, tossed, tossed along.

Then did those who were assembled and sitting together in that congregation, monks, nuns, male and female lay devotees, gods, Nâgas, goblins, Gandharvas, demons, Garu*d*as, Kinnaras, great serpents, men, and beings not human, as well as governors of a region, rulers of armies and rulers of four continents, all of them with their followers, gaze on the Lord in astonishment, in amazement, in ecstasy.

And at that moment there issued a ray from within the circle of hair between the eyebrows of the Lord[1]. It extended over eighteen hundred thousand Buddha-fields in the eastern quarter, so that all those Buddha-fields appeared wholly illuminated by its radiance, down to the great hell Avî*k*i and up to the limit of existence. And the beings in any of the six states[2] of existence became visible, all without exception. Likewise the Lords Buddhas staying, living, and existing in those Buddha-fields became all visible, and the law preached by them could be entirely heard by all beings. And the monks, nuns, lay devotees male and female, Yogins and students of Yoga, those who had obtained the fruition (of the Paths of sanctification) and those who had not, they, too, became visible. And the Bodhisattvas Mahâsattvas in those

---

[1] This reminds one of Wordsworth's lines:

'Bright apparition suddenly put forth
The Rainbow, smiling on the faded storm;
The mild assemblage of the starry heavens;
And the great Sun, earth's universal Lord.'

[2] Viz. hell, the brute creation, the world of ghosts, of demons, of men, and of gods or angels.

Buddha-fields who plied the Bodhisattva-course with ability, due to their earnest belief in numerous and various lessons and the fundamental ideas, they, too, became all visible. Likewise the Lords Buddhas in those Buddha-fields who had reached final Nirvâna became visible, all of them. And the Stûpas made of jewels and containing the relics of the extinct Buddhas became all visible in those Buddha-fields[1].

Then rose in the mind of the Bodhisattva Mahâsattva Maitreya this thought: O how great a wonder does the Tathâgata display! What may be the cause, what the reason of the Lord producing so great a wonder as this? And such astonishing, prodigious, inconceivable, powerful miracles now appear, although the Lord is absorbed in meditation! Why, let me inquire about this matter; who would be able here to explain it to me? He then thought: Here is Mañgusrî, the prince royal, who has plied his office under former Ginas and planted the roots of goodness, while worshipping many Buddhas. This Mañgusrî, the prince royal, must have witnessed before such signs of the former Tathâgatas, those Arhats, those perfectly enlightened Buddhas; of yore he must have enjoyed the grand conversations on the law. Therefore will I inquire about this matter with Mañgusrî, the prince royal.

And the four classes of the audience, monks, nuns, male and female lay devotees, numerous gods, Nâgas,

[1] It is sufficiently clear, I think, that the Buddha-fields are the heavens, and that we have in the text a description of the aspect of heaven when the stars are twinkling at dawn, shortly after or before. A Stûpa denotes the spot where a luminary, for the time being extinct, once stood; in more general acceptation it must have been synonymous with dhishnya, a fire-place, or with βωμός.

goblins, Gandharvas, demons, Garu*d*as, Kinnaras, great serpents, men, and beings not human, on seeing the magnificence of this great miracle of the Lord, were struck with astonishment, amazement and curiosity, and thought: Let us inquire why this magnificent miracle has been produced by the great power of the Lord.

At the same moment, at that very instant, the Bodhisattva Mahâsattva Maitreya knew in his mind the thoughts arising in the minds of the four classes of hearers and he spoke to Ma*ñg*u*s*rî, the prince royal: What, O Ma*ñg*u*s*rî, is the cause, what is the reason of this wonderful, prodigious, miraculous shine having been produced by the Lord? Look, how these eighteen thousand Buddha-fields appear variegated, extremely beautiful, directed by Tathâgatas and superintended by Tathâgatas.

Then it was that Maitreya, the Bodhisattva Mahâsattva, addressed Ma*ñg*u*s*rî, the prince royal, in the following stanzas:

1. Why, Ma*ñg*u*s*rî, does this ray darted by the guide of men shine forth from between his brows? this single ray issuing from the circle of hair? and why this abundant rain of Mandâravas?

2. The gods, overjoyed, let drop Ma*ñg*ûshakas and sandal powder, divine, fragrant, and delicious.

3. This earth is, on every side, replete with splendour, and all the four classes of the assembly are filled with delight, while the whole field shakes in six different ways, frightfully.

4. And that ray in the eastern quarter illuminates the whole of eighteen thousand Buddha-fields, simultaneously, so that those fields appear as gold-coloured.

5. (The universe) as far as the (hell) Avîki (and) the extreme limit of existence, with all beings of those fields living in any of the six states of existence, those who are leaving one state[1] to be born in another;

6. Their various and different actions in those states have become visible; whether they are in a happy, unhappy, low, eminent, or intermediate position, all that I see from this place.

7. I see also the Buddhas, those lions of kings, revealing and showing the essence of the law, comforting[2] many kotis of creatures and emitting sweet-sounding voices.

8. They let go forth, each in his own field, a deep, sublime, wonderful voice, while proclaiming the Buddha-laws by means of myriads of kotis of illustrations and proofs.

9. And to the ignorant creatures who are oppressed with toils and distressed in mind by birth and old age, they announce the bliss of Rest, saying: This is the end of trouble, O monks.

10. And to those who are possessed of strength and vigour and who have acquired merit by virtue or earnest belief in the Buddhas, they show the vehicle of the Pratyekabuddhas, by observing this rule of the law.

11. And the other sons of the Sugata who, striving after superior knowledge, have constantly accom-

---

[1] The word for state, gati, also means 'the position, place,' e. g. of a star.

[2] Prasvâsamânân, var. lect. prakâsamânân; Burnouf must have followed the latter reading, his translation having 'instruisent.'

plished their various tasks, them also they admonish to enlightenment.

12. From this place, O Mañgughosha, I see and hear such things and thousands of ko*t*is of other particulars besides; I will only describe some of them.

13. I see in many fields Bodhisattvas by many thousands of ko*t*is, like sands of the Ganges, who are producing enlightenment according to the different degree of their power.

14. There are some who charitably bestow wealth, gold, silver, gold money, pearls, jewels, conch shells, stones[1], coral, male and female slaves, horses, and sheep;

15. As well as litters adorned with jewels. They are spending gifts with glad hearts, developing themselves for superior enlightenment, in the hope of gaining the vehicle.

16. (Thus they think): 'The best and most excellent vehicle in the whole of the threefold world is the Buddha-vehicle magnified by the Sugatas. May I, forsooth, soon gain it after my spending such gifts.'

17. Some give carriages yoked with four horses and furnished with benches, flowers, banners, and flags; others give objects made of precious substances.

18. Some, again, give their children and wives;

[1] The text has *s*añkha*s*ilâ; according to the Tibetan version this would mean crystal, but that is impossible because *s*añkha is well known to be a conch shell. Burnouf hesitatingly renders it by 'des conques, du cristal;' see, however, Lotus, p. 314. I have been unable to find out what meaning the compound, be it a Dvandva or a Tatpurusha, is intended to convey.

others their own flesh; (or) offer, when bidden, their hands and feet, striving to gain supreme enlightenment.

19. Some give their heads, others their eyes, others their dear own body, and after cheerfully bestowing their gifts they aspire to the knowledge of the Tathâgatas.

20. Here and there, O Mañgusrî, I behold beings who have abandoned their flourishing kingdoms, harems, and continents, left all their counsellors and kinsmen,

21. And betaken themselves to the guides of the world to ask for the most excellent law, for the sake of bliss; they put on reddish-yellow robes, and shave hair and beard.

22. I see also many Bodhisattvas like monks, living in the forest, and others inhabiting the empty wilderness, engaged in reciting and reading.

23. And some Bodhisattvas I see, who, full of wisdom (or constancy), betake themselves to mountain caves, where by cultivating and meditating the Buddha-knowledge they arrive at its perception.

24. Others who have renounced all sensual desires, by purifying their own self, have cleared their sphere and obtained the five transcendent faculties, live in the wilderness, as (true) sons of the Sugata.

25. Some are standing firm, the feet put together and the hands joined in token of respect towards the leaders, and are praising joyfully the king of the leading *G*inas in thousands of stanzas.

26. Some thoughtful, meek, and tranquil, who have mastered the niceties of the course of duty, question the highest of men about the law, and retain in their memory what they have learnt.

27. And I see here and there some sons of the principal *G*ina who, after completely developing their own self, are preaching the law to many ko*t*is of living beings with many myriads of illustrations and reasons.

28. Joyfully they proclaim the law, rousing many Bodhisattvas; after conquering the Evil One with his hosts and vehicles, they strike the drum of the law.

29. I see some sons of the Sugata, humble, calm, and quiet in conduct, living under the command of the Sugatas, and honoured by men, gods, goblins, and Titans.

30. Others, again, who have retired to woody thickets, are saving the creatures in the hells by emitting radiance from their body, and rouse them to enlightenment.

31. There are some sons of the *G*ina who dwell in the forest, abiding in vigour, completely renouncing sloth, and actively engaged in walking; it is by energy that they are striving for supreme enlightenment.

32. Others complete their course by keeping a constant purity and an unbroken morality like precious stones and jewels; by morality do these strive for supreme enlightenment.

33. Some sons of the *G*ina, whose strength consists in forbearance, patiently endure abuse, censure, and threats from proud monks. They try to attain enlightenment by dint of forbearance.

34. Further, I see Bodhisattvas, who have forsaken all wanton pleasures, shun unwise companions and delight in having intercourse with genteel men (â r y a s);

35. Who, with avoidance of any distraction of thoughts and with attentive mind, during thousands of ko*t*is of years have meditated in the caves of the wilderness; these strive for enlightenment by dint of meditation.

36. Some, again, offer in presence of the *G*inas and the assemblage of disciples gifts (consisting) in food hard and soft, meat and drink, medicaments for the sick, in plenty and abundance.

37. Others offer in presence of the *G*inas and the assemblage of disciples hundreds of ko*t*is of clothes, worth thousands of ko*t*is, and garments of priceless value.

38. They bestow in presence of the Sugatas hundreds of ko*t*is of monasteries which they have caused to be built of precious substances and sandal-wood, and which are furnished with numerous lodgings (or couches).

39. Some present the leaders of men and their disciples with neat and lovely gardens abounding with fruits and beautiful flowers, to serve as places of daily recreation.

40. When they have, with joyful feelings, made such various and splendid donations, they rouse their energy in order to obtain enlightenment; these are those who try to reach supreme enlightenment by means of charitableness.

41. Others set forth the law of quietness, by many myriads of illustrations and proofs; they preach it to thousands of ko*t*is of living beings; these are tending to supreme enlightenment by science.

42. (There are) sons of the Sugata who try to reach enlightenment by wisdom; they understand the law of indifference and avoid acting at the

antinomy (of things), unattached like birds in the sky.

43. Further, I see, O Mañgughosha, many Bodhisattvas who have displayed steadiness under the rule of the departed Sugatas, and now are worshipping the relics of the *G*inas.

44. I see thousands of ko*t*is of Stûpas, numerous as the sand of the Ganges, which have been raised by these sons of the *G*ina and now adorn ko*t*is of grounds.

45. Those magnificent Stûpas, made of seven precious substances, with their thousands of ko*t*is of umbrellas and banners, measure in height no less than 5000 yo*g*anas and 2000 in circumference[1].

46. They are always decorated with flags; a multitude of bells is constantly heard sounding; men, gods, goblins, and Titans pay their worship with flowers, perfumes, and music.

47. Such honour do the sons of the Sugata render to the relics of the *G*inas, so that all directions of space are brightened as by the celestial coral trees in full blossom.

48. From this spot I behold all this; those numerous ko*t*is of creatures; both this world and heaven covered with flowers, owing to the single ray shot forth by the *G*ina.

49. O how powerful is the Leader of men! how extensive and bright is his knowledge! that a single beam darted by him over the world renders visible so many thousands of fields!

50. We are astonished at seeing this sign and

---

[1] It is evident that there is no question of earthly Stûpas, nor of hyperbolic phrases.

this wonder, so great, so incomprehensible. Explain me the matter, O Mañgusvara! the sons of Buddha are anxious to know it.

51. The four classes of the congregation in joyful expectation gaze on thee, O hero, and on me; gladden (their hearts); remove their doubts; grant a revelation, O son of Sugata!

52. Why is it that the Sugata has now emitted such a light? O how great is the power of the Leader of men! O how extensive and holy is his knowledge!

53. That one ray extending from him all over the world makes visible many thousands of fields. It must be for some purpose that this great ray has been emitted.

54. Is the Lord of men to show the primordial laws which he, the Highest of men, discovered on the terrace of enlightenment? Or is he to prophesy the Bodhisattvas their future destiny?

55. There must be a weighty reason why so many thousands of fields have been rendered visible, variegated, splendid, and shining with gems, while Buddhas of infinite sight are appearing.

56. Maitreya asks the son of *G*ina; men, gods, goblins, and Titans, the four classes of the congregation, are eagerly awaiting what answer Mañgusvara shall give in explanation.

Whereupon Mañgusrî, the prince royal, addressed Maitreya, the Bodhisattva Mahâsattva, and the whole assembly of Bodhisattvas (in these words): It is the intention of the Tathâgata, young men of good family, to begin a grand discourse for the teaching of the law, to pour the great rain of the law, to make resound the great drum of the law, to raise the great banner of the law, to kindle the great torch of the law, to blow the great conch trumpet of the law, and to strike the great tymbal of the law. Again, it is the intention of the Tathâgata, young men of good family, to make a grand exposition of the law this very day. Thus it appears to me, young men of good family, as I have witnessed a similar sign of the former Tathâgatas[1], the Arhats, the perfectly enlightened. Those former Tathâgatas, &c., they, too, emitted a lustrous ray, and I am convinced that the Tathâgata is about to deliver a grand discourse for the teaching of the law and make his grand speech on the law everywhere heard, he having shown such a foretoken. And because the Tathâgata, &c., wishes that this Dharmaparyâya meeting opposition in all the world[2] be heard everywhere, therefore does he display so great a miracle and this fore-token consisting in the lustre occasioned by the emission of a ray.

---

[1] Hence it follows that Mañgusrî is eternally young, like the rising sun, like Mithra, and like the Arhatâm deva, the latest, or youngest, of the Arhats or Ginas.

[2] The rendering of vipratyanîka, var. lect. vipratyanîyaka, is doubtful. Burnouf, who translates it by 'avec laquelle (le monde entier) doit être en désaccord,' remarks in his comment (Lotus, p. 323) that the Tibetan version assigns to pratyanîyaka the meaning of 'accordance, concord.' It is, however, extremely doubtful whether such a word as pratyanîyaka exists at all, and if pratyanîka should really be used in the sense of 'concord,' notwithstanding its generally occurring in the sense of 'opposition,' we must suppose that from the notion of 'an opposite party' has developed that of a party, paksha, in general. On that assumption we can account for vipratyanîka being used in the sense of vipaksha, repugnant, contrary, belonging to a different party. As to vipratyanîyaka, also Lalita-vistara, p. 513, this may be a wrongly Sanskritised vippakkanîyaka, to which would answer a Sanskrit vipratyanîkaka.

I remember, young men of good family, that in the days of yore, many immeasurable, inconceivable, immense, infinite, countless Æons, more than countless Æons ago, nay, long and very long before, there was born a Tathâgata called *K*andrasûryapradîpa[1], an Arhat, &c., endowed with science and conduct[2], a Sugata, knower of the world, an incomparable tamer of men, a teacher (and ruler) of gods and men, a Buddha and Lord. He showed the law; he revealed the duteous course which is holy at its commencement, holy in its middle, holy at the end, good in substance and form, complete and perfect, correct and pure. That is to say, to the disciples he preached the law containing the four Noble Truths, and starting from the chain of causes and effects, tending to overcome birth, decrepitude, sickness, death, sorrow, lamentation, woe, grief, despondency, and finally leading to Nirvâ*n*a; and to the Bodhisattvas he preached the law connected with the six Perfections[3], and terminating in the knowledge of the Omniscient, after the attainment of supreme, perfect enlightenment.

[Now, young men of good family, long before the time of that Tathâgata *K*andrasûryapradîpa, the Arhat, &c., there had appeared a Tathâgata, &c., likewise called *K*andrasûryapradîpa, after whom, O A*g*ita[4], there were twenty thousand Tathâgatas,

---

[1] I.e. having the shine of moon and sun.

[2] Otherwise, with light and motion.

[3] The six Pâramitâs, viz. of almsgiving, morality, patience, zeal or energy, meditation, and wisdom.

[4] I.e. invincible, invictus. The palpable connection between Maitreya A*g*ita and Mithras Invictus is no proof of the Buddhists having borrowed the figure from the Persians; the coincidence

&c., all of them bearing the name of *K*andrasûrya-pradîpa, of the same lineage and family name, to wit, of Bharadvâ*g*a[1]. All those twenty thousand Tathâgatas, O A*g*ita, from the first to the last, showed the law, revealed the course which is holy at its commencement, holy in its middle, holy at the end, &c. &c.[2]]

The aforesaid Lord *K*andrasûryapradîpa, the Tathâgata, &c., when a young prince and not yet having left home (to embrace the ascetic life), had eight sons, viz. the young princes Sumati, Ananta-mati, Ratnamati, Vi*s*eshamati, Vimatisamudghâtin, Ghoshamati, and Dharmamati. These eight young princes, A*g*ita, sons to the Lord *K*andrasûryapradîpa, the Tathâgata, had an immense fortune[3]. Each of them was in possession of four great continents, where they exercised the kingly sway. When they saw that the Lord had left his home to become an ascetic, and heard that he had attained supreme, perfect enlightenment, they forsook all of them the pleasures of royalty and followed the example of the Lord by resigning the world; all of them strove to

being perfectly explainable if we consider the narrow relationship of Indian and Iranian mythology. Maitreya is not strictly identical with Mitra, but a younger edition, so to speak, of him; he is the future saviour.

[1] It is clear that Bharadvâ*g*a, a well-known progenitor of one of the Brahmanic families, existed long before the creation, i.e. of the last creation of the world. There can be no question of his being a man, at least in the system of the Lotus.

[2] The words in brackets are wanting in one of the MSS.

[3] *Ri*ddhi is the word used in the text. As an ecclesiastical term it denotes 'magic power,' but that artificial meaning does not suit here.

reach superior enlightenment and became preachers of the law. While constantly leading a holy life, those young princes planted roots of goodness under many thousands of Buddhas.

It was at that time, A*g*ita, that the Lord *K*andrasûryapradîpa, the Tathâgata, &c., after expounding the Dharmaparyâya called 'the Great Exposition,' a text of great extension, serving to instruct Bodhisattvas and proper to all Buddhas, at the same moment and instant, at the same gathering of the classes of hearers, sat cross-legged on the same seat of the law, and entered upon the meditation termed 'the Station of the exposition of Infinity;' his body was motionless, and his mind had reached perfect tranquillity. And as soon as the Lord had entered upon meditation, there fell a great rain of divine flowers, Mandâravas and great Mandâravas, Ma*ñg*ûshakas and great Ma*ñg*ûshakas, covering the Lord and the four classes of hearers, while the whole Buddha-field shook in six ways; it moved, removed, trembled, trembled from one end to the other, tossed, tossed along.

Then did those who were assembled and sitting together at that congregation, monks, nuns, male and female lay devotees, gods, Nâgas, goblins, Gandharvas, demons, Garu*d*as, Kinnaras, great serpents, men and beings not human, as well as governors of a region, rulers of armies and rulers of four continents, all of them with their followers gaze on the Lord in astonishment, in amazement, in ecstasy.

And at that moment there issued a ray from within the circle of hair between the eyebrows of the Lord. It extended over eighteen hundred thousand Buddha-fields in the eastern quarter, so that all those Buddha-fields appeared wholly illuminated by its radiance, just like the Buddha-fields do now, O A*g*ita.

[At that juncture, A*g*ita, there were twenty ko*t*is of Bodhisattvas following the Lord. All hearers of the law in that assembly, on seeing how the world was illuminated by the lustre of that ray, felt astonishment, amazement, ecstasy, and curiosity[1].]

Now it happened, A*g*ita, that under the rule of the aforesaid Lord there was a Bodhisattva called Varaprabha, who had eight hundred pupils. It was to this Bodhisattva Varaprabha that the Lord, on rising from his meditation, revealed the Dharmaparyâya called 'the Lotus of the True Law.' He spoke during fully sixty intermediate kalpas, always sitting on the same seat, with immovable body and tranquil mind. And the whole assembly continued sitting on the same seats, listening to the preaching of the Lord for sixty intermediate kalpas, there being not a single creature in that assembly who felt fatigue of body or mind.

As the Lord *K*andrasûryapradîpa, the Tathâgata, &c., during sixty intermediate kalpas had been expounding the Dharmaparyâya called 'the Lotus of the True Law,' a text of great development, serving to instruct Bodhisattvas and proper to all Buddhas, he instantly announced his complete Nirvâ*n*a to the world, including the gods, Mâras and Brahmas, to all creatures, including ascetics, Brahmans, gods, men and demons, saying: To-day, O monks, this very

[1] The passage in brackets is wanting in one of the MSS.

night, in the middle watch, will the Tathâgata, by entering the element of absolute Nirvâ*n*a, become wholly extinct.

Thereupon, A*g*ita, the Lord *K*andrasûryapradîpa, the Tathâgata, &c., predestinated the Bodhisattva called *S*rîgarbha to supreme, perfect enlightenment, and then spoke thus to the whole assembly: O monks, this Bodhisattva *S*rîgarbha here shall immediately after me attain supreme, perfect enlightenment, and become Vimalanetra, the Tathâgata, &c.

Thereafter, A*g*ita, that very night, at that very watch, the Lord *K*andrasûryapradîpa, the Tathâgata, &c., became extinct by entering the element of absolute Nirvâ*n*a. And the afore-mentioned Dharmaparyâya, termed 'the Lotus of the True Law,' was kept in memory by the Bodhisattva Mahâsattva Varaprabha; during eighty intermediate kalpas did the Bodhisattva Varaprabha keep and reveal the commandment of the Lord who had entered Nirvâ*n*a. Now it so happened, A*g*ita, that the eight sons of the Lord *K*andrasûryapradîpa, Mati and the rest, were pupils to that very Bodhisattva Varaprabha. They were by him made ripe for supreme, perfect enlightenment, and in after times they saw and worshipped many hundred thousand myriads of ko*t*is of Buddhas, all of whom had attained supreme, perfect enlightenment, the last of them being Dîpa*n*kara, the Tathâgata, &c.

Amongst those eight pupils there was one Bodhisattva who attached an extreme value to gain, honour and praise, and was fond of glory, but all the words and letters one taught him faded (from his memory), did not stick. So he got the appellation of Yasaskâma[1]. He had propitiated many hundred thousand myriads of kotis of Buddhas by that root of goodness, and afterwards esteemed, honoured, respected, revered, venerated, worshipped them. Perhaps, Agita, thou feelest some doubt, perplexity or misgiving that in those days, at that time, there was another Bodhisvattva Mahâsattva Varaprabha, preacher of the law. But do not think so. Why? because it is myself who in those days, at that time, was the Bodhisattva Mahâsattva Varaprabha, preacher of the law; and that Bodhisattva named Yasaskâma, the lazy one, it is thyself, Agita, who in those days, at that time, wert the Bodhisattva named Yasaskâma, the lazy one.

And so, Agita, having once seen a similar foretoken of the Lord, I infer from a similar ray being emitted just now, that the Lord is about to expound the Dharmaparyâya called 'the Lotus of the True Law.'

And on that occasion, in order to treat the subject more copiously, Mañgusrî, the prince royal, uttered the following stanzas:

57. I remember a past period, inconceivable, illimited kalpas ago, when the highest of beings, the *G*ina of the name of *K*andrasûryapradîpa, was in existence.

58. He preached the true law, he, the leader of creatures; he educated an infinite number of kotis of beings, and roused inconceivably many Bodhisattvas to acquiring supreme Buddha-knowledge.

59. And the eight sons born to him, the leader, when he was prince royal, no sooner saw that the

---

[1] I. e. desirous of glory.

great sage had embraced ascetic life, than they resigned worldly pleasures and became monks.

60. And the Lord of the world proclaimed the law, and revealed to thousands of kotis of living beings the Sûtra, the development, which by name is called 'the excellent Exposition of Infinity.'

61. Immediately after delivering his speech, the leader crossed his legs and entered upon the meditation of 'the excellent Exposition of the Infinite.' There on his seat of the law the eminent seer continued absorbed in meditation.

62. And there fell a celestial rain of Mandâravas, while the drums (of heaven) resounded without being struck; the gods and elves in the sky paid honour to the highest of men.

63. And simultaneously all the fields (of Buddha) began trembling. A wonder it was, a great prodigy. Then the chief emitted from between his brows one extremely beautiful ray,

64. Which moving to the eastern quarter glittered, illuminating the world all over the extent of eighteen thousand fields. It manifested the vanishing and appearing of beings.

65. Some of the fields then seemed jewelled, others showed the hue of lapis lazuli, all splendid, extremely beautiful, owing to the radiance of the ray from the leader.

66. Gods and men, as well as Nâgas, goblins, Gandharvas, nymphs, Kinnaras, and those occupied with serving the Sugata became visible in the spheres and paid their devotion.

67. The Buddhas also, those self-born beings, appeared of their own accord, resembling golden columns; like unto a golden disk (within lapis

lazuli), they revealed the law in the midst of the assembly.

68. The disciples, indeed, are not to be counted: the disciples of Sugata are numberless. Yet the lustre of the ray renders them all visible in every field.

69. Energetic, without breach or flaw in their course, similar to gems and jewels, the sons of the leaders of men are visible in the mountain caves where they are dwelling.

70. Numerous Bodhisattvas, like the sand of the Ganges, who are spending all their wealth in giving alms, who have the strength of patience, are devoted to contemplation and wise, become all of them visible by that ray.

71. Immovable, unshaken, firm in patience, devoted to contemplation, and absorbed in meditation are seen the true sons of the Sugatas while they are striving for supreme enlightenment by dint of meditation.

72. They preach the law in many spheres, and point to the true, quiet, spotless state they know. Such is the effect produced by the power of the Sugata.

73. And all the four classes of hearers on seeing the power of the mighty[1] *K*andrârka-

[1] The text has tâyin, a word frequently occurring in the Lotus. I assume that the form tâpin, given in the dictionaries as an epithet of Buddha, is but a misread tâyin, and further that this is radically the same with the Pâli tâdî (tâdin). As tâyana, Pâ*n*ini I, 3, 38, is explained to have the meaning of thriving, prospering, it may be supposed that tâyin on the strength of its derivation denotes thriving, prosperous, mighty, holy, as well as making prosperous, blessing, sanctifying. Burnouf derives it from a supposed Sanskrit trâyin, and translates it by 'protector.' It is, indeed, by no means unlikely

dîpa[1] were filled with joy and asked one another: How is this?

74. And soon afterwards, as the Leader of the world, worshipped by men, gods, and goblins, rose from his meditation, he addressed his son Varaprabha, the wise Bodhisattva and preacher of the law:

75. 'Thou art wise, the eye and refuge of the world; thou art the trustworthy keeper of my law, and canst bear witness as to the treasure of laws which I am to lay bare to the weal of living beings.'

76. Then, after rousing and stimulating, praising and lauding many Bodhisattvas, did the *G*ina proclaim the supreme laws during fully sixty intermediate kalpas.

77. And whatever excellent supreme law was proclaimed by the Lord of the world while continuing sitting on the very same seat, was kept in memory by Varaprabha, the son of *G*ina, the preacher of the law.

78. And after the *G*ina and Leader had manifested the supreme law and stimulated the numerous crowd, he spoke, that day, towards the world including the gods (as follows):

79. 'I have manifested the rule of the law; I have shown the nature of the law; now, O monks, it is the time of my Nirvâ*n*a; this very night, in the middle watch.

80. 'Be zealous and strong in persuasion; apply yourselves to my lessons; (for) the *G*inas, the great

---

that tâyin was used synonymously with nâtha or nâyaka, but it seems not necessary to derive it from trâyate.

[1] This name is synonymous with *K*andrasûryapradîpa; one of the MSS. has *K*andrapradîpa.

seers, are but rarely met with in the lapse of myriads of ko*t*is of Æons.'

81. The many sons of Buddha were struck with grief and filled with extreme sorrow when they heard the voice of the highest of men announcing that his Nirvâ*n*a was near at hand.

82. To comfort so inconceivably many ko*t*is of living beings the king of kings said: 'Be not afraid, O monks; after my Nirvâ*n*a there shall be another Buddha.

83. 'The wise Bodhisattva *S*rîgarbha, after finishing his course in faultless knowledge, shall reach highest, supreme enlightenment, and become a *G*ina under the name of Vimalâgranetra.'

84. That very night, in the middle watch, he met complete extinction, like a lamp when the cause (of its burning) is exhausted. His relics were distributed, and of his Stûpas there was an infinite number of myriads of ko*t*is.

85. The monks and nuns at the time being, who strove after supreme, highest enlightenment, numerous as sand of the Ganges, applied themselves to the commandment of the Sugata.

86. And the monk who then was the preacher of the law and the keeper of the law, Varaprabha, expounded for fully eighty intermediate kalpas the highest laws according to the commandment (of the Sugata).

87. He had eight hundred pupils, who all of them were by him brought to full development. They saw many ko*t*is of Buddhas, great sages, whom they worshipped.

88. By following the regular course they became Buddhas in several spheres, and as they followed

one another in immediate succession they successively foretold each other's future destiny to Buddhaship.

89. The last of these Buddhas following one another was Dîpankara. He, the supreme god of gods, honoured by crowds of sages, educated thousands of ko*t*is of living beings.

90. Among the pupils of Varaprabha, the son of *G*ina, at the time of his teaching the law, was one slothful, covetous, greedy of gain and cleverness.

91. He was also excessively desirous of glory, but very fickle, so that the lessons dictated to him and his own reading faded from his memory as soon as learnt.

92. His name was Ya*s*askâma, by which he was known everywhere. By the accumulated merit[1] of that good action, spotted as it was,

93. He propitiated thousands of ko*t*is of Buddhas, whom he rendered ample honour. He went through the regular course of duties and saw the present Buddha *S*âkyasi*m*ha.

94. He shall be the last to reach superior enlightenment and become a Lord known by the family name of Maitreya, who shall educate thousands of ko*t*is of creatures.

---

[1] The MSS. have tenâku*s*alena karma*n*â, tenoku*s*alena karma*n*â. As teno and tenâ in the stanzas are occasionally used instead of tena, it is uncertain whether tenâk. is to be separated into tena and aku*s*ala. This much is clear, that the author of the foregoing prose text has taken the words as tenâ (Vedic the same) or teno, and ku*s*ala. The good in Ya*s*askâma was his love of renown, of good fame. Maitreya, by his very nature, holds a middle position between black night and bright daylight; Mithra also is represented as a μεσίτης.

95. He who then, under the rule of the extinct Sugata, was so slothful, was thyself, and it was I who then was the preacher of the law.

96. As on seeing a foretoken of this kind I recognise a sign such as I have seen manifested of yore, therefore and on that account I know,

97. That decidedly the chief of *G*inas, the supreme king of the *S*âkyas, the All-seeing, who knows the highest truth, is about to pronounce the excellent Sûtra which I have heard before.

98. That very sign displayed at present is a proof of the skilfulness of the leaders; the Lion of the *S*âkyas is to make an exhortation, to declare the fixed nature of the law.

99. Be well prepared and well minded; join your hands: he who is affectionate and merciful to the world is going to speak, is going to pour the endless rain of the law and refresh those that are waiting for enlightenment.

100. And if some should feel doubt, uncertainty, or misgiving in any respect, then the Wise One shall remove it for his children, the Bodhisattvas here striving after enlightenment.

CHAPTER II.

SKILFULNESS[1].

The Lord then rose with recollection and consciousness from his meditation, and forthwith addressed the venerable *S*âriputra: The Buddha knowledge, *S*âriputra, is profound, difficult to understand, difficult to comprehend. It is difficult for all disciples and Pratyekabuddhas to fathom the knowledge arrived at by the Tathâgatas, &c., and that, *S*âriputra, because the Tathâgatas have worshipped many hundred thousand myriads of ko*t*is of Buddhas; because they have fulfilled their course for supreme, complete enlightenment, during many hundred thousand myriads of ko*t*is of Æons; because they have wandered far, displaying energy and possessed of wonderful and marvellous properties; possessed of properties difficult to understand; because they have found out things difficult to understand.

The mystery[2] of the Tathâgatas, &c., is difficult to understand, *S*âriputra, because when they explain the laws (or phenomena, things) that have their

---

[1] Or, able management, diplomacy, upâyakau*s*alya. Upâya means an expedient, but with the Prâg*ñ*ikas it denotes the energy of Prag*ñ*â, the latter being Nature, otherwise called Mâyâ; see B. H. Hodgson, Essays on the Languages, Literature, and Religion of Nepâl and Tibet, p. 104; cf. pp. 72, 78, 89. From the atheistic point of view the possessor of upâyakau*s*alya can hardly be anything else but all-ruling Time; regarded from the theistic view he must be the Almighty Spirit.

[2] Sandhâ-bhâshya; on this term more in the sequel.

causes in themselves they do so by means of skilfulness, by the display of knowledge, by arguments, reasons, fundamental ideas, interpretations, and suggestions. By a variety of skilfulness they are able to release creatures that are attached to one point or another. The Tathâgatas, &c., *S*âriputra, have acquired the highest perfection in skilfulness and the display of knowledge; they are endowed with wonderful properties, such as the display of free and unchecked knowledge; the powers[1]; the absence of hesitation; the independent conditions[2]; the strength of the organs; the constituents of Bodhi[3]; the contemplations; emancipations[4]; meditations; the degrees of concentration of mind. The Tathâgatas, &c., *S*âriputra, are able to expound various things and have something wonderful and marvellous. Enough, *S*âriputra, let it suffice to say, that the Tathâgatas, &c., have something extremely

---

[1] Here will be meant the ten powers, whence the epithet of Da*s*abala applied to a Buddha; they are enumerated in S. Hardy's Manual, p. 379. Other enumerations count four, five, or seven powers.

[2] Or rather, the uncommon, not vulgar properties which distinguish the saints from the vulgar; these âve*n*ikadharmas, also called buddhadharmas, are eighteen in number; S. Hardy's Manual, p. 381.

[3] The seven Bodhyangas, viz. recollection, investigation, energy, joyfulness, calm, contemplation, and equanimity.

[4] Vimoksha, vimukti, for which see Burnouf's Appendix to the Lotus, p. 824 sqq. According to the view there expressed the eight Vimokshas are as many states of intellect which the thinking sage is going through in his effort to emancipate himself from the versatile world; cf. Lotus, p. 543. There is also a threefold Vimoksha, mentioned by Childers, Pâli Dict., p. 270; it may be compared with the threefold *k*itta-vimukti in the Yoga system; see Comm. on Yoga*s*âstra, 2, 27.

wonderful, Sâriputra. None but a Tathâgata, Sâriputra, can impart to a Tathâgata those laws which the Tathâgata knows. And all laws, Sâriputra, are taught by the Tathâgata, and by him alone; no one but he knows all laws, what they are, how they are, like what they are, of what characteristics and of what nature they are.

And on that occasion, to set forth the same subject more copiously, the Lord uttered the following stanzas:

1. Innumerable are the great heroes in the world that embraces gods and men; the totality of creatures is unable to completely know the leaders.

2. None can know their powers and states of emancipation, their absence of hesitation and Buddha properties, such as they are.

3. Of yore have I followed in presence of kotis of Buddhas the good course which is profound, subtle, difficult to understand, and most difficult to find.

4. After pursuing that career during an inconceivable number of kotis of Æons, I have on the terrace of enlightenment discovered the fruit thereof.

5. And therefore I recognise, like the other chiefs of the world, how it is, like what it is, and what are its characteristics.

6. It is impossible to explain it; it is unutterable; nor is there such a being in the world

7. To whom this law could be explained or who would be able to understand it when explained, with exception of the Bodhisattvas, those who are firm in resolve.

8. As to the disciples of the Knower of the world, those who have done their duty and received praise

from the Sugatas, who are freed from faults and have arrived at the last stage of bodily existence, the *G*ina-knowledge lies beyond their sphere.

9. If this whole sphere were full of beings like *S*ârisuta, and if they were to investigate with combined efforts, they would be unable to comprehend the knowledge of the Sugata.

10. Even if the ten points of space were full of sages like thee, ay, if they were full of such as the rest of my disciples,

11. And if those beings combined were to investigate the knowledge of the Sugata, they would, all together, not be able to comprehend the Buddha-knowledge in its whole immensity.

12. If the ten points of space were filled with Pratyekabuddhas, free from faults, gifted with acute faculties, and standing in the last stage of their existence, as numerous as reeds and bamboos in the woods;

13. And if combined for an endless number of myriads of ko*t*is of Æons, they were to investigate a part only of my superior laws, they would never find out its real meaning.

14. If the ten points of space were full of Bodhisattvas who, after having done their duty under many ko*t*is of Buddhas, investigated all things and preached many sermons, after entering a new vehicle[1];

15. If the whole world were full of them, as of dense reeds and bamboos, without any interstices, and if all combined were to investigate the law which the Sugata has realised;

[1] Or rather, a new career.

16. If they were going on investigating for many kotis of Æons, as incalculable as the sand of the Ganges, with undivided attention and subtle wit, even then that (knowledge) would be beyond their ken.

17. If such Bodhisattvas as are unable to fall back, numerous as the sand of the Ganges, were to investigate it with undivided attention, it would prove to lie beyond their ken.

18. Profound are the laws of the Buddhas, and subtle; all inscrutable and faultless. I myself know them as well as the *G*inas do in the ten directions of the world.

19. Thou, *S*âriputra, be full of trust in what the Sugata declares. The *G*ina speaks no falsehood, the great Seer who has so long preached the highest truth.

20. I address all disciples here, those who have set out to reach the enlightenment of Pratyekabuddhas, those who are roused to activity at my Nirvâ*n*a[1], and those who have been released from the series of evils.

21. It is by my superior skilfulness that I explain the law at great length to the world at large. I deliver whosoever are attached to one point or another, and show the three vehicles[2].

The eminent disciples in the assembly headed by Â*gñ*âta-Kau*nd*inya, the twelve hundred Arhats faultless and self-controlled, the other monks, nuns, male and female lay devotees using the vehicle of disciples, and those who had entered the vehicle of Pratyeka-

[1] Or, who by me are established in Nirvâ*n*a.

[2] The word yâna in the text also means 'a career, course.'

buddhas, all of them made this reflection: What may be the cause, what the reason of the Lord so extremely extolling the skilfulness of the Tathâgatas? of his extolling it by saying, 'Profound is the law by me discovered;' of his extolling it by saying, 'It is difficult for all disciples and Pratyekabuddhas to understand it.' But as yet the Lord has declared no more than one kind of emancipation, and therefore we also should acquire the Buddha-laws on reaching Nirvâ*n*a. We do not catch the meaning of this utterance of the Lord.

And the venerable *S*âriputra, who apprehended the doubt and uncertainty of the four classes of the audience and guessed their thoughts from what was passing in his own mind, himself being in doubt about the law, then said to the Lord: What, O Lord, is the cause, what the reason of the Lord so repeatedly and extremely extolling the skilfulness, knowledge, and preaching of the Tathâgata? Why does he repeatedly extol it by saying, 'Profound is the law by me discovered; it is difficult to understand the mystery of the Tathâgatas.' Never before have I heard from the Lord such a discourse on the law. These four classes of the audience, O Lord, are overcome with doubt and perplexity. Therefore may the Lord be pleased to explain what the Tathâgata is alluding to, when repeatedly extolling the profound law of the Tathâgatas.

On that occasion the venerable *S*âriputra uttered the following stanzas:

22. Now first does the Sun of men utter such a speech: 'I have acquired the powers, emancipations, and numberless meditations.'

23. And thou mentionest the terrace of enlighten-

ment without any one asking thee; thou mentionest the mystery, although no one asks thee.

24. Thou speakest unasked and laudest thine own course; thou mentionest thy having obtained knowledge and pronouncest profound words.

25. To-day a question rises in my mind and of these self-controlled, faultless beings striving after Nirvâ*n*a: Why does the *G*ina speak in this manner?

26. Those who aspire to the enlightenment of Pratyekabuddhas, the nuns and monks, gods, Nâgas, goblins, Gandharvas, and great serpents, are talking together, while looking up to the highest of men,

27. And ponder in perplexity. Give an elucidation, great Sage, to all the disciples of Sugata here assembled.

28. Myself have reached the perfection (of virtue), have been taught by the supreme Sage; still, O highest of men! even in my position I feel some doubt whether the course (of duty) shown to me shall receive its final sanction by Nirvâ*n*a.

29. Let thy voice be heard, O thou whose voice resounds like an egregious kettle-drum! proclaim thy law such as it is. The legitimate sons of *G*ina here standing and gazing at the *G*ina, with joined hands;

30. As well as the gods, Nâgas, goblins, Titans, numbering thousands of ko*t*is, like sand of the Ganges; and those that aspire to superior enlightenment, here standing, fully eighty thousand in number;

31. Further, the kings, rulers of provinces and paramount monarchs, who have flocked hither from thousands of ko*t*is of countries, are now standing with joined hands, and respectful, thinking: How are we to fulfil the course of duty?

The venerable *S*âriputra having spoken, the Lord said to him: Enough, *S*âriputra; it is of no use explaining this matter. Why? Because, *S*âriputra, the world, including the gods, would be frightened if this matter were expounded.

But the venerable *S*âriputra entreated the Lord a second time, saying: Let the Lord expound, let the Sugata expound this matter, for in this assembly, O Lord, there are many hundreds, many thousands, many hundred thousands, many hundred thousand myriads of ko*t*is of living beings who have seen former Buddhas, who are intelligent, and will believe, value, and accept the words of the Lord.

The venerable *S*âriputra addressed the Lord with this stanza:

32. Speak clearly, O most eminent of *G*inas! in this assembly there are thousands of living beings trustful, affectionate, and respectful towards the Sugata; they will understand the law by thee expounded.

And the Lord said a second time to the venerable *S*âriputra: Enough, *S*âriputra; it is of no use explaining this matter, for the world, including the gods, would be frightened, *S*âriputra, if this matter were expounded, and some monks might be proud and come to a heavy fall[1].

And on that occasion uttered the Lord the following stanza:

33. Speak no more of it that I should declare this law! This knowledge is too subtle, inscrutable, and there are so many unwise men who in their conceit and foolishness would scoff at the law revealed.

---

[1] Or, commit a great offence.

A third time the venerable *S*âriputra entreated the Lord, saying: Let the Lord expound, let the Sugata expound this matter. In this assembly, O Lord, there are many hundreds of living beings my equals, and many hundreds, many thousands, many hundred thousands, many hundred thousand myriads of ko*t*is of other living beings more, who in former births have been brought by the Lord to full ripeness. They will believe, value, and accept what the Lord declares, which shall tend to their advantage, weal, and happiness in length of time.

On that occasion the venerable *S*âriputra uttered the following stanzas:

34. Explain the law, O thou most high of men! I, thine eldest son, beseech thee. Here are thousands of ko*t*is of beings who are to believe in the law by thee revealed.

35. And those beings that in former births so long and constantly have by thee been brought to full maturity and now are all standing here with joined hands, they, too, are to believe in this law.

36. Let the Sugata, seeing the twelve hundred, my equals, and those who are striving after superior enlightenment, speak to them and produce in them an extreme joy.

When the Lord for the third time heard the entreaty of the venerable *S*âriputra, he spoke to him as follows: Now that thou entreatest the Tathâgata a third time, *S*âriputra, I will answer thee. Listen then, *S*âriputra, take well and duly to heart what I am saying; I am going to speak.

Now it happened that five thousand proud monks, nuns, and lay devotees of both sexes in the congregation rose from their seats and, after saluting with their heads the Lord's feet, went to leave the assembly. Owing to the principle of good which there is in pride they imagined having attained what they had not, and having understood what they had not. Therefore, thinking themselves aggrieved, they went to leave the assembly, to which the Lord by his silence showed assent.

Thereupon the Lord addressed the venerable *S*âriputra: My congregation, *S*âriputra, has been cleared from the chaff[1], freed from the trash; it is firmly established in the strength of faith. It is good, *S*âriputra, that those proud ones are gone away. Now I am going to expound the matter, *S*âriputra. 'Very well, Lord,' replied the venerable *S*âriputra. The Lord then began and said:

It is but now and then, *S*âriputra, that the Tathâgata preaches such a discourse on the law as this. Just as but now and then is seen the blossom of the glomerous fig-tree, *S*âriputra, so does the Tathâgata but now and then preach such a discourse on the law. Believe me, *S*âriputra; I speak what is real, I speak what is truthful, I speak what is right. It is difficult to understand the exposition of the mystery of the Tathâgata, *S*âriputra; for in elucidating the law, *S*âriputra, I use hundred thousands of various skilful means, such as different interpretations, indications, explanations, illustrations. It is not by reasoning, *S*âriputra, that the law is to be found: it is beyond the pale of reasoning, and must be

[1] One of the MSS. has nishpralâva, which ought to be nishpalâva; another has nishpudgalâva. Both imaginary words are no doubt the result of an unhappy attempt to Sanskritise a Prâkrit nippalâva by scribes unacquainted with the Sanskrit palâva (Pâli palâpa). The right form occurs below, stanza 40.

learnt from the Tathâgata. For, *S*âriputra, it is for a sole object, a sole aim, verily a lofty object, a lofty aim that the Buddha, the Tathâgata, &c., appears in the world. And what is that sole object, that sole aim, that lofty object, that lofty aim of the Buddha, the Tathâgata, &c., appearing in the world? To show all creatures the sight of Tathâgata-knowledge[1] does the Buddha, the Tathâgata, &c., appear in the world; to open the eyes of creatures for the sight of Tathâgata-knowledge does the Buddha, the Tathâgata, &c., appear in the world. This, O *S*âriputra, is the sole object, the sole aim, the sole purpose of his appearance in the world. Such then, *S*âriputra, is the sole object, the sole aim, the lofty object, the lofty aim of the Tathâgata. And it is achieved by the Tathâgata. For, *S*âriputra, I do show all creatures the sight of Tathâgata-knowledge; I do open the eyes of creatures for the sight of Tathâgata-knowledge, *S*âriputra; I do firmly establish the teaching of Tathâgata-knowledge, *S*âriputra; I do lead the teaching of Tathâgata-knowledge on the right path, *S*âriputra. By means of one sole vehicle[2], to wit, the Buddha-vehicle, *S*âriputra, do I teach creatures the law; there is no second vehicle, nor a third. This is the nature of the law, *S*âriputra, universally in the world, in all directions. For, *S*âriputra, all the Tathâgatas, &c., who in times past existed in countless, innumerable spheres in all directions for the weal of many, the happiness of many, out of pity to the world, for the benefit, weal, and happiness of the great body of creatures,

[1] Or, to rouse all creatures by the display of Tathâgata-knowledge.

[2] Rather and properly, one sole course.

and who preached the law to gods and men with able means, such as several directions and indications, various arguments, reasons, illustrations, fundamental ideas, interpretations, paying regard to the dispositions of creatures whose inclinations and temperaments are so manifold, all those Buddhas and Lords, *S*âriputra, have preached the law to creatures by means of only one vehicle, the Buddha-vehicle, which finally leads to omniscience; it is identical with showing all creatures the sight of Tathâgata-knowledge; with opening the eyes of creatures for the sight of Tathâgata-knowledge; with the awakening (or admonishing) by the display (or sight) of Tathâgata-knowledge[1]; with leading the teaching of Tathâgata-knowledge on the right path. Such is the law they have preached to creatures. And those creatures, *S*âriputra, who have heard the law from the past Tathâgatas, &c., have all of them reached supreme, perfect enlightenment.

And the Tathâgatas, &c., who shall exist in future, *S*âriputra, in countless, innumerable spheres in all directions for the weal of many, the happiness of many, out of pity to the world, for the benefit, weal, and happiness of the great body of creatures, and who shall preach the law to gods and men (&c., as above till) the right path. Such is the law they shall preach to creatures. And those creatures, *S*âriputra, who shall hear the law from the future Tathâgatas, &c., shall all of them reach supreme, perfect enlightenment.

And the Tathâgatas, &c., who now at present are

[1] One MS. has Tathâgata*g*ñânade*s*anapratibodhana; the other °dar*s*ana° instead of °de*s*ana°.

staying, living, existing, Sâriputra, in countless, innumerable spheres in all directions, &c., and who are preaching the law to gods and men (&c., as above till) the right path. Such is the law they are preaching to creatures. And those creatures, Sâriputra, who are hearing the law from the present Tathâgatas, &c., shall all of them reach supreme, perfect enlightenment.

I myself also, Sâriputra, am at the present period a Tathâgata, &c., for the weal of many (&c., till) manifold; I myself also, Sâriputra, am preaching the law to creatures (&c., till) the right path. Such is the law I preach to creatures. And those creatures, Sâriputra, who now are hearing the law from me, shall all of them reach supreme, perfect enlightenment. In this sense, Sâriputra, it must be understood that nowhere in the world a second vehicle is taught, far less a third.

Yet, Sâriputra, when the Tathâgatas, &c., happen to appear at the decay[1] of the epoch, the decay of creatures, the decay of besetting sins[2], the decay of views, or the decay of lifetime; when they appear amid such signs of decay at the disturbance of the epoch; when creatures are much tainted, full of greed and poor in roots of goodness; then, Sâriputra, the Tathâgatas, &c., use, skilfully, to designate that one and sole Buddha-vehicle by the appellation of the threefold vehicle. Now, Sâriputra, such disciples, Arhats, or Pratyekabuddhas

[1] One MS. has °kashâyeshu in the plural, literally 'the dregs.'

[2] Klesakashâya, which Burnouf renders by 'la corruption du mal.' I think we might paraphrase the term used in the text by saying, the time when the besetting sins or natural depravities show themselves at their very worst.

who do not hear their actually being called to the Buddha-vehicle by the Tathâgata, who do not perceive, nor heed it, those, *S*âriputra, should not be acknowledged as disciples of the Tathâgata, nor as Arhats, nor as Pratyekabuddhas.

Again, *S*âriputra, if there be some monk or nun pretending to Arhatship without an earnest vow to reach supreme, perfect enlightenment and saying, 'I am standing too high[1] for the Buddha-vehicle, I am in my last appearance in the body before complete Nirvâ*n*a,' then, *S*âriputra, consider such a one to be conceited. For, *S*âriputra, it is unfit, it is improper that a monk, a faultless Arhat, should not believe in the law which he hears from the Tathâgata in his presence. I leave out of question when the Tathâgata shall have reached complete Nirvâ*n*a; for at that period, that time, *S*âriputra, when the Tathâgata shall be wholly extinct, there shall be none who either knows by heart or preaches such Sûtras as this. It will be under other Tathâgatas, &c., that they are to be freed from doubts. In respect to these things believe my words, *S*âriputra, value them, take them to heart; for there is no falsehood in the Tathâgatas, *S*âriputra. There is but one vehicle, *S*âriputra, and that the Buddha-vehicle.

And on that occasion to set forth this matter more copiously the Lord uttered the following stanzas:

---

[1] According to the reading utsanna; another MS. has u*kkh*inna, the reading followed by Burnouf, for he renders it by 'exclu.' The form u*kkh*inna could the more easily creep in, because instead of utsanna we often find u*kkh*anna, which, in fact, I believe to be the true form, for the word may be derived from *s*ad, akin to Latin cedo, Greek κέκασμαι; the usual spelling, however, is utsanna.

37. No less than five thousand monks, nuns, and lay devotees of both sexes, full of unbelief and conceit,

38. Remarking this slight, went, defective in training and foolish as they were, away in order to beware of damage.

39. The Lord, who knew them to be the dregs of the congregation, exclaimed[1]: They have no sufficient merit to hear this law.

40. My congregation is now pure[2], freed from chaff; the trash is removed and the pith only remains.

41. Hear from me, *S*âriputra, how this law has been discovered by the highest man[3], and how the mighty Buddhas are preaching it with many hundred proofs of skilfulness.

42. I know the disposition and conduct, the various inclinations of ko*t*is of living beings in this world; I know their various actions and the good they have done before.

43. Those living beings I initiate in this (law) by the aid of manifold interpretations and reasons; and by hundreds of arguments and illustrations have I, in one way or another, gladdened all creatures.

44. I utter both Sûtras and stanzas; legends,

---

[1] The two preceding stanzas and the half of this stanza make no part of the Lord's speech. It appears that the maker of the prose text has worked upon the older text in poetry, and on this occasion has been at a loss how to connect the latter with the former. The matter is easily explained on the assumption that the verses contained the ancient text, and therefore were treated with the greatest scruples.

[2] *S*uddhâ; Burnouf rendering 'ayant de la foi' has followed another reading, *s*raddhâ.

[3] The term used is Purushottama, a well-known epithet of Vish*n*u.

*G*âtakas[1], and prodigies, besides hundreds of introductions and curious parables.

45. I show Nirvâ*n*a to the ignorant with low dispositions, who have followed no course of duty under many ko*t*is of Buddhas, are bound to continued existence and wretched.

46. The self-born one uses such means to manifest Buddha-knowledge, but he shall never say to them, Ye also are to become Buddhas[2].

47. Why should not the mighty[3] one, after having waited for the right time, speak, now that he perceives the right moment is come? This is the fit opportunity, met somehow, of commencing the exposition of what really is.

48. Now the word of my commandment, as contained in nine divisions[4], has been published according to the varying degree of strength of creatures. Such is the device I have shown in order to introduce (creatures) to the knowledge of the giver of boons.

49. And to those in the world who have always been pure, wise, good-minded, compassionate sons

---

[1] Moralising tales and fables, so-called birth stories. Of the Pâli version of those tales a part has been edited by Professor Fausböll and translated by Dr. Rhys Davids.

[2] The reading is uncertain; one MS. has yushme pi buddheka (!) bhavishyatheti; another yushmaipi buddhehi bhavishati (!).

[3] Tâyin; here one might translate the word by 'able, clever.'

[4] The nine divisions, according to the matter, of Scripture, are with the Southern Buddhists, Sutta, Geya, Veyyâkara*n*a, Gâthâ, Udâna, Itivuttaka, *G*âtaka, Abbhutadhamma, and Vedalla, to which answer in the Northern enumeration Sûtra, Geya, Vaiyâkara*n*a, Gâthâ, Udâna, Ityukta (or Itiv*ri*ttika), *G*âtaka, Adbhutadharma, and Vaipulya; see Burnouf, Introduction, p. 51 sqq.

of Buddha and done thei rduty under many ko*t*is of Buddhas will I make known amplified Sûtras.

50. For they are endowed with such gifts of mental disposition and such advantages of a blameless outward form [1] that I can announce to them : in future ye shall become Buddhas benevolent and compassionate.

51. Hearing which, all of them will be pervaded with delight (at the thought): We shall become Buddhas pre-eminent in the world. And I, perceiving their conduct, will again reveal amplified Sûtras.

52. And those are the disciples of the Leader, who have listened to my word of command. One single stanza learnt or kept in memory suffices, no doubt of it, to lead all of them to enlightenment.

53. There is, indeed, but one vehicle; there is no second, nor a third anywhere in the world, apart from the case of the Purushottamas using an expedient to show that there is a diversity of vehicles.

54. The Chief of the world appears in the world to reveal the Buddha-knowledge. He has but one aim, indeed, no second; the Buddhas do not bring over (creatures) by an inferior vehicle.

55. There where the self-born one has established himself, and where the object of knowledge is, of whatever form or kind; (where) the powers, the stages of meditation, the emancipations, the perfected faculties (are); there the beings also shall be established.

56. I should be guilty of envy, should I, after

[1] The text has: tathâhi te âsaya*s*ampadâhi visuddharûpâyasamanvitâ 'bhût. This abhût is rather an unhappy attempt at Sanskritising a Prâkrit ahu*m* or ahu, than a singular used for a plural. Sampad and âya are nearly synonymous terms.

reaching the spotless eminent state of enlightenment, establish any one in the inferior vehicle. That would not beseem me.

57. There is no envy whatever in me; no jealousy, no desire, nor passion. Therefore I am the Buddha, because the world follows my teaching[1].

58. When, splendidly marked with (the thirty-two) characteristics, I am illuminating this whole world, and, worshipped by many hundreds of beings, I show the (unmistakable) stamp of the nature of the law;

59. Then, *S*âriputra, I think thus: How will all beings by the thirty-two characteristics mark the self-born Seer, who of his own accord sheds his lustre all over the world?

60. And while I am thinking and pondering, when my wish has been fulfilled and my vow accomplished, I no more[2] reveal Buddha-knowledge.

61. If, O son of *S*âri[3], I spoke to the creatures, 'Vivify in your minds the wish for enlightenment,' they would in their ignorance all go astray and never catch the meaning of my good words.

62. And considering them to be such, and that they have not accomplished their course of duty in previous existences, (I see how) they are attached and devoted to sensual pleasures, infatuated by desire and blind with delusion.

---

[1] Anubodhât, which may be rendered otherwise, '(because the world) perceives me.'

[2] One MS. reads *k*a, 'and,' for na, 'not.'

[3] *S*ârisuta, otherwise *S*âriputra. *S*ârikâ or sârikâ is the Turdus Salica, one of whose other names is dûtî, masc. dûta. It is hardly a mere play of chance that *S*âriputra in *K*ullavagga VII, 4 is praised as being an excellent dûta.

63. From lust they run into distress; they are tormented in the six states of existence and people the cemetery[1] again and again; they are overwhelmed with misfortune, as they possess little virtue.

64. They are continually entangled in the thickets of (sectarian) theories, such as, 'It is and it is not; it is thus and it is not thus.' In trying to get a decided opinion on what is found in the sixty-two (heretical) theories they come to embrace falsehood and continue in it.

65. They are hard to correct, proud, hypocritical, crooked, malignant, ignorant, dull; hence they do not hear the good Buddha-call, not once in ko*t*is of births.

66. To those, son of *S*âri, I show a device and say: Put an end to your trouble. When I perceive creatures vexed with mishap I make them see Nirvâ*n*a.

67. And so do I reveal all those laws that are ever holy and correct from the very first. And the son of Buddha who has completed his course shall once be a *G*ina.

68. It is but my skilfulness which prompts me to manifest three vehicles; for there is but one vehicle and one track[2]; there is also but one instruction by the leaders.

69. Remove all doubt and uncertainty; and should

---

[1] Ka*t*â*m*si vardhenti. This is a strangely altered ka*t*asî*m* vardhenti, Pâli ka*t*asi*m* va*ddh*enti; see *K*ullavagga XII, 1, 3, and cf. the expression ka*t*asiva*ddh*ano in *G*âtaka (ed. Fausböll) I, p. 146, and the passage of Âpastamba II, 9, 23, 4 (in Bühler's transl. p. 156), where cemeteries, *S*ma*s*ânâni, by the commentator Haradatta, are said to denote 'fresh births.'

[2] Or, method.

there be any who feel doubts, (let them know that) the Lords of the world speak the truth; this is the only vehicle, a second there is not.

70. The former Tathâgatas also, living in the past for innumerable Æons, the many thousands of Buddhas who are gone to final rest, whose number can never be counted,

71. Those highest of men[1] have all of them revealed most holy laws by means of illustrations, reasons, and arguments, with many hundred proofs of skilfulness.

72. And all of them have manifested but one vehicle and introduced but one on earth; by one vehicle have they led to full ripeness inconceivably many thousands of ko*t*is of beings.

73. Yet the *G*inas possess various and manifold means through which the Tathâgata reveals to the world, including the gods, superior enlightenment, in consideration of the inclinations and dispositions (of the different beings).

74. And all in the world who are hearing or have heard the law from the mouth of the Tathâgatas, given alms, followed the moral precepts, and patiently accomplished the whole of their religious duties;

75. Who have acquitted themselves in point of zeal and meditation, with wisdom reflected on those laws, and performed several meritorious actions, have all of them reached enlightenment.

76. And such beings as were living patient, subdued, and disciplined, under the rule of the *G*inas of those times, have all of them reached enlightenment.

---

[1] Purushottamâ*h*.

77. Others also, who paid worship to the relics of the departed *G*inas, erected many thousands of Stûpas made of gems, gold, silver, or crystal,

78. Or built Stûpas of emerald, cat's eye[1], pearls, egregious lapis lazuli, or sapphire; they have all of them reached enlightenment.

79. And those who erected Stûpas from marble, sandal-wood, or eagle-wood; constructed Stûpas from Deodar or a combination of different sorts of timber;

80. And who in gladness of heart built for the *G*inas Stûpas of bricks or clay; or caused mounds of earth to be raised in forests and wildernesses in dedication to the *G*inas;

81. The little boys even, who in playing erected here and there heaps of sand with the intention of dedicating them as Stûpas to the *G*inas, they have all of them reached enlightenment.

82. Likewise have all who caused jewel images to be made and dedicated, adorned with the thirty-two characteristic signs, reached enlightenment.

83. Others who had images of Sugatas made of the seven precious substances, of copper or brass, have all of them reached enlightenment.

84. Those who ordered beautiful statues of Sugatas to be made of lead, iron, clay, or plaster have &c.

85. Those who made images (of the Sugatas) on painted walls, with complete limbs and the hundred holy signs, whether they drew them themselves or had them drawn by others, have &c.

---

[1] Karketana, a certain precious stone, which, according to the dictionaries, is a kind of cat's eye. It rather looks as if it were the Greek χαλκηδόνιος.

86. Those even, whether men or boys, who during the lesson or in play, by way of amusement, made upon the walls (such) images with the nail or a piece of wood,

87. Have all of them reached enlightenment; they have become compassionate, and, by rousing many Bodhisattvas, have saved ko*t*is of creatures.

88. Those who offered flowers and perfumes to the relics of the Tathâgatas, to Stûpas, a mound of earth, images of clay or drawn on a wall;

89. Who caused musical instruments, drums, conch trumpets, and noisy great drums to be played, and raised the rattle of tymbals at such places in order to celebrate the highest enlightenment;

90. Who caused sweet lutes, cymbals, tabors, small drums, reed-pipes, flutes of —[1] or sugar-cane to be made, have all of them reached enlightenment.

91. Those who to celebrate the Sugatas made iron cymbals resound, — (?) or small drums[2]; who sang a song sweet and lovely;

92. They have all of them reached enlightenment. By paying various kinds of worship to the relics of the Sugatas, by doing but a little for the relics, by making resound were it but a single musical instrument;

93. Or by worshipping were it but with a single

---

[1] The MSS. have ekonna*d*a, which I do not understand; Burnouf, it would seem, has read ekotsava, for his translation has 'ceux qui ne servent que pour une fête.'

[2] Two words are doubtful; one MS. has *g*alama*md*ukâ vâ—ma*md*akâ vâ; another *g*âlamaddrakâ vâ — maddrakâ vâ. It is not impossible that maddraka is essentially the same with Sanskrit mandra, which is said to be a kind of drum. Burnouf renders the words by 'qui ont battu l'eau, frappé dans leurs mains.'

flower, by drawing on a wall the images of the Sugatas, by doing worship were it even with distracted thoughts, one shall in course of time see ko*t*is of Buddhas.

94. Those who, when in presence of a Stûpa, have offered their reverential salutation, be it in a complete form or by merely joining the hands; who, were it but for a single moment, bent their head or body;

95. And who at Stûpas containing relics have one single time said: Homage be to Buddha! albeit they did it with distracted thoughts, all have attained superior enlightenment.

96. The creatures who in the days of those Sugatas, whether already extinct [1] or still in existence, have heard no more than the name of the law, have all of them reached enlightenment.

97. Many ko*t*is of future Buddhas beyond imagination and measure shall likewise reveal this device as *G*inas and supreme Lords.

98. Endless shall be the skilfulness of these leaders of the world, by which they shall educate [2] ko*t*is of beings to that Buddha-knowledge which is free from imperfection [3].

---

[1] Or, expired, and more grandly entered Nirvâ*n*a. The real meaning of the contents of stanza 74 seq. will be that all men who lived under past Sugatas, i. e. in past days, after doing acts of piety, have finished with reaching enlightenment, i. e. with dying.

[2] Vinayati, to train, educate, also means to carry away, remove.

[3] I. e. death. Such terms as perfect enlightenment, Buddha-knowledge, &c., when they are veiled or euphemistic expressions for death, may be compared with the phrase 'to see the truth,' which in some parts of Europe is quite common, especially among

99. Never has there been any being who, after hearing the law of those (leaders), shall not become Buddha [1]; for this is the fixed vow of the Tathâgatas: Let me, by accomplishing my course of duty, lead others to enlightenment.

100. They are to expound in future days many thousand ko*t*is of heads of the law; in their Tathâgataship they shall teach the law by showing the sole vehicle before-mentioned.

101. The line of the law forms an unbroken continuity and the nature of its properties is always manifest. Knowing this, the Buddhas, the highest of men, shall reveal this single vehicle [2].

102. They shall reveal the stability of the law, its being subjected to fixed rules, its unshakeable perpetuity in the world, the awaking of the Buddhas on the elevated terrace of the earth, their skilfulness.

103. In all directions of space are standing Buddhas, like sand of the Ganges, honoured by gods and men; these also do, for the weal of all beings in the world, expound superior enlightenment.

104. Those Buddhas while manifesting skilfulness display various vehicles though, at the same time, indicating the one single vehicle [3]: the supreme place of blessed rest.

---

country people, as synonymous with dying. No less common is the expression nirvâ*n*am pa*s*yati, to see Nirvâ*n*a.

[1] The text has eko 'pi satvo na kadâ*k*i teshâ*m*, *S*rutvâna dharma*m* na bhaveta buddha*h*. *S*rutvâna answers, of course, to a Prâkrit sutvâna; cf. Vedic pîtvânam, Pâ*n*ini VII, 1, 48.

[2] Viditva Buddhâ dvipadânam uttamâ, prakâ*s*ayishyanti 'mam ekayâna*m*. The elision of i is an example of Prâkrit or Pâli Sandhi, frequent in the stanzas.

[3] Yâna here properly denotes way, or place where one is going to.

105. Acquainted as they are with the conduct of all mortals, with their peculiar dispositions and previous actions; with due regard to their strenuousness and vigour, as well as their inclination, the Buddhas impart their lights to them.

106. By dint of knowledge the leaders produce many illustrations, arguments, and reasons; and considering how the creatures have various inclinations they impart various directions.

107. And myself also, the leader of the chief *G*inas, am now manifesting, for the weal of creatures now living, this Buddha enlightenment by thousands of ko*t*is of various directions.

108. I reveal the law in its multifariousness with regard to the inclinations and dispositions of creatures. I use different means to rouse each according to his own character. Such is the might of my knowledge.

109. I likewise see the poor wretches, deficient in wisdom and conduct, lapsed into the mundane whirl, retained in dismal places, plunged in affliction incessantly renewed.

110. Fettered as they are by desire like the yak by its tail, continually blinded by sensual pleasure, they do not seek the Buddha, the mighty one; they do not seek the law that leads to the end of pain.

111. Staying in the six states of existence, they are benumbed in their senses, stick unmoved to the low views, and suffer pain on pain. For those I feel a great compassion.

112. On the terrace of enlightenment I have remained three weeks in full, searching and pondering on such a matter, steadily looking up to the tree there (standing).

113. Keeping in view that king of trees with an

unwavering gaze I walked round at its foot[1] (thinking): This law is wonderful and lofty, whereas creatures are blind with dulness and ignorance.

114. Then it was that Brahma entreated me, and so did Indra, the four rulers of the cardinal points, Mahesvara, Îsvara, and the hosts of Maruts by thousands of kotis[2].

115. All stood with joined hands and respectful, while myself was revolving the matter in my mind (and thought): What shall I do? At the very time that I am uttering syllables[3], beings are oppressed with evils.

116. In their ignorance they will not heed the law I announce, and in consequence of it they will incur some penalty. It would be better were I never to speak. May my quiet extinction take place this very day!

117. But on remembering the former Buddhas and their skilfulness, (I thought): Nay, I also will manifest this tripartite Buddha-enlightenment.

118. When I was thus meditating on the law, the other Buddhas in all the directions of space appeared to me in their own body and raised their voice, crying 'Amen.

119. 'Amen, Solitary, first Leader of the world! now that thou hast come to unsurpassed knowledge,

---

[1] Tasyaiva heshthe, i.e. Prâkrit hetthe, Sanskrit adhastât.

[2] The story slightly differs from what is found in the Mahâvagga, Lalita-vistara, and other works, in so far as the number of weeks is generally reckoned as seven. There are, however, other discrepancies between the relations in the various sources, for which I must refer to Mahâvagga I, 5; Lalita-vistara, p. 511; cf. Bigandet, Legend, p. 112.

[3] The text has varnân, i.e. colours, letters.

and art meditating on the skilfulness of the leaders of the world, thou repeatest their teaching.

120. 'We also, being Buddhas, will make clear the highest word[1], divided into three parts; for men (occasionally) have low inclinations, and might perchance from ignorance not believe (us, when we say), Ye shall become Buddhas.

121. 'Hence we will rouse many Bodhisattvas by the display of skilfulness and the encouraging of the wish of obtaining fruits.'

122. And I was delighted to hear the sweet voice of the leaders of men; in the exultation of my heart I said to the blessed saints, 'The words of the eminent sages are not spoken in vain.

123. 'I, too, will act according to the indications of the wise leaders of the world; having myself been born in the midst of the degradation of creatures, I have known agitation in this dreadful world.'

124. When I had come to that conviction, O son of *S*âri, I instantly went to Benares, where I skilfully preached the law to the five Solitaries[2], that law which is the base of final beatitude.

125. From that moment the wheel of my law has been moving[3], and the name of Nirvâ*n*a made its appearance in the world, as well as the name of Arhat, of Dharma, and Saṅgha.

126. Many years have I preached and pointed to the

---

[1] Properly, the most lofty place; the word pada in the text means place, spot, word, subject, &c.

[2] Âg*ñ*âta-Kau*nd*inya and the four others mentioned in the opening chapter.

[3] In chap. VII we shall see that the wheel was put in motion at an inconceivably long period before, by the Tathâgata Mahâbhig*ñ*âg*ñ*ânâbhibhû.

stage of Nirvâ*n*a, the end of wretchedness and mundane existence. Thus I used to speak at all times.

127. And when I saw, *S*âriputra, the children of the highest of men by many thousands of ko*t*is, numberless, striving after the supreme, the highest enlightenment;

128. And when such as had heard the law of the *G*inas, owing to the many-sidedness of (their) skilfulness, had approached me and stood before my face, all of them with joined hands, and respectful;

129. Then I conceived the idea that the time had come for me to announce the excellent law and to reveal supreme enlightenment, for which task I had been born in the world.

130. This (event) to-day will be hard to be understood by the ignorant who imagine they see[1] here a sign, as they are proud and dull. But the Bodhisattvas, they will listen to me.

131. And I felt free from hesitation and highly cheered; putting aside all timidity, I began speaking in the assembly of the sons of Sugata, and roused them to enlightenment.

132. On beholding such worthy sons of Buddha (I said): Thy doubts also will be removed, and these twelve hundred (disciples) of mine, free from imperfections, will all of them become Buddhas.

133. Even as the nature of the law of the former[2] mighty saints and the future *G*inas is, so is my law

---

[1] One would rather expect 'who imagine not to see, fail to see,' but the words of the text do not admit of such an interpretation.

[2] Yathaiva teshâ*m* purimâ*n*a Tâyinâm, anâgatânâ*m* *k*a *G*inâna dharmatâ, mamâpi eshâ vikalpava*rg*itâ, tathaiva 'ha*m* de*s*ayi adya tubhya*m*.

free from any doubtfulness, and it is such as I to-day preach it to thee.

134. At certain times, at certain places, somehow do the leaders appear in the world, and after their appearance will they, whose view is boundless, at one time or another preach[1] a similar law.

135. It is most difficult to meet with this superior law, even in myriads of kotis of Æons; very rare are the beings who will adhere to the superior law which they have heard from me.

136. Just as the blossom of the glomerous fig-tree is rare, albeit sometimes, at some places, and somehow it is met with, as something pleasant to see for everybody, as a wonder to the world including the gods;

137. (So wonderful) and far more wonderful is the law I proclaim. Any one who, on hearing a good exposition of it, shall cheerfully accept it and recite but one word of it, will have done honour to all Buddhas.

138. Give up all doubt and uncertainty in this respect; I declare that I am the king of the law (Dharmarâga); I am urging others to enlightenment, but I am here without disciples.

139. Let this mystery be for thee, Sâriputra, for all disciples of mine, and for the eminent Bodhisattvas, who are to keep this mystery.

140. For the creatures, when at the period of the five depravities[2], are vile and bad; they are blinded

[1] Desayuh, plural; Burnouf seems to have read the singular.

[2] The five kashâyas are summarily indicated in Dhammapada 115 by 'râgâdi.' As the list of klesas, Lalita-vistara, p. 348 seq., commences with râga, there can be no doubt that Burnouf was right in supposing the five kashâyas to be synonymous with the corresponding number of klesas. The items of the list are variously given.

by sensual desires, the fools, and never turn their minds to enlightenment.

141. (Some) beings, having heard this one and sole vehicle[1] manifested by the *G*ina, will in days to come swerve from it, reject the Sûtra, and go down to hell.

142. But those beings who shall be modest and pure, striving after the supreme and the highest enlightenment, to them shall I unhesitatingly set forth the endless forms of this one and sole vehicle.

143. Such is the mastership of the leaders; that is, their skilfulness. They have spoken in many mysteries[2]; hence it is difficult to understand (them).

144. Therefore try to understand the mystery[3] of the Buddhas, the holy masters of the world; forsake all doubt and uncertainty: you shall become Buddhas; rejoice!

---

[1] Or, rather, learnt this way.

[2] The word in the text is sandhâva*k*anai*h*, evidently synonymous with sandhâbhâshya.

[3] Sandhâ, by Burnouf rendered 'langage énigmatique.' On comparing the different meanings of sandhâ and sandhâya, both in Sanskrit and in Pâli, I am led to suppose that sandhâ- (and sandhâya-) bhâshita (bhâshya) was a term used in the sense of 'speaking (speech) in council, a counsel,' scarcely differing from mantra. In both words secrecy is implied, though not expressed. If we take the term as synonymous with mantra, the connection between upâyakau*s*alya, diplomacy, skilfulness, and sandhâbhâshita is clear. Cf. the Gothic word rûna, both βουλή and μυστήριον; garûni, συμβούλιον. The theistical sect have taken it in the sense of 'God's counsel,' but I cannot produce a warrant for this guess. By Hiouen Thsang, the term sandhâya is translated by 'in a hidden sense,' as we know from Professor Max Müller's note, in his edition of the Vagra*kkh*edikâ, p. 23.

CHAPTER III.

A PARABLE.

Then the venerable Sâriputra, pleased, glad, charmed, cheerful, thrilling with delight and joy, stretched his joined hands towards the Lord, and, looking up to the Lord with a steady gaze, addressed him in this strain: I am astonished, amazed, O Lord! I am in ecstasy to hear such a call from the Lord. For when, before I had heard of this law from the Lord, I saw other Bodhisattvas, and heard that the Bodhisattvas would in future get the name of Buddhas, I felt extremely sorry, extremely vexed to be deprived from so grand a sight as the Tathâgata-knowledge. And whenever, O Lord, for my daily recreation I was visiting the caves of rocks or mountains, wood thickets, lovely gardens, rivers, and roots of trees, I always was occupied with the same and ever-recurring thought: 'Whereas the entrance into the fixed points[1] of the law is nominally[2] equal, we have been dismissed by the Lord with the inferior vehicle.' Instantly, however, O Lord, I felt that it

[1] Or, elements.

[2] Tulye nâma dharmadhâtupravese vayam—niryâtitâh. The terms are ambiguous, and open to various interpretations. The Tibetan version has, according to Burnouf, 'in an equal introduction to the domain of the law,' from which at least thus much results, that the text had tulye, not tulya, as Burnouf reads. Tulye pravese I take to be a so-called absolute locative case. As to the plural 'we,' it refers to Sâriputra.

was our own fault, not the Lord's. For had we regarded the Lord at the time of his giving the all-surpassing demonstration of the law, that is, the exposition of supreme, perfect enlightenment, then, O Lord, we should have become adepts in those laws. But because, without understanding the mystery of the Lord, we, at the moment of the Bodhisattvas not being assembled, heard only in a hurry, caught, meditated, minded, took to heart the first lessons pronounced on the law, therefore, O Lord, I used to pass day and night in self-reproach. (But) to-day, O Lord, I have reached complete extinction; to-day, O Lord, I have become calm; to-day, O Lord, I am wholly come to rest; to-day, O Lord, I have reached Arhatship; to-day, O Lord, I am the Lord's eldest son, born from his law, sprung into existence by the law, made by the law, inheriting from the law, accomplished by the law. My burning has left me, O Lord, now that I have heard this wonderful law, which I had not learnt before, announced by the voice from the mouth of the Lord.

And on that occasion the venerable *S*âriputra addressed the Lord in the following stanzas:

1. I am astonished, great Leader, I am charmed to hear this voice; I feel no doubt any more; now am I fully ripe for the superior vehicle.

2. Wonderful is the voice[1] of the Sugatas; it dispels the doubt and pain of living beings; my pain also is all gone now that I, freed from imperfections, have heard that voice (or, call).

3. When I was taking my daily recreation or was

[1] Rather, call.

walking in woody thickets, when betaking myself to the roots of trees or to mountain caves, I indulged in no other thought but this:

4. 'O how am I deluded by vain thoughts! whereas the faultless laws are, nominally, equal, shall I in future not preach the superior law in the world?

5. 'The thirty-two characteristic signs have failed me, and the gold colour of the skin has vanished; all the (ten) powers and emancipations have likewise been lost. O how have I gone astray at the equal laws!

6. 'The secondary signs also of the great Seers, the eighty excellent specific signs, and the eighteen uncommon properties have failed me. O how am I deluded!'

7. And when I had perceived thee, so benign and merciful to the world, and was lonely walking to take my daily recreation, I thought: 'I am excluded from that inconceivable, unbounded knowledge!'

8. Days and nights, O Lord, I passed always thinking of the same subject; I would ask the Lord whether I had lost my rank or not.

9. In such reflections, O Chief of *G*inas, I constantly passed my days and nights; and on seeing many other Bodhisattvas praised by the Leader of the world,

10. And on hearing this Buddha-law, I thought: 'To be sure, this is expounded mysteriously[1]; it is an inscrutable, subtle, and faultless science, which is announced by the *G*inas on the terrace of enlightenment.'

---

[1] Sandhâya; the Chinese translation by Kumârâ-*g*iva, according to Stan. Julien's version, has 'suivant la convenance.'

11. Formerly I was attached to (heretical) theories, being a wandering monk and in high honour (or, of the same opinions) with the heretics[1]; afterwards has the Lord, regarding my disposition, taught me Nirvâ*n*a, to detach me from perverted views.

12. After having completely freed myself from all (heretical) views and reached the laws of void, (I conceive) that I have become extinct; yet this is not deemed to be extinction.

13. But when one becomes Buddha, a superior being, honoured by men, gods, goblins, Titans, and adorned with the thirty-two characteristic signs, then one will be completely extinct.

14. All those (former) cares[2] have now been dispelled, since I have heard the voice. Now am I extinct, as thou announcest my destination (to Nirvâ*n*a) before the world including the gods.

15. When I first heard the voice of the Lord, I had a great terror lest it might be Mâra, the evil one, who on this occasion had adopted the disguise of Buddha.

16. But when the unsurpassed Buddha-wisdom had been displayed in and established with argu-

---

[1] Parivrâ*g*akas Tîrthikasammata*s* *k*a. The term parivrâ*g*aka or parivrâ*g* is occasionally applied to Buddhist monks, but here it would seem that the Brahmanistic monks are meant, the brahmasa*m*sthas of *S*aṅkara in his commentary on Brahma-Sûtra III, 4, 20. They are to be distinguished from the Tîrthika's.

[2] Or, thoughts; one MS. has vyapanîta sarvâni 'mi (read °*n*i 'mi) manyitâni; another reads, vy. sarvâ*n*i 'mi ma*kk*itâni. Manyita is a participle derived from the present tense of manyate, to mean, to mind, in the manner of *g*ahita from *g*ahâti. Ma*kk*itâni is hardly correct; it is, however, just possible that it is intended to stand for ma*k*-*k*ittâni.

ments, reasons, and illustrations, by myriads of ko*t*is, then I lost all doubt about the law I heard.

17. And when thou hadst mentioned to me[1] the thousands of ko*t*is of Buddhas, the past *G*inas who have come to final rest, and how they preached this law by firmly establishing it through skilfulness;

18. How the many future Buddhas and those who are now existing, as knowers of the real truth, shall expound or are expounding this law by hundreds of able devices;

19. And when thou wert mentioning thine own course after leaving home, how the idea of the wheel of the law presented itself to thy mind and how thou decidedst upon preaching the law;

20. Then I was convinced: This is not Mâra; it is the Lord of the world, who has shown the true course; no Mâras can here abide. So then my mind (for a moment) was overcome with perplexity;

21. But when the sweet, deep, and lovely voice of Buddha gladdened me, all doubts were scattered, my perplexity vanished, and I stood firm in knowledge.

22. I shall become a Tathâgata, undoubtedly, worshipped in the world including the gods; I shall manifest Buddha-wisdom, mysteriously[2] rousing many Bodhisattvas.

After this speech of the venerable *S*âriputra, the Lord said to him: I declare to thee, *S*âriputra, I announce to thee, in presence of this world including the gods, Mâras, and Brahmas, in presence of this

---

[1] Yadâ *k*a me Buddhasahasrako*t*ya*h*, kîrteshy (var. lect. kîrtishy) atîtân parinirv*ri*tâ*m* *G*inân. Kîrteshi is Sanskrit a*k*ikîrtas.

[2] Sandhâya. Burnouf's rendering 'aux créatures' points to satvâya, which is nothing but a misread sandhâya. Cf. stanza 37, below.

people, including ascetics and Brahmans, that thou, *S*âriputra, hast been by me made ripe for supreme, perfect enlightenment, in presence of twenty hundred thousand myriads of ko*t*is of Buddhas, and that thou, *S*âriputra, hast for a long time followed my commandments. Thou, *S*âriputra, art, by the counsel of the Bodhisattva, by the decree of the Bodhisattva, reborn here under my rule. Owing to the mighty will of the Bodhisattva thou, *S*âriputra, hast no recollection of thy former vow to observe the (religious) course; of the counsel of the Bodhisattva, the decree of the Bodhisattva. Thou thinkest that thou hast reached final rest. I, wishing to revive and renew in thee the knowledge of thy former vow to observe the (religious) course, will reveal to the disciples the Dharmaparyâya called 'the Lotus of the True Law,' this Sûtrânta, &c.

Again, *S*âriputra, at a future period, after innumerable, inconceivable, immeasurable Æons, when thou shalt have learnt the true law of hundred thousand myriads of ko*t*is of Tathâgatas, showed devotion in various ways, and achieved the present Bodhisattva-course, thou shalt become in the world a Tathâgata, &c., named Padmaprabha[1], endowed with science and conduct, a Sugata, a knower of the world, an unsurpassed tamer of men, a master of gods and men[2], a Lord Buddha.

---

[1] Padma, Nelumbium Speciosum, having a rosy hue, we must infer that *S*âriputra will be reborn at twilight.

[2] The supreme tamer of men is, in reality, Yama, personified Twilight, and as evening twilight the god of death and the ruler of the infernal regions. The word yama itself means both 'twin' (cf. twi-light) and 'tamer.' Owing to the fact that in mythology many beings are denoted by the name of 'the twins,' e. g. morning and evening, the A*s*vins, Castor and Pollux, it is often

At that time then, *S*âriputra, the Buddha-field of that Lord, the Tathâgata Padmaprabha, to be called Vira*g*a, will be level, pleasant, delightful, extremely beautiful to see, pure, prosperous, rich, quiet, abounding with food, replete with many races of men[1]; it will consist of lapis lazuli, and contain a checker-board of eight compartments distinguished by gold threads, each compartment having its jewel tree always and perpetually filled with blossoms and fruits of seven precious substances.

Now that Tathâgata Padmaprabha, &c., *S*âriputra, will preach the law by the instrumentality of three vehicles[2]. Further, *S*âriputra, that Tathâgata will not appear at the decay of the Æon, but preach the law by virtue of a vow.

That Æon, *S*âriputra, will be named Mahâratnapratima*nd*ita (i. e. ornamented with magnificent jewels). Knowest thou, *S*âriputra, why that Æon is named Mahâratnapratima*nd*ita? The Bodhisattvas of a Buddha-field, *S*âriputra, are called ratnas (jewels), and at that time there will be many Bodhisattvas in that sphere (called) Vira*g*a; innumerable, incalculable, beyond computation, abstraction made from their being computed by the Tathâgatas. On that account is that Æon called Mahâratnapratima*nd*ita.

Now, to proceed, *S*âriputra, at that period the

---

difficult to make out which pair of twins is meant in any particular case. The sun himself appears in the function of Yama, because it is he who makes twilight.

[1] One MS. reads bahu*g*anamanushyâkîr*n*a, the other bahu*g*anamarruprakîr*n*a.

[2] Cf. the threefold vehicle, trivr*i*t ratha, of the A*s*vins, Rigveda I, 34, 9. 12, 47, 2.

Bodhisattvas of that field will in walking step on jewel lotuses[1]. And these Bodhisattvas will not be plying their work for the first time, they having accumulated roots of goodness and observed the course of duty under many hundred thousand Buddhas; they are praised by the Tathâgatas for their zealous application to Buddha-knowledge; are perfectioned in the rites preparatory to transcendent knowledge; accomplished in the direction of all true laws; mild, thoughtful. Generally, *S*âriputra, will that Buddha-region teem with such Bodhisattvas.

As to the lifetime, *S*âriputra, of that Tathâgata Padmaprabha, it will last twelve intermediate kalpas, if we leave out of account the time of his being a young prince. And the lifetime of the creatures then living will measure eight intermediate kalpas. At the expiration of twelve intermediate kalpas, *S*âriputra, the Tathâgata Padmaprabha, after announcing the future destiny of the Bodhisattva called Dh*ri*tiparipûr*n*a[2] to superior perfect enlightenment, is to enter complete Nirvâ*n*a. 'This Bodhisattva Mahâsattva Dh*ri*tiparipûr*n*a, O monks, shall immediately after me come to supreme, perfect enlightenment. He shall become in the world a Tathâgata named Padmav*ri*shabhavikrâmin, an Arhat, &c., endowed with science and conduct, &c. &c.'

Now the Tathâgata Padmav*ri*shabhavikrâmin, *S*âriputra, will have a Buddha-field of quite the same description. The true law, *S*âriputra, of that Tathâgata Padmav*ri*shabhavikrâmin will, after his

[1] We may express the same idea thus: roses are springing up under their feet at every step.

[2] Dh*ri*ti, perseverance, endurance. Dh*ri*tiparipûr*n*a is, full of perseverance or endurance.

extinction, last thirty-two intermediate kalpas, and the counterfeit of his true law will last as many intermediate kalpas[1].

And on that occasion the Lord uttered the following stanzas:

23. Thou also, son of *S*âri, shalt in future be a *G*ina, a Tathâgata named Padmaprabha, of illimited sight; thou shalt educate thousands of ko*t*is of living beings[2].

24. After paying honour to many ko*t*is of Buddhas, making[3] strenuous efforts in the course of duty, and after having produced in thyself the ten powers, thou shalt reach supreme, perfect enlightenment.

25. Within a period inconceivable and immense there shall be an Æon rich in jewels (or, the Æon jewel-rich), and a sphere named Vira*g*a, the pure field of the highest of men;

26. And its ground will consist of lapis lazuli, and be set off with gold threads; it will have hundreds of jewel trees, very beautiful, and covered with blossoms and fruits.

27. Bodhisattvas of good memory, able in showing

---

[1] This counterfeit, pratirûpaka, of the true law, reminds one of the counterfeit, paitiyâro, produced by Ariman in opposition to the creation of Ormazd; mythologically it is the dark side of nature. That there is some connection between the Buddhistical pratirûpaka and the Iranian paitiyâro can hardly be doubted.

[2] A striking example of how the original Prâkrit of the verse has been adulterated in order to give it a more Sanskrit colouring is afforded by this stanza. One MS. has bhavishyasî Sârisutâ tuha*m*pi; another bhavishyase Sârisutânukampî, with marginal correction tvayampi.

[3] Upâdayitvâ, i.e. Pâli upâdiyitvâ, synonymous with ârabhya (vîryam); the var. lect. upâr*g*ayitvâ, having acquired, is an innovation, at first sight specious enough.

the course of duty which they have been taught under hundreds of Buddhas, will come to be born in that field.

28. And the afore-mentioned *G*ina, then in his last bodily existence, shall, after passing the state of prince royal, renounce sensual pleasures, leave home (to become a wandering ascetic), and thereafter reach the supreme and the highest enlightenment.

29. The lifetime of that *G*ina will be precisely twelve intermediate kalpas, and the life of men will then last eight intermediate kalpas.

30. After the extinction of the Tathâgata the true law will continue thirty-two Æons in full, for the benefit of the world, including the gods.

31. When the true law shall have come to an end, its counterfeit will stand for thirty-two intermediate kalpas. The dispersed relics of the holy one will always be honoured by men and gods.

32. Such will be the fate of that Lord. Rejoice, O son of *S*âri, for it is thou who shalt be that most excellent of men, so unsurpassed.

The four classes of the audience, monks, nuns, lay devotees male and female, gods, Nâgas, goblins, Gandharvas, demons, Garu*d*as, Kinnaras, great serpents, men and beings not human, on hearing the announcement of the venerable *S*âriputra's destiny to supreme, perfect enlightenment, were so pleased, glad, charmed, thrilling with delight and joy, that they covered the Lord severally with their own robes, while Indra the chief of gods, Brahma Sahâmpati, besides hundred thousands of ko*t*is of other divine beings, covered him with heavenly garments and bestrewed him with flowers of heaven, Mandâravas and great Mandâravas. High aloft they whirled celestial clothes and struck hundred thousands of celestial musical instruments and cymbals, high in the sky; and after pouring a great rain of flowers they uttered these words: The wheel of the law has been put in motion by the Lord, the first time at Benares at *Ri*shipatana in the Deer-park; to-day has the Lord again put in motion the supreme wheel of the law.

And on that occasion those divine beings uttered the following stanzas:

33. The wheel of the law was put in motion by thee, O thou that art unrivalled in the world, at Benares, O great hero! (that wheel which is the rotation of) the rise and decay of all aggregates.

34. There it was put in motion for the first time; now, a second time, is it turned here, O Lord. To-day, O Master, thou hast preached this law, which is hard to be received with faith[1].

35. Many laws have we heard near the Lord of the world, but never before did we hear a law like this.

36. We receive with gratitude, O great hero, the mysterious speech of the great Sages, such as this prediction regarding the self-possessed Ârya *S*âriputra.

37. May we also become such incomparable Buddhas in the world, who by mysterious speech announce supreme Buddha-enlightenment.

38. May we also, by the good we have done in this world and in the next, and by our having

[1] Du*hs*raddheyo yas te 'ya*m*, var. lect. du*hs*raddheyo 'yan teshâ*m*. It may be remarked that *s*raddhâ not only means faith, belief, but also liking, approval. Cf. the passage in Mahâvagga I, 5, 2 sq.; the verses in Lalita-vistara, p. 515.

propitiated the Buddha, be allowed to make a vow for Buddhaship.

Thereupon the venerable *S*âriputra thus spoke to the Lord: My doubt is gone, O Lord, my uncertainty is at an end on hearing from the mouth of the Lord my destiny to supreme enlightenment. But these twelve hundred self-controlled (disciples), O Lord, who have been placed by thee on the stage of *S*aikshas[1], have been thus admonished and instructed: 'My preaching of the law, O monks, comes to this, that deliverance from birth, decrepitude, disease, and death is inseparably connected with Nirvâ*n*a;' and these two thousand monks, O Lord, thy disciples, both those who are still under training and adepts, who all of them are free from false views about the soul, false views about existence, false views about cessation of existence, free, in short, from all false views, who are fancying themselves to have reached the stage of Nirvâ*n*a, these have fallen into uncertainty by hearing from the mouth of the Lord this law which they had not heard before. Therefore, O Lord, please speak to these monks, to dispel their uneasiness, so that the four classes of the audience, O Lord, may be relieved from their doubt and perplexity.

On this speech of the venerable *S*âriputra the Lord

---

[1] I. e. of those who are under training, Pâli sekho. The term is applied to the first seven degrees of persons striving for sanctification, the eighth, or Arhat, being A*s*aiksha (Asekha). It implies that they still have a remainder of human passion to eradicate, still duties to perform, still a probation to be passed through; see Childers, Pâli Dict. p. 472. The seven degrees of *S*aiksha answer to the sevenfold preparatory wisdom in the Yoga system; see Yoga-*s*âstra 2, 27.

said to him the following: Have I not told thee before, Sâriputra, that the Tathâgata, &c., preaches the law by able devices, varying directions and indications, fundamental ideas, interpretations, with due regard to the different dispositions and inclinations of creatures whose temperaments[1] are so various? All his preachings of the law have no other end but supreme and perfect enlightenment, for which he is rousing beings to the Bodhisattva-course. But, Sâriputra, to elucidate this matter more at large, I will tell thee a parable, for men of good understanding will generally readily enough catch the meaning of what is taught under the shape of a parable.

Let us suppose the following case, Sâriputra. In a certain village, town, borough, province, kingdom, or capital, there was a certain housekeeper, old, aged, decrepit, very advanced in years, rich, wealthy, opulent; he had a great house, high, spacious, built a long time ago and old, inhabited by some two, three, four, or five hundred living beings. The house had but one door, and a thatch; its terraces were tottering, the bases of its pillars rotten, the coverings[2] and plaster of the walls loose. On a sudden the whole house was from every side put in conflagration by a mass of fire. Let us suppose that the man had many little boys, say five, or ten, or even twenty, and that he himself had come out of the house.

Now, Sâriputra, that man, on seeing the house from every side wrapt in a blaze by a great mass of

[1] **Dhâtvâsaya**, properly the disposition of the constitutive elements of the body.

[2] Or, boards.

fire, got afraid, frightened, anxious in his mind, and made the following reflection: I myself am able to come out from the burning house through the door, quickly and safely, without being touched or scorched by that great mass of fire; but my children, those young boys, are staying in the burning house, playing, amusing, and diverting themselves with all sorts of sports. They do not perceive, nor know, nor understand, nor mind that the house is on fire, and do not get afraid. Though scorched by that great mass of fire, and affected with such a mass of pain, they do not mind the pain, nor do they conceive the idea of escaping.

The man, *S*âriputra, is strong, has powerful arms, and (so) he makes this reflection: I am strong, and have powerful arms; why, let me gather all my little boys and take them to my breast to effect their escape from the house. A second reflection then presented itself to his mind: This house has but one opening; the door is shut; and those boys, fickle, unsteady, and childlike as they are, will, it is to be feared, run hither and thither, and come to grief and disaster in this mass of fire. Therefore I will warn them. So resolved, he calls to the boys: Come, my children; the house is burning with a mass of fire; come, lest ye be burnt in that mass of fire, and come to grief and disaster. But the ignorant boys do not heed the words of him who is their well-wisher; they are not afraid, not alarmed, and feel no misgiving; they do not care, nor fly, nor even know nor understand the purport of the word 'burning;' on the contrary, they run hither and thither, walk about, and repeatedly look at their father; all, because they are so ignorant.

Then the man is going to reflect thus: The house is burning, is blazing by a mass of fire. It is to be feared that myself as well as my children will come to grief and disaster. Let me therefore by some skilful means get the boys out of the house. The man knows the disposition of the boys, and has a clear perception of their inclinations. Now these boys happen to have many and manifold toys to play with, pretty, nice, pleasant, dear, amusing, and precious. The man, knowing the disposition of the boys, says to them: My children, your toys, which are so pretty, precious, and admirable, which you are so loth to miss, which are so various and multifarious, (such as) bullock-carts, goat-carts, deer-carts, which are so pretty, nice, dear, and precious to you, have all been put by me outside the house-door for you to play with. Come, run out, leave the house; to each of you I shall give what he wants. Come soon; come out for the sake of these toys. And the boys, on hearing the names mentioned of such playthings as they like and desire, so agreeable to their taste, so pretty, dear, and delightful, quickly rush out from the burning house, with eager effort and great alacrity, one having no time to wait for the other, and pushing each other on with the cry of 'Who shall arrive first, the very first?'

The man, seeing that his children have safely and happily escaped, and knowing that they are free from danger, goes and sits down in the open air on the square of the village, his heart filled with joy and delight, released from trouble and hindrance, quite at ease. The boys go up to the place where their father is sitting, and say: 'Father, give us those toys to play with, those bullock-carts, goat-carts, and deer-carts.' Then, *S*âriputra, the man gives to his sons, who run swift as the wind, bullock-carts only, made of seven precious substances, provided with benches, hung with a multitude of small bells, lofty, adorned with rare and wonderful jewels, embellished with jewel wreaths, decorated with garlands of flowers, carpeted with cotton mattresses and woollen coverlets, covered with white cloth and silk, having on both sides rosy cushions, yoked with white, very fair and fleet bullocks, led by a multitude of men. To each of his children he gives several bullock-carts of one appearance and one kind, provided with flags, and swift as the wind. That man does so, *S*âriputra, because being rich, wealthy, and in possession of many treasures and granaries, he rightly thinks: Why should I give these boys inferior carts, all these boys being my own children, dear and precious? I have got such great vehicles, and ought to treat all the boys equally and without partiality. As I own many treasures and granaries, I could give such great vehicles to all beings, how much more then to my own children. Meanwhile the boys are mounting the vehicles with feelings of astonishment and wonder. Now, *S*âriputra, what is thy opinion? Has that man made himself guilty of a falsehood by first holding out to his children the prospect of three vehicles and afterwards giving to each of them the greatest vehicles only, the most magnificent vehicles?

*S*âriputra answered: By no means, Lord; by no means, Sugata. That is not sufficient, O Lord, to qualify the man as a speaker of falsehood, since it only was a skilful device to persuade his children to go out of the burning house and save their lives. Nay, besides recovering their very body, O Lord, they have received all those toys. If that man, O Lord, had given no single cart, even then he would not have been a speaker of falsehood, for he had previously been meditating on saving the little boys from a great mass of pain by some able device. Even in this case, O Lord, the man would not have been guilty of falsehood, and far less now that he, considering his having plenty of treasures and prompted by no other motive but the love of his children, gives to all, to coax[1] them, vehicles of one kind, and those the greatest vehicles. That man, Lord, is not guilty of falsehood.

The venerable Sâriputra having thus spoken, the Lord said to him: Very well, very well, Sâriputra, quite so; it is even as thou sayest. So, too, Sâriputra, the Tathâgata, &c., is free from all dangers, wholly exempt from all misfortune, despondency, calamity, pain, grief, the thick enveloping dark mists of ignorance. He, the Tathâgata, endowed with Buddha-knowledge, forces, absence of hesitation, uncommon properties, and mighty by magical power, is the father of the world[2], who has reached the highest perfection in the knowledge of skilful means, who is most merciful, long-suffering, benevolent, compassionate. He appears in this triple

[1] Slâghamâna.

[2] Here the Buddha is represented as a wise and benevolent father; he is the heavenly father, Brahma. As such he was represented as sitting on a 'lotus seat.' How common this representation was in India, at least in the sixth century of our era, appears from Varâha-Mihira's Brihat-Samhitâ, chap. 58, 44, where the following rule is laid down for the Buddha idols: 'Buddha shall be (represented) sitting on a lotus seat, like the father of the world.'

world, which is like a house the roof[1] and shelter whereof are decayed, (a house) burning by a mass of misery, in order to deliver from affection, hatred, and delusion the beings subject to birth, old age, disease, death, grief, wailing, pain, melancholy, despondency, the dark enveloping mists of ignorance, in order to rouse them to supreme and perfect enlightenment. Once born, he sees how the creatures are burnt, tormented, vexed, distressed by birth, old age, disease, death, grief, wailing, pain, melancholy, despondency; how for the sake of enjoyments, and prompted by sensual desires, they severally suffer various pains. In consequence both of what in this world they are seeking and what they have acquired, they will in a future state suffer various pains, in hell, in the brute creation, in the realm of Yama; suffer such pains as poverty in the world of gods or men, union with hateful persons or things, and separation from the beloved ones. And whilst incessantly whirling in that mass of evils they are sporting, playing, diverting themselves; they do not fear, nor dread, nor are they seized with terror; they do not know, nor mind; they are not startled, do not try to escape, but are enjoying themselves in that triple world which is like unto a burning house, and run hither and thither. Though overwhelmed by that mass of evil, they do not conceive the idea that they must beware of it.

Under such circumstances, *S*âriputra, the Tathâgata reflects thus: Verily, I am the father of these beings; I must save them from this mass of evil, and bestow on them the immense, inconceivable bliss of

[1] Or, coping.

Buddha-knowledge, wherewith they shall sport, play, and divert themselves, wherein they shall find their rest.

Then, Sâriputra, the Tathâgata reflects thus: If, in the conviction of my possessing the power of knowledge and magical faculties, I manifest to these beings the knowledge, forces, and absence of hesitation of the Tathâgata, without availing myself of some device, these beings will not escape. For they are attached to the pleasures of the five senses, to worldly pleasures; they will not be freed from birth, old age, disease, death, grief, wailing, pain, melancholy, despondency, by which they are burnt, tormented, vexed, distressed. Unless they are forced to leave the triple world which is like a house the shelter and roof whereof is in a blaze, how are they to get acquainted with[1] Buddha-knowledge?

Now, Sâriputra, even as that man with powerful arms, without using the strength of his arms, attracts his children out of the burning house by an able device, and afterwards gives them magnificent, great carts, so, Sâriputra, the Tathâgata, the Arhat, &c., possessed of knowledge and freedom from all hesitation, without using them, in order to attract the creatures out of the triple world which is like a burning house with decayed roof and shelter, shows, by his knowledge of able devices, three vehicles, viz. the vehicle of the disciples, the vehicle of the Pratyekabuddhas, and the vehicle of the Bodhisattvas. By means of these three vehicles he attracts the creatures and speaks to them thus: Do not

[1] Paribhotsyante; Burnouf's rendering, 'pourront jouir,' points to a reading paribhokshyante.

delight in this triple world, which is like a burning house, in these miserable forms, sounds, odours, flavours, and contacts [1]. For in delighting in this triple world ye are burnt, heated, inflamed with the thirst inseparable from the pleasures of the five senses. Fly from this triple world; betake yourselves to the three vehicles: the vehicle of the disciples, the vehicle of the Pratyekabuddhas, the vehicle of the Bodhisattvas. I give you my pledge for it, that I shall give you these three vehicles; make an effort to run out of this triple world. And to attract them I say: These vehicles are grand, praised by the Âryas, and provided with most pleasant things; with such you are to sport, play, and divert yourselves in a noble [2] manner. Ye will feel the great delight of the faculties [3], powers [4], constituents of Bodhi, meditations, the (eight) degrees of emancipation, self-concentration, and the results of self-concentration, and ye will become greatly happy and cheerful.

---

[1] The same idea and the same moral form the warp and woof of the sermon on the hill of Gayâsîrsha, the Âditta-pariyâya, Mahâvagga I, 21. This sermon was the second in course of time, if we leave out of account the repetitions of the first, preached near Benares. The parable also is propounded at the time when the Master moves the wheel of the law for the second time; see above, st. 34. Hence we may conclude that the sermon and parable are variations of one and the same monkish moralization on the base of a more primitive cosmological legend.

[2] Akripanam, properly, not miserably.

[3] Indriya; here apparently the five moral faculties of faith, energy, recollection, contemplation, and wisdom or prescience; cf. Spence Hardy, Manual, p. 498; Lalita-vistara, p. 37.

[4] Bala, the same as the indriya, with this difference, it would seem, that the balas are the faculties in action or more developed; cf. Spence Hardy, l. c., and Lalita-vistara, l. c.

Now, Sâriputra, the beings who have become wise have faith in the Tathâgata, the father of the world, and consequently apply themselves to his commandments. Amongst them there are some who, wishing to follow the dictate of an authoritative voice, apply themselves to the commandment of the Tathâgata to acquire the knowledge of the four great truths, for the sake of their own complete Nirvâna. These one may say to be those who, coveting the vehicle of the disciples, fly from the triple world, just as some of the boys will fly from that burning house, prompted by a desire of getting a cart yoked with deer. Other beings desirous of the science without a master, of self-restraint and tranquillity, apply themselves to the commandment of the Tathâgata to learn to understand causes and effects, for the sake of their own complete Nirvâna. These one may say to be those who, coveting the vehicle of the Pratyekabuddhas, fly from the triple world, just as some of the boys fly from the burning house, prompted by the desire of getting a cart yoked with goats. Others again desirous of the knowledge of the all-knowing, the knowledge of Buddha, the knowledge of the self-born one, the science without a master, apply themselves to the commandment of the Tathâgata to learn to understand the knowledge, powers, and freedom from hesitation of the Tathâgata, for the sake of the common weal and happiness, out of compassion to the world, for the benefit, weal, and happiness of the world at large, both gods and men, for the sake of the complete Nirvâna of all beings. These one may say to be those who, coveting the great vehicle, fly from the triple world. Therefore they are called Bodhisattvas Mahâsattvas. They may be likened to those among the boys who have fled from the burning house prompted by the desire of getting a cart yoked with bullocks.

In the same manner, *S*âriputra, as that man, on seeing his children escaped from the burning house and knowing them safely and happily rescued and out of danger, in the consciousness of his great wealth, gives the boys one single grand cart; so, too, *S*âriputra, the Tathâgata, the Arhat, &c., on seeing many ko*t*is of beings recovered[1] from the triple world, released from sorrow, fear, terror, and calamity, having escaped owing to the command of the Tathâgata, delivered from all fears, calamities, and difficulties, and having reached the bliss of Nirvâ*n*a, so, too, *S*âriputra, the Tathâgata, the Arhat, &c., considering that he possesses great wealth of knowledge, power, and absence of hesitation, and that all beings are his children, leads them by no other vehicle but the Buddha-vehicle to full development[2]. But he does not teach a particular Nirvâ*n*a for each being; he causes all beings to reach complete Nirvâ*n*a by means of the complete Nirvâ*n*a of the Tathâgata. And those beings, *S*âriputra, who are delivered from the triple world, to them the Tathâgata gives as toys to amuse themselves with the lofty pleasures of the Âryas, the pleasures

[1] Paripûr*n*ân; in one MS. there is a second-hand reading, parimuktân. I suppose that paripûr*n*a is the original reading, but that we have to take it in the sense of 'recovered, healed.'

[2] Time, *S*iva or Vish*n*u ekapâd, the One-footed, who at the same time is tripâd, three-footed, leads all living beings to final rest. The Buddha-vehicle is the ratha eka*k*akra, the one-wheeled carriage, each wheel being trinâbhi, three-naved, as in Rig-veda I, 164, 2.

of meditation, emancipation, self-concentration, and its results; (toys) all of the same kind. Even as that man, Sâriputra, cannot be said to have told a falsehood for having held out to those boys the prospect of three vehicles and given to all of them but one great vehicle, a magnificent vehicle made of seven precious substances, decorated with all sorts of ornaments, a vehicle of one kind, the most egregious of all, so, too, Sâriputra, the Tathâgata, the Arhat, &c., tells no falsehood when by an able device he first holds forth three vehicles and afterwards leads all to complete Nirvâna by the one great vehicle. For the Tathâgata, Sâriputra, who is rich in treasures and storehouses of abundant knowledge, powers, and absence of hesitation, is able to teach all beings the law which is connected with the knowledge of the all-knowing. In this way, Sâriputra, one has to understand how the Tathâgata by an able device and direction shows but one vehicle, the great vehicle.

And on that occasion the Lord uttered the following stanzas:

39. A man has[1] an old house, large, but very infirm; its terraces are decaying and the columns rotten at their bases.

40. The windows and balconies are partly ruined, the wall as well as its coverings and plaster decaying; the coping shows rents from age; the thatch is everywhere pierced with holes.

41. It is inhabited by no less than five hundred beings; containing many cells and closets filled with excrements and disgusting.

[1] The original has 'as if a man had,' &c. I have changed the construction to render it less wearisome.

42. Its roof-rafters are wholly ruined; the walls and partitions crumbling away; ko*t*is of vultures nestle in it, as well as doves, owls, and other birds.

43. There are in every corner dreadful snakes, most venomous and horrible; scorpions and mice of all sorts; it is the abode of very wicked creatures of every description.

44. Further, one may meet in it here and there beings not belonging to the human race. It is defiled with excrement and urine, and teeming with worms, insects, and fire-flies; it resounds from the howling of dogs and jackals.

45. In it are horrible hyenas that are wont to devour human carcasses; many dogs and jackals greedily seeking the matter of corpses.

46. Those animals weak from perpetual hunger go about in several places to feed upon their prey, and quarrelling fill the spot with their cries. Such is that most horrible house.

47. There are also very malign goblins, who violate human corpses; in several spots there are centipedes, huge snakes, and vipers.

48. Those animals creep into all corners, where they make nests to deposit their brood, which is often devoured by the goblins.

49. And when those cruel-minded goblins are satiated with feeding upon the flesh of other creatures, so that their bodies are big, then they commence sharply fighting on the spot.

50. In the wasted retreats are dreadful, malign urchins, some of them measuring one span, others one cubit or two cubits, all nimble in their movements.

51. They are in the habit of seizing dogs by the

feet, throwing them upside down upon the floor, pinching their necks and using them ill.

52. There also live yelling ghosts naked, black, wan, tall, and high, who, hungry and in quest of food, are here and there emitting cries of distress.

53. Some have a mouth like a needle, others have a face like a cow's; they are of the size of men or dogs, go with entangled hair, and utter plaintive cries from want of food.

54. Those goblins, ghosts, imps, like vultures, are always looking out through the windows and loop-holes, in all directions in search of food.

55. Such is that dreadful house, spacious and high, but very infirm, full of holes, frail and dreary. (Let us suppose that) it is the property of a certain man,

56. And that while he is out of doors the house is reached by a conflagration, so that on a sudden it is wrapt in a blazing mass of fire on every side.

57. The beams and rafters consumed by the fire, the columns and partitions in flame are crackling most dreadfully, whilst goblins and ghosts are yelling.

58. Vultures are driven out by hundreds; urchins withdraw with parched faces; hundreds of mischievous beasts of prey[1] run, scorched, on every side, crying and shouting[2].

59. Many poor devils move about, burnt by the fire; while burning they tear one another with the teeth, and bespatter each other with their blood.

---

[1] Vyâ*d*a.

[2] Krosanti, var. lect. kroshanti. Burnouf's version, 'sont en fureur,' points to a reading roshanti, which, however, is not appropriate, for the would-be conflagration is a description of the time of twilight.

60. Hyenas also perish there, in the act of eating one another. The excrements burn, and a loathsome stench spreads in all directions.

61. The centipedes, trying to fly, are devoured by the urchins. The ghosts, with burning hair, hover about, equally vexed with hunger and heat.

62. In such a state is that awful house, where thousands of flames are breaking out on every side. But the man who is the master of the house looks on from without.

63. And he hears his own children, whose minds are engaged in playing with their toys, in their fondness of which they amuse themselves, as fools do in their ignorance.

64. And as he hears them he quickly steps in[1] to save his children, lest his ignorant children might perish in the flames.

65. He tells them the defect of the house, and says: This, young man[2] of good family, is a miserable house, a dreadful one; the various creatures in it, and this fire to boot, form a series of evils.

66. In it are snakes, mischievous goblins, urchins, and ghosts in great number; hyenas, troops of dogs and jackals, as well as vultures, seeking their prey.

67. Such beings live in this house, which, apart

[1] This trait is wanting in the prose relation. The explanation, I fancy, is this: If the description of the glowing house refers to morning twilight, the father (Pitâmaha, or Day-god) will needs step in afterwards; if, on the other hand, the evening twilight is meant, he will already have left the house. In the former case he calls his children to activity, to their daily work; in the latter he admonishes them to take their rest, exhorts them to think of the end of life.

[2] In addressing more persons it is not uncommon that only one is addressed as representing the whole company.

from the fire, is extremely dreadful, and miserable enough; and now comes to it this fire blazing on all sides.

68. The foolish boys, however, though admonished, do not mind their father's words, deluded as they are by their toys; they do not even understand him.

69. Then the man thinks: I am now in anxiety on account of my children. What is the use of my having sons if I lose them? No, they shall not perish by this fire.

70. Instantly a device occurred to his mind: These young (and ignorant) children are fond of toys, and have none just now to play with. Oh, they are so foolish!

71. He then says to them: Listen, my sons, I have carts of different sorts, yoked with deer, goats, and excellent bullocks, lofty, great, and completely furnished.

72. They are outside the house; run out, do with them what you like; for your sake have I caused them to be made. Run out all together, and rejoice to have them.

73. All the boys, on hearing of such carts, exert themselves, immediately rush out hastily, and reach, free from harm, the open air.

74. On seeing that the children have come out, the man betakes himself to the square in the centre of the village[1], and there from the throne he is sitting on he says: Good people, now I feel at ease.

---

[1] The sun reaches the meridian point. The poetic version which makes the father enter the blazing house is consistent; the prose version has effaced a necessary trait of the story. Therefore

75. These poor sons of mine, whom I have recovered with difficulty, my own dear twenty young children, were in a dreadful, wretched, horrible house, full of many animals.

76. As it was burning and wrapt in thousands of flames, they were amusing themselves in it with playing, but now I have rescued them all. Therefore I now feel most happy.

77. The children, seeing their father happy, approached him, and said: Dear father, give us, as you have promised[1], those nice vehicles of three kinds;

78. And make true all that you promised us in the house when saying, 'I will give you three sorts of vehicles.' Do give them; it is now the right time.

79. Now the man (as we have supposed) had a mighty treasure of gold, silver, precious stones, and pearls; he possessed bullion, numerous slaves, domestics, and vehicles of various kinds;

80. Carts made of precious substances, yoked with bullocks, most excellent, with benches[2] and a row of tinkling bells, decorated with umbrellas and flags, and adorned with a network of gems and pearls.

81. They are embellished with gold, and artificial wreaths hanging down here and there; covered all around with excellent cloth and fine white muslin.

82. Those carts are moreover furnished with choice mattresses of fine silk, serving for cushions,

---

it is posterior to the version in metre, and apparently belongs to a much later period.

[1] Yathâbhibhâshitam, var. lect. °bhâvitam.

[2] Vedikâs.

and covered with choice carpets showing the images of cranes and swans, and worth thousands of kotis.

83. The carts are yoked with white bullocks, well fed, strong, of great size, very fine, who are tended by numerous persons.

84. Such excellent carts that man gives to all his sons, who, overjoyed and charmed, go and play with them in all directions.

85. In the same manner, Sâriputra, I, the great Seer, am the protector and father of all beings, and all creatures who, childlike, are captivated by the pleasures of the triple world, are my sons.

86. This triple world is as dreadful as that house, overwhelmed with a number of evils, entirely inflamed on every side by a hundred different sorts of birth, old age, and disease.

87. But I, who am detached from the triple world and serene, am living in absolute retirement[1] in a wood[2]. This triple world is my domain, and those who in it are suffering from burning heat are my sons.

88. And I told its evils because I had resolved upon saving them, but they would not listen to me, because all of them were ignorant and their hearts attached to the pleasures of sense.

89. Then I employ an able device, and tell them of the three vehicles, so showing them the means of evading[3] the numerous evils of the triple world which are known to me.

90. And those of my sons who adhere to me,

---

[1] Ekântasthâyin.

[2] Vana, a wood, also means a cloud, the cloudy region.

[3] Nirdhâvanârthâya; a var. lect. has nirvâpanârthâya, i.e. to allay.

who are mighty in the six transcendent faculties (Abhi*gñ*âs) and the triple science, the Pratyekabuddhas, as well as the Bodhisattvas unable to slide back;

91. And those (others) who equally are my sons, to them I just now am showing, by means of this excellent allegory, the single Buddha-vehicle. Receive it; ye shall all become *G*inas.

92. It is most excellent and sweet, the most exalted in the world, that knowledge of the Buddhas, the most high among men; it is something sublime and adorable.

93. The powers, meditations, degrees of emancipation and self-concentration by many hundreds of ko*t*is, that is the exalted vehicle in which the sons of Buddha take a never-ending delight.

94. In playing with it they pass days and nights, fortnights, months, seasons, years, intermediate kalpas, nay, thousands of ko*t*is of kalpas[1].

95. This is the lofty vehicle of jewels which sundry Bodhisattvas and the disciples listening to the Sugata employ to go and sport on the terrace of enlightenment.

96. Know then, Tishya[2], that there is no second

---

[1] As the mean duration of a man's life extends over thousands of ko*t*is of kalpas or Æons, it is evident that the Æon here meant is in reality an extremely small particle of time, an atom. The meaning attached to it was perhaps that of asu or prâ*n*a, a respiration. It seems to me, however, more probable that kalpa, as synonymous with rûpa, simply denotes a unit, e.g. of atoms of time.

[2] I.e. *S*âriputra, otherwise named Upatishya, i.e. secondary Tishya. The canonical etymology of the name of Upatishya is to be found in Burnouf's Introduction, p. 48, and Schiefner's Lebensbeschreibung, p. 255.

vehicle in this world anywhere to be found, in whatever direction thou shalt search, apart from the device (shown) by the most high among men.

97. Ye are my children, I am your father, who has removed you from pain, from the triple world, from fear and danger, when you had been burning for many ko*t*is of Æons.

98. And I am teaching blessed rest (Nirvâ*n*a), in so far as, though you have not yet reached (final) rest, you are delivered from the trouble of the mundane whirl, provided you seek the vehicle of the Buddhas.

99. Any Bodhisattvas here present obey my Buddha-rules. Such is the skilfulness of the *G*ina that he disciplines many Bodhisattvas.

100. When the creatures in this world delight in low and contemptible pleasures, then the Chief of the world, who always speaks the truth, indicates pain as the (first) great truth.

101. And to those who are ignorant and too simple-minded to discover the root of that pain I lay open the way: 'Awaking of full consciousness, strong desire is the origin of pain[1].'

102. Always try, unattached[2], to suppress desire. This is my third truth, that of suppression. It is an infallible means of deliverance; for by practising this method one shall become emancipated[3].

103. And from what are they emancipated, *S*âri-

---

[1] Samudâgama*h*, t*ri*sh*n*a du*h*khasya sambhava*h*. I am not certain of the translation of samudâgama, which recurs below in Chap. V, in the apparent sense of full knowledge, agreeing with what the dictionaries give.

[2] Ani*sri*tâ*h*.

[3] Na *k*o mârga*m* hi bhâvitva vimuktu bhoti (var. lect. bhotu). The words na *k*o spoil metre and sense, and must be expunged.

putra? They are emancipated from chimeras[1]. Yet they are not wholly freed; the Chief declares that they have not yet reached (final and complete) rest in this world.

104. Why is it that I do not pronounce one to be delivered before one's having reached the highest, supreme enlightenment? (Because) such is my will; I am the ruler of the law[2], who is born in this world to lead to beatitude.

105. This, *S*âriputra, is the closing word of my law which now at the last time I pronounce[3] for the weal of the world including the gods. Preach it in all quarters.

106. And if some one speaks to you these words, 'I joyfully accept,' and with signs of utmost reverence receives this Sûtra, thou mayst consider that man to be unable to slide back[4].

107. To believe in this Sûtra one must have seen former Tathâgatas, paid honour to them, and heard a law similar to this.

108. To believe in my supreme word one must have seen me; thou and the assembly of monks have seen all these Bodhisattvas.

109. This Sûtra is apt to puzzle the ignorant[5],

---

[1] Kuta*sk*a te, *S*âriputâ, vimuktâ? Asantagrâhâtu (abl.) vimukta bhonti; na[*k*a] tâva te sarvatu mukta bhonti.

[2] Dharmarâ*g*a, a well-known epithet of Yama the god of death; he is the real tamer of men, the master of gods and men, &c.

[3] Mama dharmamudrâ (properly, seal, closure of my law) yâ pa*sk*akâle (var. lect. pa*sk*imi kâle) maya adya (var. lect. mamâdya) bhâshitâ.

[4] Or, to swerve from his course, his purpose.

[5] Properly, young children, because one must have seen former Tathâgatas, i. e. lived some revolving suns before having an idea of death.

and I do not pronounce it before having penetrated to superior knowledge. Indeed, it is not within the range of the disciples, nor do the Pratyekabuddhas come to it.

110. But thou, *S*âriputra, hast good will, not to speak of my other disciples here. They will walk in my faith, though each cannot have his individual knowledge.

111. But do not speak of this matter to haughty persons, nor to conceited ones, nor to Yogins who are not self-restrained; for the fools, always revelling in sensual pleasures, might in their blindness scorn the law manifested.

112. Now hear the dire results when one scorns my skilfulness and the Buddha-rules for ever fixed in the world; when one, with sullen brow, scorns the vehicle.

113. Hear the destiny of those who have scorned such a Sûtra like this, whether during my lifetime or after my Nirvâ*n*a, or who have wronged the monks.

114. After having disappeared from amongst men, they shall dwell in the lowest hell (Avî*k*i) during a whole kalpa, and thereafter they shall fall lower and lower, the fools, passing through repeated births for many intermediate kalpas.

115. And when they have vanished from amongst the inhabitants of hell, they shall further descend to the condition of brutes, be even as dogs and jackals, and become a sport to others.

116. Under such circumstances they shall grow blackish of colour, spotted, covered with sores, itchy; moreover, they shall be hairless and feeble, (all) those who have an aversion to my supreme enlightenment.

117. They are ever despised amongst animals; hit by clods or weapons they yell; everywhere they are threatened with sticks, and their bodies are emaciated from hunger and thirst.

118. Sometimes they become camels or asses, carrying loads, and are beaten with whips[1] and sticks; they are constantly occupied with thoughts of eating, the fools who have scorned the Buddha-rule.

119. At other times they become ugly jackals, half blind and crippled[2]; the helpless creatures are vexed by the village boys, who throw clods and weapons at them.

120. Again shooting off from that place, those fools become animals with bodies of five hundred yo*g*anas, whirling round, dull and lazy.

121. They have no feet, and creep on the belly[3]; to be devoured by many ko*t*is of animals is the dreadful punishment they have to suffer for having scorned a Sûtra like this.

122. And whenever they assume a human shape, they are born crippled, maimed[4], crooked, one-eyed, blind, dull, and low, they having no faith in my Sûtra.

---

[1] Kasha, var. lect. sata, with a marginal correction sada (for sadâ). Burnouf's 'cent bâtons' is evidently based upon the reading sata.

[2] Kâ*n*akaku*nd*akâ*s k*a, var. lect. vâlaka°, with marginal correction kânaka°. The translation is doubtful; cf. st. 116 below. Ku*nd*aka I connect with ku*nt*=vikalîkara*n*e and the Greek κυλλός.

[3] Kro*d*asa*m*krin, var. lect. °sa*mg*ñin, with correction °sa*m*kkin, the reading I have followed, taking sa*m*kkin to be identical with sakkin, a Prâkrit form of Sanskrit sarpin.

[4] Ku*nd*akâlaṅgaka, for which I read °kalâṅgaka.

123. Nobody keeps their side[1]; a putrid smell is continually issuing from their mouths; an evil spirit has entered the body of those who do not believe in this supreme enlightenment.

124. Needy, obliged to do menial labour, always in another's service, feeble, and subject to many diseases they go about in the world, unprotected.

125. The man whom they happen to serve is unwilling to give them much, and what he gives is soon lost. Such is the fruit of sinfulness.

126. Even the best-prepared medicaments, administered to them by able men, do, under those circumstances, but increase their illness, and the disease has no end.

127. Some commit thefts, affrays, assaults, or acts of hostility, whereas others commit robberies of goods; (all this) befalls the sinner.

128. Never does he behold the Lord of the world, the King of kings ruling the earth[2], for he is doomed to live at a wrong time[3], he who scorns my Buddha-rule.

129. Nor does that foolish person listen to the law; he is deaf and senseless; he never finds rest, because he has scorned this enlightenment.

130. During many hundred thousand myriads of kotis of Æons equal to the sand of the Ganges he shall be dull and defective; that is the evil result from scorning this Sûtra.

---

[1] Apratyanîka, var. lect. apratyanîya. The rendering is doubtful. I take it to be synonymous with apaksha; cf. note, p. 17.

[2] Mahi, i.e. Sansk. mahîm.

[3] In the darkness of hell, i.e. in common parlance, at night-time, when nobody can behold the sun.

131. Hell is his garden (or monastery), a place of misfortune[1] his abode; he is continually living amongst asses, hogs, jackals, and dogs.

132. And when he has assumed a human shape he is to be blind, deaf, and stupid, the servant of another, and always poor.

133. Diseases, myriads of ko*t*is of wounds on the body, scab, itch, scurf, leprosy, blotch, a foul smell are, in that condition, his covering and apparel.

134. His sight is dim to distinguish the real. His anger appears mighty in him, and his passion is most violent; he always delights in animal wombs.

135. Were I to go on, *S*âriputra, for a whole Æon, enumerating the evils of him who shall scorn my Sûtra, I should not come to an end.

136. And since I am fully aware of it, I command thee, *S*âriputra, that thou shalt not expound a Sûtra like this before foolish people.

137. But those who are sensible, instructed, thoughtful, clever, and learned, who strive after the highest supreme enlightenment, to them expound its real meaning.

138. Those who have seen many ko*t*is of Buddhas, planted immeasurably many roots of goodness, and undertaken a strong vow, to them expound its real meaning.

139. Those who, full of energy and ever kindhearted, have a long time been developing the feeling of kindness, have given up body and life, in their presence thou mayst preach this Sûtra.

---

[1] Apâya, properly 'going away, disappearance,' the reverse of upâya, 'approaching.'

140. Those who show mutual love and respect, keep no intercourse with ignorant people, and are content to live in mountain caverns, to them expound this hallowed Sûtra.

141. If thou see sons of Buddha who attach themselves to virtuous friends and avoid bad friends, then reveal to them this Sûtra.

142. Those sons of Buddha who have not broken the moral vows, are pure like gems and jewels, and devoted to the study of the great Sûtras, before those thou mayst propound this Sûtra.

143. Those who are not irascible, ever sincere, full of compassion for all living beings, and respectful towards the Sugata, before those thou mayst propound this Sûtra.

144. To one who in the congregation, without any hesitation and distraction of mind, speaks to expound the law, with many myriads of ko*t*is of illustrations, thou mayst manifest this Sûtra.

145. And he who, desirous of acquiring all-knowingness, respectfully lifts his joined hands to his head, or who seeks in all directions to find some monk of sacred eloquence;

146. And he who keeps (in memory) the great Sûtras, while he never shows any liking for other books, nor even knows a single stanza from another work; to all of them thou mayst expound this sublime Sûtra.

147. He who seeks such an excellent Sûtra as this, and after obtaining it devoutly worships it, is like the man who wears a relic of the Tathâgata he has eagerly sought for.

148. Never mind other Sûtras nor other books in which a profane philosophy is taught; such books

are fit for the foolish; avoid them and preach this Sûtra.

149. During a full Æon, *S*âriputra, I could speak of thousands of ko*t*is of (connected) points, (but this suffices); thou mayst reveal this Sûtra to all who are striving after the highest supreme enlightenment.

CHAPTER IV.

DISPOSITION.

As the venerable Subhûti, the venerable Mahâ-Kâtyâyana, the venerable Mahâ-Kâsyapa, and the venerable Mahâ-Maudgalyâyana heard this law unheard of before, and as from the mouth of the Lord they heard the future destiny of Sâriputra to superior perfect enlightenment, they were struck with wonder, amazement, and rapture. They instantly rose from their seats and went up to the place where the Lord was sitting; after throwing their cloak over one shoulder, fixing the right knee on the ground and lifting up their joined hands before the Lord, looking up to him, their bodies bent, bent down and inclined, they addressed the Lord in this strain:

Lord, we are old, aged, advanced in years; honoured as seniors in this assemblage of monks. Worn out by old age we fancy that we have attained Nirvâna; we make no efforts, O Lord, for supreme perfect enlightenment; our force and exertion are inadequate to it. Though the Lord preaches the law and has long continued sitting, and though we have attended to that preaching of the law, yet, O Lord, as we have so long been sitting and so long attended the Lord's service, our greater and minor members, as well as the joints and articulations, begin to ache. Hence, O Lord, we are unable, in spite of the Lord's preaching, to realise the fact that all is vanity (or void), purposeless (or causeless, or unconditioned), and unfixed[1]; we have conceived no longing after the Buddha-laws, the divisions of the Buddha-fields, the sports[2] of the Bodhisattvas or Tathâgatas. For by having fled out of the triple world, O Lord, we imagined having attained Nirvâ*n*a, and we are decrepit from old age. Hence, O Lord, though we have exhorted other Bodhisattvas and instructed them in supreme perfect enlightenment, we have in doing so never conceived a single thought of longing. And just now, O Lord, we are hearing from the Lord that disciples also may be predestined to supreme perfect enlightenment. We are astonished and amazed, and deem it a great gain, O Lord, that to-day, on a sudden, we have heard from the Lord a voice such as we never heard before. We have acquired a magnificent jewel, O Lord, an incomparable jewel. We had not sought, nor searched, nor expected, nor required so magnificent a jewel. It has become clear to us[3], O Lord; it has become clear to us, O Sugata.

It is a case, O Lord, as if a certain man went

[1] Sûnyatânimittâpra*n*ihita*m* sarvam. The commentary on Dhammapada, ver. 92 (p. 281), gives an explanation of the Pâli terms su*ññ*ata, animitta, and appa*n*ihita. His interpretation is too artificial to be of much use. In the verse referred to we find su*ññ*ata apparently as an adjective, but till we find such an adjective in another place, it is safer to doubt its existence altogether. Apra*n*ihita is, to my apprehension, unfixed, not fixed beforehand, not determined providentially; it may also mean unpremeditated.

[2] Or, display of magical phenomena.

[3] Pratibhâti no; a would-be correction has pratilâbhino, which is inadmissible, because with this reading the pronoun vayam cannot be left out.

away from his father and betook himself to some other place. He lives there in foreign parts for many years, twenty or thirty or forty or fifty. In course of time the one (the father) becomes a great man; the other (the son) is poor; in seeking a livelihood for the sake of food and clothing he roams in all directions and goes to some place, whereas his father removes to another country. The latter has much wealth, gold, corn [1], treasures, and granaries; possesses much (wrought) gold and silver, many gems, pearls, lapis lazuli, conch shells, and stones(?), corals, gold and silver; many slaves male and female, servants for menial work and journeymen; is rich in elephants, horses, carriages, cows, and sheep. He keeps a large retinue; has his money invested in great territories [2], and does great things in business, money-lending, agriculture, and commerce.

In course of time, Lord, that poor man, in quest of food and clothing, roaming through villages, towns, boroughs, provinces, kingdoms, and royal capitals, reaches the place where his father, the owner of much wealth and gold, treasures and granaries, is residing. Now the poor man's father, Lord, the owner of much wealth and gold, treasures and granaries, who was residing in that town, had always and ever been thinking of the son he had lost fifty years ago, but he gave no utterance to his thoughts before others, and was only pining in himself and thinking: I am old, aged, advanced

---

[1] Dhânya, wanting in some MSS.

[2] Mahâ*g*anapadeshu dhanika*h*. The translation is doubtful; the words may as well mean, a creditor of people at large.

in years, and possess abundance of bullion, gold, money and corn, treasures and granaries, but have no son. It is to be feared lest death shall overtake me and all this perish unused. Repeatedly he was thinking of that son: O how happy should I be, were my son to enjoy this mass of wealth!

Meanwhile, Lord, the poor man in search of food and clothing was gradually approaching the house of the rich man, the owner of abundant bullion, gold, money and corn, treasures and granaries. And the father of the poor man happened to sit at the door of his house, surrounded and waited upon by a great crowd of Brâhmans, Kshatriyas, Vai*s*yas, and *S*ûdras; he was sitting on a magnificent throne with a footstool decorated with gold and silver, while dealing with hundred thousands of ko*t*is of gold-pieces, and fanned with a chowrie, on a spot under an extended awning inlaid with pearls and flowers and adorned with hanging garlands of jewels; sitting (in short) in great pomp. The poor man, Lord, saw his own father in such pomp sitting at the door of the house, surrounded with a great crowd of people and doing a householder's business. The poor man frightened, terrified, alarmed, seized with a feeling of horripilation all over the body, and agitated in mind, reflects thus: Unexpectedly have I here fallen in with a king or grandee. People like me have nothing to do here; let me go; in the street of the poor I am likely to find food and clothing without much difficulty. Let me no longer tarry at this place, lest I be taken to do forced labour or incur some other injury.

Thereupon, Lord, the poor man quickly departs, runs off, does not tarry from fear of a series of supposed dangers. But the rich man, sitting on the throne at the door of his mansion, has recognised his son at first sight, in consequence whereof he is content, in high spirits, charmed, delighted, filled with joy and cheerfulness. He thinks: Wonderful! he who is to enjoy this plenty of bullion, gold, money and corn, treasures and granaries, has been found! He of whom I have been thinking again and again, is here now that I am old, aged, advanced in years.

At the same time, moment, and instant, Lord, he despatches couriers, to whom he says: Go, sirs, and quickly fetch me that man. The fellows thereon all run forth in full speed and overtake the poor man, who, frightened, terrified, alarmed, seized with a feeling of horripilation all over his body, agitated in mind, utters a lamentable cry of distress, screams, and exclaims: I have given you no offence. But the fellows drag the poor man, however lamenting, violently with them. He, frightened, terrified, alarmed, seized with a feeling of horripilation all over his body, and agitated in mind, thinks by himself: I fear lest I shall be punished with capital punishment[1]; I am lost. He faints away, and falls on the earth. His father dismayed and near despondency[2] says to those fellows: Do not carry[3] the

[1] According to the reading vadhyâda*nd*ya*h*. If we read vadhyo da*nd*ya*h*, the rendering would be, executed or punished (fined). Cf. stanza 19 below.

[2] Visha*nn*as*k*a sâdâsanne *k*âsya sa pitâ bhavet; var. lect. v. syâd âsannas*k*a *k*âsya s. p. b. Both readings are corrupt; we have to read sâdâsannas*k*a. The final e of asanne is likely to be a remnant of the original Mâgadhî (not Pâli) text, the e being the nom. case sing. of masculine words in a.

[3] Mâ bhavanta ena*m* (var. lect. eva*m*) purusham âyishur

man in that manner. With these words he sprinkles him with cold water without addressing him any further. For that householder knows the poor man's humble disposition [1] and his own elevated position; yet he feels that the man is his son.

The householder, Lord, skilfully conceals from every one that it is his son. He calls one of his servants and says to him: Go, sirrah, and tell that poor man: Go, sirrah, whither thou likest; thou art free. The servant obeys, approaches the poor man and tells him: Go, sirrah, whither thou likest; thou art free. The poor man is astonished and amazed at hearing these words; he leaves that spot and wanders to the street of the poor in search of food and clothing. In order to attract him the householder practises an able device. He employs for it two men ill-favoured and of little splendour [2]. Go, says he, go to the man you saw in this place; hire him in your own name for a double daily fee, and order him to do work here in my house. And if he asks: What work shall I have to do? tell him: Help us in clearing the heap of dirt. The two

---

(var. lect. ânayeyur) iti. A would-be correction has ânayata, at any rate a blunder, because ânayantu would be required. The original reading may have been ânayishur, in common Sanskrit ânaishur. Quite different is the reading, atha khalu sa daridrapurusham ânayantv iti tam ena*m* *s*îtalena, &c., 'thereupon he (the rich man) ordered the poor man to be brought before him and,' &c.

[1] Here and repeatedly in the sequel the term hînâdhimuktatâ would much better be rendered by 'humble or low position.'

[2] Durvar*n*âv alpau*g*askau. The idiomatic meaning of durvar*n*a a. is 'having a bad complexion or colour (e.g. from ill health) and little vitality or vigour.' The artificial or so-called etymological meaning may be, 'of bad caste and of little splendour or majesty;' see, however, below at stanza 21.

fellows go and seek the poor man and engage him for such work as mentioned. Thereupon the two fellows conjointly with the poor man clear the heap of dirt in the house for the daily pay they receive from the rich man, while they take up their abode in a hovel of straw[1] in the neighbourhood of the rich man's dwelling. And that rich man beholds through a window his own son clearing the heap of dirt, at which sight he is anew struck with wonder and astonishment.

Then the householder descends from his mansion, lays off his wreath and ornaments, parts with his soft, clean, and gorgeous attire, puts on dirty raiment, takes a basket in his right hand, smears his body with dust, and goes to his son, whom he greets from afar, and thus addresses: Please, take the baskets and without delay remove the dust. By this device he manages to speak to his son, to have a talk with him and say: Do, sirrah, remain here in my service; do not go again to another place; I will give thee extra pay, and whatever thou wantest thou mayst confidently ask me, be it the price of a pot, a smaller pot, a boiler or wood[2], or be it the

[1] The MSS. vary considerably, and are moreover inconsistent in their readings of this word. One has g*ri*haparisare ka*t*apallikuñ*k*ikayâ; another, g. kapa*t*âliku*t*ikâya*m* (r. ka*t*apali° or ka*t*opali°); a third, g*ri*hapatisakare (mere nonsense for g*ri*haparisare) ka*t*apalikuñ*k*ikâyâ*m*. Paliku*t*ikâ is evidently a variation of upariku*t*î, pali being a Mâgadhî form for pari, or the Prâkrit of prati or pari. The ll is clearly wrong. Ka*t*a may mean mat, straw, and boards.

[2] The rendering of this passage is doubtful. Burnouf takes the words pot (ku*nd*a), small pot (ku*nd*ikâ), boiler (sthâlika), and kâsh*th*a to denote measures. He may be right, though in the absence of sufficient evidence for kâsh*th*a denoting a measure or value, I thought it safer to take the word in the usual sense.

price of salt, food, or clothing. I have got an old cloak, man; if thou shouldst want it, ask me for it, I will give it. Any utensil of such sort[1], when thou wantest to have it, I will give thee. Be at ease, fellow; look upon me as if I were thy father, for I am older and thou art younger, and thou hast rendered me much service by clearing this heap of dirt, and as long as thou hast been in my service thou hast never shown nor art showing wickedness, crookedness, arrogance, or hypocrisy; I have discovered in thee no vice at all of such as are commonly seen in other man-servants. From henceforward thou art to me like my own son.

From that time, Lord, the householder, addresses the poor man by the name of son, and the latter feels in presence of the householder as a son to his father. In this manner, Lord, the householder affected with longing for his son employs him for the clearing of the heap of dirt during twenty years, at the end of which the poor man feels quite at ease in the mansion to go in and out, though he continues taking his abode in the hovel of straw[2].

After a while, Lord, the householder falls sick, and feels that the time of his death is near at hand. He says to the poor man: Come hither, man, I possess abundant bullion, gold, money and corn, treasures and granaries. I am very sick, and wish to have one upon whom to bestow (my wealth); by whom it is to be received, and with whom it is to be deposited[3]. Accept it. For in the same manner as I am the

---

[1] It seems to me that this refers to ku*nd*a, &c.

[2] Here ka*t*âpaliku*ñk*e, var. lect. ka*t*akapalliku*ñk*e and ka*t*apa*t*iku*ñk*ikâyâm.

[3] MSS. ya*kk*a nidhâtavyam; we have to read yatra n°.

owner of it, so art thou, but thou shalt not suffer anything of it to be wasted.

And so, Lord, the poor man accepts the abundant bullion, gold, money and corn, treasures and granaries of the rich man, but for himself he is quite indifferent to it, and requires nothing from it, not even so much as the price of a prastha of flour; he continues living in the same hovel of straw and considers himself as poor as before.

After a while, Lord, the householder perceives that his son is able to save, mature and mentally developed; that in the consciousness of his nobility he feels abashed, ashamed, disgusted, when thinking of his former poverty. The time of his death approaching, he sends for the poor man, presents him to a gathering of his relations, and before the king or king's peer and in the presence of citizens and country-people makes the following speech: Hear, gentlemen! this is my own son, by me begotten. It is now fifty years that he disappeared from such and such a town. He is called so and so, and myself am called so and so. In searching after him I have from that town come hither. He is my son, I am his father. To him I leave all my revenues[1], and all my personal (or private) wealth shall he acknowledge (his own).

The poor man, Lord, hearing this speech was astonished and amazed; he thought by himself: Unexpectedly have I obtained this bullion, gold, money and corn, treasures and granaries.

Even so, O Lord, do we represent the sons of the

---

[1] The terms used in the text are, remarkably enough, yah kaskin mamopabhogo 'sti, which seems to differ from the following yakka me kiñkid asti pratyâtmakam dhanam.

Tathâgata, and the Tathâgata says to us: Ye are my sons, as the householder did. We were oppressed, O Lord, with three difficulties, viz. the difficulty of pain, the difficulty of conceptions [1], the difficulty of transition (or evolution); and in the worldly whirl we were disposed to what is low [2]. Then have we been prompted by the Lord to ponder on the numerous inferior laws (or conditions, things) that are similar to a heap of dirt. Once directed to them we have been practising, making efforts, and seeking for nothing but Nirvâ*n*a as our fee [3]. We were content, O Lord, with the Nirvâ*n*a obtained, and thought to have gained much at the hands of the Tathâgata because of our having applied ourselves to these laws, practised, and made efforts. But the Lord takes no notice of us, does not mix with us, nor tell us that this treasure of the Tathâgata's knowledge shall belong to us, though the Lord skilfully appoints us as heirs to this treasure of the knowledge of the Tathâgata. And we, O Lord, are not (impatiently) longing to enjoy it, because we deem it a great gain already to receive from the Lord Nirvâ*n*a as our fee. We preach to the Bodhisattvas Mahâsattvas a sublime sermon about the knowledge of the Tathâgata; we explain, show, demonstrate the knowledge of the Tathâgata, O Lord, without longing. For the Tathâgata by his skilfulness knows our disposition, whereas we ourselves do not know, nor apprehend. It is for this very

[1] Sa*m*skâra, which also means '(transitory) impressions (mental and moral).'

[2] Hînâdhimukta.

[3] Divasamudrâ, implying the notion of the fee being paid at the end of the day.

reason that the Lord just now tells us that we are to him as sons[1], and that he reminds us of being heirs to the Tathâgata. For the case stands thus: we are as sons[2] to the Tathâgata, but low (or humble) of disposition[3]; the Lord perceives the strength of our disposition and applies to us the denomination of Bodhisattvas; we are, however, charged with a double office in so far as in presence of Bodhisattvas we are called persons of low disposition and at the same time have to rouse them to Buddha-enlightenment. Knowing the strength of our disposition the Lord has thus spoken, and in this way, O Lord, do we say that we have obtained unexpectedly and without longing the jewel of omniscience, which we did not desire, nor seek, nor search after, nor expect, nor require; and that inasmuch as we are the sons of the Tathâgata.

On that occasion the venerable Mahâ-Kâ*s*yapa uttered the following stanzas:

1. We are stricken with wonder, amazement, and rapture at hearing a voice[4]; it is the lovely voice, the leader's voice, that so unexpectedly we hear to-day.

2. In a short moment we have acquired a great heap of precious jewels such as we were not thinking of, nor requiring. All of us are astonished to hear it.

3. It is like (the history of) a young[5] person who, seduced by foolish people, went away from his father and wandered to another country far distant.

---

[1] And, the Lord's real sons. [2] And, the Tathâgata's real sons.

[3] Rather, position. [4] Or call.

[5] Bâla, the word used in the text, may mean young as well as ignorant and foolish. Burnouf translates bâla*g*anena by 'par une troupe d'enfants.'

4. The father was sorry to perceive that his son had run away and in his sorrow roamed the country in all directions during no less than fifty years.

5. In search of his son he came to some great city, where he built a house and dwelt, blessed with all that can gratify the five senses.

6. He had plenty of bullion and gold, money and corn, conch shells, stones (?), and coral; elephants, horses, and footboys; cows, cattle, and sheep;

7. Interests, revenues, landed properties; male and female slaves and a great number of servants; was highly honoured by thousands of ko*t*is and a constant favourite of the king's.

8. The citizens bow to him with joined hands, as well as the villagers in the rural districts; many merchants come to him, (and) persons charged with numerous affairs[1].

9. In such way the man becomes wealthy, but he gets old, aged, advanced in years, and he passes days and nights always sorrowful in mind on account of his son.

10. 'It is fifty years since that foolish son has run away. I have got plenty of wealth and the hour of my death draws near.'

11. Meanwhile that foolish son is wandering from village to village, poor and miserable, seeking food and clothing.

12. When begging, he at one time gets something, another time he does not. He grows lean in his travels[2], the unwise boy, while his body is vitiated with scabs and itch.

---

[1] Bahûhi kâryehi k*ri*tâdhikârâ*h*.

[2] For parasara*n*eshu of the MSS., I read parisara*n*eshu,

13. In course of time he in his rovings reaches the town where his father is living, and comes to his father's mansion to beg for food and raiment.

14. And the wealthy, rich man happens to sit at the door on a throne under a canopy expanded in the sky and surrounded with many hundreds of living beings.

15. His trustees stand round him, some of them counting money and bullion, some writing bills, some lending money on interest.

16. The poor man, seeing the splendid mansion of the householder, thinks within himself: Where am I here? This man must be a king or a grandee.

17. Let me not incur some injury and be caught to do forced labour. With these reflections he hurried away inquiring after the road to the street of the poor.

18. The rich man on the throne is glad to see his own son, and despatches messengers with the order to fetch that poor man.

19. The messengers immediately seize the man, but he is no sooner caught than he faints away (as he thinks): These are certainly executioners who have approached me; what do I want clothing or food?

20. On seeing it, the rich, sagacious man (thinks): This ignorant and stupid person is of low disposition and will have no faith in my magnificence[1], nor believe that I am his father.

21. Under those circumstances he orders persons

---

a word known from classic Sanskrit and not wanting in Buddhistic Sanskrit, as appears from Lalita-vistara, p. 39.

[1] Or, have no liking for my magnificence; the term used in the text, *sraddadhâti*, admitting of both interpretations.

of low character, crooked, one-eyed, maimed, ill-clad, and blackish [1], to go and search that man who shall do menial work.

22. 'Enter my service and cleanse the putrid heap of dirt, replete with fæces and urine; I will give thee a double salary' (are the words of the message).

23. On hearing this call the poor man comes and cleanses the said spot; he takes up his abode there in a hovel [2] near the mansion.

24. The rich man continually observes him through the windows (and thinks): There is my son engaged in a low occupation [3], cleansing the heap of dirt.

25. Then he descends, takes a basket, puts on dirty garments, and goes near the man. He chides him, saying: Thou dost not perform thy work.

26. I will give thee double salary and twice more ointment for the feet; I will give thee food with salt, potherbs, and, besides, a cloak.

27. So he chides him at the time, but afterwards he wisely conciliates [4] him (by saying): Thou dost thy work very well, indeed; thou art my son, surely; there is no doubt of it.

28. Little by little he makes the man enter the house, and employs him in his service for fully twenty years, in the course of which time he succeeds in inspiring him with confidence.

29. At the same time he lays up in the house

---

[1] It is with this word, k*ri*sh*n*aka, that durvar*n*a above, p. 103, must agree.

[2] Here nive*s*anasyopaliku*ñk*ake, var. lect. °ku*ñk*ike.

[3] Hînâdhimukta; one might render it, 'placed in a low or humble position,' but 'disposition' would seem out of place.

[4] Sa*ms*leshayate.

gold, pearls, and crystal, draws up the sum total, and is always occupied in his mind with all that property.

30. The ignorant man, who is living outside the mansion, alone in a hovel, cherishes no other ideas but of poverty, and thinks to himself: Mine are no such possessions!

31. The rich man perceiving this of him (thinks): My son has arrived at the consciousness of being noble. He calls together a gathering of his friends and relatives (and says): I will give all my property to this man.

32. In the midst of the assembly where the king, burghers, citizens, and many merchantmen were present, he speaks thus: This is my son whom I lost a long time ago.

33. It is now fully fifty years—and twenty years more during which I have seen him—that he disappeared from such and such a place and that in his search I came to this place.

34. He is owner of all my property; to him I leave it all and entirely; let him do with it what he wants; I give him my whole family property.

35. And the (poor) man is struck with surprise; remembering his former poverty, his low disposition [1], and as he receives those good things of his father's and the family property, he thinks: Now am I a happy man.

36. In like manner has the leader, who knows our low disposition (or position), not declared to us: 'Ye shall become Buddhas,' but, 'Ye are, certainly, my disciples and sons.'

[1] Rather, position.

37. And the Lord of the world enjoins us: Teach, Kâsyapa, the superior path to those that strive to attain the highest summit of enlightenment, the path by following which they are to become Buddhas.

38. Being thus ordered by the Sugata, we show the path to many Bodhisattvas of great might[1], by means of myriads of kotis of illustrations and proofs.

39. And by hearing us the sons of Gina realise that eminent path to attain enlightenment, and in that case receive the prediction that they are to become Buddhas in this world.

40. Such is the work we are doing strenuously[2], preserving this law-treasure and revealing it to the sons of Gina, in the manner of that man who had deserved the confidence of that (other man).

41. Yet, though we diffuse the Buddha-treasure[3] we feel ourselves to be poor; we do not require the knowledge of the Gina, and yet, at the same time, we reveal it.

42. We fancy an individual[4] Nirvâna; so far, no further does our knowledge reach; nor do we ever rejoice at hearing of the divisions of Buddha-fields.

43. All these laws are faultless, unshaken, exempt from destruction and commencement; but there is no law[5] in them. When we hear this, however, we cannot believe[6].

---

[1] Mahâbala; this term is obviously intended to be synonymous with mahâsattva.

[2] Tâyin, which here I have ventured to render by 'strenuous,' on the strength of Pânini I, 3, 38, where we learn that tâyate, like kramate, denotes making progress, going on successfully.

[3] One MS. ghosha, call, instead of kosha.

[4] I. e. separate.

[5] I. e. moral law.

[6] And, we cannot approve, agree.

44. We have put aside all aspiration to superior Buddha-knowledge a long time ago; never have we devoted ourselves to it. This is the last and decisive word spoken by the *G*ina.

45. In this bodily existence, closing with Nirvâ*n*a, we have continually accustomed our thoughts to the void; we have been released from the evils of the triple world we were suffering from, and have accomplished the command of the *G*ina.

46. To whom(soever) among the sons of *G*ina who in this world are on the road to superior enlightenment we revealed (the law), and whatever law we taught, we never had any predilection[1] for it.

47. And the Master of the world, the Self-born one, takes no notice of us, waiting his time; he does not explain the real connection of the things[2], as he is testing our disposition.

48. Able in applying devices at the right time, like that rich man (he says): 'Be constant in subduing your low disposition,' and to those who are subdued he gives his wealth.

49. It is a very difficult task which the Lord of the world is performing, (a task) in which he displays his skilfulness, when he tames his sons of low disposition and thereupon imparts to them his knowledge.

50. On a sudden have we to-day been seized with surprise, just as the poor man who acquired riches; now for the first time have we obtained the fruit under the rule of Buddha, (a fruit) as excellent as faultless.

51. As we have always observed the moral pre-

---

[1] Sp*ri*hâ. One may also translate, 'we never were partial to it.'

[2] Bhûtapadârthasandhi.

cepts under the rule of the Knower of the world, we now receive the fruit of that morality which we have formerly practised.

52. Now have we obtained the egregious, hallowed[1], exalted, and perfect fruit of our having observed an excellent and pure spiritual life under the rule of the Leader.

53. Now, O Lord, are we disciples, and we shall proclaim supreme enlightenment everywhere, reveal the word of enlightenment, by which we are formidable disciples[2].

54. Now have we become Arhats[3], O Lord; and deserving of the worship of the world, including the gods, Mâras and Brahmas, in short, of all beings[4].

55. Who is there, even were he to exert himself during ko*t*is of Æons, able to thwart thee, who accomplishes in this world of mortals such difficult things as those, and others even more difficult[5]?

---

[1] *S*ânta, also, tranquil, ever free from disturbance.

[2] *S*râvaka bhîshmakalpa. This may be rendered 'disciples like Bhîshma.' Now it is well known from the Mahâbhârata that Bhîshma, the son of *S*ântanu, was a great hero and sage, and it is by no means impossible that the word used in the text contains an allusion to that celebrated person. According to the dictionaries bhîshma occurs as an epithet of *S*iva.

[3] We may translate it by 'saints,' but properly arhat means any worthy, a master, an honoured personage, in short, Guru. On comparing the Greek ἄρχειν, ἄρχεσθαι, we may infer that one of the oldest meanings of the word was 'a foregoer,' and in a restricted sense, a forefather, a departed one, an ancestor, so that the becoming an Arhat, an ancestor, and dying comes to be the same. The prominent part played by the Arhats is, in my opinion, a remnant of primeval Pit*ri*-worship, the chiefest of the ancestors being Dharmarâ*g*a, Yama.

[4] It is difficult not to perceive the true meaning of such passages.

[5] This passage is still more explicit, if possible, than the former.

56. It would be difficult to offer resistance with hands, feet, head, shoulder, or breast, (even were one to try) during as many complete Æons as there are grains of sand in the Ganges.

57. One may charitably give food, soft and solid, clothing, drink, a place for sleeping and sitting, with clean coverlets; one may build monasteries of sandal-wood, and after furnishing them with double pieces of fine white muslin[1] present them;

58. One may be assiduous in giving medicines of various kinds to the sick, in honour of the Sugata; one may spend alms during as many Æons as there are grains of sand in the Ganges—even then one will not be able to offer resistance[2].

59. Of sublime nature, unequalled power, miraculous might, firm in the strength of patience is the Buddha; a great ruler is the *G*ina, free from imperfections. The ignorant cannot bear (or understand) such things as these[3].

60. Always returning, he preaches the law to those whose course (of life) is conditioned[4], he, the Lord of the law, the Lord of all the world, the great Lord[5], the Chief among the leaders of the world.

The Buddha is here clearly Dharmarâ*g*a, Yama, the chief of Arhats, or Manes, the personification of death.

[1] Dûshyayugehi.

[2] Even virtuous actions cannot avert death, the tamer of men, the master of gods and men.

[3] Sahanti bâlâ na im' îd*r*i*s*âni.

[4] Nimitta*k*ârî*n*a. The corresponding Sanskrit form would be nimitta*k*âri*n*âm. I am not sure of the meaning of this term. Burnouf has 'ceux qui portent des signes favorables,' which points to a reading nimittadhârî*n*a.

[5] Î*s*varu sarvaloke, Mahe*s*varo; he, the Dharmarâ*g*a, Yama, &c., is also the same with Î*s*vara and Mahe*s*vara, well-known epithets of *S*iva, the destroyer, time, death.

61. Fully aware of the circumstances (or places) of (all) beings he indicates their duties, so multifarious, and considering the variety of their dispositions he inculcates the law with thousands of arguments.

62. He, the Tathâgata, who is fully aware of the course of all beings and individuals, preaches a multifarious law, while pointing to this superior enlightenment.

CHAPTER V.

ON PLANTS.

Thereupon the Lord addressed the venerable Mahâ-Kâsyapa and the other senior great disciples, and said: Very well, very well, Kâsyapa; you have done very well to proclaim the real qualities of the Tathâgata. They are the real qualities of the Tathâgata, Kâsyapa, but he has many more, innumerable, incalculable, the end of which it would be difficult to reach, even were one to continue enumerating them for immeasurable Æons. The Tathâgata, Kâsyapa, is the master of the law, the king, lord, and master of all laws. And whatever law for any case has been instituted by the Tathâgata, remains unchanged. All laws, Kâsyapa, have been aptly instituted by the Tathâgata. In his Tathâgata-wisdom he has instituted them in such a manner that all those laws finally lead to the stage of those who know all[1]. The Tathâgata also distinctly knows the meaning of all laws. The Tathâgata, the Arhat, &c. is possessed of the faculty of penetrating all laws, possessed of the highest perfection of knowledge, so that he is able to decide all laws, able to display the knowledge of the all-knowing, impart the knowledge of the all-knowing,

[1] 'All-knowing' is one of the most frequent euphemistic phrases to denote the state of the dead. Hence all-knowing (sarvagña) and knowing nothing (agña) virtually come to the same, and the commentator on Bhâgavata-Purâna X, 78, 6 could therefore aptly identify agña and sarvagña.

and lay down (the rules of) the knowledge of the all-knowing.

It is a case, Kâsyapa, similar to that of a great cloud big with rain, coming up in this wide universe over all grasses, shrubs, herbs, trees of various species and kind, families of plants of different names growing on earth, on hills, or in mountain caves, a cloud covering the wide universe to pour down its rain everywhere and at the same time. Then, Kâsyapa, the grasses, shrubs, herbs, and wild trees in this universe, such as have young and tender stalks, twigs, leaves, and foliage, and such as have middle-sized stalks, twigs, leaves, and foliage, and such as have the same fully developed, all those grasses, shrubs, herbs, and wild trees, smaller and greater (other) trees will each, according to its faculty and power, suck the humid element from the water emitted by that great cloud, and by that water which, all of one essence, has been abundantly poured down by the cloud, they will each, according to its germ, acquire a regular development, growth, shooting up, and bigness; and so they will produce blossoms and fruits, and will receive, each severally, their names. Rooted in one and the same soil, all those families of plants and germs are drenched and vivified by water of one essence throughout.

In the same manner, Kâsyapa, does the Tathâgata, the Arhat, &c. appear in the world. Like unto a great cloud coming up, the Tathâgata appears and sends forth his call to the whole world, including gods, men, and demons[1]. And even as a

[1] Parganya or Indra, Jupiter pluvius, is at the same time the thunderer, Jupiter tonans.

great cloud, Kâsyapa, extending over the whole universe, in like manner, Kâsyapa, the Tathâgata, the Arhat, &c., before the face of the world, including gods, men, and demons, lifts his voice and utters these words: I am the Tathâgata, O ye gods and men! the Arhat, the perfectly enlightened one; having reached the shore myself, I carry others to the shore; being free, I make free; being comforted, I comfort; being perfectly at rest, I lead others to rest. By my perfect wisdom I know both this world and the next, such as they really are. I am all-knowing, all-seeing. Come to me, ye gods and men! hear the law. I am he who indicates the path; who shows the path, as knowing the path, being acquainted with the path. Then, Kâsyapa, many hundred thousand myriads of kotis of beings come to hear the law of the Tathâgata; and the Tathâgata, who knows the difference as to the faculties and the energy of those beings, produces various Dharmaparyâyas, tells many tales, amusing, agreeable, both instructive and pleasant, tales by means of which all beings not only become pleased with the law in this present life, but also after death will reach happy states, where they are to enjoy many pleasures and hear the law. By listening to the law they will be freed from hindrances and in due course apply themselves to the law of the all-knowing, according to their faculty, power, and strength.

Even as the great cloud, Kâsyapa, after expanding over the whole universe, pours out the same water and recreates by it all grasses, shrubs, herbs, and trees; even as all these grasses, shrubs, herbs, and trees, according to their faculty, power, and strength, suck in the water and thereby attain the full development assigned to their kind; in like manner, Kâsyapa, is the law preached by the Tathâgata, the Arhat, &c., of one and the same essence, that is to say, the essence of it is deliverance, the final aim being absence of passion, annihilation, knowledge of the all-knowing[1]. As to that, Kâsyapa, (it must be understood) that the beings who hear the law when it is preached by the Tathâgata, who keep it in their memory and apply themselves to it, do not know, nor perceive, nor understand their own self. For, Kâsyapa, the Tathâgata only really knows who, how, and of what kind those beings are; what[2], how, and whereby they are meditating; what, how, and whereby they are contemplating; what, why, and whereby they are attaining. No one but the Tathâgata, Kâsyapa, is there present, seeing all intuitively, and seeing the state of those beings in different stages, as of the lowest, highest, and mean grasses, shrubs, herbs, and trees. I am he, Kâsyapa, who, knowing the law which is of but one essence, viz. the essence of deliverance, (the law) ever peaceful, ending in Nirvâna, (the law) of eternal rest, having but one stage and placed in voidness, (who knowing this) do not on a sudden reveal to all the knowledge of the all-knowing, since I pay regard to the dispositions of all beings.

You are astonished, Kâsyapa, that you cannot fathom the mystery[3] expounded by the Tathâgata. It is, Kâsyapa, because the mystery expounded by

[1] The dead man knows all, i.e. has experienced all he was to experience in his span of life.

[2] The MSS. here and in the sequel have yañka instead of yakka, a trace of the original Prâkrit text.

[3] Sandhâbhâshita.

the Tathâgatas, the Arhats, &c. is difficult to be understood.

And on that occasion, the more fully to explain the same subject, the Lord uttered the following stanzas:

1. I am the Dharmarâga, born in the world as the destroyer of existence[1]. I declare the law to all beings after discriminating their dispositions.

2. Superior men of wise understanding[2] guard the word, guard the mystery, and do not reveal it to living beings.

3. That science is difficult to be understood; the simple, if hearing it on a sudden, would be perplexed; they would in their ignorance fall out of the way and go astray.

4. I speak according to their reach and faculty; by means of various meanings[3] I accommodate my view (or the theory).

5. It is, Kâsyapa[4], as if a cloud rising above the

[1] It is known from the Katha Upanishad that the Dharmarâga, Death, knows all about death and the next world, and is questioned about it by Nakiketas.

[2] Dhîrabuddhi.

[3] Or, permutable meanings, anyamanyehi arthehi.

[4] The translation is uncertain, because the MSS. most distinctly read Kâsyapo, which may be a clerical error for Kâsyapâ, a common form of the vocative in Prâkrit. As, however, Kasyapo is a personification of gloom, the gray of twilight, the construction of kâsyapo meghah, as a gloomy or dark or gray cloud, is perfectly intelligible. As to Kâsyapa in the vocative, this also may be explained, because he is near the setting sun, the Dharmarâga delivering his speech on immortality at the third juncture. There he, Mahâ-Kasyapa (wrongly written Kâsyapa), immediately succeeds the Buddha after the Nirvâna as the president of the first council of monks. I need not add that the prevailing opinion amongst scholars is different; they see real history in the tradition about the first council.

horizon shrouds all space (in darkness) and covers the earth.

6. That great rain-cloud, big with water, is wreathed with flashes of lightning and rouses with its thundering call all creatures.

7. By warding off the sunbeams, it cools the region; and gradually lowering so as to come in reach of hands, it begins pouring down its water all around.

8. And so, flashing on every side, it pours out an abundant mass of water equally, and refreshes this earth.

9. And all herbs which have sprung up on the face of the earth, all grasses, shrubs, forest trees, other trees small and great;

10. The various field fruits and whatever is green; all plants on hills, in caves and thickets;

11. All those grasses, shrubs, and trees are vivified by the cloud that both refreshes the thirsty earth and waters the herbs.

12. Grasses and shrubs absorb the water of one essence which issues from the cloud according to their faculty and reach.

13. And all trees, great, small, and mean, drink that water according to their growth and faculty, and grow lustily.

14. The great plants whose trunk, stalk, bark, twigs, pith, and leaves are moistened by the water from the cloud develop their blossoms and fruits.

15. They yield their products, each according to its own faculty, reach, and the particular nature of the germ; still the water emitted (from the cloud) is of but one essence.

16. In the same way, Kâsyapa, the Buddha

comes into the world like a rain-cloud[1], and, once born, he, the world's Lord, speaks and shows the real course of life.

17. And the great Seer, honoured in the world, including the gods, speaks thus: I am the Tathâgata, the highest of men, the *G*ina; I have appeared in this world like a cloud.

18. I shall refresh all beings whose bodies are withered, who are clogged to the triple world. I shall bring to felicity those that are pining away with toils, give them pleasures and (final) rest.

19. Hearken to me, ye hosts of gods and men; approach to behold me: I am the Tathâgata, the Lord, who has no superior, who appears in this world to save[2].

20. To thousands of ko*t*is of living beings I preach a pure and most bright law that has but one scope, to wit, deliverance and rest.

21. I preach with ever the same voice, constantly taking enlightenment as my text. For this is equal for all; no partiality is in it, neither hatred nor affection.

22. I am inexorable[3], bear no love nor hatred towards any one, and proclaim the law to all creatures without distinction, to the one as well as the other.

---

[1] In the legend, it is well known, he enters the womb of the Great Mother, Mahâ-Mâyâ (identical with Prak*ri*ti, Aditi, both Nature and Earth), as an elephant. The discrepancy between the two legends is more apparent than real, for in Indian poetry the clouds are called elephants.

[2] Like Apollo σωτήρ.

[3] Anunîyatâ mahya na kâ*k*id asti. I suppose that anunîya answers to Sanskrit anuneya.

23. Whether walking, standing, or sitting, I am exclusively occupied with this task of proclaiming the law. I never get tired of sitting on the chair I have ascended.

24. I recreate the whole world like a cloud shedding its water without distinction; I have the same feelings for respectable people as for the low; for moral persons as for the immoral;

25. For the depraved as for those who observe the rules of good conduct; for those who hold sectarian views and unsound tenets as for those whose views are sound and correct.

26. I preach the law to the inferior (in mental culture) as well as to persons of superior understanding and extraordinary faculties; inaccessible to weariness, I spread in season the rain of the law.

27. After hearing me, each according to his faculty, the several beings find their determined place in various situations, amongst gods, men, beautiful beings[1], amongst Indras, Brahmas, or the monarchs, rulers of the universe.

28. Hear, now, I am going to explain what is meant by those plants of different size, some of them being low in the world, others middle-sized and great.

29. Small plants are called the men who walk in the knowledge of the law, which is free from evil after the attaining of Nirvâ*n*a, who possess the six transcendent faculties and the triple science.

---

[1] Manorameshu, perhaps women are meant. A var. lect. has manoratheshu, i.e. amongst fancies, fanciful beings, chimeras. This reading would rather lead us to see in those beautiful or charming beings some kind of geniuses, cherubim, alias Vidyâdharas.

30. Mean plants are called the men who, dwelling in mountain caverns, covet the state of a Pratyekabuddha, and whose intelligence is moderately purified.

31. Those who aspire to become leading men (thinking), I will become a Buddha, a chief of gods and men, and who practise exertion and meditation, are called the highest plants.

32. But the sons of Sugata, who sedulously practise benevolence and a peaceful conduct, who have arrived at certainty about their being leading men, these are called trees.

33. Those who move forward the wheel that never rolls back, and with manly strength stand firm in the exercise of miraculous power, releasing many kotis of beings, those are called great trees[1].

34. Yet it is one and the same law which is preached by the Gina, like the water emitted by the cloud is one and the same; different only are the faculties as described, just as the plants on the face of the earth.

35. By this parable thou mayst understand the skilfulness of the Tathâgata, how he preaches one law, the various developments whereof may be likened to drops of rain.

36. I also pour out rain: the rain of the law

---

[1] It is not easy to make out what kind of terrestrial beings are severally alluded to in stanzas 29–33. I first thought that the small plants were simply the Brahmakârins, the mean ones the Vânaprasthas or hermits, and the highest plants the Yatis; but it seems more reasonable to suppose that real sons of Buddha are meant; cf. the stanzas 39–41. The Buddhists alluded to in stanza 32 are simple monks, whereas those of the following stanza are preachers, able exponents of the law, and clever propagandists of the Bauddha religion.

by which this whole world is refreshed; and each according to his faculty takes to heart this well-spoken law[1] that is one in its essence.

37. Even as all grasses and shrubs, as well as plants of middle size, trees and great trees at the time of rain look bright in all quarters;

38. So it is the very nature of the law to promote the everlasting weal of the world; by the law the whole world is recreated, and as the plants (when refreshed) expand their blossoms, the world does the same when refreshed.

39. The plants that in their growth remain middle-sized, are Arhats (saints) stopping when they have overcome frailties, (and) the Pratyekabuddhas who, living in woody thickets[2], accomplish this well-spoken law.

40. (But) the many Bodhisattvas who, thoughtful and wise, go their way all over the triple world, striving after supreme enlightenment, they continue increasing in growth like trees.

41. Those who, endowed with magical powers and being adepts in the four degrees of meditation, feel delight at hearing of complete voidness[3] and emit thousands of rays, they are called the great trees on earth.

42. So then, Kâsyapa, is the preaching of the law, like the water poured out by the cloud everywhere alike; by which plants and men(?) thrive, endless (and eternal) blossoms (are produced)[4].

---

[1] The term used might be rendered by 'gospel.'

[2] Pratyekabuddhâ vanashandakârino, &c. Burnouf must have had quite a different reading.

[3] Or unreality, sûnyatâ.

[4] Yehî (the Sanskrit would require the dual) vivarddhanti

43. I reveal the law which has its cause in itself; at due time I show Buddha-enlightenment; this is my supreme skilfulness and that of all leaders of the world.

44. What I here say is true in the highest sense of the word; all my disciples attain Nirvâ*n*a; by following the sublime path of enlightenment all my disciples shall become Buddhas.

And further, Kâ*s*yapa, the Tathâgata, in his educating[1] creatures, is equal (i.e. impartial) and not unequal (i.e. partial). As the light of the sun and moon, Kâ*s*yapa, shines upon all the world, upon the virtuous and the wicked, upon high and low, upon the fragrant and the ill-smelling; as their beams are sent down upon everything equally, without inequality (partiality); so, too, Kâ*s*yapa, the intellectual light of the knowledge of the omniscient, the Tathâgatas, the Arhats, &c., the preaching of the true law proceeds equally in respect to all beings in the five states of existence, to all who according to their particular disposition are devoted to the great vehicle, or to the vehicle of the Pratyekabuddhas, or to the vehicle of the disciples. Nor is there any deficiency or excess in the brightness of the Tathâgata-knowledge[2] up to one's becoming fully acquainted with the law. There are not three vehicles, Kâ*s*yapa; there are but beings who act differently; therefore it is declared that there are three vehicles.

When the Lord had thus spoken, the venerable

(Sansk. °nte) mahoshadhîyo manushya (Sansk. manushyâ*h*?) pushpâ*n*i anantakâni.

[1] And removing.

[2] Tathâgata*g*ñânaprabhâyâ*h*; var. lect. Tathâgatapra*g*ñâyâ*h*.

Mahâ-Kâ*s*yapa said to him: Lord, if there are not three vehicles, for what reason then is the designation of disciples (*S*râvakas), Buddhas, and Bodhisattvas kept up in the present times?

On this speech the Lord answered the venerable Mahâ-Kâ*s*yapa as follows: It is, Kâ*s*yapa, as if a potter made different vessels out of the same clay. Some of those pots are to contain sugar, others ghee, others curds and milk; others, of inferior quality, are vessels of impurity. There is no diversity in the clay used; no, the diversity of the pots is only due to the substances which are put into each of them. In like manner, Kâ*s*yapa, is there but one vehicle, viz. the Buddha-vehicle; there is no second vehicle, no third.

The Lord having thus spoken, the venerable Mahâ-Kâ*s*yapa said: Lord, if the beings are of different disposition, will there be for those who have left the triple world one Nirvâ*n*a, or two, or three? The Lord replied: Nirvâ*n*a, Kâ*s*yapa, is a consequence of understanding that all laws (things) are equal. Hence there is but one Nirvâ*n*a, not two, not three[1]. Therefore, Kâ*s*yapa, I will tell thee a parable, for men of good understanding will generally readily enough catch the meaning of what is taught under the shape of a parable.

It is a case, Kâ*s*yapa, similar to that of a certain blind-born man, who says: There are no handsome or ugly shapes; there are no men able to see handsome or ugly shapes; there exists no sun nor moon; there are no asterisms nor planets; there are no

[1] Cf. Ecclesiastes ix. 2: 'All things come alike to all: there is one event to the righteous, and to the wicked; to the good and to the clean, and to the unclean.'

men able to see planets. But other persons say to the blind-born: There are handsome and ugly shapes; there are men able to see handsome and ugly shapes; there is a sun and moon; there are asterisms and planets; there are men able to see planets. But the blind-born does not believe them, nor accept what they say. Now there is a physician who knows all diseases. He sees that blind-born man and makes to himself this reflection: The disease of this man originates in his sinful actions in former times. All diseases possible to arise are fourfold: rheumatical, cholerical, phlegmatical, and caused by a complication of the (corrupted) humours. The physician, after thinking again and again on a means to cure the disease, makes to himself this reflection: Surely, with the drugs in common use it is impossible to cure this disease, but there are in the Himâlaya, the king of mountains, four herbs, to wit: first, one called Possessed-of-all-sorts-of-colours-and-flavours; second, Delivering-from-all-diseases; third, Delivering-from-all-poisons; fourth, Procuring-happiness-to-those-standing-in-the-right-place. As the physician feels compassion for the blind-born man he contrives some device to get to the Himâlaya, the king of mountains. There he goes up and down and across to search. In doing so he finds the four herbs. One he gives after chewing it with the teeth; another after pounding; another after having it mixed with another drug and boiled; another after having it mixed with a raw drug; another after piercing with a lancet somewhere a vein[1]; another after singeing it in fire;

[1] Sarîrasthâna*m* viddhvâ, var. lect. sarasthâna*m* v., with a marginal correction sarîrasthâna*m* v. I consider the original reading to have been sîrâsthâna*m*.

another after combining it with various other substances so as to enter in a compound potion, food, &c. Owing to these means being applied the blind-born recovers his eyesight, and in consequence of that recovery he sees outwardly and inwardly[1], far and near, the shine of sun and moon, the asterisms, planets, and all phenomena. Then he says: O how foolish was I that I did not believe what they told me, nor accepted what they affirmed. Now I see all; I am delivered from my blindness and have recovered my eyesight; there is none in the world who could surpass me. And at the same moment Seers of the five transcendent faculties[2], strong in the divine sight and hearing, in the knowledge of others' minds, in the memory of former abodes, in magical science and intuition, speak to the man thus: Good man, thou hast just recovered thine eyesight, nothing more, and dost not know yet anything. Whence comes this conceitedness to thee? Thou hast no wisdom, nor art thou a clever man. Further they say to him: Good man, when sitting in the interior of thy room, thou canst not see nor distinguish forms

[1] Bahir adhyâtmam, (the things) external and in relation to one's own self.

[2] I. e. simply the five senses. The term Abhi*gñ*â can hardly originally have meant 'transcendent faculty or knowledge,' because it is a derivation from a compound abhi*g*ânâti. Neither in Sanskrit nor in Prâkrit can abhi*gñ*â denote anything else but perception, acknowledgment, recognition. Yet it cannot be denied that those who used it intended by it to convey the meaning of something grand and imposing, especially the senses of a spiritual man, as distinguished from the profanum vulgus. As to the Seers, *Ri*shis, here mentioned, I think that they are the senses personified, otherwise called devas, gods. Deva, to denote an organ of sense, occurs frequently, e. g. Mu*nd*aka Upanishad III, 1, 8.

outside, nor discern which beings are animated with kind feelings and which with hostile feelings; thou canst not distinguish nor hear at the distance of five yoganas the voice of a man or the sound of a drum, conch trumpet, and the like; thou canst not even walk as far as a kos without lifting up thy feet; thou hast been produced and developed in thy mother's womb without remembering the fact; how then wouldst thou be clever, and how canst thou say: I see all? Good man, thou takest[1] darkness for light, and takest light for darkness.

Whereupon the Seers are asked by the man: By what means and by what good work shall I acquire such wisdom and with your favour acquire those good qualities (or virtues)? And the Seers say to that man: If that be thy wish, go and live in the wilderness or take thine abode in mountain caves, to meditate on the law and cast off evil passions. So shalt thou become endowed with the virtues of an ascetic[2] and acquire the transcendent faculties. The man catches their meaning and becomes an ascetic. Living in the wilderness, the mind intent upon one sole object, he shakes off worldly desires, and acquires the five transcendent faculties. After that acquisition he reflects thus: Formerly I did not do the right thing; hence no good accrued to me[3]. Now,

---

[1] Samgânâsi, var. lect. samgânîshe.

[2] Dhutaguna, Pâli the same, besides dhûtaguna. In Pâli the dhutangas or dhû° denote thirteen ascetic practices; see Childers, Pâli Dict. s. v. The Dhutagunas are, according to the same author's statement, other names for the Dhutâṅgas, but I venture to think that they are the twenty-eight virtues of a Dhutâṅga, as enumerated in Milinda Pañho (ed. Trenckner), p. 351.

[3] Pûrvam anyat karma kritavân, tena me na kaskid guno 'dhigatah.

however, I can go whither my mind prompts me; formerly I was ignorant, of little understanding, in fact, a blind man.

Such, Kâsyapa, is the parable I have invented to make thee understand my meaning. The moral to be drawn from it is as follows. The word 'blind-born,' Kâsyapa, is a designation for the creatures staying in the whirl of the world with its six states; the creatures who do not know the true law and are heaping up the thick darkness of evil passions. Those are blind from ignorance[1], and in consequence of it they build up conceptions[2]; in consequence of the latter name-and-form, and so forth, up to the genesis of this whole huge mass of evils[3].

So the creatures blind from ignorance remain in the whirl of life, but the Tathâgata, who is out of the triple world, feels compassion, prompted by which, like a father for his dear and only son, he appears in the triple world and sees with his eye of wisdom that the creatures are revolving in the circle of the mundane whirl, and are toiling without finding the right means to escape from the rotation. And

[1] Or, false knowledge, avidyâ, which in the Chain of Causation (pratîtyasamutpâda, Pâli pati*kk*asamutpâda) occupies exactly the same place as in other systems of Indian philosophy. In reality the avidyâ was not only the origin of all evils, but also the remedy, the panacea. It was, however, thought convenient to veil that conclusion and to call the future state of complete ignorance 'all-knowingness.'

[2] Rather, products (sa*m*skâra) of the imaginative power, of fancy. These form the second item in the enumeration of Causes and Effects.

[3] The genesis of diseases, death, &c. The merely ideal nature of this genesis is proved by the fact that the sage who has overcome avidyâ is just as liable to diseases and death as the most ignorant creature.

on seeing this he comes to the conclusion: Yon beings, according to the good works they have done in former states, have feeble aversions and strong attachments; (or) feeble attachments and strong aversions; some have little wisdom, others are clever; some have soundly developed views, others have unsound views. To all of them the Tathâgata skilfully shows three vehicles [1].

The Seers in the parable, those possessing the five transcendent faculties and clear-sight, are the Bodhisattvas [2] who produce enlightened thought, and by the acquirement of acquiescence in the eternal law [3] awake us to supreme, perfect enlightenment.

The great physician in the parable is the Tathâgata. To the blind-born may be likened the creatures

---

[1] With this we may compare the term trivartman (of three paths), applied to the individual or living being, *S*vetâ*s*vatara Upanishad V, 7. *S*aṅkara explains it by devayânâdi; in the more ancient and natural meaning, the word may have been applied to the three divisions of time. Cf. the same Upanishad I, 4, where the brahma*k*akra, the brahma-wheel, is said to be triv*ri*t, threefold.

[2] In the Yoga called buddhisattva, the reasoning faculty. The Bodhisattvas are the five Dhyâni-Bodhisattvas Samantabhadra, &c., who do no more differ from the five Dhyâni-Buddhas Vairokana, &c., than the balas do from the indriyas. Cf. Burnouf, Introd. p. 118.

[3] Anutpattikadharmakshântim pratilabhya, var. lect. anutpattikî*m* kshântîm p. Anutpattika, being a Bahuvrîhi, necessarily means 'having no origin, no beginning,' alias anâdi. The eternal law is that of rise and decay, and in so far the purport of the phrase seems not materially to differ from the translation in Goldstücker's Dict., 'enduring conditions which have not yet taken place.' The word 'acquiescence' in my version gives but one side of the meaning, for it also denotes 'undergoing.' In reality the sanctimonious phrase comes to this: every thinking being suffers the eternal law, i. e. he must die.

blind with infatuation. Attachment, aversion, and infatuation are likened to rheum, bile, and phlegm. The sixty-two false theories also must be looked upon as such (i. e. as doshas, 'humours and corrupted humours of the body,' 'faults and corruptions'). The four herbs are like vanity (or voidness), causelessness (or purposelessness), unfixedness, and reaching Nirvâ*n*a. Just as by using different drugs different diseases are healed, so by developing the idea of vanity (or voidness), purposelessness, unfixedness, (which are) the principles of emancipation, is ignorance suppressed; the suppression of ignorance is succeeded by the suppression of conceptions (or fancies); and so forth, up to the suppression of the whole huge mass of evils. And thus one's mind will dwell no more on good nor on evil.

To the man who recovers his eyesight is likened the votary of the vehicle of the disciples and of Pratyekabuddhas. He rends the ties of evil passion in the whirl of the world; freed from those ties he is released from the triple world with its six states of existence. Therefore the votary of the vehicle of the disciples may think and speak thus: There are no more laws to be penetrated; I have reached Nirvâ*n*a. Then the Tathâgata preaches to him: How can he who has not penetrated all laws have reached Nirvâ*n*a? The Lord rouses him to enlightenment, and the disciple, when the consciousness of enlightenment has been awakened in him, no longer stays in the mundane whirl, but at the same time has not yet reached Nirvâ*n*a[1]. As he has arrived at

[1] I. e. he is not yet actually dead, but dead to the world; he is a *G*îvan-mukta.

true insight, he looks upon this triple world in every direction as void, resembling the produce of magic, similar to a dream, a mirage, an echo. He sees that all laws (and phenomena) are unborn and undestroyed, not bound and not loose, not dark and not bright. He who views the profound laws in such a light, sees, as if he were not seeing, the whole triple world full of beings of contrary and omnifarious fancies and dispositions.

And on that occasion, in order to more amply explain the same subject, the Lord uttered the following stanzas:

45. As the rays of the sun and moon descend alike on all men, good and bad, without deficiency (in one case) or surplus (in the other);

46. So the wisdom of the Tathâgata shines like the sun and moon [1], leading all beings without partiality.

47. As the potter, making clay vessels, produces from the same clay pots for sugar, milk, ghee, or water;

48. Some for impurities, others for curdled milk, the clay used by the artificer [2] for the vessels being of but one sort;

49. As a vessel is made to receive all its distinguishing qualities according to the quality of the substance laid into it [3], so the Tathâgatas, on account of the diversity of taste,

---

[1] Tathâgatasya pragña *k*a bhâsad' âdityaa*k*andravat. Bhâsad' stands for bhâsadi, Sansk. bhâsate. A var. lect. has Tathâgatasya pragñâbhâ samâ hy â., i.e. 'the lustre of the Tathâgata's wisdom is equal (to all), like the sun and moon.'

[2] Bhârgava, to which we may assign the meaning of 'a skilful workman, artificer,' because it is one of the synonyms of tvash*tri*.

[3] Yâd*ri*k prakshipyate dravyam bhâgana*m* tena labhyate (read,

50. Mention a diversity of vehicles, though the Buddha-vehicle be the only indisputable one. He who ignores the rotation of mundane existence, has no perception of blessed rest;

51. But he who understands that all laws are void and without reality (and without individual character) penetrates the enlightenment of the perfectly enlightened Lords in its very essence.

52. One who occupies a middle position of wisdom[1] is called a Pratyeka*g*ina (i. e. Pratyekabuddha); one lacking the insight of voidness[2] is termed a disciple.

53. But after understanding all laws one is called a perfectly-enlightened one; such a one is assiduous in preaching the law to living beings by means of hundreds of devices.

54. It is as if some blind-born man, because he sees no sun, moon, planets, and stars, in his blind ignorance (should say): There are no visible things[3] at all.

55. But a great physician taking compassion on the blind man, goes to the Himâlaya, where (seeking) across, up and down,

56. He fetches from the mountain four plants;

---

lambhyate) sarvâ(n) vi*s*eshe 'pi (Prâkrit for vi*s*eshân api, though the stanza bears the traces of having originally been in Sanskrit) tathâ ru*k*ibhedât Tathâgatâ*h*. A var. lect. has kshate (one syllable wanting) instead of la(m)bhyate; what is intended is rakshate, it keeps.

[1] Pra*g*ñâmadhyavyavasthânât Pratyeka*g*ina u*k*yate.

[2] I am at a loss to explain how this statement is to be reconciled with the bearings of the passage in prose before, unless we assume that the philosophers here alluded to are followers of other creeds, who believe in the existence of a soul. Their views are in opposition to those of the Buddha; yet they are to be spoken of with moderate respect, because they do not belong to the profanum vulgus.

[3] Rather here, phenomena.

the herb Of-all-colours-flavours-and-cases[1], and others. These he intends to apply.

57. He applies them in this manner: one he gives to the blind man after chewing it, another after pounding, again another by introducing it with the point of a needle into the man's body.

58. The man having got his eyesight, sees the sun, moon, planets, and stars, and arrives at the conclusion that it was from sheer ignorance that he spoke thus as he had formerly done.

59. In the same way do people of great ignorance, blind from their birth, move in the turmoil of the world, because they do not know the wheel of causes and effects, the path of toils[2].

60. In the world so blinded by ignorance appears the highest of those who know all, the Tathâgata, the great physician, of compassionate nature.

61. As an able teacher he shows the true law; he reveals supreme Buddha-enlightenment to him who is most advanced.

62. To those of middling wisdom the Leader preaches a middling enlightenment; again another enlightenment he recommends to him who is afraid of the mundane whirl.

63. The disciple who by his discrimination has escaped from the triple world thinks he has reached pure, blest Nirvâna[3], but it is only by knowing all

---

[1] The reading is doubtful: sarvavarnarasasthânân nagâl labhata oshadhîm, evamâdîs katasro 'tha, &c.; var. lect. °sthânânugâm l., &c. This may mean, fit for all colours, flavours, and cases.

[2] Pratî(t)yotpâdakakrasya—duhkhavartmânah.

[3] In other words, he has indeed attained a qualified (sopadhisesha, Pâli upâdisesa or sa-upâdisesha) Nirvâna, or as non-Buddhists say, gîvanmukti.

laws (and the universal laws) that the immortal[1] Nirvâ*n*a is reached.

64. In that case it is as if the great Seers, moved by compassion, said to him : Thou art mistaken ; do not be proud of thy knowledge.

65. When thou art in the interior of thy room, thou canst not perceive what is going on without, fool as thou art.

66. Thou who, when staying within, dost not perceive even now what people outside are doing or not doing, how wouldst thou be wise, fool as thou art?

67. Thou art not able to hear a sound at a distance of but five yo*g*anas, far less at a greater distance.

68. Thou canst not discern who are malevolent or benevolent towards thee. Whence then comes that pride to thee?

69. If thou hast to walk so far as a kos, thou canst not go without a beaten track[2]; and what happened to thee when in thy mother's womb thou hast immediately forgotten.

70. In this world he is called all-knowing who possesses the five transcendent faculties, but when thou who knowest nothing pretendest to be all-knowing, it is an effect of infatuation.

71. If thou art desirous of omniscience, direct thy attention to transcendent wisdom ; then betake thy-

[1] I.e. eternal, because in this system the dead is dead for ever. This immortal, everlasting Nirvâ*n*a is, of course, the anupadhi*s*esha, Pâli anupâdisesa N.

[2] Or, perhaps, without a guide, padavîn tu vinâ 'gati*h*. This does not agree with the prose version, but it is not rare to meet with such discrepancies.

self to the wilderness and meditate on the pure law; by it thou shalt acquire the transcendent faculties.

72. The man catches the meaning, goes to the wilderness, meditates with the greatest attention, and, as he is endowed with good qualities, ere long acquires the five transcendent faculties.

73. Similarly all disciples fancy having reached Nirvâna, but the Gina instructs them (by saying): This is a (temporary) repose, no final rest.

74. It is an artifice of the Buddhas to enunciate this dogma[1]. There is no (real) Nirvâna without all-knowingness; try to reach this.

75. The boundless knowledge of the three paths (of time), the six utmost perfections (Pâramitâs), voidness, the absence of purpose (or object), the absence of finiteness[2];

76. The idea of enlightenment and the other laws leading to Nirvâna, both such as are mixed with imperfection and such as are exempt from it, such as are tranquil and comparable to ethereal space;

77. The four Brahmavihâras[3] and the four Saṅgrahas[4], as well as the laws sanctioned by eminent sages for the education of creatures;

78. (He who knows these things) and that all phenomena have the nature of illusion and dreams,

---

[1] Of temporary repose, it would seem.

[2] Or, absence of fixed purpose, pranidhânavivargitam.

[3] Otherwise termed Appamaññâ in Pâli; they are identical with the four bhâvanâs, or exercises to develop benevolence, compassion, cheerful sympathy, and equanimity, well known from the Yoga; see Yogasâstra I, 33.

[4] Commonly called saṅgrahavastûni, Pâli saṅgahavatthûni, articles of sociability, viz. liberality, affability, promoting another's interest, and pursuit of a common aim; see e.g. Lalita-vistara, p. 39, l. 1.

that they are pithless as the stem of the plantain[1], and similar to an echo;

79. And who knows that the triple world throughout is of that nature, not fast and not loose, he knows rest.

80. He who considers all laws[2] to be alike, void, devoid of particularity and individuality, not derived from an intelligent cause; nay, who discerns that nothingness is law[3];

81. Such a one has great wisdom and sees the whole of the law entirely. There are no three vehicles by any means; there is but one vehicle in this world.

82. All laws (or the laws of all) are alike, equal, for all, and ever alike. Knowing this, one understands immortal, blest Nirvâ*n*a.

---

[1] Cf. the words of the funeral song in Yâ*g*ñavalkya III, 8: 'Foolish is he who would seek pithfulness in humanity, which is pithless as the plantain's stem and resembling a water bubble.'

[2] Or all things; or the laws of all things.

[3] Sarvadharmân samâ(*ñ*)*k kh*ûnyâ(n) nirnânâkara*n*âtmakâ*m* (r. °kân), na *k*aitân (I think *k*aittân) prekshate nâpi ki*mk*id dharmâ*m* (sic) vipa*s*yate. The other MS. has sarvadharmâ*m* (r. °mân) samâ(n) *s*ûnyân nirnânâkara*n*âtmikân, na *k*etâ*m* prekshate nâpi ki*mk*id dharma*m* vina*s*yati. The great difficulty lies in the second half verse, which is evidently corrupt and wrongly Sanskritised, so that the correctness of the translation in this respect is problematical.

CHAPTER VI.

ANNOUNCEMENT OF FUTURE DESTINY.

After pronouncing these stanzas the Lord addressed the complete assembly of monks: I announce to you, monks, I make known to you that the monk Kâ*s*yapa, my disciple, here present, shall do homage to thirty thousand ko*t*is of Buddhas; shall respect, honour, and worship them; and shall keep the true law of those Lords and Buddhas. In his last bodily existence[1] in the world Avabhâsa (i. e. lustre), in the age (Æon) Mahâvyûha (i.e. great division) he shall be a Tathâgata, an Arhat, &c. &c., by the name of Ra*s*miprabhâsa (i.e. beaming with rays). His lifetime shall last twelve intermediate kalpas, and his true law twenty intermediate kalpas; the counterfeit of his true law shall last as many intermediate kalpas. His Buddha-field will be pure, clean, devoid of stones, grit, gravel; of pits and precipices; devoid of gutters and dirty pools[2]; even, pretty, beautiful, and pleasant to see; consisting of lapis lazuli, adorned with jewel-trees, and looking like a checker-board with eight compartments set off with gold threads. It will be strewed

---

[1] Pa*sk*ima samu*kkh*raya, which also means western rise, elevation.

[2] Apagatasyandanikagûtho*d*illa, var. lect. °tho*d*igalla. My rendering of the last part of the compound is conjectural.

with flowers, and many hundred thousand Bodhisattvas are to appear in it. As to disciples, there will be innumerable hundred thousands of myriads of ko*t*is of them. Neither Mâra the evil one, nor his host will be discoverable in it, though Mâra and his followers shall afterwards be there; for they will apply themselves to receive the true law under the command of that very Lord Ra*s*miprabhâsa.

And on that occasion the Lord uttered the following stanzas:

1. With my Buddha-eye, monks, I see that the senior Kâ*s*yapa here shall become a Buddha at a future epoch, in an incalculable Æon, after he shall have paid homage to the most high of men.

2. This Kâ*s*yapa shall see fully thirty thousand ko*t*is of *G*inas, under whom he shall lead a spiritual life for the sake of Buddha-knowledge.

3. After having paid homage to those highest of men and acquired that supreme knowledge, he shall in his last bodily existence be a Lord of the world, a matchless, great Seer.

4. And his field will be magnificent, excellent, pure, goodly, beautiful, pretty, nice, ever delightful, and set off with gold threads.

5. That field, monks, (appearing like) a board divided into eight compartments, will have several jewel-trees, one in each compartment, from which issues a delicious odour.

6. It will be adorned with plenty of flowers, and embellished with variegated blossoms; in it are no pits nor precipices; it is even, goodly, beautiful.

7. There will be found hundreds of ko*t*is of Bodhisattvas, subdued of mind and of great magical

power, mighty keepers[1] of Sûtrântas of great extension.

8. As to disciples, faultless, princes of the law, standing in their last period of life, their number can never be known, even if one should go on counting for Æons, and that with the aid of divine knowledge.

9. He himself shall stay twelve intermediate kalpas, and his true law twenty complete Æons; the counterfeit is to continue as many Æons, in the domain of Ra*s*miprabhâsa.

Thereupon the venerable senior Mahâ-Maudgalyâyana, the venerable Subhûti, and the venerable Mahâ-Kâtyâyana, their bodies trembling, gazed up to the Lord with unblenching eyes, and at the same moment severally uttered, in mental concert, the following stanzas:

10. O hallowed one (Arhat), great hero, *S*âkya-lion, most high of men! out of compassion to us speak the Buddha-word.

11. The highest of men, the *G*ina, he who knows the fatal term, will, as it were, sprinkle us with nectar by predicting our destiny also.

12. (It is as if) a certain man, in time of famine, comes and gets good food, but to whom, when the food is already in his hands, they say that he should wait[2].

13. Similarly it was with us, who after minding

---

[1] Vaipulyasûtrântadharâ*n*a tâyinâm. Here the word tâyin would seem to be used in the sense of 'able,' agreeing with the meaning of tâyana in Pâ*n*ini I, 3, 38.

[2] Durbhiksha âgata*h* kas*k*in naro labdhvâ subho*g*ana*m*, 'pratîksha' bhûya u*k*yeta hastaprâptasmi bho*g*ane. The Prâkrit underlying this literary dialect is easily reconstrued.

the lower vehicle, at the calamitous conjuncture of a bad time [1], were longing for Buddha-knowledge.

14. But the perfectly-enlightened great Seer has not yet favoured us with a prediction (of our destiny), as if he would say: Do not eat the food that has been put into your hand.

15. Quite so, O hero, we were longing as we heard the exalted voice (and thought): Then shall we be at rest [2], when we shall have received a prediction.

16. Utter a prediction, O great hero, so benevolent and merciful! let there be an end of our feeling of poverty!

And the Lord, who in his mind apprehended the thoughts arising in the minds of those great senior disciples, again addressed the complete assembly of monks: This great disciple of mine, monks, the senior Subhûti, shall likewise pay homage to thirty hundred thousand myriads of ko*t*is of Buddhas; shall show them respect, honour, reverence, veneration, and worship. Under them shall he lead a spiritual life and achieve enlightenment. After the performance of such duties shall he, in his last bodily existence, become a Tathâgata in the world, an Arhat, &c. &c., by the name of *S*a*s*iketu [3].

His Buddha-field will be called Ratnasambhava and his epoch Ratnaprabhâsa [4]. And that Buddha-field will be even, beautiful, crystalline, variegated with jewel-trees, devoid of pits and precipices, devoid

---

[1] Dushkâlabhagnasandhau.

[2] And felicitous, blest, beatified (nirv*ri*ta).

[3] I. e. moon-signal, or having the moon for ensign.

[4] Var. lect. Ratnâvabhâsa.

of sewers[1], nice, covered with flowers. And there will men have their abode in palaces (or towers) given them for their use. In it will be many disciples, innumerable, so that it would be impossible to terminate the calculation. Many hundred thousand myriads of ko*t*is of Bodhisattvas also will be there. The lifetime of that Lord is to last twelve intermediate kalpas; his true law is to continue twenty intermediate kalpas, and its counterfeit as many. That Lord will, while standing poised in the firmament[2], preach the law to the monks, and educate many thousands of Bodhisattvas and disciples.

And on that occasion the Lord uttered the following stanzas:

17. I have something to announce, monks, something to make known; listen then to me: The senior Subhûti, my disciple, shall in days to come be a Buddha.

18. After having seen of most mighty Buddhas thirty myriads of ko*t*is in full, he shall enter upon the straight[3] course to obtain this knowledge.

19. In his last bodily existence shall the hero, possessed of the thirty-two distinctive signs, become a great Seer, similar to a column of gold, beneficial and bounteous to the world.

20. The field where that friend of the world[4] shall save myriads of ko*t*is of living beings will be most beautiful, pretty, and delightful to people at large.

---

[1] Doubtful, the MSS. having gûtho*d*igilla and gûtho*d*igalla.

[2] Properly, standing as a great meteor, mahâvaihâyasa*m* sthitvâ; vaihâyasa is exactly the Greek μετέωρος.

[3] Anuloma, direct, straight; the reverse of vakragati, the retrograde motion of planets, &c.

[4] Lokabandhu.

21. In it will be many Bodhisattvas to turn the wheel that never rolls back (or never deviates); endowed with keen faculties they will, under that *G*ina, be the ornaments of the Buddha-field.

22. His disciples are so numerous as to pass calculation and measure; gifted with the six transcendent faculties, the triple science and magic power; firm in the eight emancipations.

23. His magic power, while he reveals supreme enlightenment, is inconceivable. Gods and men, as numerous as the sands of the Ganges, will always reverentially salute him with joined hands.

24. He shall stay twelve intermediate kalpas; the true law of that most high of men is to last twenty intermediate kalpas and the counterfeit of it as many.

Again the Lord addressed the complete assembly of monks: I announce to you, monks, I make known that the senior Mahâ-Kâtyâyana here present, my disciple, shall pay homage to eight thousand ko*t*is of Buddhas; shall show them respect, honour, reverence, veneration, and worship; at the expiration of those Tathâgatas he shall build Stûpas, a thousand yo*g*anas in height, fifty yo*g*anas in circumference, and consisting of seven precious substances, to wit, gold, silver, lapis lazuli, crystal, red pearl[1], emerald, and, seventhly, coral[2]. Those Stûpas he shall worship

[1] Lohitamukti, according to Buddhist authorities, red pearl. The word is of so frequent occurrence that there can be no question of muktes in the genitive case being a clerical error for muktâyâs. If the word ever had any existence out of Buddhist writings, mukti must have been a variation of muktâ.

[2] Musâragalva; whether this precious stone really be coral, as Buddhist dictionaries assert, is rather doubtful. As the enumerated substances represent the seven colours—originally the

with flowers, incense, perfumed wreaths, ointments, powder, robes, umbrellas, banners, flags, triumphal streamers. Afterwards he shall again pay a similar homage to twenty ko*t*is of Buddhas; show them respect, honour, reverence, veneration, and worship. Then in his last bodily existence [1], his last corporeal appearance, he shall be a Tathâgata in the world, an Arhat, &c. &c., named *G*âmbûnada-prabhâsa (i.e. gold-shine), endowed with science and conduct, &c. His Buddha-field will be thoroughly pure, even, nice, pretty, beautiful, crystalline, variegated with jewel-trees, interlaced with gold threads, strewed with flowers, free from beings of the brute creation, hell, and the host of demons, replete with numerous men and gods, adorned with many hundred thousand disciples and many hundred thousand Bodhisattvas. The measure of his lifetime shall be twelve intermediate kalpas; his true law shall continue twenty intermediate kalpas and its counterfeit as many.

And on that occasion the Lord uttered the following stanzas:

25. Listen all to me, ye monks, since I am going to utter an infallible word [2]. Kâtyâyana here, the senior, my disciple, shall render worship to the Leaders.

26. He shall show veneration of various kinds and in many ways to the Leaders, after whose

rainbow colours, I think—the interpretation either of lohitamukti or of musâragalva must be wrong, perhaps both are false.

[1] Properly, western elevation or rise.

[2] The Buddha may in sober truth say so, because the astronomer can predict future risings and settings. He here shows himself to be Brahma, in his function of the first of astronomers, to whom the ancient Brahma-Siddhânta is referred.

expiration he shall build Stûpas, worshipping them with flowers and perfumes.

27. In his last bodily existence he shall be a *G*ina, in a thoroughly pure field, and after acquiring full knowledge he shall preach to a thousand ko*t*is of living beings.

28. He shall be a mighty Buddha and illuminator, highly honoured in this world, including the gods, under the name of *G*âmbunada-prabhâsa [1], and save ko*t*is of gods and men.

29. Many Bodhisattvas as well as disciples, beyond measure and calculation, will in that field adorn the reign of that Buddha, all of them freed from existence and exempt from existence [2].

Again the Lord addressed the complete assembly of monks: I announce to you, monks, I make known, that the senior Mahâ-Maudgalyâyana here present, my disciple, shall propitiate twenty-eight thousand Buddhas [3] and pay those Lords homage of various kinds; he shall show them respect, &c., and after their expiration build Stûpas consisting of seven precious substances, to wit, gold, silver, lapis lazuli, crystal, red pearl, emerald, and, seventhly, coral; (Stûpas) a thousand yo*g*anas in height and five hundred yo*g*anas in circumference, which Stûpas he shall worship in different ways, with flowers, incense, perfumed wreaths, ointments, powder, robes, umbrellas, banners, flags, and triumphal streamers.

---

[1] One MS. has a second-hand reading, °dâbhâsa.

[2] Vibhava; Burnouf must have read vibhaya, 'exempts de terreur.'

[3] The number of twenty-eight—the cyphers not being taken into account—probably indicates the number of days (Buddhas) during which the planet is standing in some stage of its course.

Afterwards he shall again pay a similar worship to twenty[1] hundred thousand ko*t*is of Buddhas; he shall show respect, &c., and in his last bodily existence become in the world a Tathâgata, &c., named Tamâlapatra*k*andanagandha[2], endowed with science and conduct, &c. The field of that Buddha will be called Manobhirâma; his period Ratipratipûr*n*a. And that Buddha-field will be even, nice, pretty, beautiful, crystalline, variegated with jewel-trees, strewn with detached flowers, replete with gods and men, frequented by hundred thousands of Seers, that is to say, disciples and Bodhisattvas. The measure of his lifetime shall be twenty-four intermediate kalpas; his true law is to last forty intermediate kalpas and its counterfeit as many.

And on that occasion the Lord uttered the following stanzas:

30. The scion of the Mudgala-race, my disciple here, after leaving[3] human existence shall see twenty thousand mighty[4] *G*inas and eight (thousand) more of these faultless beings.

31. Under them he shall follow a course of duty, trying to reach Buddha-knowledge; he shall pay homage in various ways to those Leaders and to the most high of men.

32. After keeping their true law, of wide reach and sublime, for thousands of ko*t*is of Æons, he shall at the expiration of those Sugatas worship their Stûpas.

---

[1] As many days in another stage.

[2] I. e. having the odour (or resemblance) of Xanthochymus and sandal. From the dark colour I infer that Saturn is meant, for this planet is represented as being black.

[3] *G*ahitva.

[4] Tâyin.

33. In honour of those most high *G*inas, those mighty beings[1] so beneficial to the world, he shall erect Stûpas consisting of precious substances, and decorated with triumphal streamers, worshipping them with flowers, perfumes, and the sounds of music.

34. At the period of his last bodily existence he shall, in a nice and beautiful field, be a Buddha bounteous and compassionate to the world, under the name of Tamâlapatra*k*andanagandha.

35. The measure of that Sugata's life shall be fully twenty-four intermediate kalpas, during which he shall be assiduous in declaring the Buddha-rule to men and gods.

36. That *G*ina shall have many thousands of ko*t*is of disciples, innumerable as the sands of the Ganges, gifted with the six transcendent faculties and the triple science, and possessed of magic power, under the command of that Sugata.

37. Under the reign of that Sugata there shall also appear numerous Bodhisattvas, many thousands of them, unable to slide back (or to deviate), developing zeal, of extensive knowledge and studious habits.

38. After that *G*ina's expiration his true law shall measure in time twenty-four[2] intermediate kalpas in full; its counterfeit shall have the same measure.

39. These are my five mighty disciples whom I

---

[1] Tâyin.

[2] The original reading has been meddled with; one MS. has vi*m*sa*k* *k*ava*m* (second-hand, *k*a vi*m*) syântarakalpa; another, vi*m*sa*k* *k*a vi*s*ântarak°. The original Prâkrit may have had something like vi*m*sa*m* *k*atu*m*.

have destined to supreme enlightenment and to become in future self-born *G*inas; now hear from me their course[1].

[1] In this chapter only four disciples are mentioned; the fifth must be *S*âriputra, whose destination has been predicted before.

CHAPTER VII.

ANCIENT DEVOTION[1].

Of yore, monks, in the past, incalculable, more than incalculable, inconceivable, immense, measureless Æons since, nay, at a period, an epoch far beyond, there appeared in the world a Tathâgata, &c., named Mahâbhi*gñâgñ*ânâbhibhû, endowed with science and conduct[2], a Sugata, &c. &c., in the sphere Sambhava (i. e. origin, genesis), in the period Mahârûpa. (You ask), monks, how long ago is it that the Tathâgata was born? Well, suppose some man was to reduce to powder the whole mass of the earth element as much as is to be found in this whole universe; that after taking one atom of dust from this world he is to walk a thousand worlds farther in easterly direction to deposit that single atom; that after taking a second atom of dust and walking a thousand worlds farther he deposits that second atom, and proceeding in this way at last gets the whole of the earth element deposited in eastern

---

[1] Pûrvayoga, which recurs as the heading of chaps. XXII and XXV, would at first sight seem to mean 'former conjunction,' but that does not answer any more than 'ancient devotion.' I think that yoga here is an alteration of yuga, age, period, or a Prâkritism for yauga, i. e. referring to an age. A Sanskrit pûrvayauga would be formed like pûrva-yâyâta, &c.; cf. Pâ*n*ini VI, 2, 103. The original meaning of pûrva-yoga is, I suppose, pre-history. Cf. pubbayogo ti pubbakamma*m*, Milinda Pañho, p. 2.

[2] I. e. with light and motion.

direction. Now, monks, what do you think of it, is it possible by calculation to find the end or limit of these worlds? They answered: Certainly not, Lord; certainly not, Sugata. The Lord said: On the contrary, monks, some arithmetician or master of arithmetic might, indeed, be able by calculation to find the end or limit of the worlds, both those where the atoms have been deposited and where they have not, but it is impossible by applying the rules of arithmetic to find the limit of those hundred thousands of myriads of Æons; so long, so inconceivable, so immense is the number of Æons which have elapsed since the expiration of that Lord, the Tathâgata Mahâbhi*gñâgñ*ânâbhibhû. Yet, monks, I perfectly remember that Tathâgata who has been extinct for so long a time [1], as if he had reached extinction to-day or yesterday [2], because of my possessing the mighty knowledge and sight of the Tathâgata.

And on that occasion the Lord pronounced the following stanzas:

1. I remember [3] the great Seer Abhi*gñâgñ*ânâbhibhû, the most high of men, who existed many ko*t*is of Æons ago as the superior *G*ina of the period.

2. If, for example, some men after reducing this

---

[1] Hence follows that the Buddha has existed since time immemorial; in other words, that he is Âdibuddha.

[2] I have taken the liberty to render *s*vas by 'yesterday,' though I have no other warrant for the word ever being taken in this sense except the context and the fact that in sundry languages the notions of to-morrow and yesterday are occasionally expressed by the same term, e.g. Hindî kal (properly morning, to-morrow, Sansk. kalyam, kâlyam); the English 'yesterday' is the very same word with Gothic gistradagis, to-morrow.

[3] Anusmarâmi, omitted by Burnouf.

universe to atoms of dust took one atom to deposit it a thousand regions farther on;

3. If he deposited a second, a third atom, and so proceeded until he had done with the whole mass of dust, so that this world were empty and the mass of dust exhausted;

4. To that immense mass of the dust of these worlds, entirely reduced to atoms, I liken the number of Æons past.

5. So immense is the number of ko*t*is of Æons past since that extinct Sugata; the whole of (existing) atoms is no (adequate) expression of it; so many are the Æons which have expired since.

6. That Leader who has expired so long ago, those disciples and Bodhisattvas, I remember all of them as if it were to-day or yesterday. Such is the knowledge of the Tathâgatas.

7. So endless, monks, is the knowledge of the Tathâgata; I know what has taken place many hundreds of Æons ago, by my precise and faultless memory.

To proceed, monks, the measure of the lifetime of the Tathâgata Mahâbhi*g*ñâ*g*ñânâbhibhû, the Arhat, &c. was fifty-four hundred thousand myriads of ko*t*is of Æons.

In the beginning when the Lord had not yet reached supreme, perfect enlightenment and had just occupied the summit of the terrace of enlightenment[1], he discomfited and defeated the whole host of Mâra, after which he thought: I am to reach

[1] Bodhima*nd*avarâgragata eva; vâr. lect. bodhima*nd*avarâgata eva, i.e. just having come to the terrace of enlightenment. Vara here is vára, circuit; it adds little to the notion of the simple bodhima*nd*a, this also being a round terrace.

perfect enlightenment[1]. But those laws (of perfect enlightenment) had not yet dawned upon him. He stayed on the terrace of enlightenment at the foot of the tree of enlightenment during one intermediate kalpa. He stayed there a second, a third intermediate kalpa, but did not yet attain supreme, perfect enlightenment. He remained a fourth, a fifth, a sixth, a seventh, an eighth, a ninth, a tenth intermediate kalpa on the terrace of enlightenment at the foot of the tree of enlightenment[2], continuing sitting cross-legged without in the meanwhile rising. He stayed, the mind motionless, the body unstirring and untrembling, but those laws had not yet dawned upon him.

Now, monks, while the Lord was just on the summit of the terrace of enlightenment, the gods of Paradise (Trâyastri*ms*as) prepared him a magnificent royal throne, a hundred yo*g*anas high, on occupying which the Lord attained supreme, perfect enlightenment; and no sooner had the Lord occupied the seat of enlightenment than the Brahmakâyika gods scattered a rain of flowers all around the seat of enlightenment over a distance of a hundred yo*g*anas; in the sky they let loose storms by which the flowers, withered, were swept away. From the beginning of the rain of flowers, while the Lord was sitting on the seat of enlightenment, it poured without interruption during fully ten intermediate kalpas[3],

---

[1] It is difficult not to see that we have here, as well as in the opening of the Mahâvagga and in Lalita-vistara, chap. 21, a description of the rising of the sun, the beginning of a kalpa, a myth of the creation of the visible world.

[2] The so-called Bo-tree.

[3] An intermediate kalpa is the twentieth part of an incalculable kalpa, which in reality is equal to one day of twenty-four hours,

covering the Lord. That rain of flowers having once begun falling continued to the moment of the Lord's complete Nirvâ*n*a. The angels belonging to the division of the four guardians of the cardinal points made the celestial drums of the gods resound[1]; they made them resound without interruption in honour of the Lord who had attained the summit of the terrace of enlightenment. Thereafter, during fully ten intermediate kalpas, they made uninterruptedly resound those celestial musical instruments up to the moment of the complete extinction of the Lord.

Again, monks, after the lapse of ten intermediate kalpas the Lord Mahâbhi*g*ñâ*g*ñânâbhibhû, the Tathâgata, &c., reached supreme, perfect enlightenment[2]. Immediately on knowing his having become enlightened the sixteen[3] sons born to that Lord when a prince royal, the eldest of whom was named *G*ñânâkara—which sixteen young princes, monks, had severally toys to play with, variegated and pretty—those sixteen princes, I repeat, monks, left their toys, their amusements, and since they knew that the Lord Mahâbhi*g*ñâ*g*ñânâbhibhû, the Tathâgata, &c., had attained supreme, perfect knowledge, went, surrounded and attended by their weeping mothers and nurses, along with the noble, rich king *K*akravartin, many ministers, and hundred thousands of myriads of ko*t*is of living beings, to the place where the Lord Mahâbhi*g*ñâ*g*ñânâbhibhû, the

consequently ten intermediate kalpas are equal to one day (half day-night) of twelve hours, from sunrise until sunset at the equinox.

1 It must have been a stormy day, far from rare about the time of the equinoxes.

2 Just at sunset.

3 Sixteen is the number of the kalâs (digits) of the moon.

Tathâgata, &c., was seated on the summit of the terrace of enlightenment. They went up to the Lord in order to honour, respect, worship, revere, and venerate him, saluted his feet with their heads, made three turns round him keeping him to the right[1], lifted up their joined hands, and praised the Lord, face to face, with the following stanzas:

8. Thou art the great physician[2], having no superior, rendered perfect in endless Æons[3]. Thy benign wish of saving all mortals (from darkness) has to-day been fulfilled.

9. Most difficult things hast thou achieved[4] during the ten intermediate kalpas now past; thou hast been sitting all that time without once moving thy body, hand, foot, or any other part[5].

10. Thy mind also was tranquil and steady, motionless, never to be shaken; thou knewest no distraction[6]; thou art completely quiet and faultless.

11. Joy with thee[7]! that thou so happily and safely,

---

[1] And, moving from east to south, and so forth.

[2] Like Apollo. Therefore the Buddha immediately after his bodhi, i. e. awakening, pronounces the four Âryasatyâni, which are nothing else but the well-known four chief points in the medical art,—the disease, the cause of the disease, necessity to remove that cause, and the remedy.

[3] And, of infinite body; and, whose pharmacology is boundless; anantakalpa is the term used.

[4] Out of a figure similar and akin to Hercules, the active Nârâyana has become a sage tranquil, peaceful, and refraining from action.

[5] Desa. This immovability must be taken cum grano salis, in so far as the sun is represented to continue in the same portion of the ecliptic for one day.

[6] Vikshepa as an astronomical term means celestial latitude; the sun knows no deviation from the ecliptic, of course.

[7] Dishtyâsi.

without any hurt, hast reached supreme enlightenment. How great a fortune is ours! we congratulate ourselves, O Lion amongst kings!

12. These unhappy[1] creatures, vexed in all ways, deprived of eyes, as it were, and joyless, do not find the road leading to the end of toils, nor develop energy for the sake of deliverance.

13. Dangers are for a long time on the increase, and the laws (or phenomena, things) are deprived of the (possession of a) celestial body; the word of the *G*ina is not being heard; the whole world is plunged in thick darkness.

14. But to-day (or now) hast thou, Majesty of the world, reached this hallowed, high, and faultless spot; we as well as the world are obliged to thee, and approach to seek our refuge with thee, O Protector!

When, O monks, those sixteen princes in the condition of boys, childlike and young, had with such stanzas celebrated the Lord Mahâbhi*g*ñâ*g*ñânâbhibhû, the Tathâgata, &c., they urged the Lord to move on the wheel of the law[2]: Preach the law, O Lord; preach the law, O Sugata, for the weal of the public, the happiness of the public, out of compassion for the world; for the benefit, weal, and happiness of the people generally, both of gods and men. And on that occasion they uttered the following stanzas:

15. Preach the law, O thou who art marked with a hundred auspicious signs, O Leader, O incomparable great Seer! thou hast attained exalted,

[1] Anâyika, derived from an and âya.

[2] I. e. to rise a second day, to awaken from his Nirvâ*n*a.

sublime knowledge; let it shine in the world, including the gods.

16. Release us as well as these creatures; display the knowledge of the Tathâgatas, that we also and, further, these beings may obtain this supreme[1] enlightenment.

17. Thou knowest every course (of duty) and knowledge; thou knowest the (mental and moral) disposition and the good works done in a former state; the (natural) bent of all living beings. Move on the most exalted, sublime wheel!

Then, monks, as the Lord Mahâbhi*g*ñâ*g*ñânâbhibhû, the Tathâgata, &c., reached supreme, perfect enlightenment, fifty hundred thousand myriads of ko*t*is of spheres in each of the ten directions of space were shaken in six different ways and became illumined with a great lustre. And in the intervals between all those spheres, in the dreary places of dark gloom, where even the sun and moon, so powerful, mighty, and splendid, have no advantage of the shining power they are endowed with, have no advantage of the colour and brightness they possess, even in those places a great lustre arose instantly. And the beings who appeared[2] in those intervals behold each other, acknowledge each other, (and exclaim): Lo, there are other beings also here appearing! lo, there are other beings also here appearing! The palaces and aerial cars of the gods in all those spheres up to the Brahma-world shook in six different ways and became illumined with a

[1] Or, foremost; the word used being agra.

[2] Upapanna, by so-called aupapâduka (Pâli opapâtika), apparitional birth, birth by metamorphosis. Clouds e.g. are so born.

great lustre, surpassing the divine majesty of the gods. So then, monks, a great earthquake and a great, sublime lustre arose simultaneously. And the aerial cars of the Brahma-angels to the east, in these fifty hundred thousand myriads of ko*t*is of spheres, began excessively to glitter, glow, and sparkle in splendour and glory. And those Brahma-angels made this reflection: What may be foreboded by these aerial cars so excessively glittering, glowing, and sparkling in splendour and glory? Thereupon, monks, the Brahma-angels in the fifty hundred thousand myriads of ko*t*is of spheres went all to each other's abodes and communicated the matter to one another. After that, monks, the great Brahma-angel, named Sarvasattvatrât*ri* (i.e. Saviour of all beings)[1], addressed the numerous host of Brahma-angels in the following stanzas:

18. Our aerial cars to-day (or now) are all bristling[2] with rays in an extraordinary degree, and blazing in beautiful splendour and brilliancy. What may be the cause of it?

19. Come, let us investigate the matter, what divine being has to-day sprung into existence, whose power, such as was never seen before, here now appears?

20. Or should it be the Buddha, the king of kings, who to-day has been born somewhere in the world, and whose birth is announced by such a token that all the points of the horizon are now blazing in splendour?

Thereupon, monks, the great Brahma-angels in the

[1] Probably a veiled name of the regent of the eastern quarter, Indra, one of whose epithets is Sutrâman.

[2] Harshita.

fifty hundred thousand myriads of ko*t*is of spheres mounted all together their own divine aerial cars, took with them divine bags, as large as Mount Sumeru, with celestial flowers, and went through the four quarters successively until they arrived at the western quarter, where those great Brahma-angels, O monks, stationed in the western quarter, saw the Lord Mahâbhi*g*ñâ*g*ñânâbhibhû, the Tathâgata, &c., on the summit of the exalted terrace of enlightenment, seated on the royal throne at the foot of the tree of enlightenment[1], surrounded and attended by gods, Nâgas, goblins, Gandharvas, demons, Garu*d*as, Kinnaras, great serpents, men, and beings not human, while his sons, the sixteen young princes, were urging him to move forward the wheel of the law. On seeing which the Brahma-angels came up to the Lord, saluted his feet with their heads, walked many hundred thousand times round him from left to right, strewing (flowers) and overwhelming both him and the tree of enlightenment, over a distance of ten yo*g*anas, with those flower-bags as large as Mount Sumeru. After that they presented to the Lord their aerial cars (with the words): Accept, O Lord, these aerial cars out of compassion to us; use, O Sugata, those cars out of compassion to us.

On that occasion, monks, after presenting their own cars to the Lord, the Brahma-angels celebrated the Lord, face to face, with the following seasonable stanzas:

21. A (or the) wonderful, matchless *G*ina, so beneficial and merciful, has arisen in the world. Thou art born a protector, a ruler (and teacher), a master; to-day all quarters are blessed.

[1] The sun rises the second day.

22. We have come as far as fully fifty thousand ko*t*is of worlds from here to humbly salute the *G*ina by surrendering our lofty aeriel cars all together.

23. We possess these variegated and bright cars, owing to previous works; accept them to oblige us, and make use of them to thine heart's content, O Knower of the world!

After the great Brahma-angels, monks, had celebrated the Lord Mahâbhi*gñ*â*gñ*ânâbhibhû, the Tathâgata, &c., face to face, with these seasonable stanzas, they besought him, saying: May the Lord move forward the wheel of the law! May the Lord preach final rest! May the Lord release all beings! Be favourable, O Lord, to this world! Preach the law, O Lord, to this world, including gods, Mâras, and Brahma-angels; to all people, including ascetics and Brahmans, gods[1], men, and demons! It will tend to the weal of the public, to the happiness of the public; out of mercy to the world, for the benefit and happiness of the people at large, both gods and men.

Thereupon, monks, those fifty hundred thousand myriads of ko*t*is of Brahma-angels addressed the Lord, with one voice, in common chorus[2], with the following stanza:

24. Show the law, O Lord; show it, O most high of men! Show the power of thy kindness; save the tormented beings.

25. Rare[3] is the light[4] of the world like the

[1] The gods have been enumerated just before; therefore it would seem that gods, men, and demons here are veiled expressions for kings or Kshatriyas, Vai*s*yas, and *S*ûdras.

[2] MSS. sometimes samasaṅgîtyâ, but more frequently sama*m* s., i. e. all together in chorus or concert.

[3] And, precious, durlabha.

[4] Pradyota.

blossom of the glomerated fig-tree. Thou hast arisen, O great Hero; we pray to thee, the Tathâgata.

And the Lord, O monks, silently intimated his assent to the Brahma-angels.

Somewhat later, monks, the aerial cars of the Brahma-angels in the south-eastern quarter in the fifty hundred thousand myriads of spheres began excessively to glitter, glow, and sparkle in splendour and glory. And those Brahma-angels made this reflection: What may be foreboded by these aerial cars so excessively glittering, glowing, and sparkling in splendour and glory? Thereupon, monks, the Brahma-angels in the fifty hundred thousand myriads of ko*t*is of spheres went all to each other's abodes and communicated the matter to one another. After that, monks, the great Brahma-angel, named Adhimâtrakâru*n*ika (i.e. exceedingly compassionate), addressed the numerous host of Brahma-angels with the following stanzas:

26. What foretoken is it we see to-day (or now), friends? Who or what is foreboded by the celestial cars shining with such uncommon glory?

27. May, perhaps, some blessed divine being have come hither, by whose power all these aerial cars are illumined?

28. Or may the Buddha, the most high of men, have appeared in this world, that by his power these celestial cars are in such a condition as we see them?

29. Let us all together go and search; no trifle can be the cause of it; such a foretoken, indeed, was never seen before[1].

---

[1] Viz. in the same kalpa, i.e. on that same day.

30. Come, let us go and visit ko*t*is of fields, along the four quarters; a Buddha will certainly now have made his appearance in this world.

Thereupon, monks, the great Brahma-angels in the fifty hundred thousand myriads of ko*t*is of spheres mounted all together their own divine aerial cars, took with them divine bags, as large as Mount Sumeru, with celestial flowers, and went through the four quarters successively until they arrived at the north-western quarter, where those great Brahma-angels, stationed in the north-western quarter, saw the Lord Mahâbhi*gñâgñ*ânâbhibhû [&c., as above till compassion to us].

On that occasion, monks, after presenting their own cars to the Lord the Brahma-angels celebrated the Lord, face to face, with the following seasonable stanzas:

31. Homage to thee, matchless great Seer, chief god of gods, whose voice is sweet as the lark's[1]. Leader in the world, including the gods, I salute thee, who art so benign and bounteous to the world.

32. How wonderful, O Lord, is it that after so long a time thou appearest in the world[2]. Eighty hundred complete Æons this world of the living was without Buddha[3].

---

[1] Kalaviṅka, which I have freely rendered in this manner, commonly denotes a sparrow, but the corresponding Pâli word kuravîka is supposed to be the Indian cuckoo, the koil, which in Indian poetry may be said to answer to our nightingale; in so far one might perhaps render kalaviṅka by nightingale.

[2] Consequently it was not for the first time that he appeared.

[3] I do not understand this reckoning, unless Æon (kalpa) here be taken in the sense of intermediate kalpa. A mahâkalpa is the period elapsing from the commencement of the world's destruction (i. e. sunset) to its complete restoration (i. e. sunrise). So, indeed,

33. It was deprived of the most high of men; hell was prevailing and the celestial bodies constantly went on waning during eighty hundred complete Æons.

34. But now he has appeared, owing to our good works, who is (our) eye, refuge, resting-place[1], protection, father, and kinsman[2]; he, the benign and bounteous one, the King of the law.

After the great Brahma-angels, monks, had celebrated the Lord Mahâbhig*ñ*âg*ñ*ânâbhibhû, the Tathâgata, &c., face to face, with these seasonable stanzas, they besought him: May the Lord move forward the wheel of the law! [as above till both gods and men.]

Thereupon, monks, those fifty hundred thousand myriads of ko*t*is of Brahma-angels addressed the Lord, with one voice, in common chorus, with the following stanzas:

35. Move forward the exalted wheel, O great ascetic! reveal the law in all directions; deliver all beings oppressed with suffering[3]; produce amongst mortals gladness and joy!

36. Let them by hearing the law partake of enlightenment and reach divine places. Let all shake off their demon body and be peaceful, meek, and at ease[4].

---

the Buddha has been absent for a kalpa, such a kalpa = mahâkalpa contains 4 asaṅkhyeya-kalpas; each asaṅkhyeya-kalpa has 20 intermediate kalpas; hence a mahâkalpa = 80 intermediate kalpas.

[1] Lena, Sansk. layana. In Burnouf's translation we find this word rendered by appui.

[2] The sun is lokabandhu, the kinsman and friend of the world, of mankind.

[3] Or relieve all beings oppressed with toil.

[4] It is not easy to say what is really meant by those divine

And the Lord, O monks, silently intimated his assent to these Brahma-angels also.

Somewhat later, monks, the aerial cars of the Brahma-angels in the southern quarter [&c., as above till to one another]. After that, monks, the great Brahma-angel, named Sudharma[1], addressed the numerous host of Brahma-angels in stanzas:

37. It cannot be without cause or reason, friends, that to-day (or now) all these celestial cars are so brilliant; this bespeaks some portent somewhere in the world. Come, let us go and investigate the matter.

38. No such portent has appeared in hundreds of Æons past. Either some god has been born or a Buddha has arisen in this world.

Thereupon, monks, the great Brahma-angels in the fifty hundred thousand myriads of ko*t*is of spheres mounted [&c., as above[2] till compassion to us].

On that occasion, monks, after presenting their own cars to the Lord, the Brahma-angels celebrated the Lord, face to face, with the following seasonable stanzas:

39. Most rare (and precious) is the sight of the Leaders. Be welcome, thou dispeller of worldly defilement. It is after a long time that thou now appearest in the world; after hundreds of complete Æons one (now) beholds thee.

40. Refresh the thirsty creatures, O Lord of the

---

places; I think the temples and shrines to be visited in the morning.

[1] Of course Dharma, Yama, the regent of the south. The name here applied to him is derived from Sudharmâ, Yama's hall.

[2] Save the substitution of 'northern quarter' to 'north-western quarter.'

world! Now first thou art seen[1]; it is not easy to behold thee. As rare (or precious) as the flowers of the glomerated fig-tree is thine appearance, O Lord.

41. By thy power these aerial cars of ours are so uncommonly illumined now, O Leader. To show us thy favour accept them, O thou whose look pierces everywhere!

After the great Brahma-angels, monks, had celebrated the Lord Mahâbhi*gñâgñ*ânâbhibhû, the Tathâgata, &c., face to face, with these seasonable stanzas, they besought him: May the Lord move forward the wheel of the law! [as above till gods and men.]

Thereupon, monks, those fifty hundred thousand myriads of ko*t*is of Brahma-angels addressed the Lord, with one voice, in common chorus, with the following stanzas:

42. Preach the law, O Lord and Leader! move forward the wheel of the law, make the drum of the law resound, and blow the conch-trumpet of the law.

43. Shed the rain of the true law over this world and proclaim the sweet-sounding good word; manifest the law required, save myriads of ko*t*is of beings.

And the Lord, monks, silently intimated his assent to the Brahma-angels.

Repetition; the same occurred in the south-west, in the west, in the north-west, in the north, in the north-east, in the nadir.

Then, monks, the aerial cars of the Brahma-angels in the nadir[2], in those fifty hundred thousand myriads of ko*t*is of spheres [&c., as above till

[1] We must in thought add, in full glory, because we are at noontide.

[2] Yenâdhodigbhâga.

to one another]. After that, monks, the great Brahma-angel, named *S*ikhin, addressed the numerous host of Brahma-angels with the following stanzas:

44. What may be the cause, O friends, that our cars are so bright with splendour, colour, and light? What may be the reason of their being so exceedingly glorious?

45. We have seen nothing like this before nor heard of it from others. These (cars) are now bright with splendour and exceedingly glorious; what may be the cause of it?

46. Should it be some god who has been bestowed upon[1] the world in recompense of good works, and whose grandeur thus comes to light? Or is perhaps a Buddha born in the world?

Thereupon, monks, the great Brahma-angels in the fifty hundred thousand myriads of ko*t*is of spheres mounted all together their own divine aerial cars, took with them divine bags, as large as Mount Sumeru, with celestial flowers, and went through the four quarters successively until they arrived at the zenith, where those great Brahma-angels, stationed at the zenith, saw the Lord Mahâbhi*gñ*â*gñ*ânâbhibhû [&c., as above till compassion to us].

On that occasion, monks, after presenting their own cars to the Lord, the Brahma-angels celebrated the Lord, face to face, with the following seasonable stanzas:

47. How goodly is the sight of the Buddhas, the mighty[2] Lords of the world; those Buddhas who are to deliver all beings in this triple world.

---

[1] Samarpita. [2] Tâyin.

48. The all-seeing Masters of the world send their looks in all directions of the horizon, and by opening the gate of immortality [1] they make people reach the (safe) shore [2].

49. An inconceivable number of Æons now past were void, and all quarters wrapt in darkness, as the chief *G*inas did not appear.

50. The dreary hells, the brute creation and demo nswere on the increase; thousands of ko*t*is of living beings fell into the state of ghosts [3].

51. The heavenly bodies were on the wane; after their disappearance they entered upon evil ways; their course became wrong because they did not hear the law of the Buddhas.

52. All creatures lacked dutiful behaviour [4], purity, good state [5], and understanding; their happiness was lost, and the consciousness of happiness was gone.

53. They did not observe the rules of morality; were firmly rooted in the false law [6]; not being led by the Lord of the world, they were precipitated into a false course.

54. Hail! thou art come at last, O Light of the world! thou, born to be bounteous towards all beings.

---

[1] In the Mahâbhârata III, 156, and Yogayâtrâ I, 1, the sun is called 'the opened gate of deliverance,' mokshadvâram apâv*ri*tam.

[2] Âtârenti; the var. lect. avatârenti is out of place and destroys the metre.

[3] Preta, properly 'deceased, a deceased one.' The real meaning of the passage is that men at night fall asleep.

[4] Properly, movement, *k*aryâ.

[5] Gati, going, gait; the latter is really meant.

[6] Asaddharme pratish*th*ita; the real meaning may be, 'firmly established in the condition of non-existence,' i. e. in sleep.

55. Hail! thou hast safely arrived at supreme Buddha-knowledge; we feel thankful before thee, and so does the world, including the gods.

56. By thy power, O mighty Lord, our aerial cars are glittering; to thee we present them, great Hero; deign to accept them, great Solitary.

57. Out of grace to us, O Leader, make use of them, so that we, as well as all (other) beings, may attain supreme enlightenment.

After the great Brahma-angels, O monks, had celebrated the Lord Mahâbhi*gñâgñ*ânâbhibhû, the Tathâgata, &c., face to face, with seasonable stanzas, they besought him: May the Lord move forward the wheel of the law! [&c., as above till both gods and men.]

Thereupon, monks, those fifty hundred thousand myriads of ko*t*is of Brahma-angels addressed the Lord, with one voice, in common chorus, with the following two stanzas:

58. Move forward the exalted, unsurpassed wheel! beat the drum of immortality! release all beings from hundreds of evils, and show the path of Nirvâ*n*a.

59. Expound the law we pray for; show thy favour to us and this world. Let us hear thy sweet and lovely voice which thou hast exercised during thousands of ko*t*is of Æons.

Now, monks, the Lord Mahâbhi*gñâgñ*ânâbhibhû, the Tathâgata, &c., being acquainted with the prayer of the hundred thousand myriads of ko*t*is of Brahma-angels and of the sixteen princes, his sons, commenced at that juncture to turn the wheel that has three turns and twelve parts, the wheel never moved by any ascetic, Brahman, god, demon, nor by any one else. (His preaching) consisted in this: This is pain; this is the origin of pain; this is the suppression of pain; this is the treatment leading to suppression of pain. He moreover extensively set forth how the series of causes and effects is evolved, (and said): It is thus, monks. From ignorance proceed conceptions (or fancies); from conceptions (or fancies) proceeds understanding[1]; from understanding name and form; from name and form the six senses[2]; from the six senses proceeds contact; from contact sensation; from sensation proceeds longing; from longing proceeds striving[3]; from striving as cause issues existence; from existence birth; from birth old age, death, mourning, lamentation, sorrow, dismay, and despondency. So originates this whole mass of misery. From the suppression of ignorance results the suppression of conceptions; from the suppression of conceptions results that of understanding; from the suppression of understanding results that of name and form; from the suppression of name and form results that of the six senses; from the suppression of the six senses results that of contact; from the suppression of contact results that of sensation; from the suppression of sensation results that of longing; from the suppression of longing results that of striving; from the suppression of striving results that of existence; from the suppression of existence results that of birth; from the suppression of birth results that of old age, death, mourning, lamentation, sorrow, dismay, and

[1] Or, distinctive knowledge, judgment.
[2] And, the objects of the six senses.
[3] Upâdâna, also taking up, and material.

despondency. In this manner the whole mass of misery is suppressed.

And while this wheel of the law, monks, was being moved onward[1] by the Lord Mahâbhi*gñâ*g*ñâ*nâbhibhû, the Tathâgata, &c., in presence of the world, including the gods, demons, and Brahma-angels; of the assemblage, including ascetics and Brahmans; then, at that time, on that occasion, the minds of sixty[2] hundred thousand myriads of ko*t*is of living beings were without effort freed from imperfections and became all possessed of the triple science, of the sixfold transcendent wisdom, of the emancipations and meditations. In due course, monks, the Lord Mahâbhi*gñâ*g*ñâ*nâbhibhû, the Tathâgata, &c., again gave a second exposition of the law; likewise a third and a fourth exposition[3]. And at each exposition, monks, the minds of hundred thousands of myriads of ko*t*is of beings, like the sands of the river Ganges, were without effort freed from imperfections. Afterwards, monks, the congregation of disciples of that Lord was so numerous as to surpass all calculation.

Meanwhile, monks, the sixteen princes, the youths, had, full of faith, left home to lead the vagrant life of mendicants, and had all of them become novices, clever, bright, intelligent, pious, followers of the course (of duty) under many hundred thousand Buddhas, and striving after supreme, perfect en-

---

[1] Var. lect. sahapravartti *k*eda*m* buddhakshetra*m* tena Bhagavatâ, &c., 'and while this Buddha-field moved on along with the Lord,' or 'while this B. moved on with the Lord.'

[2] Sixty is the number of gha*t*ikâs, Indian half-hours, making one day.

[3] Cf. the four vyûhas, appearances, divisions of the Lord Vish*n*u.

lightenment. These sixteen novices, monks, said to the Lord Mahâbhi*gñâgñ*ânâbhibhû, the Tathâgata, &c., the following: O Lord, these many hundred thousand myriads of ko*t*is of disciples of the Tathâgata have become very mighty, very powerful, very potent, owing to the Lord's teaching of the law. Deign, O Lord, to teach us also, for mercy's sake, the law with a view to supreme, perfect enlightenment, so that we also may follow the teaching of the Tathâgata[1]. We want, O Lord, to see the knowledge of the Tathâgata; the Lord can himself testify to this, for thou, O Lord, who knowest the disposition of all beings, also knowest ours.

Then, monks, on seeing that those princes, the youths, had chosen the vagrant life of mendicants and become novices, the half of the whole retinue of the king *K*akravartin, to the number of eighty hundred thousand myriads of ko*t*is of living beings[2], chose the vagrant life of mendicants.

Subsequently, monks, the Lord Mahâbhi*gñâgñâ*nâbhibhû, the Tathâgata, &c., viewing the prayer of those novices at the lapse[3] of twenty thousand Æons, amply and completely revealed the Dharmaparyâya called 'the Lotus of the True Law,' a text[4] of great extent, serving to instruct Bodhisattvas and proper for all Buddhas, in presence of all the four classes of auditors.

---

[1] Yad vayam-api Tathâgatasyânu*s*ikshemahi, which may also be rendered, that we also may profit by the teaching, &c.

[2] The use of the term prâ*n*in, a living being, an animal, to denote lifeless objects, is quite analogous to that of ζῷον in Greek.

[3] Or, within the lapse, atyayena.

[4] Sûtrânta, a word formed after the model of Siddhânta or Râddhânta.

In course of time, monks, those sixteen novices grasped, kept, and fully penetrated the Lord's teaching.

Subsequently, monks, the Lord Mahâbhi*gñâgñ*ânâbhibhû, the Tathâgata, &c., foretold those sixteen novices their future destiny to supreme, perfect enlightenment. And while the Lord Mahâbhi*gñâgñ*ânâbhibhû, the Tathâgata, &c., was propounding the Dharmaparyâya of the Lotus of the True Law, the disciples as well as the sixteen novices were full of faith, and many hundred thousand myriads of ko*t*is of beings acquired perfect certainty[1].

Thereupon, monks, after propounding the Dharmaparyâya of the Lotus of the True Law during eight thousand Æons without interruption, the Lord Mahâbhi*gñâgñ*ânâbhibhû, the Tathâgata, &c., entered the monastery to retire for the purpose of meditation[2], and in that retirement, monks, the Tathâgata continued in the monastery during eighty-four thousand ko*t*is of Æons.

Now, monks, when the sixteen novices perceived that the Lord was absorbed, they sat down on the seats, the royal thrones which had been prepared for each of them, and[3] amply expounded, during eighty-four hundred thousand myriads of ko*t*is[4], the Dhar-

---

[1] Nirvi*k*ikitsâprâpta; a var. lect. has vi*k*ikitsâprâpta, which means exactly the reverse, at least if we take vi*k*ikitsâ in its usual acceptation.

[2] Pratisa*m*layana, seclusion, retirement for the purpose of meditation, absorbing oneself in meditation; Pâli pa*t*isallâ*n*a.

[3] In one MS. added in the margin, 'after rendering homage to the Lord M., the Tathâgata.'

[4] One would expect eighty-four thousand ko*t*is, the same number as above. Burnouf has in both cases eighty-four thousand Æons, and that would seem to be the preferable reading.

maparyâya of the Lotus of the True Law to the four classes. By doing this, monks, each of those novices, as Bodhisattvas fully developed, instructed, excited, stimulated, edified, confirmed[1] in respect to supreme, perfect enlightenment 60 x 60[2] hundred thousand myriads of ko*t*is of living beings, equal to the sands of the river Ganges.

Now, monks, at the lapse of eighty-four thousand Æons the Lord Mahâbhi*gñ*â*gñ*ânâbhibhû, the Tathâgata, &c., rose from his meditation, in possession of memory and consciousness, whereafter he went up to the seat of the law, designed for him, in order to occupy it.

As soon as the Lord had occupied the seat of the law, monks, he cast his looks over the whole circle of the audience and addressed the congregation of monks: They are wonderfully gifted, monks, they are prodigiously gifted, these sixteen novices, wise, servitors to many hundred thousand myriads of ko*t*is of Buddhas, observers of the course (of duty), who have received Buddha-knowledge, transmitted Buddha-knowledge, expounded Buddha-knowledge. Honour these sixteen novices, monks, again and again; and all, be they devoted to the vehicle of the disciples, the vehicle of the Pratyekabuddhas, or the vehicle of the Bodhisattvas,

---

[1] Avadhâritavân; var. lect. avatâritavân, 'brought (them) to, initiated (them) in.'

[2] Shash*t*im shash*t*i (var. lect. shash*t*ishash*t*i) Gaṅgânadîvâlikâsamâni prâ*n*iko*t*inayuta*s*atasahasrâ*n*i; the second reading admits of being rendered, hundred thousands of myriads of ko*t*is of living beings, equal to the sands of 60 × 60 rivers (like the) Ganges. The number 360 is that of the days in a year, the five supernumerary days (avama) not being taken into account.

who shall not reject nor repudiate the preaching of these young men of good family, O monks, shall quickly gain supreme, perfect enlightenment, and obtain Tathâgata-knowledge.

In the sequel also, monks, have these young men of good family repeatedly revealed this Dharmaparyâya of the Lotus of the True Law under the mastership of that Lord. And the 60 × 60 hundred thousand myriads of ko*t*is of living beings, equal to the sands of the river Ganges[1], who by each of the sixteen novices, the Bodhisattvas Mahâsattvas, in the quality of Bodhisattva, had been roused to enlightenment, all those beings followed the example of the sixteen novices in choosing along with them the vagrant life of mendicants, in their several existences; they enjoyed their sight and heard the law from their mouth. They propitiated forty ko*t*is[2] of Buddhas, and some are doing so up to this day.

I announce to you, monks, I declare to you: Those sixteen princes, the youths, who as novices under the mastership of the Lord were interpreters of the law, have all reached supreme, perfect enlightenment, and all of them are staying, existing, living even now, in the several directions of space, in different Buddha-fields, preaching the law to many hundred thousand myriads of ko*t*is of disciples and Bodhisattvas, to wit: In the east, monks, in the world[3] Abhirati the Tathâgata named Akshobhya,

---

[1] Or, as above in note 2, page 176.

[2] Var. lect. has 40 × 100,000 × 10,000 ko*t*is.

[3] Lokadhâtu; it appears from this passage that this term, though it may be rendered by 'world' or 'universe,' in reality means what is implied by its etymology, viz. a fixed point of the world. It is needless to remark that the points of the compass are meant.

the Arhat, &c., and the Tathâgata Merukû*t*a, the Arhat, &c.[1] In the south-east, monks, is the Tathâgata Si*m*haghosha, &c., and the Tathâgata Si*m*hadhva*g*a, &c.[2] In the south, monks, is the Tathâgata named Âkâ*s*apratish*th*ita, &c., and the Tathâgata named Nityaparinirv*ri*ta[3], &c. In the south-west, monks, is the Tathâgata named Indradhva*g*a, &c., and the Tathâgata named Brahmadhva*g*a, &c. In the west, monks, is the Tathâgata named Amitâyus[4], &c., and the Tathâgata named Sarvalokadhâtûpadravodvegapratyuttîr*n*a, &c. In the north-west, monks, is the Tathâgata named Tamâlapatra*k*andanagandhâbhi*gñ*a[5], &c., and the Tathâgata Merukalpa, &c. In the north, monks, is the Tathâgata named Meghasvarapradîpa[6], &c., and the Tathâgata

[1] I am at a loss to explain by what trick the S. E. E. point is called 'summit of the Meru.'

[2] The names of these two Tathâgatas mean severally, having a lion's voice, and having a lion for ensign. 'Lion' is one of the constant veiled expressions for hari, yellow, ruddy, Vish*n*u, lion, &c., because hari possesses all these different meanings. The Buddhas here intended may be Agni and Anila or Antariksha (=vâyu, air), both of them known by the name of hari. Cf. Journal of the Royal Asiatic Society, VI (new series), p. 287 seq.

[3] So have my MSS.; Nityaparinivr*ri*ta, 'always extinct or quiet,' is Yama, Death.

[4] Identical with Amitâbha; he is the ruler of the blessed dead in the city of Bliss (Sukhâvatî), and therefore a variety of Yama. His being placed in the west is explainable, because Yama and Varu*n*a in a certain function coincide, and the latter otherwise appears as the ruler of the west. The following worthy with endless name, 'Having past all worldly calamities and emotions,' is another designation of Amitâyus, i. e. he whose life is of unlimited duration.

[5] According to the Camb. MSS.; the name 'cognizant of the scent of Xanthochymus and sandal' denotes the Wind, the ruler of the north-west.

[6] Var. lect. Meghasvaradîpa; Burnouf has a third form, Megha-

named Meghasvararâ*g*a, &c. In the north-east, monks, is the Tathâgata named Sarvalokabhayâ*g*ita*kkh*ambhitatvavidhva*m*sanakara[1], the Arhat, &c., and, the sixteenth, myself, *S*âkyamuni, the Tathâgata, the Arhat, &c., who have attained supreme, perfect enlightenment in the centre of this Saha-world[2].

Further, monks, those beings who have heard the law from us when we were novices, those many hundred thousand myriads of ko*t*is of beings, numerous as the sands of the river Ganges, whom we have severally initiated in supreme, perfect enlightenment, they are up to this day standing on the stage of disciples and matured for supreme, perfect enlightenment. In regular turn they are to attain supreme, perfect enlightenment, for it is difficult, monks, to penetrate the knowledge of the Tathâgatas. And which are those beings, monks, who,

svara. Dîpa or pradîpa, torch, candle, light, is necessary, because the ruler of the north is the moon; meghasvara, sound of the clouds, must somehow denote the sky. Râ*g*an, king, is king Soma (identified with the moon).

[1] Var. lect. °bhayadevâga*kkh*a°, and, according to Burnouf, °bhayâstambhitatva°. The compound contains four epithets of *S*iva, the ruler of the north-east; sarvalokabhaya, the terror of all the world; a*g*ita, unconquerable (the var. lect. devâga is probably devâgra, the chief or supreme of gods); *k*ambhitatvakara, he who causes stiffness; vidhva*m*sanakara, the destroyer. *K*ambhita is the regular Prâkrit form for stambhita, and here, without doubt, the original reading.

[2] Which seems to imply that *S*âkyamuni is both the ruler of the north-west and the central point. As a ruler of the north-west we find *S*ikhin in B*r*ihat Sa*m*hitâ, chap. 53, 51; in Buddhist writings *S*ikhin is synonymous with Brahma Sahâmpati. So it would seem as if *S*âkyamuni in this passage were considered to be one with Brahma.

innumerable, incalculable like the sands of the Ganges, those hundred thousands of myriads of ko*t*is of living beings, whom I, when I was a Bodhisattva under the mastership of that Lord, have taught the law of omniscience? Yourselves, monks, were at that time those beings.

And those who shall be my disciples in future, when I shall have attained complete Nirvâ*n*a, shall learn the course (of duty) of Bodhisattvas, without conceiving the idea of their being Bodhisattvas. And, monks, all who shall have the idea of complete Nirvâ*n*a, shall reach it. It should be added, monks, as[1] I stay under different names in other worlds, they shall there be born again seeking after the knowledge of the Tathâgatas, and there they shall anew hear this dogma: The complete Nirvâ*n*a of the Tathâgatas is but one; there is no other, no second Nirvâ*n*a of the Tathâgatas. Herein, monks, one has to see a device of the Tathâgatas and a direction[2] for the preaching of the law. When the Tathâgata, monks, knows that the moment of his complete extinction has arrived, and sees that the assemblage is pure, strong in faith, penetrated with the law of voidness, devoted to meditation, devoted to great meditation, then, monks, the Tathâgata, because the time has arrived, calls together all Bodhisattvas and all disciples to teach them thus: There

---

[1] Or, perhaps, when; api tu khalu punar, bhikshavo, yad aham anyâsu lokadhâtushu anyonyair (to r. anyânyair?) nâmadheyair viharâmi; in one MS. a correcting hand has written in the margin vihareya*m*.

[2] Abhinirhâra; I am not sure of the correctness of this rendering; in Pâli abhinîhâra is interpreted to be 'earnest wish or aspiration;' abhinîharati, to turn, direct.

is, O monks, in this world no second vehicle at all, no second Nirvâ*n*a, far less a third. It is an able device of the Tathâgata, monks, that on seeing creatures[1] far advanced on the path of perdition, delighting in the low and plunged in the mud of sensual desires, the Tathâgata teaches them that Nirvâ*n*a to which they are attached.

By way of example, monks, suppose there is some dense forest five hundred yo*g*anas in extent which has been reached by a great company of men. They have a guide to lead them on their journey to the Isle of Jewels, which guide, being able, clever, sagacious, well acquainted with the difficult passages of the forest, is to bring the whole company[2] out of the forest. Meanwhile that great troop of men, tired, weary, afraid, and anxious, say: 'Verily, Master, guide, and leader, know that we are tired, weary, afraid, and anxious; let us return; this dense forest stretches so far.' The guide, who is a man of able devices, on seeing those people desirous of returning, thinks within himself: It ought not to be that these poor creatures should not reach that great Isle of Jewels. Therefore out of pity for them he makes use of an artifice. In the middle of that forest he produces a magic city more than a hundred or two hundred yo*g*anas in extent. Thereafter he says to those men: 'Be not afraid, sirs, do not return; there you see a populous place where you may take repose and perform all you have to do; there stay in the enjoyment of happy rest[3]. Let him who after

[1] Satvân, var. lect. satvadhâtû*m*; Burnouf has 'la réunion des êtres.'

[2] Sârtha, usually a company of merchants, a caravan.

[3] And, of Nirvâ*n*a, nirvâ*n*aprâptâ viharadhvam.

reposing there wants to do so, proceed to the great Isle of Jewels.'

Then, monks, the men who are in the forest are struck with astonishment, and think: We are out of the forest; we have reached the place of happy rest; let us stay here. They enter that magic city, in the meaning that they have arrived at the place of their destination, that they are saved and in the enjoyment of rest. They think: We are at rest, we are refreshed[1]. After a while, when the guide perceives that their fatigue is gone, he causes the magic city to disappear, and says to them: 'Come, sirs, there you see the great Isle of Jewels quite near; as to this great city, it has been produced by me for no other purpose but to give you some repose.'

In the same manner, monks, is the Tathâgata, the Arhat, &c., your guide, and the guide of all other beings. Indeed, monks, the Tathâgata, &c., reflects thus: Great is this forest of evils which must be crossed, left, shunned. It ought not to be that these beings, after hearing the Buddha-knowledge, should suddenly turn back and not proceed to the end because they think: This Buddha-knowledge is attended with too many difficulties to be gone through to the end. Under those circumstances the Tathâgata, knowing the creatures to be feeble of character, (does) as the guide (who) produces the magic city in order that those people may have repose, and after their having taken repose, he tells them that the city is one produced by magic. In the same manner, monks, the Tathâgata, &c., to give a repose to the creatures, very skilfully teaches and proclaims two stages of

[1] *S*îtîbhûta.

Nirvâ*n*a, viz. the stage of the disciples and that of the Pratyekabuddhas. And, monks, when the creatures are there halting, then the Tathâgata, &c., himself, pronounces these words: 'You have not accomplished your task, monks; you have not finished what you had to do. But behold, monks! the Buddha-knowledge is near; behold and be convinced[1]: what to you (seems) Nirvâ*n*a, that is not Nirvâ*n*a. Nay, monks, it is an able device of the Tathâgatas, &c., that they expound three vehicles.'

And in order to explain this same subject more in detail, the Lord on that occasion uttered the following stanzas:

60. The Leader of the world, Abhi*gñ*â*gñ*ânâbhibhû, having occupied the terrace of enlightenment, continued ten complete intermediate kalpas without gaining enlightenment, though he saw the things in their very essence.

61. Then the gods, Nâgas, demons, and goblins, zealous to honour the *G*ina, sent down a rain of flowers on the spot where the Leader awakened to enlightenment.

62. And high in the sky they beat the cymbals to worship and honour the *G*ina, and they were vexed that the *G*ina delayed so long in coming to the highest place.

63. After the lapse of ten intermediate kalpas the Lord Anâbhibhû[2] attained enlightenment; then

---

[1] Vyava*k*ârayadhvam; I have not met this word elsewhere, and am not certain of its precise meaning; Burnouf renders it by 'réfléchissez-y.'

[2] I.e. 'he who has no one surpassing him;' it is virtually the same with Abhibhû.

all gods, men, serpents, and demons were glad and overjoyed.

64. The sixteen sons of the Leader of men, those heroes, being at the time young princes, rich in virtues, came along with thousands of ko*t*is of living beings to honour the eminent chiefs of men.

65. And after saluting the feet of the Leader they prayed: Reveal the law and refresh us as well as this world with thy good word, O Lion amongst kings.

66. After a long time thou art seen (again) in the ten points of this world; thou appearest, great Leader, while the aerial cars of the Brahma-angels are stirring to reveal a token to living beings.

67. In the eastern quarter fifty thousand ko*t*is of fields have been shaken, and the lofty angelic cars[1] in them have become excessively brilliant.

68. The Brahma-angels on perceiving this foretoken went and approached the Chief of the Leaders of the world, and, covering him with flowers, presented all of them their cars to him.

69. They prayed him to move forward the wheel of the law, and celebrated him with stanzas and songs. But the king of kings was silent, (for he thought): The time has not yet arrived for me to proclaim the law.

70. Likewise in the south, west, north, the nadir, zenith, and in the intermediate points of the compass there were thousands of ko*t*is of Brahma-angels.

71. Unremittingly covering the Lord (with flowers) they saluted the feet of the Leader, presented all their aerial cars, celebrated him, and again prayed:

---

[1] Literally, Brahma-cars.

72. Move forward the wheel, O thou whose sight is infinite! Rarely art thou met in (the course of) many ko*t*is of Æons. Display the benevolence thou hast observed in so many former generations[1]; open the gate of immortality.

73. On hearing their prayer, he whose sight is infinite exposed the multifarious law and the four Truths, extensively. All existences (said he) spring successively from their antecedents.

74. Starting from Ignorance, the Seer proceeded to speak of death, endless woe[2]; all those evils spring from birth. Know likewise that death is the lot of mankind[3].

75. No sooner had he expounded the multifarious, different, endless laws, than eighty myriads of ko*t*is of creatures who had heard them quickly attained the stage of disciples.

76. On a second occasion[4] the *G*ina expounded many laws, and beings like the sands of the Ganges became instantly purified and disciples.

77. From that moment the assembly of that Leader of the world was innumerable; no man would be able to reach the term (of its number), even were he to go on counting for myriads of ko*t*is of Æons.

78. Those sixteen princes also, his own dear sons,

---

[1] Maitrîm bahupûrvasevitâm.

[2] MSS. prabhâshate mara*n*am ananta*m* du*h*kham; Burnouf has 'parle de la mort dont la douleur est sans fin.'

[3] The translation is uncertain; m*ri*tyu*ñ* *k*a mânushyam imeva *g*ânatha. I take imeva, like emeva in other passages (e.g. in st. 103), for the hemeva (Sansk. evam eva) of the A*s*oka inscriptions. One might also render: 'Know that death (mortality) and humanity (human lot) are one and the same.'

[4] Or, at a second moment, ksha*n*e.

who had become mendicants[1] and novices, said to the *G*ina: 'Expound, O Chief, the superior law;

79. 'That we may become sages, knowers of the world, such as thyself art, O supreme of all *G*inas, and that all these beings may become such as thyself art, O hero, O clear-sighted one[2].'

80. And the *G*ina, considering the wish of his sons, the young princes, explained the highest superior enlightenment by means of many myriads of ko*t*is of illustrations.

81. Demonstrating with thousands of arguments and elucidating the knowledge of transcendent wisdom, the Lord of the world indicated the veritable course (of duty) such as was followed by the wise Bodhisattvas.

82. This very Sûtra of great extension, this good Lotus of the True Law, was by the Lord delivered in many thousands of stanzas, so numerous as to equal the sands of the Ganges.

83. After delivering this Sûtra, the *G*ina entered the monastery for the purpose of becoming absorbed[3] in meditation; during eighty-four complete Æons the Lord of the world continued meditating, sitting on the same seat.

84. Those novices, perceiving that the Chief remained in the monastery without coming out of it, imparted to many ko*t*is of creatures that Buddha-

---

[1] *K*ellakabhûta, var. lect. *k*elukabh. and *k*ailakabhûta. The *K*ailaka 'is he who contents himself with such a portion of clothes as barely suffices to cover his nakedness, rejecting everything more as superfluous.' Hodgson Essays, p. 52, cf. pp. 30 and 64.

[2] Or, according to the reading followed by Burnouf, 'clear-sighted as thyself, O hero.'

[3] Vilakshayîti.

knowledge, which is free from imperfections and blissful.

85. On the seats which they had made to be prepared, one for each, they expounded this very Sûtra under the mastership of the Sugata of that period. A service of the same kind they render to me[1].

86. Innumerable as the sands of sixty thousand (rivers like the) Ganges were the beings then taught; each of the sons of the Sugata converted (or trained) endless beings.

87. After the *G*ina's complete Nirvâ*n*a they commenced a wandering life and saw ko*t*is of Buddhas; along with those pupils they rendered homage to the most exalted amongst men.

88. Having observed the extensive and sublime course of duty and reached enlightenment in the ten points of space, those sixteen sons of the *G*ina became themselves *G*inas, two by two, in each point of the horizon.

89. And all those who had been their pupils became disciples of those *G*inas, and gradually obtained possession of enlightenment by various means.

90. I myself was one of their number, and you have all been taught by me. Therefore you are my disciples now also, and I lead you all to enlightenment by (my) devices.

91. This is the cause dating from old, this is the motive of my expounding the law, that I lead you to superior enlightenment. This being the case, monks, you need not be afraid.

92. It is as if there were a forest dreadful, terrific, barren, without a place of refuge or shelter, replete

---

[1] Adhikâru kurvanti mamaivarûpa*m*.

with wild beasts, deprived of water, frightful for persons of no experience.

93. (Suppose further that) many thousand men have come to the forest, that waste track of wilderness which is fully five hundred yoganas in extent.

94. And he who is to act as their guide through that rough and horrible forest is a rich man, thoughtful, intelligent, wise, well instructed, and undaunted.

95. And those beings, numbering many kotis, feel tired, and say to the guide: 'We are tired, Master; we are not able to go on; we should like now to return.'

96. But he, the dexterous and clever guide, is searching in his mind for some apt device. Alas! he thinks, by going back these foolish men will be deprived of the possession of the jewels.

97. Therefore let me by dint of magic power now produce a great city adorned with thousands of kotis of buildings and embellished by monasteries and parks.

98. Let me produce ponds and canals; (a city) adorned with gardens and flowers, provided with walls and gates, and inhabited by an infinite number of men and women.

99. After creating that city he speaks to them in this manner: 'Do not fear, and be cheerful; you have reached a most excellent city; enter it and do your business, speedily.

100. 'Be joyful and at ease; you have reached the limit of the whole forest.' It is to give them a time for repose that he speaks these words, and, in fact, they recover from their weariness.

101. As he perceives that they have sufficiently

reposed, he collects them and addresses them again: 'Come, hear what I have to tell you: this city have I produced by magic.

102. 'On seeing you fatigued, I have, lest you should go back, made use of this device; now strain your energy to reach the Isle.'

103. In the same manner, monks, I am the guide, the conductor of thousands of ko*t*is of living beings; in the same manner I see creatures toiling and unable to break the shell of the egg of evils[1].

104. Then I reflect on this matter: These beings have enjoyed repose, have been tranquillised; now I will remind[2] them of the misery of all things (and I say): 'At the stage of Arhat you shall reach your aim.'

105. At that time, when you shall have attained that state, and when I see all of you have become Arhats, then will I call you all together and explain to you how the law really is.

106. It is an artifice of the Leaders, when they, the great Seers, show three vehicles, for there is but one vehicle, no second; it is only to help (creatures) that two vehicles are spoken of.

107. Therefore I now tell you, monks: Rouse to the utmost your lofty energy for the sake of the knowledge of the all-knowing; as yet, you have not come so far as to possess complete Nirvâ*n*a.

108. But when you shall have attained the knowledge of the all-knowing and the ten powers proper to *G*inas, you shall become Buddhas marked by

---

[1] Kle*s*â*nd*ako*s*a.

[2] The rendering of this passage is doubtful; the text runs thus: sarvasya du*h*khasya 'nubodha eshu.

the thirty-two characteristic signs and have rest for ever.

109. Such is the teaching of the Leaders: in order to give quiet they speak of repose, (but) when they see that (the creatures) have had a repose, they, knowing this to be no final resting-place, initiate them in the knowledge of the all-knowing.

CHAPTER VIII.

ANNOUNCEMENT OF THE FUTURE DESTINY OF THE FIVE HUNDRED MONKS.

On hearing from the Lord that display of skilfulness and the instruction by means of mysterious speech; on hearing the announcement of the future destiny of the great Disciples, as well as the foregoing tale concerning ancient devotion and the leadership[1] of the Lord, the venerable Pûrna, son of Maitrâyanî, was filled with wonder and amazement, thrilled[2] with pure-heartedness[3], a feeling of delight and joy. He rose from his seat, full of delight and joy, full of great respect for the law, and while prostrating himself before the Lord's feet, made within himself the following reflection: Wonderful, O Lord; wonderful, O Sugata; it is an extremely difficult thing that the Tathâgatas, &c., perform, the conforming to this world, composed of so many elements, and preaching the law to all creatures with many proofs of their skilfulness, and skilfully releasing them when attached to this or that. What could we

[1] Vrishabhitva, a curious and irregular form instead of vrishabhatva.

[2] Sphuta, in the sense of vyâpta; Pâli phuta.

[3] Nirâmishakittena. Nirâmisha is both 'free from worldly taint, sensual desire,' and 'without having a lure, not eager for reward,' i.e. disinterested. Both meanings are so intimately connected that it is not always easy to decide which we should prefer, e.g. Lalita-vistara, p. 215, and Manu VI, 49.

do, O Lord, in such a case? None but the Tathâgata knows our inclination and our ancient course. Then, after saluting with his head the Lord's feet, Pûrna went and stood apart, gazing up to the Lord with unmoved eyes and so showing his veneration.

And the Lord, regarding the mental disposition of the venerable Pûrna, son of Maitrâyanî, addressed the entire assembly of monks in this strain: Ye monks, see[1] this disciple, Pûrna, son of Maitrâyanî, whom I have designated as the foremost of preachers in this assembly, praised for his many virtues, and who has applied himself in various ways to comprehend the true law. He is the man to excite, arouse, and stimulate the four classes of the audience; unwearied in the preaching of the law; as capable to preach the law as to oblige his fellow-followers of the course of duty. The Tathâgata excepted, monks, there is none able to equal Pûrna, son of Maitrâyanî, either essentially or in accessories. Now, monks, do you suppose that he keeps my true law only? No, monks, you must not think so. For I remember, monks, that in the past, in the times of the ninety-nine Buddhas, the same Pûrna kept the true law under the mastership of those Buddhas. Even as he is now with me, so he has, in all periods, been the foremost of the preachers of the law; has in all periods been a consummate knower of Voidness; has in all periods acquired the (four) distinctive qualifications of an Arhat[2]; has in all periods reached mastership in the transcendent

---

[1] Pasyata, var. lect. pasyadhvam.

[2] Pratisamvid, in meaning answering to Pâli patisambhidâ.

wisdom of the Bodhisattvas. He has been a strongly convinced[1] preacher of the law, exempt from doubt, and quite pure. Under the mastership of those Buddhas he has during his whole existence observed a spiritual life, and everywhere they termed him 'the Disciple.' By this means he has promoted the interest of innumerable, incalculable hundred thousands of myriads of ko*t*is of beings, and brought innumerable and incalculable beings to full ripeness for supreme and perfect enlightenment. In all periods he has assisted the creatures in the function of a Buddha, and in all periods he has purified his own Buddha-field, always striving to bring creatures to ripeness. He was also, monks, the foremost among the preachers of the law under the seven Tathâgatas, the first of whom is Vipa*s*yin and the seventh myself[2].

And as to the Buddhas, monks, who have in future to appear in this Bhadra-kalpa, to the number of a thousand less four, under the mastership of them also shall this same Pûr*n*a, son of Maitrâya*n*î, be the foremost among the preachers of the law and the keeper of the true law. Thus he shall keep the true law of innumerable and incalculable Lords and Buddhas in future, promote the interest of innumerable and incalculable beings, and bring innumerable and incalculable beings to full ripeness for supreme and perfect enlightenment. Constantly and assiduously he shall be instant in purifying his own Buddha-field and bringing creatures to ripeness.

[1] Suvini*sk*ita.

[2] The seven so-called Mânushi-Buddhas; a rather transparent disguise of the fact that in cosmological mythology there are seven Manus, rulers of certain periods.

After completing such a Bodhisattva-course, at the end of innumerable, incalculable Æons, he shall reach supreme and perfect enlightenment; he shall in the world be the Tathâgata called Dharmaprabhâsa, an Arhat, &c., endowed with science and conduct, a Sugata, &c. He shall appear in this very Buddha-field.

Further, monks, at that time the Buddha-field spoken of will look as if formed by thousands of spheres similar to the sands of the river Ganges. It will be even, like the palm of the hand, consist of seven precious substances, be without hills, and filled with high edifices of seven precious substances[1]. There will be cars of the gods stationed in the sky; the gods will behold men, and men will behold the gods. Moreover, monks, at that time that Buddha-field shall be exempt from places of punishment and from womankind, as all beings shall be born by apparitional birth. They shall lead a spiritual life, have ideal[2] bodies, be self-lighting, magical, moving in the firmament, strenuous, of good memory, wise, possessed of gold-coloured bodies, and adorned with the thirty-two characteristics of a great man. And at that time, monks, the beings in that Buddha-field will have two things to feed upon, viz. the delight in the law and the delight in meditation. There will

[1] The Buddha-field of Pûr*n*a, i.e. full, is so extremely pure, because he is, I suppose, the full moon. He is called the son of Maitrâya*n*î, because the full moon is born on the 15th day of the month. Maitrâya*n*î is a slightly disguised Maitrî, otherwise called Anurâdhâ, the 15th asterism, in the ancient series. Hence we may infer that the story of Pûr*n*a is comparatively old. No wonder that Pûr*n*a is surpassed by none, the Buddha excepted.

[2] Manomaya.

be an immense, incalculable number of hundred thousands of myriads of ko*t*is of Bodhisattvas; all endowed with great transcendent wisdom, accomplished in the (four) distinctive qualifications of an Arhat, able in instructing creatures. He (that Buddha) will have a number of disciples, beyond all calculation, mighty in magic, powerful, masters in the meditation of the eight emancipations. So immense are the good qualities that Buddha-field will be possessed of. And that Æon shall be called Ratnâvabhâsa (i. e. radiant with gems), and that world Suvi*s*uddha (i. e. very pure). His lifetime shall last immense, incalculable Æons; and after the complete extinction of that Lord Dharmaprabhâsa, the Tathâgata, &c., his true law shall last long, and his world shall be full of Stûpas made of precious substances. Such inconceivable good qualities, monks, shall the Buddha-field of that Lord be possessed of.

So spoke the Lord, and thereafter he, the Sugata, the Master, added the following stanzas:

1. Listen to me, monks, and hear how my son has achieved his course of duty, and how he, well-trained and skilful, has observed the course of enlightenment.

2. Viewing these beings to be lowly-disposed and to be startled at the lofty vehicle, the Bodhisattvas become disciples and exercise Pratyekabuddhaship.

3. By many hundreds of able devices they bring numerous Bodhisattvas to full ripeness and declare: We are but disciples, indeed, and we are far away from the highest and supreme enlightenment.

4. It is by learning from them this course (of duty) that ko*t*is of beings arrive at full ripeness,

who (at first), lowly-disposed and somewhat lazy, in course of time all become Buddhas.

5. They follow a course in ignorance (thinking): We, disciples, are of little use, indeed! In despondency they descend into all places of existence (successively), and (so) clear their own field.

6. They show in their own persons that they are not free from affection, hatred, and infatuation; and on perceiving (other) beings clinging to (heretical) views[1], they go so far as to accommodate themselves to those views.

7. By following such a course my numerous disciples skilfully save creatures; simple people would go mad, if they were taught the whole course of life (or story).

8. Pûrna here, monks, my disciple, has formerly fulfilled his course (of duty) under thousands of kotis of Buddhas, he has got possession of this true law by seeking after Buddha-knowledge.

9. And at all periods has he been the foremost of the disciples, learned, a brilliant orator, free from hesitation; he has, indeed, always been able to excite to gladness and at all times ready to perform the Buddha-task.

10. He has always been accomplished in the sublime transcendent faculties and endowed with the distinctive qualifications of an Arhat; he knew the faculties and range of (other) beings, and has always preached the perfectly pure law.

11. By exposing the most eminent of true laws he has brought thousands of kotis of beings to full ripeness for this supreme, foremost vehicle, whilst purifying his own excellent field.

[1] Drishtîvilagna.

12. In future also he shall likewise honour thousands of ko*t*is of Buddhas, acquire knowledge of the most eminent of good laws, and clean his own field.

13. Always free from timidity he shall preach the law with thousands of ko*t*is of able devices, and bring many beings to full ripeness for the knowledge of the all-knowing that is free from imperfections.

14. After having paid homage to the Chiefs of men and always kept the most eminent of laws, he shall in the world be a Buddha self-born, widely renowned everywhere by the name of Dharmaprabhâsa.

15. And his field shall always be very pure and always set off with seven precious substances; his Æon shall be (called) Ratnâvabhâsa, and his world Suvi*s*uddha.

16. That world shall be pervaded with many thousand ko*t*is of Bodhisattvas, accomplished masters in the great transcendent sciences, pure in every respect, and endowed with magical power.

17. At that period the Chief shall also have an assemblage of thousands of ko*t*is of disciples, endowed with magical power, adepts at the meditation of the (eight) emancipations, and accomplished in the (four) distinctive qualifications of an Arhat.

18. And all beings in that Buddha-field shall be pure and lead a spiritual life. Springing into existence by apparitional birth, they shall all be gold-coloured and display the thirty-two characteristic signs.

19. They shall know no other food but pleasure in the law and delight in knowledge. No womankind shall be there, nor fear of the places of punishments or of dismal states.

20. Such shall be the excellent field of Pûr*n*a, who is possessed of all good qualities; it shall abound with all goodly things[1], a small part (only) of which has here been mentioned.

Then this thought arose in the mind of those twelve hundred self-controlled (Arhats): We are struck with wonder and amazement. (How) if the Tathâgata would predict to us severally our future destiny as the Lord has done to those other great disciples? And the Lord apprehending in his own mind what was going on in the minds of these great disciples addressed the venerable Mahâ-Kâ*s*yapa: Those twelve hundred self-controlled hearers whom I am now beholding from face to face, to all those twelve hundred self-controlled hearers, Kâ*s*yapa, I will presently foretell their destiny. Amongst them, Kâ*s*yapa, the monk Kau*nd*inya, a great disciple, shall, after sixty-two hundred thousand myriads of ko*t*is of Buddhas, become a Tathâgata, an Arhat, &c., under the name of Samantaprabhâsa, endowed with science and conduct, a Sugata, &c. &c.; but of those (twelve hundred), Kâ*s*yapa, five hundred shall become Tathâgatas of the same name. Thereafter shall all those five hundred great disciples reach supreme and perfect enlightenment, all bearing the name of Samantaprabhâsa; viz. Gayâ-Kâ*s*yapa, Nadî-Kâ*s*yapa, Uruvilvâ-Kâ*s*yapa, Kâla, Kâlodâyin, Aniruddha, Kapphi*n*a, Vakkula[2], *K*unda[3], Svâgata[4],

[1] Âkîr*nn*a sarvehi subhadrakehi; Burnouf takes it as a masculine, rendering it by 'créatures fortunées.'

[2] Also spelt Vakula; see p. 2.

[3] Probably the same with Mahâ-*K*unda in Mahâvagga I, 6, 36; *K*ullavagga I, 18, 1.

[4] Pâli Sâgata, Mahâvagga V, 1, 3.

and the rest of the five hundred self-controlled (Arhats).

And on that occasion the Lord uttered the following stanzas:

21. The scion of the Ku*nd*ina family, my disciple here, shall in future be a Tathâgata, a Lord of the world, after the lapse of an endless period; he shall educate hundreds of ko*t*is of living beings.

22. After seeing many endless Buddhas, he shall in future, after the lapse of an endless period, become the *G*ina Samantaprabhâsa, whose field shall be thoroughly pure.

23. Brilliant, gifted with the powers of a Buddha, with a voice far resounding in all quarters, waited upon by thousands of ko*t*is of beings, he shall preach supreme and eminent enlightenment.

24. There shall be most zealous Bodhisattvas, mounted on lofty aereal cars, and moving, meditative, pure in morals, and assiduous in doing good.

25. After hearing the law from the highest of men, they shall invariably go to other fields, to salute thousands of Buddhas and show them great honour.

26. But ere long they shall return to the field of the Leader called Prabhâsa, the Tathâgata[1]. So great shall be the power of their course (of duty).

27. The measure of the lifetime of that Sugata shall be sixty thousand Æons, and, after the complete extinction of that mighty one[2], his true law shall remain twice as long in the world.

28. And the counterfeit of it shall continue three

---

[1] Var. lect. 'the most high (or best) of men.'

[2] Tâyin.

times as long. When the true law of that holy one shall he exhausted, men and gods shall be vexed.

29. There shall appear a complete number of five hundred Chiefs, supreme amongst men, who shall bear the same name with that *G*ina, Samantaprabha, and follow one another in regular succession.

30. All shall have like divisions, magical powers, Buddha-fields, and hosts (of followers). Their true law also shall be the same and stand equally long.

31. All shall have in this world, including the gods, the same voice as Samantaprabhâsa, the highest of men, such as I have mentioned before.

32. Moved by benevolence and compassion they shall in succession foretell each other's destiny, with the words: This is to be my immediate successor, and he is to command the world as I do at present.

33. Thus, Kâ*s*yapa, keep now in view[1] here these self-controlled (Arhats), no less than five hundred (in number), as well as my other disciples, and speak of this matter to the other disciples.

On hearing from the Lord the announcement of their own future destiny, the five hundred Arhats, contented, satisfied, in high spirits and ecstasy, filled with cheerfulness, joy, and delight, went up to the place where the Lord was sitting, reverentially saluted with their heads his feet, and spoke thus: We confess our fault, O Lord, in having continually and constantly persuaded ourselves that we had arrived

[1] Dhârehi. I am not sure of the correctness of this translation; the word usually means 'to keep,' but this seems out of place, unless it be assumed that the injunction is given in anticipation, because Kâ*s*yapa succeeded to the Lord after the latter's Nirvâ*n*a. Burnouf has: 'Voilà-comme tu dois considérer ici en ce jour ces Auditeurs,' &c.

at final Nirvâna, as (persons who are) dull, inept, ignorant of the rules. For, O Lord, whereas we should have thoroughly penetrated the knowledge of the Tathâgatas, we were content with such a trifling degree of knowledge.

It is, O Lord, as if some man having come to a friend's house got drunk or fell asleep, and that friend bound a priceless gem within[1] his garment, with the thought: Let this gem be his. After a while, O Lord, that man rises from his seat and travels further; he goes to some other country, where he is befallen by incessant difficulties, and has great trouble to find food and clothing. By dint of great exertion he is hardly able to obtain a bit of food, with which (however) he is contented and satisfied. The old friend of that man, O Lord, who bound within the man's garment that priceless gem, happens to see him again and says: How is it, good friend, that thou hast such difficulty in seeking food and clothing, while I, in order that thou shouldst live in ease, good friend, have bound within thy garment a priceless gem, quite sufficient to fulfil all thy wishes? I have given thee that gem, my good friend, the very gem I have bound within thy garment. Still thou art deliberating: What has been bound? by whom? for what reason and purpose? It is something foolish[2], my good friend, to be contented, when thou hast with (so much) difficulty to procure food and clothing. Go, my good friend, betake thyself, with this gem, to some great city,

---

[1] Vastrânte, vasanânte; below in stanza 40 we find vasanântarasmi.

[2] Etad bâlagâttyam.

exchange the gem for money, and with that money do all that can be done with money.

In the same manner, O Lord, has the Tathâgata formerly, when he still followed the course of duty of a Bodhisattva, raised in us also ideas of omniscience, but we, O Lord, did not perceive, nor know it. We fancied, O Lord, that on the stage of Arhat we had reached Nirvâna. We live in difficulty, O Lord, because we content ourselves with such a trifling degree of knowledge. But as our strong aspiration after the knowledge of the all-knowing has never ceased, the Tathâgata teaches us the right: 'Have no such idea of Nirvâna, monks; there are in your intelligence[1] roots of goodness which of yore I have fully developed. In this you have to see an able device of mine that from the expressions used by me, in preaching the law, you fancy Nirvâna to take place at this moment[2].' And after having taught us the right in such a way, the Lord now predicts our future destiny to supreme and perfect knowledge.

And on that occasion the five hundred self-controlled (Arhats), Âgñâta-Kaundinya and the rest, uttered the following stanzas:

34. We are rejoicing and delighted to hear this unsurpassed word of comfort that we are destined to the highest, supreme enlightenment. Homage be to thee, O Lord of unlimited sight!

35. We confess our fault before thee; we were so childish, nescient, ignorant that we were fully contented with a small part of Nirvâna, under the mastership of the Sugata.

---

[1] Santâne.

[2] Or, at present, etarhi.

36. This is a case like that of a certain man who enters the house of a friend, which friend, being rich and wealthy, gives him much food, both hard and soft.

37. After satiating him with nourishment, he gives him a jewel of great value. He ties it with a knot within the upper robe and feels satisfaction at having given that jewel.

38. The other man, unaware of it, goes forth and from that place travels to another town. There he is befallen with misfortune and, as a miserable beggar, seeks his food in affliction.

39. He is contented with the pittance he gets by begging without caring for dainty food; as to that jewel, he has forgotten it; he has not the slightest remembrance of its having been tied in his upper robe.

40. Under these circumstances he is seen by his old friend who at home gave him that jewel. This friend properly reprimands him and shows him the jewel within his robe.

41. At this sight the man feels extremely happy. The value of the jewel is such that he becomes a very rich man, of great power, and in possession of all that the five senses can enjoy.

42. In the same manner, O Lord, we were unaware of our former aspiration[1], (the aspiration) laid in us by the Tathâgata himself in previous existences from time immemorial.

43. And we were living in this world, O Lord, with dull understanding and in ignorance, under the

[1] Pra*n*idhâna; from the context one would gather that the real meaning had been 'predestination.'

mastership of the Sugata; for we were contented with a little of Nirvâna; we required nothing higher, nor even cared for it.

44. But the Friend of the world has taught us better: 'This is no blessed Rest[1] at all; the full knowledge of the highest men[2], that is blessed Rest, that is supreme beatitude.'

45. After hearing this sublime, grand, splendid, and matchless prediction, O Lord, we are greatly elated with joy, when thinking of the prediction (we shall have to make to each other) in regular succession.

---

[1] Nirvriti.

[2] Purushottamânâm.

CHAPTER IX.

ANNOUNCEMENT OF THE FUTURE DESTINY OF ÂNANDA, RÂHULA, AND THE TWO THOUSAND MONKS.

On that occasion the venerable Ânanda made this reflection: Should we also receive a similar prediction? Thus thinking, pondering, wishing, he rose from his seat, prostrated himself at the Lord's feet and uttered the following words. And the venerable Râhula also, in whom rose the same thought and the same wish as in Ânanda, prostrated himself at the Lord's feet, and uttered these words: 'Let it be our turn also, O Lord; let it be our turn also, O Sugata. The Lord is our father and procreator, our refuge and protection. For in this world, including men, gods, and demons, O Lord, we are particularly distinguished[1], as people say: These are the Lord's sons, the Lord's attendants; these are the keepers of the law-treasure of the Lord. Therefore, Lord, it would seem meet[2], were the Lord ere long to predict our destiny to supreme and perfect enlightenment.'

Two thousand other monks, and more, both such as were still under training and such as were not, likewise rose from their seats, put their upper robes upon one shoulder, stretched their joined hands

[1] Or respected, *k*itrîk*ri*ta; cf. Pâli *k*ittîkâra and Sansk. *k*itrîkâra, Lalita-vistara, p. 347.

[2] Pratirûpa.

towards the Lord and remained gazing up to him, all pre-occupied with the same thought, viz. of this very Buddha-knowledge: Should we also receive a prediction of our destiny to supreme and perfect enlightenment.

Then the Lord addressed the venerable Ânanda in these words: Thou, Ânanda, shalt in future become a Tathâgata by the name of Sâgaravaradharabuddhivikrîditâbhigña [1], an Arhat, &c., endowed with science and conduct, &c. After having honoured, respected, venerated, and worshipped sixty-two kotis of Buddhas, kept in memory the true law of those Buddhas and received this command, thou shalt arrive at supreme and perfect enlightenment, and bring to full ripeness for supreme, perfect enlightenment twenty hundred thousand myriads of kotis of Bodhisattvas similar to the sands of twenty Ganges [2]. And thy Buddha-field shall consist of lapis lazuli and be superabundant. The sphere shall be named Anavanâmita-vaigayanta and the Æon Manogñasabdâbhigargita. The lifetime of that Lord Sâgaravaradharabuddhivikrîditâbhigña, the Tathâgata, &c., shall measure an immense number of Æons, Æons

---

[1] The epithet Sâgaravaradharavipulabuddhi, i.e. having the great intelligence of Sâgaravaradhara, is bestowed on the Bodhisattva destined to be born as Sâkyamuni, Lalita-vistara, p. 10. As the next preceding epithet, l. c. mahâpadmagarbhekshana, seems to point to the sun, I infer that Sâgaravara, the choicest of oceans, denotes Soma, and Sâgaravaradhara, the keeper of that ocean, the moon.

[2] According to the reading vimsatim Gangânadîvâlikopamâni; var. lect. has vimsati-Gangâ°, so that Burnouf's rendering 'égal à celui des sables de vingt fleuves du Gange' is admissible. On the other hand it must be remarked that we shall meet in the sequel with the phrase bahûni Gangânadîvâlikopamâni Buddhakotinayutasata sahasrâni.

the term of which is not to be found by calculation. So many hundred thousand myriads of ko*t*is of incalculable Æons shall last the lifetime of that Lord. Twice as long, Ânanda, after the complete extinction of that Lord, shall his true law stand, and twice as long again shall continue its counterfeit. And further, Ânanda, many hundred thousand myriads of ko*t*is of Buddhas, similar to the sands of the river Ganges, shall in all directions of space speak the praise of that Tathâgata Sâgaravaradharabuddhivikrî*d*itâbhi*gñ*a, the Arhat, &c.

1. I announce to you, congregated monks, that Ânanda-Bhadra, the keeper of my law, shall in future become a *G*ina, after having worshipped sixty ko*t*is of Sugatas.

2. He shall be widely renowned by the name of Sâgarabuddhidhârin Abhi*gñ*âprâpta [1], in a beautiful, thoroughly clear field, (termed) Anavanatâ Vai*g*ayantî (i. e. triumphal banner unlowered).

3. There shall be Bodhisattvas like the sands of the Ganges and even more, whom he shall bring to full ripeness; he shall be a *G*ina endowed with great (magical) power, whose word shall widely resound in all quarters of the world.

4. The duration of his life shall be immense. He shall always be benign and merciful to the world. After the complete extinction of that *G*ina and mighty saint [2], his true law shall stand twice as long.

5. The counterfeit (shall continue) twice as long

---

[1] These names may be translated by 'possessor of an intellect (unfathomable) as the ocean, having arrived at transcendent wisdom.'

[2] Tâyin.

under the rule[1] of that *G*ina. Then also shall beings like grains of sand of the Ganges produce in this world what is the cause of Buddha-enlightenment.

In that assembly were eight thousand Bodhisattvas who had newly entered the vehicle. To them this thought presented itself: Never before did we have such a sublime prediction to Bodhisattvas, far less to disciples. What may be the cause of it? what the motive? The Lord, who apprehended in his mind what was going on in the minds of those Bodhisattvas, addressed them in these words: Young men of good family, I and Ânanda have in the same moment, the same instant conceived the idea of supreme and perfect enlightenment in the presence of the Tathâgata Dharmagahanâbhyudgatarâ*g*a[2], the Arhat, &c. At that period, young men of good family, he (Ânanda) constantly and assiduously applied himself to great learning, whereas I was applying myself to strenuous labour. Hence I sooner arrived at supreme and perfect enlightenment, whilst Ânanda-Bhadra was the keeper of the law-treasure of the Lords Buddhas; that is to say, young men of good family, he made a vow[3] to bring Bodhisattvas to full development.

When the venerable Ânanda heard from the Lord the announcement of his own destiny to supreme and perfect enlightenment, when he learned the good qualities of his Buddha-field and its divisions, when he heard of the vow he had made in the

---

[1] I.e. reign, epoch inaugurated by him.

[2] Var. lect. Dharmagaganâ° and Dharmagamanâ°.

[3] Pra*n*idhâna.

past, he felt pleased, exultant, ravished, joyous, filled with cheerfulness and delight. And at that juncture he remembered the true law of many hundred thousand myriads of ko*t*is of Buddhas and his own vow of yore.

And on that occasion the venerable Ânanda uttered the following stanzas:

6. Wonderful, boundless are the *G*inas[1] who remind us of the law preached by the extinct *G*inas and mighty saints[2]. Now I remember it as if it had happened to-day or yesterday[3].

7. I am freed from all doubts; I am ready for enlightenment. Such is my skilfulness, (as) I am the servitor[4], and keep the true law for the sake of enlightenment.

Thereupon the Lord addressed the venerable Râhula-Bhadra in these words: Thou, Râhula, shalt be in future a Tathâgata of the name of Saptaratnapadmavikrântagâmin[5], an Arhat, &c., endowed with science and conduct, &c. After having honoured, respected, venerated, worshipped a number of Tathâgatas, &c., equal to the atoms of ten worlds, thou shalt always be the eldest son of those Lords Buddhas, just as thou art mine at present. And, Râhula, the measure of the lifetime of that Lord Saptaratnapadmavikrântagâmin, the Tathâgata, &c., and the abundance of all sorts of good qualities (belonging to him) shall be exactly the same as of

---

[1] This may be interpreted as being a pluralis majestatis.

[2] Tâyin.

[3] Adya *s*vo vâ; cf. note 2, p. 154.

[4] Pari*k*âraka, synonymous with upasthâyaka, one who is in attendance, in readiness, an attendant, a servitor, a satellite.

[5] So my MSS.; Burnouf has Saptaratnapadmavikrâmin.

the Lord Sâgaravaradharabuddhivikrî*d*itâbhi*gñ*a, the Tathâgata, &c.; likewise shall the divisions of the Buddha-field and its qualities be the same as those possessed by that Lord. And, Râhula, thou shalt be the eldest son of that Tathâgata Sâgaravaradharabuddhivikrî*d*itâbhi*gñ*a, the Arhat, &c. Afterwards thou shalt arrive at supreme and perfect enlightenment.

8. Râhula here, my own eldest son, who was born to me when I was a prince royal, he, my son, after my reaching enlightenment, is a great Seer, an heir to the law[1].

9. The great number of ko*t*is of Buddhas which he shall see in future, is immense. To all these *G*inas he shall be a son, striving after enlightenment.

10. Unknown is this course (of duty) to Râhula[2], but I know his (former) vow. He glorifies the Friend of the world[3] (by saying): I am, forsooth, the Tathâgata's son.

11. Innumerable myriads of ko*t*is of good qualities, the measure of which is never to be found, appertain to this Râhula, my son; for it has been said: He exists by reason of enlightenment.

The Lord now again regarded those two thousand disciples, both such as were still under training and such as were not, who were looking up to him with serene, mild, placid minds. And the Lord then addressed the venerable Ânanda: Seest thou, Ânanda, these two thousand disciples, both such as are still under training and such as are not? 'I

[1] Cf. the myth according to which Râhu, the personified eclipse, came in for his share before Brahma, the father of the world.

[2] Or of Râhula.

[3] Lokabandhu, from elsewhere known as an epithet of the sun.

do, Lord; I do, Sugata.' The Lord proceeded: All these two thousand monks, Ânanda, shall simultaneously accomplish the course of Bodhisattvas, and after honouring, respecting, venerating, worshipping Buddhas as numerous as the atoms of fifty worlds, and after acquiring the true law, they shall, in their last bodily existence, attain supreme and perfect enlightenment at the same time, the same moment, the same instant, the same juncture in all directions of space, in different worlds, each in his own Buddha-field. They shall become Tathâgatas, Arhats, &c., by the name of Ratnaketurâgas[1]. Their lifetime shall last a complete Æon. The division and good qualities of their Buddha-fields shall be equal; equal also shall be the number of the congregation of their disciples and Bodhisattvas; equal also shall be their complete extinction, and their true law shall continue an equal time.

And on that occasion the Lord uttered the following stanzas:

12. These two thousand disciples, Ânanda, who here are standing before me, to them, the sages, I now predict that in future they shall become Tathâgatas.

13. After having paid eminent worship to the Buddhas, by means of infinite comparisons and examples, they shall, when standing in their last bodily existence, reach my extreme enlightenment.

14. They shall all, under the same name, in every direction, at the same moment and instant, and

---

[1] In astrological works, in the enumeration of Grahas (sun, moon, planets, &c.), the Ketus are constantly named after Râhu. It is hardly fortuitous that here we find these 'kings of Ketus' mentioned immediately after Râhula.

sitting at the foot of the most exalted tree, become Buddhas, after they shall have reached the knowledge.

15. All shall bear the same name of Ketus[1] of the Ratna, by which they shall be widely famed in this world. Their excellent fields shall be equal, and equal the congregation of disciples and Bodhisattvas.

16. Strong in magic power, they shall all simultaneously, in every direction of space, reveal the law in this world and all at once[2] become extinct; their true law shall last equally long.

And the disciples, both such as were still under training and such as were not, on hearing from the Lord, face to face, the prediction concerning each of them, were pleased, exultant, ravished, joyous, filled with cheerfulness and delight, and addressed the Lord with the following stanzas:

17. We are satisfied, O Light of the world, to hear this prediction; we are pleased, O Tathâgata, as if sprinkled with nectar.

18. We have no doubt, no uncertainty that we shall become supreme amongst men; to-day we have obtained felicity, because we have heard that prediction.

---

[1] Ketumâlâ, apparently 'cluster of Ketus,' is the appellation of the western region; Ketumat is a ruler of the western quarter, i.e. the personification of the west. The phrase rendered by 'standing in their last bodily existence' (pas*k*ime samu*kk*h*raye), in stanza 13, also means 'standing in their elevation in the west.'

[2] MSS. have sadâpi, but this is obviously a clerical error for sahâpi.

CHAPTER X.

THE PREACHER.

The Lord then addressed the eighty thousand Bodhisattvas Mahâsattvas by turning to Bhaishagyarâga as their representative. Seest thou, Bhaishagyarâga, in this assembly the many gods, Nâgas, goblins, Gandharvas, demons, Garudas, Kinnaras, great serpents, men, and beings not human, monks, nuns, male and female lay devotees, votaries of the vehicle of disciples, votaries of the vehicle of Pratyekabuddhas, and those of the vehicle of Bodhisattvas, who have heard this Dharmaparyâya from the mouth of the Tathâgata? 'I do, Lord; I do, Sugata.' The Lord proceeded: Well, Bhaishagyarâga, all those Bodhisattvas Mahâsattvas who in this assembly have heard, were it but a single stanza, a single verse (or word), or who even by a single rising thought have joyfully accepted this Sûtra, to all of them, Bhaishagyarâga, among the four classes of my audience I predict their destiny to supreme and perfect enlightenment. And all whosoever, Bhaishagyarâga, who, after the complete extinction of the Tathâgata, shall hear this Dharmaparyâya and after hearing, were it but a single stanza, joyfully accept it, even with a single rising thought, to those also, Bhaishagyarâga, be they young men or young ladies of good family, I predict their destiny to supreme and perfect enlightenment. Those young men or ladies of good family, Bhaishagyarâga, shall be worshippers of many hundred thousand myriads of kotis of Buddhas. Those young men or ladies of good family, Bhaishagyarâga, shall have made a vow under hundred thousands of myriads of kotis of Buddhas. They must be considered as being reborn amongst the people of Gambudvîpa[1], out of compassion to all creatures. Those who shall take, read, make known, recite, copy, and after copying always keep in memory and from time to time regard were it but a single stanza of this Dharmaparyâya; who by that book[2] shall feel veneration for the Tathâgatas, treat them with the respect due to Masters[3], honour, revere, worship them; who shall worship that book with flowers, incense, perfumed garlands, ointment, powder, clothes, umbrellas, flags, banners, music, &c., and with acts of reverence such as bowing and joining hands; in short, Bhaishagyarâga, any young men or young ladies of good family who shall keep or joyfully accept were it but a single stanza of this Dharmaparyâya, to all of them, Bhaishagyarâga, I predict their being destined to supreme and perfect enlightenment.

Should some man or woman, Bhaishagyarâga, happen to ask: How now have those creatures to be who in future are to become Tathâgatas, Arhats, &c.? then that man or woman should be referred to the example of that young man or young lady of good family. 'Whoever is able to keep, recite, or teach,

[1] I. e. India.

[2] Tasmin pustake, literally 'at that book,' i. e. when that book is being read, written, heard, &c.

[3] *Sâstrigauravena* satkarishyanti. I take the instrumental case here to be the instrumental of manner.

were it but a single stanza of four lines, and whoever shows respect for this Dharmaparyâya, that young man or young lady of good family shall in future become a Tathâgata, &c.; be persuaded of it.' For, Bhaishagyarâga, such a young man or young lady of good family must be considered to be a Tathâgata, and by the whole world, including the gods, honour should be done to such a Tathâgata who keeps were it but a single stanza of this Dharmaparyâya, and far more, of course, to one who grasps, keeps, comprehends, makes known, copies, and after copying always retains in his memory this Dharmaparyâya entirely and completely, and who honours that book with flowers, incense, perfumed garlands, ointment, powder, clothes, umbrellas, flags, banners, music, joined hands, reverential bows and salutations. Such a young man or young lady of good family, Bhaishagyarâga, must be held to be accomplished in supreme and perfect enlightenment; must be held to be the like of a Tathâgata, who out of compassion and for the benefit of the world, by virtue of a former vow, makes his appearance here in Gambudvîpa, in order to make this Dharmaparyâya generally known. Whosoever, after leaving[1] his own lofty conception of the law[2] and the lofty Buddha-field occupied by him, in order to make generally known this Dharmaparyâya, after my

[1] Sthâpayitvâ, which commonly means 'apart from, barring.'

[2] Yah svam (var. lect. yas tam)—dharmâbhisamskâram. If we follow the former reading, sthâpayitvâ can hardly be taken in the sense of 'apart from;' in the other case it would be possible, though I should be at a loss to guess the purport of the phrase. The real meaning of dharmâbhisamskâra is, probably, 'position in life' or 'religion.' Cf. stanza 4 below.

complete Nirvâ*n*a, may be deemed to have appeared[1] in the predicament of a Tathâgata[2], such a one, Bhaishagyarâga, be it a young man or a young lady of good family, must be held to perform the function of the Tathâgata, to be a deputy of the Tathâgata. As such, Bhaishagyarâga, should be acknowledged the young man or the young lady of good family, who communicates this Dharmaparyâya, after the complete Nirvâ*n*a of the Tathâgata, were it but in secret or by stealth or to one single creature that he communicated or told it.

Again, Bhaishagyarâga, if some creature vicious, wicked, and cruel-minded should in the (current) Age speak something injurious in the face of the Tathâgata, and if some should utter a single harsh word, founded or unfounded, to those irreproachable preachers of the law and keepers of this Sûtrânta, whether lay devotees or clergymen, I declare that the latter sin is the graver. For, Bhaishagyarâga, such a young man or young lady of good family must be held to be adorned with the apparel of the Tathâgata. He carries the Tathâgata on his shoulder, Bhaishagyarâga, who after having copied this Dharmaparyâya and made a volume of it, carries it on his shoulder. Such a one, wherever he goes, must be saluted by all beings with joined hands, must be honoured, respected, worshipped, venerated, revered by gods and men with flowers, incense, perfumed garlands, ointment, powder, clothes, umbrellas, flags, banners, musical instruments, with

---

[1] Upapanna, an ambiguous term; it may also mean 'fit.'

[2] Tathâgata-bhûta; a var. lect. has Tathâgata-dûta, a messenger, a deputy of the Tathâgata.

food, soft and hard, with nourishment and drink, with vehicles, with heaps of choice and gorgeous jewels. That preacher of the law must be honoured by heaps of gorgeous jewels being presented to that preacher of the law. For it may be that by his expounding this Dharmaparyâya, were it only once, innumerable, incalculable beings who hear it shall soon become accomplished in supreme and perfect enlightenment.

And on that occasion the Lord uttered the following stanzas:

1. He who wishes to be established in Buddhahood and aspires to the knowledge of the Self-born [1], must honour those who keep this doctrine.

2. And he who is desirous of omniscience and thinks: How shall I soonest reach it? must try to know this Sûtra by heart, or at least honour one who knows it.

3. He has been sent by the Lord of the world to convert (or catechise) men, he who out of compassion for mankind recites this Sûtra [2].

4. After giving up a good position, that great man [3] has come hither, he who out of compassion for mankind keeps this Sûtra (in memory).

5. It is by force of his position, that in the last times he is seen preaching this unsurpassed Sûtra.

6. That preacher of the law must be honoured

---

[1] Svayambhû*g*ñâna, which, to my apprehension, is an alteration of brahmavidyâ.

[2] From such a passage as this one might be tempted to believe that it had been the intention of the author of this verse to represent Buddha as eternal; cf. Burnouf's remarks in his Introduction, p. 119.

[3] I. e. the preacher or catechiser.

with divine and human flowers and all sorts of perfumes; be decked with divine cloth and strewed with jewels.

7. One should always reverentially salute him with joined hands, as if he were the Chief of *G*inas or the Self-born, he who in these most dreadful, last days keeps this Sûtra of the Extinct (Buddha).

8. One should give food, hard and soft, nourishment and drink, lodging in a convent, ko*t*is of robes to honour the son of *G*ina, when he has propounded, be it but once, this Sûtra.

9. He performs the task of the Tathâgatas and has been sent by me to the world of men, he who in the last days shall copy, keep, or hear this Sûtra.

10. The man who in wickedness of heart or with frowning brow should at any time of a whole Æon utter something injurious in my presence, commits a great sin.

11. But one who reviles and abuses those guardians of this Sûtrânta, when they are expounding this Sûtra, I say that he commits a still greater sin.

12. The man who, striving for superior enlightenment, shall in a complete Æon praise me in my face with joined hands, with many myriads of ko*t*is of stanzas,

13. Shall thence derive a great merit, since he has glorified me in gladness of heart. But a still greater merit shall he acquire who pronounces the praise of those (preachers).

14. One who shall during eighteen thousand ko*t*is of Æons pay worship to those objects of veneration[1], with words, visible things, flavours, with divine scents and divine kinds of touch,

[1] Pusteshu. I think that these pustas, models, images, denote

15. If such a one, by his paying that worship to the objects of veneration during eighteen thousand ko*t*is of Æons, happens to hear this Sûtra, were it only once, he shall obtain an amazingly great advantage.

I announce to thee, Bhaisha*g*yarâ*g*a, I declare to thee, that many are the Dharmaparyâyas which I have propounded, am propounding, and shall propound. And among all those Dharmaparyâyas, Bhaisha*g*yarâ*g*a, it is this which is apt to meet with no acceptance with everybody, to find no belief with everybody. This, indeed, Bhaisha*g*yarâ*g*a, is the transcendent spiritual esoteric lore of the law, preserved by the power of the Tathâgatas, but never divulged; it is an article (of creed)[1] not yet made known. By the majority of people, Bhaisha*g*yarâ*g*a, this Dharmaparyâya is rejected during the lifetime of the Tathâgata; in far higher degree such will be the case after his complete extinction.

Nevertheless, Bhaisha*g*yarâ*g*a, one has to consider those young men or young ladies of good family to be invested with the robes of the Tathâgata; to be regarded and blessed by the Tathâgatas living in other worlds, that they shall have the force of individual persuasion, the force that is rooted in virtue,

---

the exemplary preachers who are likened to the Tathâgata, and sent by him (Tathâgata-bhûta and Tathâgata-dûta), spoken of in the preceding verses as well as in the prose passages above. Instead of models, I have used the phrase, objects of veneration. for clearness sake. Burnouf's original rendering 'images' is, so far as I can see, preferable to his correction of it into 'books.' There is no question of books, only of a single work, the Lotus; and it is clear that we must try to make the contents of the last two stanzas agree with the final part of the preceding prose.

[1] Or point of view, standpoint.

and the force of a pious vow. They shall dwell apart in the convents of the Tathâgata, Bhaishagyarâga, and shall have their heads stroked by the hand of the Tathâgata, those young men and young ladies of good family, who after the complete extinction of the Tathâgata shall believe, read, write, honour this Dharmaparyâya and recite it to others.

Again, Bhaishagyarâga, on any spot of the earth where this Dharmaparyâya is expounded, preached, written, studied, or recited in chorus, on that spot, Bhaishagyarâga, one should build a Tathâgata-shrine, magnificent, consisting of precious substances, high, and spacious; but it is not necessary to depose in it relics of the Tathâgata. For the body of the Tathâgata is, so to say, collectively deposited there. Any spot of the earth where this Dharmaparyâya is expounded or taught or recited or rehearsed in chorus or written or kept in a volume, must be honoured, respected, revered, worshipped as if it were a Stûpa, with all sorts of flowers, incense, perfumes, garlands, ointment, powder, clothes, umbrellas, flags, banners, triumphal streamers, with all kinds of song, music, dancing, musical instruments, castanets [1], and shouts in chorus. And those, Bhaishagyarâga, who approach a Tathâgata-shrine to salute or see it, must be held to be near supreme and perfect enlightenment. For, Bhaishagyarâga, there are many laymen as well as priests who observe the course of a Bodhisattva without, however, coming so far as to see, hear, write or worship this Dharmaparyâya. So long as they do not hear this Dharmaparyâya, they are not yet proficient in the course of a Bodhisattva. But

[1] Tâdâvakara.

those who hear this Dharmaparyâya and thereupon accept, penetrate, understand, comprehend it, are at the time near supreme, perfect enlightenment, so to say, immediately near it.

It is a case, Bhaishagyarâga, similar to that of a certain man, who in need and in quest of water, in order to get water, causes a well to be dug in an arid tract of land. So long as he sees that the sand being dug out is dry and white, he thinks: the water is still far off. After some time he sees that the sand being dug out is moist, mixed with water, muddy, with trickling drops, and that the working men who are engaged in digging the well are bespattered with mire and mud. On seeing that foretoken, Bhaishagyarâga, the man will be convinced and certain that water is near. In the same manner, Bhaishagyarâga, will these Bodhisattvas Mahâsattvas be far away from supreme and perfect enlightenment so long as they do not hear, nor catch, nor penetrate, nor fathom, nor mind this Dharmaparyâya. But when the Bodhisattvas Mahâsattvas shall hear, catch, penetrate, study, and mind this Dharmaparyâya, then, Bhaishagyarâga, they will be, so to say, immediately near supreme, perfect enlightenment. From this Dharmaparyâya, Bhaishagyarâga, will accrue to creatures supreme and perfect enlightenment. For this Dharmaparyâya contains an explanation of the highest mystery, the secret article[1] of the law which the Tathâgatas, &c., have revealed for the perfecting of the Bodhisattvas Mahâsattvas. Any Bodhisattva, Bhaishagyarâga, who is startled, feels anxiety, gets frightened at this Dharmaparyâya,

[1] Or point.

may be held, Bhaishagyarâga, to have (but) newly entered the vehicle[1]. If, however, a votary of the vehicle of the disciples is startled, feels anxiety, gets frightened at this Dharmaparyâya, such a person, devoted to the vehicle of the disciples, Bhaishagyarâga, may be deemed a conceited man.

Any Bodhisattva Mahâsattva, Bhaishagyarâga, who after the complete extinction of the Tathâgata, in the last times, the last period shall set forth this Dharmaparyâya to the four classes of hearers, should do so, Bhaishagyarâga, after having entered the abode[2] of the Tathâgata, after having put on the robe of the Tathâgata, and occupied the pulpit of the Tathâgata. And what is the abode of the Tathâgata, Bhaishagyarâga? It is the abiding[3] in charity (or kindness) to all beings; that is the abode of the Tathâgata, Bhaishagyarâga, which the young man of good family has to enter. And what is the robe of the Tathâgata, Bhaishagyarâga? It is the apparel of sublime forbearance; that is the robe of the Tathâgata, Bhaishagyarâga, which the young man of good family has to put on. What is the pulpit of the Tathâgata, Bhaishagyarâga? It is the entering into the voidness (or complete abstraction) of all laws (or things); that is the pulpit, Bhaishagyarâga, on which the young man of good family has to sit in order to set forth this Dharmaparyâya to the four classes of hearers. A Bodhisattva ought to propound this Dharmaparyâya with unshrinking mind, before the face of the congregated Bodhisattvas, the four classes

[1] The Mahâyâna, apparently.

[2] Layana, recess, retreat, refuge, cell, lair, stronghold, asylum, abode.

[3] Vihâra, both walk and abode, and further, monastery.

of hearers, who are striving for the vehicle of Bodhisattvas, and I, staying in another world, Bhaishagyarâga, will by means of fictious creatures[1] make the minds of the whole congregation favourably disposed to that young man of good family, and I will send fictious monks, nuns, male and female lay devotees in order to hear the sermon of the preacher, who are unable to gainsay or contradict him[2]. If afterwards he shall have retired to the forest, I will send thither many gods, Nâgas, goblins, Gandharvas, demons, Garudas, Kinnaras, and great serpents to hear him preach, while I, staying in another world, Bhaishagyarâga, will show my face to that young man of good family, and the words and syllables of this Dharmaparyâya which he happens to have forgotten will I again suggest to him[3] when he repeats his lesson.

And on that occasion the Lord uttered the following stanzas:

16. Let one listen to this exalted Sûtra, avoiding all distractedness; for rare is the occasion (given) for hearing it, and rare also the belief in it.

---

[1] Nirmitaih; the word is masculine, as appears from the sequel.

[2] I cannot tell what real phenomena are underlying these creations of the Buddha after his Nirvâna; but this much seems clear, that we have in this piece a description of the practical course a young preacher has to go through in order to become fit for his task.

[3] Pratyukkârayishyâmi, literally, I will cause him to re-utter. The real purport, unless I am much mistaken, is: on a following day (Buddha) will restore what the student has forgotten from his lesson, provided he reads the passage again; or, if we take the words in a spiritual sense, the mental light of the student will again supply what he has forgotten of his lesson. Cf. stanza 31.

17. It is a case similar to that of a certain man who in want of water goes to dig a well in an arid tract of land, and sees how again and again only dry sand is being dug up.

18. On seeing which he thinks: the water is far off; a token of its being far off is the dry white sand which appears in digging.

19. But when he (afterwards) sees again and again the sand moist and smooth, he gets the conviction that water cannot be very far off.

20. So, too, are those men far from Buddha-knowledge who have not heard this Sûtra and have failed to repeatedly meditate on it.

21. But those who have heard and oft meditated on this profound king amongst Sûtras, this authoritative book [1] for disciples,

22. Are wise and near Buddha-knowledge, even as from the moisture of sand may be inferred that water is near.

23. After entering the abode of the *G*ina, putting on his robe and sitting down on my seat, the preacher should, undaunted, expound this Sûtra.

24. The strength of charity (or kindness) is my abode; the apparel of forbearence is my robe; and voidness (or complete abstraction) is my seat; let (the preacher) take his stand on this and preach.

25. Where clods, sticks, pikes, or abusive words and threats fall to the lot of the preacher, let him be patient, thinking of me.

26. My body has existed entire in thousands of

---

[1] Vinis*k*aya, decision, here hardly differing from tantra or siddhânta. After the model of the latter has been framed the term Sûtrânta; and the Lotus, as we know, is a Sûtrânta.

ko*t*is of regions; during a number of ko*t*is of Æons beyond comprehension I teach the law to creatures.

27. To that courageous man who shall proclaim this Sûtra after my complete extinction I will also send many creations[1].

28. Monks, nuns, lay devotees, male and female, will honour him as well as the classes of the audience.

29. And should there be some to attack him with clods, sticks, injurious words, threats, taunts, then the creations shall defend him.

30. And when he shall stay alone, engaged in study, in a lonely place, in the forest or the hills,

31. Then will I show him my luminous body and enable him to remember the lesson he forgot[2].

32. While he is living lonely in the wilderness, I will send him gods and goblins in great number to keep him company.

33. Such are the advantages he is to enjoy; whether he is preaching to the four classes, or living, a solitary, in mountain caverns and studying his lesson, he will see me.

34. His readiness of speech knows no impediment; he understands the manifold requisites of exegesis; he satisfies thousands of ko*t*is of beings because he is, so to say, inspired (or blessed) by the Buddha[3].

---

[1] Bahunirmitân. As a class of angels is called Parinirmita Va*s*avartin, it may be that the idea the word nirmita was intended to convey to the simple-minded is that of angels.

[2] Here the Buddha seems to be the personification of the faculty of memory, of mental light.

[3] Buddhena. Burnouf seems to have read Buddhai*h*, the plural.

35. And the creatures who are entrusted to his care shall very soon all become Bodhisattvas, and by cultivating his intimacy they shall behold Buddhas as numerous as the sands of the Ganges.

CHAPTER XI.

APPARITION OF A STÛPA.

Then there arose a Stûpa, consisting of seven precious substances, from the place of the earth opposite the Lord, the assembly being in the middle[1], a Stûpa five hundred *yoganas* in height and proportionate in circumference. After its rising, the Stûpa, a meteoric phenomenon[2], stood in the sky sparkling, beautiful, nicely decorated with five thousand[3] successive terraces of flowers[4], adorned with many thousands of arches, embellished by thousands of banners and triumphal streamers, hung with thousands of jewel-garlands and with hour-plates and bells, and emitting the scent of Xanthochymus and sandal, which scent filled this whole world. Its row of umbrellas rose so far on high as to touch the abodes of the four guardians of the

---

[1] Between the Lord (i. e. the Sun) and the Stûpa of seven Ratnas, i. e. here, it would seem, the rainbow of seven colours. We shall see that the Stûpa has also another function, that of symbolising the celestial dhishnya in which sun and moon are standing. Cf. E. Senart, Essai sur la légende du Buddha, p. 436.

[2] Vaihâyasam, in the neuter gender, whereas stûpa is masculine.

[3] The number of colours is now five, then seven. Moreover there ought to be a parallelism between the five colours and the five planets, and, on the other hand, between the seven ratnas, or colours, and the grahas, including sun and moon. In Rigveda we find saptarasmi and pañkarasmi.

[4] Pushpagrahanivedikâ.

horizon and the gods. It consisted of seven precious substances, viz. gold, silver, lapis lazuli, Musâragalva, emerald, red coral, and Karketana-stone [1]. This Stûpa of precious substances once formed, the gods of paradise strewed and covered it with Mandârava and great Mandâra flowers [2]. And from that Stûpa of precious substances there issued this voice: Excellent, excellent, Lord Sâkyamuni! thou hast well expounded this Dharmaparyâya of the Lotus of the True Law. So it is, Lord; so it is, Sugata.

At the sight of that great Stûpa of precious substances, that meteoric phenomenon in the sky, the four classes of hearers were filled with gladness, delight, satisfaction and joy. Instantly they rose from their seats, stretched out their joined hands, and remained standing in that position. Then the Bodhisattva Mahâsattva Mahâpratibhâna, perceiving the world, including gods, men, and demons, filled with curiosity, said to the Lord: O Lord, what is the cause, what is the reason of so magnificent a Stûpa of precious substances appearing in the world? Who is it, O Lord, who causes that sound to go out from the magnificent Stûpa of precious substances? Thus asked, the Lord spake to Mahâpratibhâna, the Bodhisattva Mahâsattva, as follows: In this great Stûpa of precious substances, Mahâpratibhâna, the proper body [3] of the Tathâgata is contained condensed; his is the Stûpa; it is he who causes this sound to go out.

---

[1] The raising of a seven-jewelled Stûpa is also narrated in the Vinaya Pitaka of the Mahâsânghika school, according to Beal in the Indian Antiquary, vol. xi, p. 47. The particulars of the description in that narrative bear little resemblance to those found in our text.

[2] There fell smaller and bigger drops of rain.

[3] Âtmabhâva, also the very nature, the essential being.

In the point of space below, Mahâpratibhâna, there are innumerable thousands of worlds [1]. Further on is the world called Ratnavisuddha [2], there is the Tathâgata named Prabhûtaratna, the Arhat, &c. This Lord of yore made this vow: Formerly, when following the course of a Bodhisattva, I have not arrived at supreme, perfect enlightenment before I had heard this Dharmaparyâya of the Lotus of the True Law, serving for the instruction of Bodhisattvas. But from the moment that I had heard this Dharmaparyâya of the Lotus of the True Law, I have become fully ripe for supreme, perfect enlightenment. Now, Mahâpratibhâna, that Lord Prabhûtaratna, the Tathâgata, &c., at the juncture of time when his complete extinction was to take place, announced in presence of the world, including the gods: After my complete extinction, monks, one Stûpa must be made of precious substances of this frame (or form) of the proper body of the Tathâgata [3]; the other Stûpas, again, should be made in dedication (or in reference) to me. Thereupon, Mahâpratibhâna, the Lord Prabhûtaratna, the Tathâgata, &c., pronounced this blessing: Let my Stûpa here, this Stûpa of my proper bodily frame (or form), arise wherever in any Buddha-field in the ten directions of space, in all worlds, the Dharmaparyâya of the Lotus of the True Law is propounded, and let

[1] Var. lect. innumerable hundred thousand myriads of kotis of worlds.

[2] I.e. clear by jewels (stars), or, quite the reverse, cleared from jewels. Most probably, however, we have to take it in the former sense. The world so called is, apparently, the starry vault, beyond the atmosphere where the rainbow is glittering.

[3] Asya Tathâgatâtmabhâvavigrahasya.

it stand in the sky above the assembled congregation when this Dharmaparyâya of the Lotus of the True Law is being preached by some Lord Buddha or another, and let this Stûpa of the frame (or form) of my proper body give a shout of applause to those Buddhas while preaching this Dharmaparyâya of the Lotus of the True Law[1]. It is that Stûpa, Mahâpratibhâna, of the relics of the Lord Prabhûtaratna, the Tathâgata, &c., which, while I was preaching this Dharmaparyâya of the Lotus of the True Law in this Saha-world, arose above this assembled congregation and, standing as a meteor in the sky, gave its applause.

Then said Mahâpratibhâna, the Bodhisattva Mahâsattva, to the Lord: Show us, O Lord, through thy power the frame of the afore-mentioned Tathâgata. Whereon the Lord spake to the Bodhisattva Mahâsattva Mahâpratibhâna as follows: This Lord Prabhûtaratna, Mahâpratibhâna, has made a grave and pious vow. That vow consisted in this: When the Lords, the Buddhas, being in other Buddha-fields, shall preach this Dharmaparyâya of the Lotus of the

[1] We shall see that the 'extinct Lord Prabhûtaratna' is to sit in the middle of the Stûpa along with the Buddha. The moon is 'completely extinct' when in conjunction with the sun, and it seems sufficiently clear that Prabhûtaratna, the Tathâgata, the Arhat, &c., is the moon at the time of amâvâsyâ, conjunction. The Stûpa, in the centre of which sun and moon are sitting together at that period, cannot be the rainbow, so that we have in the sequel again to take Stûpa in the sense of dhishnya, asterism; see note 1, p. 227. The crescent surmounting the Stûpa-symbols on coins (see Senart, l. c.) is not exactly the representation of the 'extinct Lord'—who is difficult to be represented—but of the same nature. The appearance of this symbol on those coins is by itself sufficient to show the high antiquity of a refined nature-worship in Buddhism.

True Law, then let this Stûpa of the frame of my proper body be near the Tathâgata[1] to hear from him this Dharmaparyâya of the Lotus of the True Law. And when those Lords, those Buddhas wish to uncover the frame of my proper body and show it to the four classes of hearers, let then the Tathâgata-frames, made by the Tathâgatas in all quarters, in different Buddha-fields, from their own proper body, and preaching the law to creatures, under different names in several Buddha-fields, let all those Tathâgata-frames, made from the proper body, united together, along with this Stûpa containing the frame of my own body, be opened and shown to the four classes of hearers. Therefore, Mahâpratibhâna, have I made many Tathâgata-frames[2] which in all quarters, in several Buddha-fields in thousands of worlds, preach the law to creatures. All those ought to be brought hither.

Thereupon the Bodhisattva Mahâsattva Mahâpratibhâna said to the Lord: Then, O Lord, shall we reverentially salute all those bodily emanations of the Tathâgata and created by the Tathâgata.

And instantly the Lord darted from the circle of hair on his brow a ray, which was no sooner darted than the Lords, the Buddhas stationed in the east in fifty hundred thousand myriads of ko*t*is of worlds, equal to the sands of the river Ganges, became all visible, and the Buddha-fields there, consisting of crystal, became visible, variegated with jewel trees, decorated

---

[1] The place of the moon just before entering Nirvâ*n*a must of course be near the sun's seat of the law.

[2] It is hardly necessary to remark that by the luminous bodies, the attendants of Prabhûtaratna, i. e. the stars, are meant.

with strings of fine cloth, replete with many hundred thousands of Bodhisattvas, covered with canopies, decked with a network of seven precious substances and gold[1]. And in those fields appeared the Lords, the Buddhas, teaching with sweet and gentle voice the law to creatures; and those Buddha-fields seemed replete with hundred thousands of Bodhisattvas. So, too, it was in the south-east; so in the south; so in the south-west; so in the west; so in the north-west; so in the north; so in the north-east; so in the nadir; so in the zenith; so in the ten directions of space; in each direction were to be seen many hundred thousand myriads of kotis of Buddha-fields, similar to the sands of the river Ganges, in many worlds similar to the sands of the river Ganges, Lords Buddhas in many hundred thousand myriads of kotis of Buddha-fields.

Those Tathâgatas, &c., in the ten directions of space then addressed each his own troop of Bodhisattvas: We shall have to go, young men of good family, to the Saha-world near the Lord Sâkyamuni, the Tathâgata, &c., to humbly salute the Stûpa of the relics of Prabhûtaratna, the Tathâgata, &c. Thereupon those Lords, those Buddhas resorted with their own satellites, each with one or two, to this Saha-world. At that period this all-embracing world was adorned with jewel trees; it consisted of lapis lazuli, was covered with a network of seven precious substances and gold, smoking with the odorous incense of magnificent jewels, everywhere strewn with Mandârava and great Mandârava flowers,

[1] Here we see that gold does not belong to the seven ratnas. The whole list of the seven colours seems to have undergone some alterations.

decorated with a network of little bells[1], showing a checker board divided by gold threads into eight compartments, devoid of villages, towns, boroughs, provinces, kingdoms, and royal capitals, without Kâla-mountain, without the mountains Mu*k*ilinda and great Mu*k*ilinda, without a mount Sumeru, without a *K*akravâla (i. e. horizon) and great *K*akravâla (i. e. extended horizon), without other principal mountains, without great oceans, without rivers and great rivers, without bodies of gods, men, and demons, without hells, without brute creation, without a kingdom of Yama. For it must be understood that at that period all beings in any of the six states of existence in this world had been removed to other worlds, with the exception of those who were assembled at that congregation[2]. Then it was that those Lords, those Buddhas, attended by one or two satellites, arrived at this Saha-world and went one after the other to occupy their place close to the foot of a jewel tree. Each of the jewel trees was five hundred yo*g*anas in height, had boughs, leaves, foliage, and circumference in proportion[3], and was provided with blossoms and fruits. At the foot of each jewel tree stood prepared a throne, five yo*g*anas in height, and adorned with magnificent jewels. Each Tathâgata went to occupy his throne and sat on it cross-legged. And so all the Tathâgatas of the whole sphere sat cross-legged at the foot of the jewel trees.

---

[1] Kaṅka*n*î*g*âlâlaṅk*r*i*ta.

[2] The hells at least, which are places of darkness, could not be present when the stars are shining brightly.

[3] My MSS. read pa*ñk*ayo*g*ana*s*atâny u*kk*aistvenâbhût, anupûrva*s*âkhâpatrapalâ*s*apari*n*âha*h*. In the sequel we meet with another reading agreeing with Burnouf's.

At that moment the whole sphere was replete with Tathâgatas, but the beings produced from the proper body of the Lord *S*âkyamuni had not yet arrived, not even from a single point of the horizon. Then the Lord *S*âkyamuni, the Tathâgata, &c., proceeded to make room for those Tathâgata-frames that were arriving one after the other. On every side in the eight directions of space (appeared) twenty hundred thousand myriads of ko*t*is of Buddha-fields of lapis lazuli, decked with a network of seven precious substances and gold, decorated with a fringe of little bells, strewn with Mandârava and great Mandârava flowers, covered with heavenly awnings, hung with wreaths of heavenly flowers, smoking with heavenly odorous incense. All those twenty hundred thousand myriads of ko*t*is of Buddha-fields were without villages, towns, boroughs, &c.; without Kâla-mountain, &c.; without great oceans, &c.; without bodies of gods, &c. All those Buddha-fields were so arranged by him as to form one Buddha-field, one soil, even, lovely, set off with trees of seven precious substances, trees five hundred yo*g*anas in height and circumference, provided with boughs, flowers, and fruits in proportion[1]. At the foot of each tree stood prepared a throne, five yo*g*anas in height and width, consisting of celestial gems, glittering and beautiful. The Tathâgatas arriving one after the other occupied the throne near the foot of each tree, and sat cross-legged. In like manner the Tathâgata *S*âkyamuni prepared twenty hundred thousand myriads of ko*t*is of other

[1] The reading is somewhat doubtful: ârohapari*n*âhonupûrva- (var. lect. °ha*h*, anupûrva-)*s*âkhâpatrapushpaphalopeta(*h*).

worlds, in every direction of space, in order to give room to the Tathâgatas who were arriving one after the other. Those twenty hundred thousand myriads of ko*t*is of worlds in every direction of space were likewise so made by him as to be without villages, towns, &c. [as above]. They were without bodies of gods, &c. [as above]; all those beings had been removed to other worlds. These Buddha-fields also were of lapis lazuli, &c. [as above]. All those jewel trees measured five hundred yo*g*anas, and near them were thrones, artificially made and measuring five yo*g*anas. Then those Tathâgatas sat down cross-legged, each on a throne at the foot of a jewel tree.

At that moment the Tathâgatas produced by the Lord *S*âkyamuni, who in the east were preaching the law to creatures in hundred thousands of myriads of ko*t*is of Buddha-fields, similar to the sands of the river Ganges, all arrived from the ten points of space and sat down in the eight quarters. Thereupon thirty ko*t*is of worlds in each direction were occupied[1] by those Tathâgatas from all the eight quarters. Then, seated on their thrones, those Tathâgatas deputed their satellites into the presence of the Lord *S*âkyamuni, and after giving them bags with jewel flowers enjoined them thus: Go, young men of good family, to the G*ri*dhrakû*t*a mountain, where the Lord *S*âkyamuni, the Tathâgata, &c., is; salute him reverentially and ask, in our name, after the state of health, well-being, lustiness, and comfort both of himself and the crowd of Bodhisattvas and disciples. Strew

[1] Burnouf seems to have read atikrânta, for his translation has 'franchirent,' whereas my MSS. have âkrânta. One of the MSS. has lokadhâtuko*t*ibhyo instead of °ko*t*yo.

him with this heap of jewels and speak thus: Would the Lord Tathâgata deign to open this great Stûpa of jewels? It was in this manner that all those Tathâgatas deputed their satellites.

And when the Lord Sâkyamuni, the Tathâgata, perceived that his creations, none wanting, had arrived; perceived that they were severally seated on their thrones, and perceived that the satellites of those Tathâgatas, &c., were present, he, in consideration of the wish expressed by those Tathâgatas, &c., rose from his seat and stood in the sky, as a meteor. And all the four classes of the assembly rose from their seats, stretched out their joined hands, and stood gazing up to the face of the Lord. The Lord then, with the right fore-finger[1], unlocked the middle of the great Stûpa of jewels, which showed like a meteor, and so severed the two parts. Even as the double doors of a great city gate separate when the bolt is removed, so the Lord opened the great Stûpa, which showed like a meteor, by unlocking it in the middle with the right fore-finger. The great Stûpa of jewels had no sooner been opened than the Lord Prabhûtaratna, the Tathâgata, &c., was seen sitting cross-legged on his throne, with emaciated[2] limbs and faint body, as if absorbed in abstract meditation, and he pronounced these words: Excellent, excellent, Lord Sâkyamuni; thou hast well expounded this Dharmaparyâya of the Lotus of the True Law. I repeat, thou hast well expounded this Dharmaparyâya of the Lotus of the True Law,

---

[1] Dakshinayâ hastâṅgulyâ.

[2] Parisushkagâtra, var. lect. parisuddha°, with thoroughly pure or correct limbs. Burnouf had committed no mistake in reading parisushka°, though he accuses himself of having done so.

Lord *S*âkyamuni, to the (four) classes of the assembly. I myself, Lord, have come hither to hear the Dharmaparyâya of the Lotus of the True Law.

Now the four classes of the assembly, on perceiving the Lord Prabhûtaratna, the Tathâgata, &c., who had been extinct for many hundred thousand myriads of ko*t*is of Æons, speaking in this way, were filled with wonder and amazement. Instantly they covered the Lord Prabhûtaratna, the Tathâgata, &c., and the Lord *S*âkyamuni, the Tathâgata, &c., with heaps of divine and human flowers. And then the Lord Prabhûtaratna, the Tathâgata, &c., ceded to the Lord *S*âkyamuni, the Tathâgata, &c., the half of the seat on that very throne within that same great Stûpa of jewels and said: Let the Lord *S*âkyamuni, the Tathâgata, &c., sit down here. Whereon the Lord *S*âkyamuni, the Tathâgata, &c., sat down upon that half-seat together with the other Tathâgata, so that both Tathâgatas were seen as meteors in the sky, sitting on the throne in the middle of the great Stûpa of jewels.

And in the minds of those four classes of the assembly rose this thought: We are far off from the two Tathâgatas; therefore let us also, through the power of the Tathâgata, rise up to the sky. As the Lord apprehended in his mind what was going on in the minds of those four classes of the assembly, he instantly, by magic power, established the four classes as meteors in the sky. Thereupon the Lord *S*âkyamuni, the Tathâgata, addressed the four classes: Who amongst you, monks, will endeavour to expound this Dharmaparyâya of the Lotus of the True Law in this Saha-world? The fatal term, the time (of death), is now at hand; the Tathâgata longs for complete extinction, monks, after entrusting to you this Dharmaparyâya of the Lotus of the True Law.

And on that occasion the Lord uttered the following stanzas:

1. Here you see, monks, the great Seer, the extinct Chief, within the Stûpa of jewels, who now has come to hear the law. Who would not call up his energy for the law's sake?

2. Albeit completely extinct for many kotis of Æons, he yet now comes to hear the law; for the law's sake he moves hither and thither; very rare (and very precious) is a law like this.

3. This Leader practised[1] a vow when he was in a former existence; even after his complete extinction he wanders through this whole world in all ten points of space.

4. And all these (you here see) are my proper bodies, by thousands of kotis, like[2] the sands of the Ganges; they have appeared that the law may be fulfilled[3] and in order to see this extinct Master.

5. After laying out[4] for each his peculiar field, as well as having (created) all disciples, men and gods, in order to preserve the true law, as long as the reign of the law shall last,

6. I have by magic power cleared many worlds,

---

[1] Nishevita. [2] Yathâ.

[3] Dharmakrityasya kritena, literally, for the sake of the task or office of the law.

[4] *Kh*oritvâ, Sansk. *kh*uritvâ and *kh*orayitvâ, to inlay, make inlaid work, cut figures, fashion. *S*âkyamuni is most distinctly represented as a creator—in the Indian sense, of course—in the same way as Brahma Hiranyagarbha is a creator.

destined as seats for those Buddhas, and transported all creatures.

7. It has (always) been my anxious care how this line of the law might be manifested. So (you see) Buddhas here in immense number staying at the foot of trees like a great multitude of lotuses.

8. Many ko*t*is of bases of trees are brightened by the Leaders sitting on the thrones which are perpetually occupied by them and brightened as darkness is by fire.

9. A delicious fragrance spreads from the Leaders of the world over all quarters, (a fragrance) by which, when the wind is blowing, all these creatures are intoxicated.

10. Let him who after my extinction shall keep this Dharmaparyâya quickly pronounce his declaration in the presence of the Lords of the world.

11. The Seer Prabhûtaratna who, though completely extinct, is awake, will hear the lion's roar of him who shall take this resolution [1].

12. Myself, in the second place, as well as the many Chiefs who have flocked hither by ko*t*is, will hear that resolution from the son of *G*ina, who is to exert himself to expound this law.

13. And thereby shall I always be honoured as well as Prabhûtaratna, the self-born *G*ina, who perpetually wanders through the quarters and intermediate quarters in order to hear such a law as this.

14. And these (other) Lords of the world here present, by whom this soil is so variegated and splendid, to them also will accrue ample and manifold honour from this Sûtra being preached.

---

[1] Vyavasâya.

15. Here on this seat you see me, together with the Lord next to me, in the middle of the Stûpa; likewise many other Lords of the world here present, in many hundreds of fields.

16. Ye, young men of good family, mind, for mercy's sake towards all beings, that it is a very difficult task to which the Chief urges you.

17. One might expound many thousands of Sûtras, like to the sands of the Ganges, without overmuch difficulty.

18. One who after grasping the Sumeru in the fist were to hurl it a distance of kotis of fields, would do nothing very difficult.

19. Nor would it be so very difficult if one could shake this whole universe by the thumb to hurl it a distance of kotis of fields.

20. Nor would one who, after taking stand on the limit of the existing world, were to expound the law and thousands of other Sûtras, do something so very difficult.

21. But to keep and preach this Sûtra in the dreadful period succeeding the extinction of the Chief of the world, that is difficult[1].

22. To throw down the totality of ether-element after compressing it in one fist, and to leave it behind after having thrown it away, is not difficult.

23. But to copy a Sûtra like this in the period after my extinction, that is difficult[2].

24. To collect the whole earth-element at a nail's

[1] Yet the stars perform that extremely difficult task apparently with the greatest ease.

[2] Nay, it is impossible, if one does not avail oneself of a lamp or other artificial light.

end, cast it away, and then walk off to the Brahma-world[1],

25. Is not difficult, nor would it require a strength surpassing everybody's strength to do this work of difficulty.

26. Something more difficult than that will he do who in the last days after my extinction shall pronounce this Sûtra, were it but a single moment.

27. It will not be difficult for him to walk in the midst of the conflagration at the (time of the) end of the world, even if he carries with him a load of hay.

28. More difficult it will be to keep this Sûtra after my extinction and teach it to a single creature.

29. One may keep the eighty-four thousand divisions of the law[2] and expound them, with the

---

[1] Brahmaloka may mean either one of the twenty Brahma heavens, or all of them collectively. There are four arûpabrahmalokas, and sixteen rûpabrahmalokas.

[2] Dharmaskandha, Pâli Dhammakkhandha; see Burnouf, Introd. p. 34 seq.; B. H. Hodgson, Essays, p. 14; Childers, Pâli Dict. p. 117, where the following definition is given: 'The Tipi*t*aka is divided into eighty-four thousand dhammakkhandhas, "articles" or "sections of the Law." They are divisions according to subject. Buddhaghosa, as an illustration of the meaning of this term, says that a Sutta, or discourse, dealing with one subject forms one dh., while a Sutta embracing several subjects forms several.' It is worth while to compare this number of divisions with the eighty-four thousand monasteries erected by king A*s*oka in the eighty-four (thousand) towns of India, as we know from the historical work Dîpava*m*sa VI, 95 seq., where we read (according to Dr. Oldenberg's transl.): 'Full and complete eighty-four thousand most precious sections of the Truth (dhammakkhandha) have been taught by the most excellent Buddha; I will build eighty-four thousand monasteries, honouring each single section of the Truth by one monastery.'

instructions and such as they have been set forth, to ko*t*is of living beings;

30. This is not so difficult; nor is it, to train at the present time monks, and confirm my disciples in the five parts of transcendent knowledge.

31. But more difficult is it to keep this Sûtra, believe in it, adhere to it, or expound it again and again.

32. Even he who confirms many thousands of ko*t*is of Arhats, blest with the possession of the six transcendent faculties (Abhi*gñ*âs), like sands of the Ganges[1],

33. Performs something not so difficult by far as the excellent man does who after my extinction shall keep my sublime law.

34. I have often, in thousands of worlds, preached the law, and to-day also I preach it with the view that Buddha-knowledge may be obtained.

35. This Sûtra is declared the principal of all Sûtras; he who keeps in his memory this Sûtra, keeps the body of the *G*ina.

36. Speak, O young men of good family, while the Tathâgata is (still) in your presence, who amongst you is to exert himself[2] in later times to keep the Sûtra.

37. Not only I myself shall be pleased, but the Lords of the world in general, if one would keep for a moment this Sûtra so difficult to keep.

38. Such a one shall ever be praised by all the Lords of the world, famed as an eminent hero, and quick in arriving at transcendent wisdom.

---

[1] The latter half of the stanza runs thus: sha*d*abhi*gñ*âmahâbhâgân yathâ Gaṅgâya vâlikâ.

[2] Or, shall be capable.

39. He shall be entrusted with the leadership[1] amongst the sons of the Tathâgatas, he who, after having reached the stage of meekness[2], shall keep this Sûtra.

40. He shall be the eye of the world, including gods and men, who shall speak this Sûtra after the extinction of the Chief of men.

41. He is to be venerated by all beings, the wise man who in the last times shall preach this Sûtra (were it but) a single moment.

Thereupon the Lord addressed the whole company of Bodhisattvas and the world, including gods and demons, and said: Of yore, monks, in times past I have, unwearied and without repose, sought after the Sûtra of the Lotus of the True Law, during immense, immeasurable Æons; many Æons before I have been a king, during many thousands of Æons. Having once taken the strong resolution to arrive at supreme, perfect enlightenment, my mind did not swerve from its aim. I exerted myself to fulfil the six Perfections (Pâramitâs), bestowing immense alms: gold, money, gems, pearls, lapis lazuli, conch-shells, stones (?), coral, gold and silver, emerald, Musâragalva, red pearls; villages, towns, boroughs, provinces, kingdoms, royal capitals; wives, sons, daughters, slaves, male and female; elephants, horses, cars, up to the sacrifice of life and body, of limbs and members, hands, feet, head. And never did the thought of self-complacency[3] rise in me. In

---

[1] Dhuravâha.

[2] Dântabhûmi. Dânta is tamed, subject, meek; and also a young tamed bullock.

[3] Âgraha*k*ittam.

those days the life of men lasted long, so that for a time of many hundred thousand years I was exercising the rule of a King of the Law for the sake of duty, not for the sake of enjoyment[1]. After installing in government the eldest prince royal, I went in quest of the best law in the four quarters, and had promulgated with sound of bell the following proclamation: He who procures for me the best law[2] or points out what is useful, to him will I become a servant. At that time there lived a Seer; he told me: Noble king, there is a Sûtra, called the Lotus of the True Law, which is an exposition of the best law. If thou consent to become my servant, I will teach thee that law. And I, glad, content, exulting and ravished at the words I heard from the Seer, became his pupil[3], and said: I will do for thee the work of a servant. And so having agreed upon becoming the servant of the Seer, I performed the duties of a servitor, such as fetching grass, fuel, water, bulbs, roots, fruit, &c. I held also the office of a doorkeeper. When I had done such kind of work at day-time, I at night kept his feet while he

---

[1] This golden age evidently coincided with the reign of king Yima in Iran, of king Frôði in Denmark, of king Manu in India; in short, with the dawn of humanity.

[2] Or, the best right.

[3] Upeyitavân. The original must have had upeyivân. The whole story, so different in language, style, phraseology, choice of words and spirit from anything else in the Lotus, has been so profoundly altered that almost every word must be taken in another sense than what originally was attached to it. I am not sure that those who modified the ancient tale understood the meaning of upeyivân; even the grammatical form was a puzzle, if not to them, at least to the scribes.

was lying on his couch[1], and never did I feel fatigue of body or mind. In such occupations I passed a full millennium.

And for the fuller elucidation of this matter the Lord on that occasion uttered the following stanzas:

42. I have a remembrance of past ages when I was Dhârmika[2], the King of the Law, and exercised the royal sway for duty's sake, not for love's sake, in the interest of the best law[3].

43. I let go out in all directions this proclamation: I will become a servant to him who shall explain Dharma[4]. At that time there was a far-seeing Sage, a revealer of the Sûtra called the True Law[5].

44. He said to me: If thou wish to know Dharma, become my servant[6]; then I will explain it to thee. As I heard these words I rejoiced and carefully performed such work as a servant ought to do.

45. I never felt any bodily nor mental weariness since I had become a servant for the sake of the true law. I did my best[7] for real truth's sake[8], not with a view to win honour or enjoy pleasure.

---

[1] *S*ayanasya ma*ñk*a*k*e pâdân dhârayâmâsa, which is sheer nonsense; we have to read *s*ayânasya. The plural pâdân shows that not the feet are meant—for that is pâdau in the dual—but the lower end of the couch; the plural, if applied to one person, is always metaphorical.

[2] The text of these verses is one mass of corruption, as is proved by the repeated offences against the metre.

[3] Perhaps those who changed the original text intended to join the last sentence to the following.

[4] In the intention of the original author: (what is) Right.

[5] Sûtrasya saddharmanâmna*h*; this term being prosodically inadmissible, the original must have had another word.

[6] Rather absurd; the original must have had 'my pupil.'

[7] Pra*n*idhi, here synonymous with avadhâna, prayatna.

[8] Vastutvaheto*h*, which is nonsense; probably to read vas-

46. That king meanwhile, strenuously and without engaging in other pursuits, roamed in every direction during thousands of kotis of complete Æons without being able to obtain the Sûtra called Dharma[1].

Now, monks, what is your opinion? that it was another who at that time, at that juncture was the king? No, you must certainly not hold that view. For it was myself, who at that time, at that juncture was the king. What then, monks, is your opinion? that it was another who at that time, at that juncture was the Seer? No, you must certainly not hold that view. For it was this Devadatta himself, the monk[2], who at that time, at that juncture was the Seer. Indeed, monks, Devadatta was my good friend. By the aid of Devadatta[3] have I accomplished the six perfect virtues (Pâramitâs). Noble kindness, noble compassion, noble sympathy, noble indifference, the thirty-two signs of a great man, the eighty lesser marks[4], the gold-coloured tinge, the ten powers, the fourfold absence of hesitation[5], the four articles of sociability, the eighteen uncommon

---

tutatvahetoh. A later hand has added a marginal reading sarvasatva, obviously intended to give a Buddhistic tinge to the tale.

[1] The traces of alteration are so clearly visible that it is not necessary to point them out.

[2] Ayam-eva sa Devadatto bhikshus tena kâlena tena samayena rishir abhût. Hence it follows that Devadatta is present at the gathering. His name not being mentioned before, he must be concealed under another name; I take him to be identical with Prabhûtaratna.

[3] Devadattam âgamya, properly, having come to or reached D.

[4] Anuvyañgana; they have been thoroughly treated of by Burnouf in an Appendix to the Lotus, p. 583 seq.; cf. Hodgson's Essays, p. 90, and S. Hardy's Manual, p. 369.

[5] Vaisâradya; Burnouf, Lotus, p. 396; S. Hardy, Eastern Monachism, p. 291.

properties, magical power, ability to save beings in all directions of space,—all this (have I got) after having come to Devadatta. I announce to you, monks, I declare to you: This Devadatta, the monk, shall in an age to come, after immense, innumerable Æons, become a Tathâgata named Devarâ*g*a (i. e. King of the gods), an Arhat, &c., in the world Devasopâna (i. e. Stairs of the gods). The lifetime of that Tathâgata Devarâ*g*a, monks, shall measure twenty intermediate kalpas. He shall preach the law in extension, and beings equal to the sands of the river Ganges shall through him forsake all evils and realise Arhatship. Several beings shall also elevate their minds to Pratyekabuddhaship, whereas beings equal to the sands of the river Ganges shall elevate their minds to supreme, perfect enlightenment, and become endowed with unflinching patience. Further, monks, after the complete extinction of the Tathâgata Devarâ*g*a, his true law shall stay twenty intermediate kalpas. His body shall not be seen divided into different parts (and relics); it shall remain as one mass within a Stûpa of seven precious substances, which Stûpa is to be sixty hundred yo*g*anas in height and forty yo*g*anas in extension[1]. All, gods and men, shall do worship to it with flowers, incense, perfumed garlands, unguents, powder, clothes, umbrellas, banners, flags, and celebrate it with stanzas and songs. Those who shall turn round that Stûpa from left to right or humbly salute it, shall some of them realise Arhatship, others attain Pratyekabuddhaship; others, gods and men, in immense number, shall raise their minds to supreme, perfect enlightenment, never to return.

---

[1] Âyâmena, which also means length.

Thereafter the Lord again addressed the assembly of monks: Whosoever in future, monks, be he a young man or a young lady of good family, shall hear this chapter of the Sûtra of the Lotus of the True Law, and by doing so be relieved from doubt, become pure-minded, and put reliance on it, to such a one the door of the three states of misfortune shall be shut: he shall not fall so low as to be born in hell, among beasts, or in Yama's kingdom. When born in the Buddha-fields in the ten points of space he shall at each repeated birth hear this very Sûtra, and when born amongst gods or men he shall attain an eminent rank. And in the Buddha-field where he is to be born he shall appear by metamorphosis on a lotus of seven precious substances, face to face with the Tathâgata.

At that moment a Bodhisattva of the name of Pra*gñ*âkû*t*a, having come from beneath the Buddha-field of the Tathâgata Prabhûtaratna, said to the Tathâgata Prabhûtaratna: Lord, let us resort to our own Buddha-field. But the Lord *S*âkyamuni, the Tathâgata, said to the Bodhisattva Pra*gñ*âkû*t*a: Wait a while, young man of good family, first have a discussion with my Bodhisattva Ma*ñg*u*s*rî, the prince royal, to settle some point of the law. And at the same moment, lo, Ma*ñg*u*s*rî, the prince royal, rose seated on a centifolious lotus that was large as a carriage yoked with four horses, surrounded and attended by many Bodhisattvas, from the bosom of the sea, from the abode of the Nâga-king Sâgara (i. e. Ocean). Rising high into the sky he went through the air to the G*ri*dhrakû*t*a mountain to the presence of the Lord. There Ma*ñg*u*s*rî, the prince royal, alighted from his lotus, reverentially saluted the feet of the Lord *S*âkyamuni and Prabhûtaratna, the Tathâgata, went up to the Bodhisattva Pra*gñ*â-kû*t*a and, after making the usual complimentary questions as to his health and welfare, seated himself at some distance. The Bodhisattva Pra*gñ*âkû*t*a then addressed to Ma*ñ*gu*s*rî, the prince royal, the following question: Ma*ñ*gu*s*rî, how many beings hast thou educated[1] during thy stay in the sea? Ma*ñ*gu*s*rî answered: Many, innumerable, incalculable beings have I educated, so innumerable that words cannot express it, nor thought conceive it. Wait a while, young man of good family, thou shalt presently see a token. No sooner had Ma*ñ*gu*s*rî, the prince royal, spoken these words than instantaneously many thousands of lotuses rose from the bosom of the sea up to the sky, and on those lotuses were seated many thousands of Bodhisattvas, who flocked through the air to the G*ri*dhrakû*t*a mountain, where they stayed, appearing as meteors. All of them had been educated by Ma*ñ*gu*s*rî, the prince royal, to supreme, perfect enlightenment[2]. The Bodhisattvas amongst them who had formerly striven after the great vehicle extolled the virtues of the great vehicle and the six perfect virtues (Pâramitâs). Such as had been disciples extolled the vehicle of disciples. But all acknowledged the voidness (or vanity) of all laws (or things), as well as the virtues of the great vehicle. Ma*ñ*gu*s*rî, the prince royal, said to the Bodhisattva Pra*gñ*âkû*t*a: Young man of good family, while I was staying in the bosom of the great ocean I have by all means

[1] Properly, lead, lead out.

[2] Here Ma*ñ*gu*s*rî appears in the character of Hermes ψυχοπομπός.

educated creatures, and here thou seest the result. Whereupon the Bodhisattva Pragñâkûta questioned Mañgusrî, the prince royal, in chanting the following stanzas:

47. O thou blessed one, who from thy wisdom art called the Sage[1], by whose power is it that thou to-day (or now) hast educated those innumerable beings? Tell it me upon my question, O thou god amongst men[2].

48. What law hast thou preached, or what Sûtra, in showing the path of enlightenment, so that those who are there with you have conceived the idea of enlightenment? that, once having gained a safe ford[3], they have been decisively established in omniscience?

Mañgusrî answered: In the bosom of the sea I have expounded the Lotus of the True Law and no other Sûtra. Pragñâkûta said: That Sûtra is profound, subtle, difficult to seize; no other Sûtra equals it. Is there any creature able to understand this jewel of a Sûtra or to arrive at supreme, perfect enlightenment? Mañgusrî replied: There is, young man of good family, the daughter of Sâgara, the Nâga-king, eight years old, very intelligent, of keen faculties, endowed with prudence in acts of body, speech, and mind, who has caught and kept all the teachings, in substance and form, of the Tathâgatas, who has acquired in one moment a thousand meditations and proofs of the essence of all laws[4]. She

---

[1] Mahâbhadra pragñayâ sûranâman. I take sûra in the sense of sûri, though it is also possible that sûra stands for sûra, a hero.

[2] Naradeva.

[3] Labdhagâthâh; I think we have to read labdhagâdhâh, and have translated accordingly.

[4] The reading is uncertain; sarvadharmasatvasamâdhânasamâ-

does not swerve from the idea of enlightenment, has great aspirations, applies to other beings the same measure as to herself; she is apt to display all virtues and is never deficient in them. With a bland smile on the face and in the bloom of an extremely handsome appearance she speaks words of kindliness and compassion[1]. She is fit to arrive at supreme, perfect enlightenment. The Bodhisattva Pra*gñâ*kû*t*a said: I have seen how the Lord *S*âkyamuni, the Tathâgata, when he was striving after enlightenment, in the state of a Bodhisattva, performed innumerable good works[2], and during many Æons never slackened in his arduous task. In the whole universe there is not a single spot so small as a mustard-seed where he has not surrendered his body for the sake of creatures[3]. Afterwards he arrived at enlightenment. Who then would believe that she should have been able to arrive at supreme, perfect knowledge in one moment?

At that very moment appeared the daughter of Sâgara, the Nâga-king, standing before their face. After reverentially saluting the feet of the Lord she stationed herself at some distance and uttered on that occasion the following stanzas:

---

dhisahasraikaksha*n*apratilâbhinî. A marginal correction by a later hand adds sarva between dharma and satva.

[1] The daughter of Sâgara, the Ocean, is Lakshmî, the smiling goddess of Beauty and Fortune, but from some traits in the sequel it would seem that she is identified with Târâ, the wife of B*ri*haspati and the Moon.

[2] As Hercules performed his ἆθλα.

[3] As the sun shoots his rays everywhere, it is quite natural that his dhâtus, i.e. particles, relics, have been spread all over the surface of the earth, and it is no untruth that the footprints (the pâdas, rays) of the Lord *S*âkyamuni are to be found in Laos, in Ceylon, &c.

49. Spotless, bright, and of unfathomable light is that ethereal body, adorned with the thirty-two characteristic signs, pervading space in all directions.

50. He is possessed of the secondary marks and praised by every being, and accessible to all, like an open market-place[1].

51. I have obtained enlightenment according to my wish; the Tathâgata can bear witness to it; I will extensively reveal the law that releases from sufferance.

Then the venerable *S*âriputra said to that daughter of Sâgara, the Nâga-king: Thou hast conceived the idea of enlightenment, young lady of good family, without sliding back, and art gifted with immense wisdom, but supreme, perfect enlightenment is not easily won. It may happen, sister, that a woman displays an unflagging energy, performs good works for many thousands of Æons, and fulfils the six perfect virtues (Pâramitâs), but as yet there is no example of her having reached Buddhaship, and that because a woman cannot occupy the five ranks, viz. 1. the rank of Brahma; 2. the rank of Indra; 3. the rank of a chief guardian of the four quarters; 4. the rank of *K*akravartin; 5. the rank of a Bodhisattva incapable of sliding back[2].

Now the daughter of Sâgara, the Nâga-king, had at the time a gem which in value outweighed the whole universe. That gem the daughter of Sâgara, the Nâga-king, presented to the Lord, and the Lord graciously accepted it. Then the daughter of Sâgara,

[1] Antarâpa*n*avad yathâ. I am not certain of the correctness of my translation. Burnouf has 's'il était leur concitoyen.'

[2] All these beings are in Sanskrit of masculine gender; hence their rank cannot be taken by beings having feminine names.

the Nâga-king, said to the Bodhisattva Pra*gñ*â-kû*t*a and the senior priest *S*âriputra: Has the Lord readily accepted[1] the gem I presented him or has he not? The senior priest answered: As soon as it was presented by thee, so soon it was accepted by the Lord. The daughter of Sâgara, the Nâga-king, replied: If I were endowed with magic power, brother *S*âriputra, I should sooner have arrived at supreme, perfect enlightenment, and there would have been none to receive this gem.

At the same instant, before the sight of the whole world and of the senior priest *S*âriputra, the female sex of the daughter of Sâgara, the Nâga-king, disappeared; the male sex appeared[2] and she manifested herself as a Bodhisattva, who immediately went to the South to sit down at the foot of a tree made of seven precious substances, in the world Vimala (i. e. spotless), where he showed himself enlightened and preaching the law, while filling all directions of space with the radiance of the thirty-two characteristic signs and all secondary marks. All beings in the Saha-world beheld that Lord while he received the homage of all, gods, Nâgas, goblins, Gandharvas, demons, Garu*d*as, Kinnaras, great serpents, men, and beings not human, and was engaged

---

[1] A marginal reading from a later hand adds: anukampâm upâdâya, by grace, by mercy, graciously.

[2] In ancient times such a change of sex is nothing strange. Sundry words for 'star,' e.g. târâ, târakâ, Latin stella, are feminine, whereas the names of some particular stars are masculine; so Târâ, the daughter of the Sea, Stella Marina, may have been identified with Tishya, or the Iranian Tishtrya, who equally rises from the sea; cf. Tishter Yasht (ed. Westergaard, p. 177). The daughter of the ocean seems to be identical with Ardvî Sûra, celebrated in Abân Yasht.

in preaching the law. And the beings who heard the preaching of that Tathâgata became incapable of sliding back in supreme, perfect enlightenment. And that world Vimala and this Saha-world shook in six different ways. Three thousand living beings from the congregational circle of the Lord *S*âkyamuni gained the acquiescence in the eternal law[1], whereas three hundred thousand beings obtained the prediction of their future destiny to supreme, perfect enlightenment.

Then the Bodhisattva Pra*g*ñâkû*t*a and the senior priest *S*âriputra were silent.

[1] Anutpattikadharmakshânti.

CHAPTER XII.

EXERTION.

Thereafter the Bodhisattva Bhaisha*g*yarâ*g*a and the Bodhisattva Mahâpratibhâna, with a retinue of twenty hundred thousand Bodhisattvas, spoke before the face of the Lord the following words: Let the Lord be at ease in this respect; we will after the extinction of the Tathâgata expound this Paryâya to (all) creatures[1], though we are aware, O Lord, that at that period there shall be malign beings, having few roots of goodness, conceited, fond of gain and honour, rooted in unholiness, difficult to tame, deprived of good will, and full of unwillingness. Nevertheless, O Lord, we will at that period read, keep, preach, write, honour, respect, venerate, worship this Sûtra; with sacrifice of body and life, O Lord, we will divulge this Sûtra. Let the Lord be at ease.

Thereupon five hundred monks of the assembly, both such as were under training and such as were not, said to the Lord: We also, O Lord, will exert ourselves to divulge this Dharmaparyâya, though in other worlds. Then all the disciples of the Lord, both such as were under training and such as were

---

[1] One would expect that this speech immediately followed st. 41 in the foregoing chapter, but the rules of composition in Buddhistic writings are so peculiar that it is unsafe to apply criticism.

not, who had received from the Lord the prediction as to their (future) supreme enlightenment, all the eight thousand monks raised their joined hands towards the Lord and said: Let the Lord be at ease. We also will divulge this Dharmaparyâya, after the complete extinction of the Lord, in the last days, the last period, though in other worlds. For in this Saha-world, O Lord, the creatures are conceited, possessed of few roots of goodness, always vicious in their thoughts, wicked, and naturally perverse.

Then the noble matron Gautamî, the sister of the Lord's mother, along with six hundred[1] nuns, some of them being under training, some being not, rose from her seat, raised the joined hands towards the Lord and remained gazing up to him. Then the Lord addressed the noble matron Gautamî: Why dost thou stand so dejected, gazing up to the Tathâgata? (She replied): I have not been mentioned by the Tathâgata, nor have I received from him a prediction of my destiny to supreme, perfect enlightenment. (He said): But, Gautamî, thou hast received a prediction with the prediction regarding the whole assembly. Indeed, Gautamî, thou shalt from henceforward, before the face of thirty-eight

[1] Ciphers do not count, so that only six must be reckoned. These six with Gautamî form the number of seven. The seven Matres or Mother-goddesses are known from Indian mythology. Kumâra, the prince royal (Skanda), is sometimes said to have six mothers, sometimes seven, sometimes one. The six are said to be the six clearly visible K*ri*ttikâs (Pleiads); the seventh is the less distinct star of the Pleiads. His one mother is Durgâ. It is by mistake that the dictionaries fix the number of K*ri*ttikâs at six; there are seven, as appears e.g. from Mahâbhârata III, 230, 11.

hundred thousand myriads of ko*t*is of Buddhas[1], be a Bodhisattva and preacher of the law. These six thousand[2] nuns also, partly perfected in discipline, partly not, shall along with others become Bodhisattvas[3] and preachers of the law before the face of the Tathâgatas. Afterwards, when thou shalt have completed the course of a Bodhisattva, thou shalt become, under the name of Sarvasattvapriyadar*s*ana (i. e. lovely to see for all beings), a Tathâgata, an Arhat, &c., endowed with science and conduct, &c. &c. And that Tathâgata Sarvasattvapriyadar*s*ana, O Gautamî, shall give a prediction by regular succession to those six thousand Bodhisattvas concerning their destiny to supreme, perfect enlightenment.

Then the nun Ya*s*odharâ, the mother of Râhula, thought thus: The Lord has not mentioned my name. And the Lord comprehending in his own mind what was going on in the mind of the nun Ya*s*odharâ said to her: I announce to thee, Ya*s*odharâ, I declare to thee: Thou also shalt before the face of ten thousand ko*t*is[4] of Buddhas become a Bodhisattva and preacher of the law, and after regularly completing the course of a Bodhisattva thou shalt become a Tathâgata, named Ra*s*mi*s*atasahasraparipûr*n*adhva*g*a, an Arhat, &c., endowed with science and conduct, &c. &c., in the

---

[1] In the margin has been added by a later hand: 'after paying honour, respect, reverence, worship, and veneration.' A little further on we find the same marginal addition.

[2] A few lines before the number was six hundred. Both numbers come to the same, for ciphers do not count.

[3] Here it is not added that Gautamî cum suis has to change sex (i.e. gender) in order to be fit for Bodhisattvaship. In fact, the K*ri*ttikâs are always feminine in Sanskrit.

[4] Burnouf has read, ten hundred thousand myriads of ko*t*is.

world Bhadra; and the lifetime of that Lord Rasmi*s*atasahasraparipûr*n*adhva*g*a shall be unlimited.

When the noble matron Gautamî, the nun, with her suite of six thousand nuns, and Ya*s*odharâ, the nun, with her suite of four thousand nuns, heard from the Lord their future destiny to supreme, perfect enlightenment, they uttered, in wonder and amazement, this stanza:

1. O Lord, thou art the trainer, thou art the leader; thou art the master of the world, including the gods; thou art the giver of comfort, thou who art worshipped by men and gods. Now, indeed, we feel satisfied.

After uttering this stanza the nuns said to the Lord: We also, O Lord, will exert ourselves to divulge this Dharmaparyâya in the last days, though in other worlds.

Thereafter the Lord looked towards the eighty hundred thousand Bodhisattvas who were gifted with magical spells and capable of moving forward the wheel that never rolls back. No sooner were those Bodhisattvas regarded by the Lord than they rose from their seats, raised their joined hands towards the Lord and reflected thus: The Lord invites us to make known the Dharmaparyâya. Agitated by that thought they asked one another: What shall we do, young men of good family, in order that this Dharmaparyâya may in future be made known as the Lord invites us to do? Thereupon those young men of good family, in consequence of their reverence for the Lord and their own pious vow in their previous course, raised a lion's roar[1] before the Lord: We, O Lord, will in future, after the

[1] One might say, a cry of martial exultation.

complete extinction of the Lord, go in all directions in order that creatures shall write, keep, meditate, divulge this Dharmaparyâya, by no other's power but the Lord's. And the Lord, staying in another world, shall protect, defend, and guard us.

Then the Bodhisattvas unanimously in a chorus addressed the Lord with the following stanzas:

2. Be at ease, O Lord. After thy complete extinction, in the horrible last period of the world, we will proclaim this sublime Sûtra.

3. We will suffer, patiently endure, O Lord, the injuries, threats, blows and threats with sticks[1] at the hands of foolish men.

4. At that dreadful last epoch men will be malign, crooked, wicked, dull, conceited, fancying to have come to the limit when they have not.

5. 'We do not care but to live in the wilderness and wear a patched cloth; we lead a frugal life;' so will they speak to the ignorant[2].

6. And persons greedily attached to enjoyments will preach the law to laymen and be honoured as if they possessed the six transcendent qualities.

7. Cruel-minded and wicked men, only occupied with household cares, will enter our retreat in the forest and become our calumniators.

8. The Tîrthikas[3], themselves bent on profit and honour, will say of us that we are so, and—shame on such monks!—they will preach their own fictions[4].

---

[1] Da*nd*a-udgira*n*a, for which I think we have to read da*nd*a-udgûra*n*a.

[2] Durmatîn.

[3] Dissenters, as the foremost of whom generally appear the *G*ainas, from the Buddhist point of view.

[4] Tîrthikâ vat' ime bhikshû svâni kâvyâni de*s*ayu*h*. Here

9. Prompted by greed of profit and honour they will compose Sûtras of their own invention and then, in the midst of the assembly, accuse us of plagiarism[1].

10. To kings, princes, king's peers, as well as to Brahmans and commoners, and to monks of other confessions,

11. They will speak evil of us and propagate the Tîrtha-doctrine[2]. We will endure all that out of reverence for the great Seers.

12. And those fools who will not listen to us, shall (sooner or later) become enlightened[3], and therefore will we forbear to the last.

13. In that dreadful, most terrible period of frightful general revolution will many fiendish monks stand up as our revilers.

14. Out of respect for the Chief of the world we will bear it, however difficult it be; girded with the girdle of forbearance will I[4] proclaim this Sûtra.

15. I[5] do not care for my body or life, O Lord,

---

we have the interjection vata (bata) in the sense of a nindâ, reproach, contempt. The Buddhists are fond of denouncing schismatics or heretics as impostors, and their works as forgeries; a model of such an accusation brought forward by the orthodox against the 'wicked' monks, the Vaggiputtakas, is to be found in Dîpavamsa V, 30 seqq.

[1] Or, perhaps, speak slander of us. The term used, anukuttanâ, is unknown to me from other passages, so that I have had recourse to etymology: anu, after, kuttanâ, stamping.

[2] These passages are not very explicit, but this much is clear that the Tîrthikas are somehow akin to the Buddhists, and distinguished from monks of other confession, who are wholly out of the pale of Bauddha sects. The whole history of the church in India is one of family quarrels, at least down to the days of Hiouen Thsang.

[3] Or, Buddhas, i.e. will sooner or later die.

[4] Prakâsaye, a singular which I do not feel at liberty to render by a plural.

[5] Again a singular, anarthiko 'smi.

but as keepers of thine entrusted deposit we care for enlightenment.

16. The Lord himself knows that in the last period there are (to be) wicked monks who do not understand mysterious speech[1].

17. One will have to bear frowning looks, repeated disavowal (or concealment), expulsion from the monasteries, many and manifold abuses[2].

18. Yet mindful of the command of the Lord of the world we will in the last period undauntedly proclaim this Sûtra in the midst of the congregation.

19. We will visit towns and villages everywhere, and transmit to those who care for it thine entrusted deposit, O Lord.

20. O Chief of the world, we will deliver thy message; be at ease then, tranquil and quiet, great Seer.

21. Light of the world, thou knowest the disposition of all who have flocked hither from every direction, (and thou knowest that) we speak a word of truth.

---

[1] Sandhâbhâshya, here rather 'conciliatory speech;' this is the meaning which sandhâya sambhâshana has in Sanskrit.

[2] The rendering of the last words bahukuttî bahûvidhâh is conjectural. Burnouf has, 'emprisonner et frapper de diverses manières,' but hereby two meanings are assigned to kuttî.

CHAPTER XIII.

PEACEFUL LIFE.

Mañgusrî, the prince royal, said to the Lord: It is difficult, Lord, most difficult, what these Bodhisattvas Mahâsattvas will attempt out of reverence for the Lord. How are these Bodhisattvas Mahâsattvas to promulgate this Dharmaparyâya at the end of time, at the last period? Whereupon the Lord answered Mañgusrî, the prince royal: A Bodhisattva Mahâsattva, Mañgusrî, he who is to promulgate this Dharmaparyâya at the end of time, at the last period, must be firm in four things. In which things? The Bodhisattva Mahâsattva, Mañgusrî, must be firm in his conduct and proper sphere if he wishes to teach this Dharmaparyâya. And how, Mañgusrî, is a Bodhisattva Mahâsattva firm in his conduct and proper sphere? When the Bodhisattva Mahâsattva, Mañgusrî, is patient, meek, has reached the stage of meekness; when he is not rash, nor envious; when, moreover, Mañgusrî, he clings to no law whatever and sees the real character of the laws (or things); when he is refraining from investigating and discussing these laws, Mañgusrî; that is called the conduct of a Bodhisattva Mahâsattva. And what is the proper sphere of a Bodhisattva Mahâsattva, Mañgusrî? When the Bodhisattva Mahâsattva, Mañgusrî, does not serve, not court, not wait upon kings; does not serve, not court, not wait upon princes; when he does not approach them; when he does not serve, not court, not wait upon persons of another sect, *K*arakas, Parivrâ*g*akas, Âgîvakas[1], Nirgranthas[2], nor persons passionately fond of fine literature; when he does not serve, not court, not wait upon adepts at worldly spells[3], and votaries of a worldly philosophy[4], nor keep any intercourse with them; when he does not go to see *K*â*nd*âlas, jugglers, vendors of pork, poulterers, deer-hunters, butchers, actors and dancers, wrestlers, nor resort to places whither others flock for amusement and sport; when he keeps no intercourse with them unless from time to time to preach the law to them when they come to him, and that freely[5]; when he does not serve, not court, not wait upon monks, nuns, lay devotees, male and female, who are adherents of the vehicle of disciples, nor keep intercourse with them; when he does not come in contact with them at the place of promenade or in the monastery, unless from time to time to preach the law to them when they come to him, and even that freely. This, Ma*ñg*u*s*rî, is the proper sphere of a Bodhisattva Mahâsattva.

Again, Ma*ñg*u*s*rî, the Bodhisattva Mahâsattva does not take hold of some favourable opportunity or another to preach the law to females every now and anon, nor is he desirous of repeatedly seeing females; nor does he think it proper to visit families and then too often address a girl, virgin, or young wife, nor does he greet them too fondly in return. He does

---

[1] Three kinds of mendicant friars not belonging to the Buddhist, nor to the *G*aina persuasion.

[2] *G*aina monks.

[3] Lokâyatamantradhâraka.

[4] Lokâyatikas, the Sadducees or Epicureans of India.

[5] Ani*s*rita; Burnouf renders it, 'sans même s'arrêter.'

not preach the law to a hermaphrodite, keeps no intercourse with such a person, nor greets too friendly in return. He does not enter a house alone in order to receive alms, unless having the Tathâgata in his thoughts. And when he happens to preach the law to females, he does not do so by passionate attachment to the law, far less by passionate attachment to a woman. When he is preaching, he does not display his row of teeth, let alone a quick emotion on his physiognomy. He addresses no novice, male or female, no nun, no monk, no young boy, no young girl, nor enters upon a conversation with them; he shows no great readiness in answering their address [1], nor cares to give too frequent answers. This, *Mañgusrî*, is called the first proper sphere of a Bodhisattva Mahâsattva.

Further, *Mañgusrî*, a Bodhisattva Mahâsattva looks upon all laws (and things) as void; he sees them duly established [2], remaining unaltered, as they are in reality, not liable to be disturbed, not to be moved backward, unchangeable, existing in the highest sense of the word (or in an absolute sense), having the nature of space, escaping explanation and expression by means of common speech, not born, composed and simple, aggregated and isolated [3], not expressible in words, independently established, manifesting them-

---

[1] Pratisa*m*lâpanaguruka, literally 'making much of returning (one's) addressing.'

[2] Yathâvatpratish*th*itân, aviparîtasthâyino yathâbhûtân, &c. Burnouf adds, 'privées de toute essence,' i.e. nirâtmakân.

[3] In the rendering of the last four terms I have followed Burnouf, as the reading in the Camb. MS. is evidently corrupt: asa*m*sk*ri*tânasa*m*tânâsa*m*mânâsannâbhilâpena pravyâh*ri*tân. The original reading may have been asa*m*sk*ri*tân nâsa*m*sk*ri*tân, not composed, not simple; nâsamân na samân, not unlike

selves owing to a perversion of perception. In this way then, Mañgusrî, the Bodhisattva Mahâsattva constantly views all laws, and if he abides in this course, he remains in his own sphere. This, Mañgusrî, is the second proper sphere of a Bodhisattva Mahâsattva.

And in order to expound this matter in greater detail, the Lord uttered the following stanzas:

1. The Bodhisattva who, undaunted and unabashed, wishes to set forth this Sûtra in the dreadful period hereafter,

2. Must keep to his course (of duty) and proper sphere; he must be retired and pure, constantly avoid intercourse with kings and princes.

3. Nor should he keep up intercourse with king's servants, nor with *K*â*nd*âlas, jugglers, and Tîrthikas in general[1].

4. He ought not to court conceited men, but catechise such as keep to the religion[2]. He must also avoid such monks as follow the precepts of the Arhat[3], and immoral men.

5. He must be constant in avoiding a nun who is fond of banter and chatter; he must also avoid notoriously loose female lay devotees.

6. He should shun any intercourse with such female lay devotees as seek their highest happiness

(i.e. equal to all), nor like; or, nâsa*m*tân (in grammatical Sansk. nâsato) na sa*m*tân, not non-existent, not existent.

[1] Burnouf adds, 'ceux qui vendent des liqueurs fermentées,' which is wanting in my MS.: *kand*âlair mush*t*ikais*k*âpi tîrthikais*k*âpi sarvasa*h*.

[2] According to the reading, vinayed âgamasthitâ(n). A marginal reading has vinayenâ°, a reading followed by Burnouf.

[3] Or, Arhats: Arhantasa*m*matâ(n) bhikhshûn. The *G*ainas are meant.

in this transient world. This is called the proper conduct of a Bodhisattva.

7. But when one comes to him to question him about the law for the sake of superior enlightenment, he should, at any time, speak freely, always firm and undaunted.

8. He should have no intercourse with women and hermaphrodites; he should also shun the young wives and girls in families.

9. He must never address them to ask after their health[1]. He must also avoid intercourse with vendors of pork and mutton.

10. With any persons who slay animals of various kind for the sake of profit, and with such as sell meat he should avoid having any intercourse.

11. He must shun the society of whoremongers, players, musicians, wrestlers, and other people of that sort.

12. He should not frequent whores, nor other sensual persons; he must avoid any exchange of civility with them.

13. And when the sage has to preach for a woman, he should not enter into an apartment with her alone, nor stay to banter.

14. When he has often to enter a village in quest of food, he must have another monk with him or constantly think of the Buddha.

15. Herewith have I shown the first sphere of proper conduct[2]. Wise are they who, keeping this Sûtra in memory, live according to it.

16. And when one observes[3] no law at all, low,

---

[1] Kau*s*alya*m* hâsa p*rikkh*itu*m*. I take hâsa to stand for âsa (Sansk. âsâm), if it be no error for tâsa (Sansk. tâsâm).

[2] Â*k*âragoc*k*aro hy esha.

[3] *K*arate.

superior or mean, composed or uncomposed, real or not real;

17. When the wise man does not remark, 'This is a woman,' nor marks, 'This is a man;' when in searching he finds no laws (or things), because they have never existed;

18. This is called the observance[1] of the Bodhisattvas in general. Now listen to me when I set forth what should be their proper sphere.

19. All laws (i.e. the laws, the things) have been declared to be non-existing, not appearing, not produced, void, immovable, everlasting; this is called the proper sphere of the wise.

20. They have been divided into existing and non-existing, real and unreal, by those who had wrong notions; other laws also, of permanency, of being produced, of birth from something already produced[2], are wrongly assumed.

21. Let (the Bodhisattva) be concentrated in mind, attentive, ever firm as the peak of Mount Sumeru, and in such a state (of mind) look upon all laws (and things) as having the nature of space[3],

22. Permanently equal to space, without essence, immovable, without substantiality[4]. These, indeed, are the laws, all and for ever. This is called the proper sphere of the wise.

23. The monk observing this rule of conduct given by me may, after my extinction, promulgate this Sûtra in the world, and shall feel no depression.

24. Let the sage first, for some time, coerce his

---

[1] Â*k*âra.

[2] *G*âtâda bhûti (Sansk. *g*âtâd bhûti*h*).

[3] I. e. as being void.

[4] Satyena; in the margin âtmanâ.

thoughts, exercise meditation with complete absorption, and correctly perform all that is required for attaining spiritual insight[1], and then, after rising (from his pious meditation), preach with unquailing mind.

25. The kings of this earth and the princes who listen to the law protect him. Others also, both laymen (or burghers) and Brahmans, will be found together in his congregation.

Further, Mañgusrî, the Bodhisattva Mahâsattva who, after the complete extinction of the Tathâgata at the end of time, the last period, the last five hundred years[2], when the true law is in a state of decay, is going to propound this Dharmaparyâya, must be in a peaceful state (of mind) and then preach the law, whether he knows it by heart or has it in a book. In his sermon he will not be too prone to carping at others, not blame other preaching friars, not speak scandal nor propagate scandal. He does not mention by name other monks, adherents of the vehicle of disciples, to propagate scandal. He cherishes even no hostile feelings against them, because he is in a peaceful state. All who come, one after the other, to hear the sermon he receives with benevolence, and preaches the law to them without invidiousness[3]. He refrains from entering upon a

---

[1] Kâlena *k*o *k*ittayamâtu (Sansk. °yamât) pa*nd*ita*h* pravilayana*m* tatha gha*tt*ayitvâ, vipa*s*yidharmam imu sarva yoniso utthâya, &c. I take gha*tt*ayitvâ in the sense of gha*t*ayitvâ=yuktvâ.

[2] I.e. in the latter part of the millennium. According to the declaration of the Buddha in *K*ullavagga X, 1, 6, the true law (Saddhamma) is to stand a millennium, though at the same time, owing to the institution of female monks, the number of 1000 years should be reduced to half.

[3] Anupârigrâhikayâ, ananyusû*k*anayâ dharma*m* de*s*ayati; °sû*k*anayâ is certainly wrong; cf. stanza 30 below.

dispute; but if he is asked a question, he does not answer in the way of (those who follow) the vehicle of disciples[1]; on the contrary, he answers as if he had attained Buddha-knowledge.

And on that occasion the Lord uttered the following stanzas:

26. The wise man[2] is always at ease[3], and in that state he preaches the law, seated on an elevated pulpit which has been prepared for him on a clean and pretty spot.

27. He puts on a clean, nice, red robe, dyed with good colours[4], and a black woollen garment and a long undergarment;

28. Having duly washed his feet and rubbed his head and face with smooth ointments[5], he ascends the pulpit, which is provided with a footbank and covered with pieces of fine cloth of various sorts, and sits down.

29. When he is thus seated on the preacher's pulpit and all who have gathered round him are

---

[1] Srâvakayânena. It is instructive to see that the Buddha here espouses the party of the great vehicle.

[2] I. e. preacher, minister of religion. The word used, pa*nd*ita, has passed into the languages of the Indian Archipelago in the sense of a minister of religion.

[3] Sukhasthita, which in the preceding passage I have rendered by 'being in a peaceful state,' because there the mental state is more prominent.

[4] *K*auksha*m* *k*a so *k*îvara prâvaritvâ suraktaraṅga*m* supra*s*astaraṅgai*h*.

[5] According to the ten commandments (Dasa*s*îla) the use of ointments is forbidden to the monks, but the preacher need not be a monastic man. In Nepâl it is the Vagra-Â*k*ârya who devotes himself to the active ministry of religion; see Hodgson's Essays, p. 52.

attentive, he proceeds to deliver many discourses, pleasing by variety, before monks and nuns,

30. Before male and female lay devotees, kings and princes. The wise man always (takes care to) deliver a sermon diversified in its contents and sweet, free from invidiousness[1].

31. If occasionally he is asked some question, even after he has commenced, he will explain the matter anew in regular order, and he will explain it in such a way that his hearers gain enlightenment.

32. The wise man is indefatigable; not even the thought of fatigue will rise in him; he knows no listlessness, and so displays to the assembly the strength of charity.

33. Day and night the wise man preaches this sublime law with myriads of ko*t*is of illustrations; he edifies and satisfies his audience without ever requiring anything.

34. Solid food, soft food, nourishment and drink, cloth, couches, robes, medicaments for the sick, all this does not occupy his thoughts, nor does he want anything from the congregation.

35. On the contrary, the wise man is always thinking: How can I and these beings become Buddhas? I will preach this true law, upon which the happiness of all beings depends[2], for the benefit of the world.

36. The monk who, after my extinction, shall preach in this way, without envy, shall not meet with trouble, impediment, grief or despondency.

37. Nobody shall frighten him, beat or blame

---

[1] Ananyasûyantu; perhaps we must read anabhyasûyantu.

[2] Etat samasatvasukhopadhâna*m* saddharma*m* *s*râvemi hitâya loke.

him; never shall he be driven away, because he is firm in the strength of forbearance.

38. The wise man who is peaceful, so disposed as I have just said, possesses hundreds of ko*t*is of advantages, so many that one would not be able to enumerate them in hundreds of Æons.

Again, Ma*ñg*u*s*rî, the Bodhisattva Mahâsattva who lives after the extinction of the Tathâgata at the end of time when the true law is in decay, the Bodhisattva Mahâsattva who keeps this Sûtra is not envious, not false, not deceitful; he does not speak disparagingly of other adherents of the vehicle of Bodhisattvas, nor defame, nor humble them. He does not bring forward the shortcomings of other monks, nuns, male and female lay devotees, neither of the adherents of the vehicle of disciples nor of those of the vehicle of Pratyekabuddhas. He does not say: You young men of good family, you are far off from supreme, perfect enlightenment; you give proof of not having arrived at it; you are too fickle in your doings and not capable of acquiring true knowledge. He does not in this way bring forward the shortcomings of any adherent of the vehicle of the Bodhisattvas. Nor does he show any delight in disputes about the law, or engage in disputes about the law, and he never abandons the strength of charity towards all beings. In respect to all Tathâgatas he feels as if they were his fathers, and in respect to all Bodhisattvas as if they were his masters. And as to the Bodhisattvas Mahâsattvas in all directions of space, he is assiduous in paying homage to them by good will and respect. When he preaches the law, he preaches no less and no more than the law, without partial predilection for (any part of) the law, and he does not show greater favour to one than to another, even from love of the law.

Such, Mañgusrî, is the third quality with which a Bodhisattva Mahâsattva is endowed who is to expound this Dharmaparyâya after the extinction of the Tathâgata at the end of time when the true law is in decay; who will live at ease[1] and not be annoyed in the exposition of this Dharmaparyâya. And in the synod[2] he will have allies, and he will find auditors at his sermons who will listen to this Dharmaparyâya, believe, accept, keep, read, penetrate, write it and cause it to be written, and who, after it has been written and a volume made of it, will honour, respect, esteem, and worship it.

This said the Lord, and thereafter he, the Sugata, the Master, added the following:

39. The wise man, the preacher, who wishes to expound this Sûtra must absolutely renounce falsehood, pride, calumny, and envy.

40. He should never speak a disparaging word of anybody; never engage in a dispute on religious belief; never say to such as are guilty of shortcomings, You will not obtain superior knowledge.

41. He is always sincere, mild, forbearing; (as) a (true) son of Sugata he will repeatedly preach the law without any feeling of vexation.

42. 'The Bodhisattvas in all directions of space, who out of compassion for creatures are moving in the world, are my teachers;' (thus thinking) the wise man respects them as his masters.

---

[1] Sukhya[m] sparsam viharati, which answers to the Pâli phrase phâsu viharati.

[2] Dharmasangîtyâm.

43. Cherishing the memory of the Buddhas, the supreme amongst men, he will always feel towards them as if they were his fathers, and by forsaking all idea of pride he will escape hindrance.

44. The wise man who has heard this law, should be constant in observing it. If he earnestly strives after a peaceful life, ko*t*is of beings will surely protect him.

Further, Ma*ñg*u*s*rî, the Bodhisattva Mahâsattva, living at the time of destruction of the true law after the extinction of the Tathâgata, who is desirous of keeping this Dharmaparyâya, should live as far as possible away from laymen and friars, and lead a life of charity. He must feel affection for all beings who are striving for enlightenment and therefore make this reflection: To be sure, they are greatly perverted in mind, those beings who do not hear, nor perceive, nor understand the skilfulness and the mystery[1] of the Tathâgata, who do not inquire for it, nor believe in it, nor even are willing to believe in it. Of course, these beings do not penetrate, nor understand this Dharmaparyâya. Nevertheless will I, who have attained[2] this supreme, perfect knowledge, powerfully[3] bend to it the mind of every one, whatever may be the position he occupies, and bring about that he accepts, understands, and arrives at full ripeness.

By possessing also this fourth quality, Ma*ñg*u*s*rî, a Bodhisattva Mahâsattva, who is to expound the law after the extinction of the Tathâgata, will be

---

[1] Sandhâbhâshita.

[2] Abhisambudhya.

[3] Balena; in the margin added by a later hand, *ri*ddhi; this is the reading followed by Burnouf, 'par la force de mes facultés surnaturelles.'

unmolested, honoured, respected, esteemed, venerated by monks, nuns, and lay devotees, male and female, by kings, princes, ministers, king's officers, by citizens and country people, by Brahmans and laymen; the gods of the sky will, full of faith, follow his track to hear the law, and the angels will follow his track to protect him; whether he is in a village or in a monastery, they will approach him day and night to put questions about the law, and they will be satisfied, charmed with his explanation. For this Dharmaparyâya, Ma*ñg*u*s*rî, has been blessed by all Buddhas. With the past, future, and present Tathâgata, Ma*ñg*u*s*rî, this Dharmaparyâya is for ever blessed. Precious[1] in all worlds, Ma*ñg*u*s*rî, is the sound, rumour, or mentioning of this Dharmaparyâya.

It is a case, Ma*ñg*u*s*rî, similar to that of a king, a ruler of armies, who by force has conquered his own kingdom, whereupon other kings, his adversaries, wage war against him. That ruler of armies has soldiers of various description to fight with various enemies. As the king sees those soldiers fighting, he is delighted with their gallantry, enraptured, and in his delight and rapture he makes to his soldiers several donations, such as villages and village grounds, towns and grounds of a town; garments and head-gear; hand-ornaments, necklaces, gold threads, earrings, strings of pearls, bullion, gold, gems, pearls, lapis lazuli, conch-shells, stones (?), corals; he, moreover, gives elephants, horses, cars, foot soldiers, male and female slaves, vehicles, and litters. But to none he makes a present

[1] Durlabha, also meaning rare, difficult to be got.

of his crown jewel, because that jewel only fits on the head of a king. Were the king to give away that crown jewel, then that whole royal army, consisting of four divisions, would be astonished and amazed. In the same manner, Mañgusrî, the Tathâgata, the Arhat, &c., exercises the reign of righteousness (and of the law) in the triple world which he has conquered by the power of his arm and the power of his virtue. His triple world is assailed by Mâra, the Evil One. Then the Âryas, the soldiers of the Tathâgata, fight with Mâra. Then, Mañgusrî, the king of the law, the lord of the law, expounds to the Âryas, his soldiers, whom he sees fighting, hundred thousands of Sûtras in order to encourage the four classes. He gives them the city of Nirvâna, the great city of the law; he allures them with that city of Nirvâna, but he does not preach to them such a Dharmaparyâya as this. Just as in that case, Mañgusrî, that king, ruler of armies, astonished at the great valour of his soldiers in battle gives them all his property, at last even his crown jewel, and just as that crown jewel has been kept by the king on his head to the last, so, Mañgusrî, the Tathâgata, the Arhat, &c., who as the great king of the law in the triple world exercises his sway with justice, when he sees disciples and Bodhisattvas fighting against the Mâra of fancies or the Mâra of sinful inclinations, and when he sees that by fighting they have destroyed affection, hatred, and infatuation, overcome the triple world and conquered all Mâras, is satisfied, and in his satisfaction he expounds to those noble (ârya) soldiers this Dharmaparyâya which meets opposition in all the world, the unbelief of all the world, a Dharmaparyâya never before preached, never before explained. And the Tathâgata bestows on all disciples the noble crown jewel, that most exalted crown jewel which brings omniscience to all. For this, Mañ*g*u*s*rî, is the supreme preaching of the Tathâgatas; this is the last Dharmaparyâya of the Tathâgatas; this is the most profound discourse on the law, a Dharmaparyâya meeting opposition in all the world. In the same manner, Mañ*g*u*s*rî, as that king of righteousness and ruler of armies took off the crown jewel which he had kept so long a time and gave it (at last) to the soldiers, so, Mañ*g*u*s*rî, the Tathâgata now reveals this long-kept mystery of the law exceeding all others, (the mystery) which must be known by the Tathâgatas.

And in order to elucidate this matter more in detail, the Lord on that occasion uttered the following stanzas:

45. Always displaying the strength of charity, always filled with compassion for all creatures, expounding this law, the Sugatas have approved this exalted Sûtra.

46. The laymen, as well as the mendicant friars, and the Bodhisattvas who shall live at the end of time, must all show the strength of charity, lest those who hear the law reject it.

47. But I, when I shall have reached enlightenment and be established in Tathâgataship, will initiate (others), and after having initiated disciples[1] preach everywhere this superior enlightenment.

48. It is (a case) like that of a king, ruler of armies, who gives to his soldiers various things, gold, elephants, horses, cars, foot soldiers; he also

[1] Tato upaneshyi upâyayitvâ sa*m*s*r*âvayishye imam agrabodhim.

gives towns and villages, in token of his contentment.

49. In his satisfaction he gives to some hand-ornaments, silver and gold thread; pearls, gems, conch-shells, stones (?), coral; he also gives slaves of various description.

50. But when he is struck with the incomparable daring of one amongst the soldiers, he says: Thou hast admirably done this; and, taking off his crown, makes him a present of the jewel.

51. Likewise do I, the Buddha, the king of the law, I who have the force of patience and a large treasure of wisdom, with justice govern the whole world, benign, compassionate, and pitiful.

52. And seeing how the creatures are in trouble, I pronounce thousands of ko*t*is of Sûtrântas, when I perceive the heroism of those living beings who by pure-mindedness overcome the sinful inclinations of the world.

53. And the king of the law, the great physician, who expounds hundreds of ko*t*is of Paryâyas, when he recognises that creatures are strong, shows them this Sûtra, comparable to a crown jewel.

54. This is the last Sûtra proclaimed in the world, the most eminent of all my Sûtras, which I have always kept and never divulged. Now I am going to make it known; listen all.

55. There are four qualities to be acquired by those who at the period after my extinction desire supreme enlightenment and perform my charge[1]. The qualities are such as follows.

56. The wise man knows no vexation, trouble,

[1] Vyâpara*n*a.

sickness; the colour of his skin is not blackish; nor does he dwell in a miserable town.

57. The great Sage has always a pleasant look, deserves to be honoured, as if he were the Tathâgata himself, and little angels shall constantly be his attendants.

58. His body can never be hurt by weapons, poison, sticks, or clods, and the mouth of the man who utters a word of abuse against him shall be closed.

59. He is a friend to all creatures in the world. He goes all over the earth as a light, dissipating the gloom of many kotis of creatures, he who keeps this Sûtra after my extinction.

60. In his sleep he sees visions in the shape of Buddha; he sees monks and nuns appearing on thrones and proclaiming the many-sided law.

61. He sees in his dream gods and goblins, (numerous) as the sands of the Ganges, as well as demons and Nâgas of many kinds, who lift their joined hands and to whom he expounds the eminent law.

62. He sees in his dream the Tathâgata preaching the law to many kotis of beings with lovely voice, the Lord with golden colour.

63. And he stands there with joined hands glorifying the Seer, the highest of men, whilst the *G*ina, the great physician, is expounding the law to the four classes.

64. And he, glad to have heard the law, joyfully pays his worship, and after having soon reached the knowledge which never slides back, he obtains, in dream, magical spells.

65. And the Lord of the world, perceiving his good

intention, announces to him his destiny of becoming a leader amongst men: Young man of good family (says he), thou shalt here reach in future supreme, holy knowledge.

66. Thou shalt have a large field and four classes (of hearers), even as myself, that respectfully and with joined hands shall hear from thee the vast and faultless law.

67. Again he sees his own person occupied with meditating on the law in mountain caverns; and by meditating he attains the very nature of the law and, on obtaining complete absorption, sees the *G*ina.

68. And after seeing in his dream the gold-coloured one, him who displays a hundred hallowed signs, he hears the law, whereafter he preaches it in the assembly. Such is his dream.

69. And in his dream he also forsakes his whole realm, harem, and numerous kinsfolk; renouncing all pleasures he leaves home (to become an ascetic), and betakes himself to the place of the terrace of enlightenment.

70. There, seated upon a throne at the foot of a tree to seek enlightenment, he will[1], after the lapse of seven days, arrive at the knowledge of the Tathâgatas.

71. On having reached enlightenment he will rise up from that place to move forward the faultless wheel and preach the law during an inconceivable number of thousands of ko*t*is of Æons.

72. After having revealed perfect enlightenment and led many ko*t*is of beings to perfect rest, he

[1] Anuprâpsyate.

himself will be extinguished like a lamp when the oil is exhausted. So is that vision.

73. Endless, Mañgughosha, are the advantages which constantly are his who at the end of time shall expound this Sûtra of superior enlightenment that I have perfectly explained.

CHAPTER XIV.

ISSUING OF BODHISATTVAS FROM THE GAPS OF THE EARTH.

Out of the multitude of Bodhisattvas Mahâsattvas who had flocked from other worlds, Bodhisattvas eight (times) equal to the sands of the river Ganges[1] then rose from the assembled circle. Their joined hands stretched out towards the Lord to pay him homage, they said to him: If the Lord will allow us, we also would, after the extinction of the Lord, reveal this Dharmaparyâya in this Saha-world; we would read, write, worship it, and wholly devote ourselves[2] to that law. Therefore, O Lord, deign to grant to us also this Dharmaparyâya. And the Lord answered: Nay, young men of good family, why should you occupy yourselves with this task? I have here in this Saha-world thousands of Bodhisattvas equal to the sands of sixty Ganges rivers, forming the train of one Bodhisattva; and of such Bodhisattvas there is a number equal to the sands of sixty Ganges rivers, each of these Bodhisattvas having an equal number

[1] The text has ash*t*au Gaṅgânadîvâlikâsamâ Bodhisatvâs. Burnouf renders the passage by 'en nombre égal à celui des sables de huit Ganges.' Perhaps we must understand eight to mean eight thousand, just as e.g. Dîpava*m*sa VI, 98 the word eighty-four denotes eighty-four thousand.

[2] Yogam âpadyemahi.

in their train, who at the end of time, at the last period after my extinction, shall keep, read, proclaim this Dharmaparyâya.

No sooner had the Lord uttered these words than the Saha-world burst open on every side, and from within the clefts arose many hundred thousand myriads of ko*t*is of Bodhisattvas with gold-coloured bodies and the thirty-two characteristic signs of a great man, who had been staying in the element of ether underneath this great earth, close to this Saha-world. These then on hearing the word of the Lord came up from below the earth. Each of these Bodhisattvas had a train of thousands of Bodhisattvas similar to the sands of sixty Ganges[1] rivers; (each had) a troop, a great troop, as teacher of a troop. Of such Bodhisattvas Mahâsattvas having a troop, a great troop, as teachers of a troop, there were hundred thousands of myriads of ko*t*is equal to the sands of sixty Ganges[2] rivers, who emerged from the gaps of the earth in this Saha-world. Much more there were to be found of Bodhisattvas Mahâsattvas having a train of Bodhisattvas similar to the sands of fifty Ganges rivers; much more there were to be found of Bodhisattvas Mahâsattvas having a train of Bodhisattvas similar to the sands of forty Ganges rivers; of 30[3], 20, 10, 5, 4, 3, 2, 1 Ganges river; of $\frac{1}{2}, \frac{1}{4}, \frac{1}{6}, \frac{1}{10}, \frac{1}{20}, \frac{1}{50}, \frac{1}{100}, \frac{1}{1000}, \frac{1}{100,000}, \frac{1}{10,000,000}, \frac{1}{100 \times 10,000,000}, \frac{1}{1000 \times 10,000,000}$,

[1] Or, a train of sixty thousand Bodhisattvas similar to the sands of the river Ganges.

[2] Shash*t*y eva, which is ungrammatical, for shash*t*ir eva, or it is a corrupt reading.

[3] The text goes on repeating the same words, save the difference of number; I have given the contents in a shortened form.

$\frac{1}{100 \times 1000 \times 10{,}000{,}000}$, $\frac{1}{100 \times 1000 \times 10{,}000 \times 10{,}000{,}000}$ part of the river Ganges. Much more there were to be found of Bodhisattvas Mahâsattvas having a train of many hundred thousand myriads of ko*t*is of Bodhisattvas; of one ko*t*i; of one hundred thousand; of one thousand; of 500; of 400; of 300; of 200; of 100; of 50; of 40; of 30; of 20; of 10; of 5, 4, 3, 2. Much more there were to be found of Bodhisattvas Mahâsattvas having one follower. Much more there were to be found of Bodhisattvas Mahâsattvas standing isolated. They cannot be numbered, counted, calculated, compared, known by occult science, the Bodhisattvas Mahâsattvas who emerged from the gaps of the earth to appear in this Saha-world. And after they had successively emerged they went up to the Stûpa of precious substances which stood in the sky, where the Lord Prabhûtaratna, the extinct Tathâgata, was seated along with the Lord *S*âkyamuni on the throne. Whereafter they saluted the feet of both Tathâgatas, &c., as well as the images of Tathâgatas produced by the Lord *S*âkyamuni from his own body, who all together were seated on thrones at the foot of various jewel trees on every side in all directions, in different worlds. After these Bodhisattvas had many hundred thousand times saluted, and thereon circumambulated the Tathâgatas, &c., from left to right, and celebrated them with various Bodhisattva hymns, they went and kept themselves at a little distance, the joined hands stretched out to honour the Lord *S*âkyamuni, the Tathâgata, &c., and the Lord Prabhûtaratna, the Tathâgata, &c.

And while those Bodhisattvas Mahâsattvas who had emerged from the gaps of the earth were saluting and celebrating the Tathâgatas by various Bodhisattva hymns, fifty intermediate kalpas in full rolled away, during which fifty intermediate kalpas the Lord *S*âkyamuni remained silent, and likewise the four classes of the audience. Then the Lord produced such an effect of magical power that the four classes fancied that it had been no more than one afternoon[1], and they saw this Saha-world assume the appearance of hundred thousands of worlds[2] replete with Bodhisattvas[3]. The four Bodhisattvas Mahâsattvas who were the chiefest of that great host of Bodhisattvas, viz. the Bodhisattva Mahâsattva called Vi*s*ish*t*a*k*âritra (i. e. of eminent conduct), the Bodhisattva Mahâsattva called Ananta*k*âritra (i. e. of endless conduct), the Bodhisattva Mahâsattva called Vi*s*uddha*k*âritra (i. e. of correct conduct), and the Bodhisattva Mahâsattva called Supratish*th*ita*k*âritra (i. e. of very steady conduct), these four Bodhisattvas Mahâsattvas standing at

[1] If we take kalpa or Æon (i.e. a day of twenty-four hours) to contain eighty intermediate kalpas, it is impossible that either fifty or five intermediate kalpas should be equal to an afternoon. A so-called Asankhyeya kalpa has twenty intermediate kalpas, and is, in reality, equal to six hours, so that five intermediate kalpas will embrace a time of 1½ hour. If we might take an Asankhyeya to be the equivalent of a day of twenty-four hours, the reckoning would be correct, for then five intermediate kalpas would be equal to six hours; we can, however, produce no authority for Asankhyeya kalpa ever being used in the (esoteric) sense of a day and night.

[2] Lokadhâtu*s*atasahasrâkârâparigr*i*hîtâm, which ought to be °kârap°, or °kâra*m* p°. Instances of the peculiar construction of parigr*i*hîta after the analogy of prâpta are found, Lalita-vistara, pp. 109, 112, 181, 368. A marginal would-be correction has °kâsa*m* p°.

[3] The afternoon being at an end, the innumerable spheres of the stars become visible.

the head of the great host, the great multitude of Bodhisattvas stretched out the joined hands towards the Lord and addressed him thus: Is the Lord in good health? Does he enjoy well-being and good ease? Are the creatures decorous, docile, obedient, correctly performing their task[1], so that they give no trouble to the Lord?

And those four Bodhisattvas Mahâsattvas addressed the Lord with the two following stanzas:

1. Does the Lord of the world, the illuminator, feel at ease? Dost thou feel free from bodily disease, O Perfect One?

2. The creatures, we hope, will be decorous, docile, performing the orders[2] of the Lord of the world, so as to give no trouble.

And the Lord answered the four Bodhisattvas Mahâsattvas who were at the head of that great host, that great multitude of Bodhisattvas: So it is, young men of good family, I am in good health, well-being, and at ease. And these creatures of mine are decorous, docile, obedient, well performing what is ordered; they give no trouble when I correct them[3]; and that, young men of good family, because these creatures, owing to their being already prepared under the ancient, perfectly enlightened Buddhas, have but to see and hear me to put trust

---

[1] Suvi*s*odhakâ*h*. The rendering doubtful; see next note.

[2] Su*s*odhaka. This, as well as suvi*s*odhaka, properly means 'well cleaning,' and applies, at least originally, to servants or pupils who are charged with sweeping the house or precincts. I have tried to give the expression a spiritual look; Burnouf renders it by 'faciles à purifier,' which is quite plausible, because in a similar compound, subodha, we find bodha used in a passive sense, the word meaning 'easy to be understood.'

[3] Na *k*a kheda*m* *g*anayanti vi*s*odhyamânâs.

in me, to understand and fathom the Buddha-knowledge. And those who fulfilled their duties in the stage of disciples have now been introduced by me into Buddha-knowledge and well instructed in the highest truth.

And at that time the Bodhisattvas Mahâsattvas uttered the following stanzas:

3. Excellent, excellent, O great Hero! we are happy to hear that those creatures are decorous, docile, well performing their duty[1];

4. And that they listen to thy profound knowledge, O Leader, and that after listening to it they have put trust in it and understand it.

This said, the Lord declared his approval to the four Bodhisattvas Mahâsattvas who were at the head of that great host, that great multitude of Bodhisattvas Mahâsattvas, saying: Well done, young men of good family, well done, that you so congratulate the Tathâgata.

And at that moment the following thought arose in the mind of the Bodhisattva Mahâsattva Maitreya and the eight hundred thousand myriads of ko*t*is of Bodhisattvas similar to the sands of the river Ganges[2]: We never yet saw so great a host, so great a multitude of Bodhisattvas; we never yet heard of such a multitude, that after issuing from the gaps of the earth has stood in the presence of the Lord to honour, respect, venerate, worship him and greet him with joyful shouts[3]. Whence have these Bodhisattvas Mahâsattvas flocked hither?

---

[1] Su*s*odhaka; cf. above.

[2] Ash*t*ânâ*m* Gaṅgânadîvâlikopamânâ*m* Bodhisatvako*t*inayutasatasahasrâ*n*â*m*. Burnouf renders, 'à celui des sables de huit Ganges.'

[3] Pratisammodante.

Then the Bodhisattva Mahâsattva Maitreya, feeling within himself doubt and perplexity, and inferring from his own thoughts those of the eight hundred thousand myriads of ko*t*is of Bodhisattvas similar to the sands of the river Ganges, stretched out his joined hands towards the Lord and questioned him about the matter by uttering the following stanzas:

5. Here are many thousand myriads of ko*t*is of Bodhisattvas, numberless, whom we never saw before; tell us, O supreme of men!

6. Whence and how do these mighty persons come? Whence have they come here under the form of great bodies[1]?

7. All are great Seers, wise and strong in memory, whose outward appearance is lovely to see; whence have they come?

8. And each of those Bodhisattvas, O Lord of the world, has an immense train, like the sands of the Ganges.

9. The train of (each) glorious Bodhisattva is equal to the sands of sixty Ganges in full[2]. All are striving after enlightenment.

10. Of such heroes and mighty possessors of a troop the followers are equal to the sands of sixty Ganges[3].

---

[1] The rendering is doubtful; the text has mahâtmabhâvarûpe*n*a.

[2] Gaṅgâvâlikasamâ shash*t*i paripûr*nn*â yasasvina*h*, parivâro Bodhisatvasya. It is in the teeth of grammar to render the passage in this way, but from the following we must infer that no other translation will suit the case.

[3] The translation is uncertain; the text has eva*m* rûpâ*n*a vîrâ*n*â*m* varshavantâna tâyinâ*m*, shash*t*ir eva pramâ*n*ena Gaṅgavâlikâ ime. Instead of varshavantâna I would read vargavantâna, which

11. There are others, still more numerous, with an unlimited train, like the sands of fifty, forty, and thirty Ganges;

12, 13. Who have a train equal to the (sands of) twenty Ganges. Still more numerous are the mighty sons of Buddha, who have each a train (equal to the sands) of ten, of five Ganges. Whence, O Leader, has such an assembly flocked hither?

14. There are others who have each a train of pupils and companions equal to the sands of four, three, or two Ganges.

15. There are others more numerous yet; it would be impossible to calculate their number in thousands of ko*t*is of Æons.

16. (Equal to) a half Ganges, one third, one tenth, one twentieth, is the train of those heroes, those mighty Bodhisattvas.

17. There are yet others who are incalculable; it would be impossible to count them even in hundreds of ko*t*is of Æons.

18. Many more yet there are, with endless trains; they have in their attendance ko*t*is, and ko*t*is and again ko*t*is, and also half ko*t*is.

19. Other great Seers again, beyond computation, very wise Bodhisattvas are seen in a respectful posture.

20. They have a thousand, a hundred, or fifty attendants; in hundreds of ko*t*is of Æons one would not be able to count them.

21. The suite of (some of these) heroes consists of twenty, of ten, five, four, three, or two; those are countless.

Burnouf seems to have had before him, for his translation has 'suivis chacun de leur assemblée.'

22. As to those who are walking alone and come to their rest alone, they have now flocked hither in such numbers as to be beyond computation.

23. Even if one with a magic wand in his hand would try for a number of Æons equal to the sands of the Gangesto count them, he would not reach the term.

24. Where do all those noble, energetic heroes, those mighty Bodhisattvas, come from?

25. Who has taught them the law (or duty)? and by whom have they been destined to enlightenment? Whose command do they accept? Whose command do they keep?

26. Bursting forth at all points of the horizon through the whole extent of the earth they emerge, those great Sages endowed with magical faculty and wisdom.

27. This world on every side is being perforated, O Seer, by the wise Bodhisattvas, who at this time are emerging.

28. Never before have we seen anything like this. Tell us the name of this world, O Leader.

29. We have repeatedly roamed in all directions of space, but never saw these Bodhisattvas.

30. We never saw a single infant[1] of thine, and now, on a sudden, these appear to us. Tell us their history, O Seer.

31. Hundreds, thousands, ten thousands of Bodhisattvas, all equally filled with curiosity, look up to the highest of men.

32. Explain to us, O incomparable, great hero, who knowest no bounds[2], where do these heroes, these wise Bodhisattvas, come from?

---

[1] Stanapa.

[2] Nirâvadhe, which I identify with Sansk. niravadhe, the voc.

Meanwhile the Tathâgatas, &c., who had flocked from hundred thousands of myriads of ko*t*is of worlds, they, the creations of the Lord *S*âkyamuni, who were preaching the law to the beings in other worlds; who all around[1] the Lord *S*âkyamuni, the Tathâgata, &c., were seated with crossed legs on magnificent jewel thrones[2] at the foot of jewel trees in every direction of space; as well as the satellites of those Tathâgatas were struck with wonder and amazement at the sight of that great host, that great multitude of Bodhisattvas emerging from the gaps of the earth and established in the element of ether, and they (the satellites) asked each their own Tathâgata: Where, O Lord, do so many Bodhisattvas Mahâsattvas, so innumerable, so countless, come from? Whereupon those Tathâgatas, &c., answered severally to their satellites: Wait awhile, young men of good family; this Bodhisattva Mahâsattva here, called Maitreya, has just received from the Lord *S*âkyamuni a revelation about his destiny to supreme, perfect enlightenment. He has questioned the Lord *S*âkyamuni, the Tathâgata, &c., about the matter, and the Lord *S*âkyamuni, the Tathâgata, &c., is going to explain it; then you may hear.

Thereupon the Lord addressed the Bodhisattva Maitreya: Well done, A*g*ita, well done; it is a sublime subject, A*g*ita, about which thou questionest me. Then the Lord addressed the entire host of Bodhisattvas: Be attentive all, young men of good

---

case of niravadhi. Burnouf has, 'toi qui es affranchi de l'accumulation [des éléments constitutifs de l'existence].'

[1] Samantâd; Burnouf's 'en présence' is wanting in my MS.

[2] Or, thrones of magnificent jewels.

family; be well prepared and steady on your post, you and the entire host of Bodhisattvas; the Tathâgata, the Arhat, &c., is now going to exhibit the sight of the knowledge of the Tathâgata, young men of good family, the leadership of the Tathâgata, the work of the Tathâgata, the sport[1] of the Tathâgata, the might of the Tathâgata, the energy of the Tathâgata.

And on that occasion the Lord pronounced the following stanzas:

33. Be attentive all, young men of good family; I am to utter an infallible word; refrain from disputing[2] about it, O sages: the science of the Tathâgata is beyond reasoning.

34. Be all steady and thoughtful; continue attentive all. To-day you will hear a law as yet unknown, the wonder of the Tathâgatas.

35. Never have any doubt, ye sages, for I shall strengthen you, I am the Leader who speaketh infallible truth, and my knowledge is unlimited.

36. Profound are the laws known to the Sugata, above reasoning and beyond argumentation. These laws I am going to reveal; ye, hear which and how they are.

After uttering these stanzas the Lord addressed the Bodhisattva Mahâsattva Maitreya: I announce to thee, A*g*ita, I declare to thee: These Bodhisattvas Mahâsattvas, A*g*ita, so innumerable, incalculable, inconceivable, incomparable, uncountable, whom you never saw before, who just now have issued from

[1] I.e. magic display of creative power, lîlâ, synonymous with mâyâ.

[2] Vivâda, the original reading, though afterwards effaced and replaced by vishâda, despondency.

the gaps of the earth, these Bodhisattvas Mahâsattvas, Agita, have I roused, excited, animated, fully developed to supreme, perfect enlightenment after my having arrived at supreme, perfect enlightenment in this world. I have, moreover, fully matured, established, confirmed, instructed, perfected these young men of good family in their Bodhisattvaship. And these Bodhisattvas Mahâsattvas, Agita, occupy in this Saha-world the domain of the ether-element below. Only thinking of the lesson they have to study, and devoted to thoroughly comprehend it, these young men of good family have no liking for social gatherings, nor for bustling crowds; they do not put off their tasks, and are strenuous[1]. These young men of good family, Agita, delight in seclusion[2], are fond of seclusion. These young men of good family do not dwell in the immediate vicinity of gods and men, they not being fond of bustling crowds. These young men of good family find their luxury in the pleasure of the law, and apply themselves to Buddha-knowledge.

And on that occasion the Lord uttered the following stanzas:

37. These Bodhisattvas, immense, inconceivable and beyond measure, endowed with magic power, wisdom, and learning, have progressed in knowledge for many kotis of Æons.

38. It is I who have brought them to maturity for enlightenment, and it is in my field that they

[1] It will be remarked that these Bodhisattvas are represented as pupils or young monks under training, Srâmaneras.

[2] Vivekârâmâh; viveka at the same time means 'discrimination.'

have their abode; by me alone have they been brought to maturity; these Bodhisattvas are my sons.

39. All have devoted themselves to a hermit life[1] and are assiduous in shunning places of bustle; they walk detached, these sons of mine, following my precepts in their lofty course.

40. They dwell in the domain of ether, in the lower portion of the field, those heroes who, unwearied, are striving day and night to attain superior knowledge.

41. All strenuous, of good memory, unshaken in the immense strength of their intelligence, those serene sages preach the law, all radiant, as being my sons.

42. Since the time when I reached this superior (or foremost) enlightenment, at the town of Gayâ, at the foot of the tree, and put in motion the all-surpassing wheel of the law, I have brought to maturity all of them for superior enlightenment.

43. These words I here speak are faultless, really true; believe me, all of you who hear me: verily, I have reached superior enlightenment, and it is by me alone that all have been brought to maturity.

The Bodhisattva Mahâsattva Maitreya and those numerous hundred thousands of myriads of ko*t*is of Bodhisattvas were struck with wonder, amazement, and surprise, (and thought): How is it possible that within so short a moment, within the lapse of so short a time so many Bodhisattvas, so countless, have been roused and made fully ripe to reach supreme, perfect enlightenment? Then the Bodhi-

[1] Âra*n*yadhutâbhiyukta; âra*n*yadhuta, essentially the same as Pâli ârañ*ñ*akaṅga, is one of the thirteen Dhutâṅgas.

sattva Mahâsattva Maitreya asked the Lord: How then, O Lord, has the Tathâgata, after he left, when a prince royal, Kapilavastu, the town of the *S*âkyas, arrived at supreme, perfect enlightenment on the summit of the terrace of enlightenment, not far from the town of Gayâ, somewhat more than forty years since, O Lord? How then has the Lord, the Tathâgata, within so short a lapse of time, been able to perform the endless task of a Tathâgata, to exercise the leadership of a Tathâgata, the energy of a Tathâgata? How has the Tathâgata, within so short a time, been able to rouse and bring to maturity for supreme, perfect enlightenment this host of Bodhisattvas, this multitude of Bodhisattvas, a multitude so great that it would be impossible to count the whole of it, even if one were to continue counting for hundred thousands of myriads of ko*t*is of Æons? These Bodhisattvas, so innumerable, O Lord, so countless, having long followed a spiritual course of life and planted roots of goodness under many hundred thousands of Buddhas, have in the course of many hundred thousands of Æons become finally ripe.

It is just as if some man, young and youthful, a young man with black hair and in the prime of youth, twenty-five years of age, would represent centenarians as his sons, and say: 'Here, young men of good family, you see my sons;' and if those centenarians would declare: 'This is the father who begot us.' Now, Lord, the speech of that man would be incredible, hard to be believed by the public. It is the same case with the Tathâgata, who but lately has arrived at supreme, perfect enlightenment, and with these Bodhisattvas Mahâsattvas, so immense in number, who for many hundred thousand myriads of ko*t*is of Æons, having observed a spiritual course of life, have long since come to certainty in regard to Tathâgata-knowledge; who are able to plunge in and again rise from the hundred thousand sorts of meditation[1]; who are adepts at the preparatories to noble transcendent wisdom, have accomplished the preparatories to noble transcendent wisdom[2]; who are clever on the Buddha-ground, able in the (ecclesiastical) Council and in Tathâgata duties; who are the wonder[3] and admiration of the world; who are possessed of great vigour, strength, and power. And the Lord says: From the very beginning have I roused, brought to maturity, fully developed them to be fit for this Bodhisattva position. It is I who have displayed this energy and vigour after arriving at supreme, perfect enlightenment. But, O Lord, how can we have faith in the words of the Tathâgata, when he says: The Tathâgata speaks infallible truth? The Tathâgata must know that the Bodhisattvas who have newly entered the vehicle are apt to fall into doubt on this head; after the extinction of the Tathâgata those who hear this Dharmaparyâya will not accept, not believe, not trust it. Hence, O Lord, they will design acts tending to the ruin of the law. Therefore, O Lord, deign to explain us this matter, that we may be free from perplexity, and that the Bodhisattvas who in future shall hear it, be they young

[1] Samâdhimukha*s*atasahasrasamâpadyanavyutthânaku*s*alâh. I suppose that for mukha, point, principal point, side, face, we have to read sukha, ecstasy.

[2] Mahâbhig*ñ*âparikarmaniryâtâ mahâbhig*ñ*âk*ri*taparikarmâ*n*a*h*.

[3] Pa*nd*itâ Buddhabhûmau saṅgîtiku*s*alâ*h*, Tathâgatadharmâ*n*â*m*.

men of good family or young ladies, may not fall into doubt.

On that occasion the Bodhisattva Mahâsattva Maitreya addressed the Lord with the following stanzas:

44. When thou wert born in Kapilavastu, the home of the *S*âkyas, thou didst leave it and reach enlightenment at the town of Gayâ[1]. That is a short time ago, O Lord of the world.

45. And now thou hast so great a crowd of followers, these sages who for many ko*t*is of Æons have fulfilled their duties, stood firm in magic power, unshaken, well disciplined, accomplished in the might of wisdom;

46. These, who are untainted as the lotus is by water; who to-day have flocked hither after rending the earth, and are standing all with joined hands, respectful and strong in memory, the sons of the Master of the world[2].

47. How will these Bodhisattvas believe this great wonder? Expel (all) doubt, tell the cause, and show how the matter really is.

---

[1] The succint form in which the events of the legendary life of the *S*âkya prince are told is remarkable, especially if we bear in mind that the first going out (nishkrama*n*a) of a young boy (kumâra) usually takes place four months after his birth; the rite of 'giving rice food,' annaprâ*s*ana, takes place in the sixth month; this rite has its counterpart in Su*g*âtâ's providing Gautama with milk porridge and honey. Another rite, that of shaving the hair with the exception of a tuft on the crown, the *k*û*d*âkarman, commonly follows the annaprâ*s*ana; in the case of Gautama, however, it is represented to be subsequent on the kumâra having left his home. In so far as he cut off his hair at the time of his entering a spiritual life, the act agrees with the *k*û*d*âkarman at the upanayana or initiation of boys.

[2] Lokâdhipatisya putrâ*h*.

48. It is as if there were some man, a young man with black hair, twenty years old or somewhat more, who presented as his sons some centenarians,

49. And the latter, covered with wrinkles and grey-haired, declared the (young) man to be their father. But such (a young man) never having sons of such appearance, it would be difficult to believe, O Lord of the world, that they were sons to so young a man.

50. In the same manner, O Lord, we are unable to conceive how these numerous Bodhisattvas of good memory and excelling in wisdom, who have been well instructed during thousands of ko*t*is of Æons;

51. Who are firm, of keen intelligence, lovely and agreeable to sight, free from hesitation in the decisions on law, praised by the Leaders of the world;

52. Who in freedom live in the wood[1]; who unattached in the element of ether constantly display their energy, who are the sons of Sugata striving after this Buddha-ground;

53. How will this be believed when the Leader of the world shall be completely extinct? After hearing it from the Lord's own mouth we shall never more feel any doubt.

54. May Bodhisattvas never come to grief by having doubt on this head. Grant us, O Lord, a truthful account how these Bodhisattvas have been brought to maturity by thee.

---

[1] Vane, which, especially in the more ancient language, also means a cloud, the region of clouds.

CHAPTER XV.

DURATION OF LIFE OF THE TATHÂGATA.

Thereupon the Lord addressed the entire host of Bodhisattvas: Trust me, young men of good family, believe in the Tathâgata speaking a veracious word. A second time the Lord addressed the Bodhisattvas: Trust me, young gentlemen of good family, believe in the Tathâgata speaking a veracious word. A third and last time the Lord addressed the Bodhisattvas: Trust me, young men of good family, believe in the Tathâgata speaking a veracious word. Then the entire host of Bodhisattvas with Maitreya, the Bodhisattva Mahâsattva at their head, stretched out the joined hands and said to the Lord: Expound this matter, O Lord; expound it, O Sugata; we will believe in the word of the Tathâgata. A second time the entire host, &c. &c. A third time the entire host, &c. &c.

The Lord, considering that the Bodhisattvas repeated their prayer up to three times, addressed them thus: Listen then, young men of good family. The force of a strong resolve which I assumed[1] is such, young men of good family, that this world, including gods, men, and demons, acknowledges: Now has the Lord Sâkyamuni, after going out from the home of the Sâkyas, arrived at supreme, perfect enlightenment, on the summit of the terrace of

[1] Or, the power of supremacy which forms my attribute, mamâdhishthânabalâdhânam.

enlightenment at the town of Gayâ. But, young men of good family, the truth is that many hundred thousand myriads of ko*t*is of Æons ago I have arrived at supreme, perfect enlightenment. By way of example, young men of good family, let there be the atoms of earth of fifty hundred thousand myriads of ko*t*is of worlds; let there exist some man who takes one of those atoms of dust and then goes in an eastern direction fifty hundred thousand myriads of ko*t*is of worlds further on, there to deposit that atom of dust; let in this manner the man carry away from all those worlds the whole mass of earth, and in the same manner, and by the same act as supposed, deposit all those atoms in an eastern direction[1]. Now, would you think, young men of good family, that any one should be able to imagine, weigh, count, or determine (the number of) those worlds? The Lord having thus spoken, the Bodhisattva Mahâsattva Maitreya and the entire host of Bodhisattvas replied: They are incalculable, O Lord, those worlds, countless, beyond the range of thought. Not even all the disciples and Pratyekabuddhas, O Lord, with their Ârya-knowledge, will be able to imagine, weigh, count, or determine them. For us also, O Lord, who are Bodhisattvas standing on the place from whence there is no turning back, this point lies beyond the sphere of our comprehension; so innumerable, O Lord, are those worlds.

This said, the Lord spoke to those Bodhisattvas Mahâsattvas as follows: I announce to you, young men of good family, I declare to you: However numerous

[1] This passage is a repetition, in shorter form, of what is found in chapter VII; see p. 153.

be those worlds where that man deposits those atoms of dust and where he does not, there are not, young men of good family, in all those hundred thousands of myriads of ko*t*is of worlds so many dust atoms as there are hundred thousands of myriads of ko*t*is of Æons since I have arrived at supreme, perfect enlightenment[1]. From the moment, young men of good family, when I began preaching the law to creatures in this Saha-world and in hundred thousands of myriads of ko*t*is of other worlds, and (when) the other Tathâgatas, Arhats, &c., such as the Tathâgata Dîpankara and the rest whom I have mentioned in the lapse of time (preached), (from that moment) have I, young men of good family, for the complete Nirvâ*n*a of those Tathâgatas, &c., created all that with the express view to skilfully preach the law[2]. Again, young men of good family, the Tathâgata, considering the different degrees of faculty and strength of succeeding generations,

---

[1] *S*âkyamuni here declares, in the most emphatic manner, not only that he has existed from eternity, but that he is the All-wise, the Buddha from the beginning. The world thinks that he has become all-wise at Gayâ, a short time before, but in reality he has been the All-wise from eternity. In other words, the meaning of his being a common man who had reached enlightenment under the Bodhi-tree near Gayâ, is declared by himself to be a delusion. Further, it will be remarked that *S*âkyamuni and the Tathâgata Mahâbhi*g*ñâ*g*ñânâbhibhû in chapter VII are identical, though apparently diversified.

[2] Teshâ*m* *k*a Tathâgatânâm Arhatâ*m* samyaksambuddhânâ*m* parinirvâ*n*âya mayaiva tâni, kulaputrâ, upâyakau*s*alyadharmade*s*anâyâ (abhi) nirhâranirmitâni. Burnouf translates as if he read te—°nirmitâ*h*, so that 'those Tathâgatas—have been created.' Both readings come essentially to the same; in either case *S*âkyamuni is the creator, the really existing being; the other Tathâgatas are emanations from him or apparent beings.

reveals at each (generation) his own name, reveals a state in which Nirvâ*n*a has not yet been reached[1], and in different ways he satisfies the wants of (different) creatures through various Dharmaparyâyas[2]. This being the case, young men of good family, the Tathâgata declares to the creatures, whose dispositions are so various and who possess so few roots of goodness, so many evil propensities: I am young of age, monks; having left my father's home, monks, I have lately arrived at supreme, perfect enlightenment[3]. When, however, the Tathâgata, who so long ago arrived at perfect enlightenment, declares himself to have but lately arrived at perfect enlightenment, he does so in order to lead creatures to full ripeness and make them go in. Therefore have these Dharmaparyâyas been revealed; and it is for the education of creatures, young men of good family, that the Tathâgata has revealed all Dharmaparyâyas. And, young men of good family, the word that the Tathâgata delivers on behalf of the education of creatures, either under his own appearance or under another's, either on his own authority[4] or under the mask[5] of another, all that the Tathâ-

[1] Instead of the last clause we find in the margin, 'reveals (or declares) at each his own Nirvâ*n*a.' The material difference is slight, for the temporal appearances of the everlasting being are final and multifarious, but the being itself is one and everlasting. *S*âkyamuni is, in reality, the one and everlasting brahma.

[2] The Tathâgata, in his proper being well understood, is not only the Devâtideva, the supreme god of gods, of Buddhism, but of all religions in the world; from him are all scriptures.

[3] In various periods mankind wants renewed revelation; hence Vish*n*u, for Dharma's sake, descends on earth.

[4] Âtmârambanena (sic), properly, on his own base.

[5] Aparâvara*n*ena. One may also render it by 'under the cloak of another.'

gata declares, all those Dharmaparyâyas spoken by the Tathâgata are true. There can be no question of untruth from the part of the Tathâgata in this respect. For the Tathâgata sees the triple world as it really is: it is not born, it dies not; it is not conceived, it springs not into existence; it moves not in a whirl, it becomes not extinct; it is not real, nor unreal; it is not existing, nor non-existing; it is not such, nor otherwise[1], nor false. The Tathâgata sees the triple world, not as the ignorant, common people, he seeing things always present to him; indeed, to the Tathâgata, in his position, no laws are concealed. In that respect any word that the Tathâgata speaks is true, not false. But in order to produce the roots of goodness in the creatures, who follow different pursuits and behave according to different notions, he reveals various Dharmaparyâyas with various fundamental principles. The Tathâgata then, young men of good family, does what he has to do. The Tathâgata who so long ago was perfectly enlightened is unlimited in the duration of his life, he is everlasting. Without being extinct, the Tathâgata makes a show of extinction, on behalf of those who have to be educated. And even now, young gentlemen of good family, I have not accomplished my ancient Bodhisattva-course, and the measure of my lifetime is not full. Nay, young men of good family, I shall yet have twice as many hundred thousand myriads of ko*t*is of Æons before the measure of my lifetime be full[2].

---

[1] Or, it is not as it ought to be, nor wrong.

[2] Virtually he has existed from the very beginning, from an infinite period; infinity multiplied by two remains infinity.

I announce final extinction, young men of good family, though myself I do not become finally extinct[1]. For in this way, young men of good family, I bring (all) creatures to maturity, lest creatures in whom goodness is not firmly rooted, who are unholy, miserable, eager of sensual pleasures, blind and obscured by the film of wrong views, should, by too often seeing me, take to thinking: 'The Tathâgata is staying[2],' and fancy that all is a child's play[3]; (lest they) by thinking 'we are near that Tathâgata' should fail to exert themselves in order to escape the triple world and not conceive how precious[4] the Tathâgata is. Hence, young men of good family, the Tathâgata skilfully utters these words: The apparition of the Tathâgatas, monks, is precious (and rare). For in the course of many hundred thousand myriads of ko*t*is of Æons creatures may happen to see a Tathâgata or not to see him[5]. Therefore and upon that ground, young men of good family, I say: The apparition of the Tathâgatas, monks, is precious (and rare).

---

[1] All this is perfectly true in the mouth of a personification of the sun, of time, of eternity, or of λόγος, but quite unintelligible in the mouth of some individual of the human race. Moments of time expire, time never ceases. The termination of every day, month, year, &c. must remind us of our being mortal, and is a call from the Buddha to us, an inducement to lead a virtuous and holy life.

[2] I. e. time stands still; we shall never die.

[3] In the margin added, not realise the idea of his (i. e. time's) preciousness.

[4] Durlabha.

[5] Nobody is certain whether the present day is his last or not; in other words, whether he has seen the Tathâgata for the last time, or shall see him again to-morrow, &c. Therefore the Tathâgata is so precious.

By being more and more convinced of the apparition of the Tathâgatas being precious (or rare) they will feel surprised and sorry, and whilst not seeing the Tathâgata they will get a longing to see him. The good roots developing from their earnest thought relating to the Tathâgata[1] will lastingly tend to their weal, benefit, and happiness; in consideration of which the Tathâgata announces final extinction, though he himself does not become finally extinct, on behalf of the creatures who have to be educated. Such, young men of good family, is the Tathâgata's manner of teaching[2]; when the Tathâgata speaks in this way, there is from his part no falsehood.

Let us suppose an analogous case, young men of good family. There is some physician, learned, intelligent, prudent, clever in allaying all sorts of diseases. That man has many sons, ten, twenty, thirty, forty, fifty, or a hundred[3]. The physician once being abroad, all his children incur a disease from poison or venom. Overcome with the grievous pains[4] caused by that poison or venom which burns them they lie rolling on the ground. Their father, the physician, comes home from his journey at the time when his sons are suffering from that poison or venom. Some of them have perverted notions, others have right notions, but all suffer the same pain. On seeing their father they cheerfully greet

---

[1] I.e. the good designs germinating in man when he is thinking of the shortness of life, the transitoriness of time.

[2] Desanâparyâya.

[3] A marginal reading improves upon the more ancient text by adding, or a thousand.

[4] Duhkhâbhir vedanâbhih.

him and say: Hail, dear father, that thou art come back in safety and welfare! Now deliver us from our evil, be it poison or venom; let us live, dear father. And the physician, seeing his sons befallen with disease, overcome with pain and rolling on the ground, prepares a great remedy, having the required colour, smell, and taste, pounds it on a stone and gives it as a potion to his sons, with these words: Take this great remedy, my sons, which has the required colour, smell, and taste. For by taking this great remedy, my sons, you shall soon be rid of this poison or venom; you shall recover and be healthy. Those amongst the children of the physician that have right notions, after seeing the colour of the remedy, after smelling the smell and tasting the flavour, quickly take it, and in consequence of it are soon totally delivered from their disease. But the sons who have perverted notions cheerfully greet their father and say: Hail, dear father, that thou art come back in safety and welfare; do heal us. So they speak, but they do not take the remedy offered, and that because, owing to the perverseness of their notions, that remedy does not please them, in colour, smell, nor taste. Then the physician reflects thus: These sons of mine must have become perverted in their notions owing to this poison or venom, as they do not take the remedy nor hail me[1]. Therefore will I by some able device induce these sons to take this remedy. Prompted by this desire he speaks to those sons as follows: I am old, young men of good family, decrepit, advanced in years, and my term of life is near at hand; but be not sorry, young men

[1] One would rather have expected, joyfully accept my injunction.

of good family, do not feel dejected; here have I prepared a great remedy for you; if you want it, you may take it. Having thus admonished them, he skilfully betakes himself to another part of the country and lets his sick sons know that he has departed life. They are extremely sorry and bewail him extremely: So then he is dead, our father and protector; he who begat us; he, so full of bounty! now are we left without a protector. Fully aware of their being orphans and of having no refuge, they are continually plunged in sorrow, by which their perverted notions make room for right notions. They acknowledge that remedy possessed of the required colour, smell, and taste to have the required colour, smell, and taste, so that they instantly take it, and by taking it are delivered from their evil. Then, on knowing that these sons are delivered from evil, the physician shows himself again. Now, young men of good family, what is your opinion? Would any one charge[1] that physician with falsehood on account of his using that device? No, certainly not, Lord; certainly not, Sugata. He proceeded: In the same manner, young men of good family, I have arrived at supreme, perfect enlightenment since an immense, incalculable number of hundred thousands of myriads of kotis of Æons, but from time to time I display such able devices to the creatures, with the view of educating them, without there being in that respect any falsehood on my part.

In order to set forth this subject more extensively the Lord on that occasion uttered the following stanzas:

[1] *Kodayet*; a would-be correction by a later hand has *samvadet*.

1. An inconceivable number of thousands of ko*t*is of Æons, never to be measured, is it since I reached superior (or first) enlightenment and never ceased to teach the law.

2. I roused many Bodhisattvas and established them in Buddha-knowledge. I brought myriads of ko*t*is of beings, endless, to full ripeness in many ko*t*is of Æons.

3. I show the place of extinction, I reveal to (all) beings a device[1] to educate them, albeit I do not become extinct at the time, and in this very place continue preaching the law.

4. There I rule myself as well as all beings, I[2]. But men of perverted minds, in their delusion, do not see me standing there[3].

5. In the opinion that my body is completely extinct, they pay worship, in many ways, to the relics, but me they see not. They feel (however) a certain aspiration by which their mind becomes right[4].

6. When such upright (or pious), mild, and gentle creatures leave off their bodies, then I assemble the crowd of disciples and show myself here[5] on the G*ri*dhrakû*t*a.

7. And then I speak thus to them, in this very

[1] Upâyam. It has been remarked above that upâya likewise denotes the world, the energy of nature (pra*g*ñâ).

[2] Tatrâham âtmânam adhish*th*ihâmi, sarvâ*n*a satvâna tathaiva *k*âha*m*. Adhish*th*â is constructed both with the accusative case and the genitive.

[3] Tatraiva.

[4] I. e. comes into the right disposition, or becomes pious.

[5] This important word has been omitted by Burnouf. The Tathâgata represents himself to be Dharmarâ*g*a, the judge of the departed, the god rewarding the pious and brave after their death.

place: I was not completely extinct at that time; it was but a device of mine, monks; repeatedly am I born in the world of the living.

8. Honoured by other beings, I show them my superior enlightenment, but you would not obey my word, unless the Lord of the world enter Nirvâna.

9. I see how the creatures are afflicted, but I do not show them my proper being. Let them first have an aspiration to see me; then I will reveal to them the true law.

10. Such has always been my firm resolve during an inconceivable number of thousands of kotis of Æons, and I have not left this Gridhrakûta for other abodes[1].

11. And when creatures behold this world and imagine that it is burning, even then my Buddha-field is teeming with gods and men.

12. They dispose of manifold amusements, kotis of pleasure gardens, palaces, and aerial cars; (this field) is embellished by hills of gems and by trees abounding with blossoms and fruits.

13. And aloft gods are striking musical instruments and pouring a rain of Mandâras[2] by which they are covering me, the disciples and other sages who are striving after enlightenment.

14. So is my field here, everlastingly; but others fancy that it is burning; in their view this world is most terrific, wretched, replete with number of woes[3].

---

[1] *S*ayyâsana.

[2] The form constantly used in Buddhist writings, both in Pâli and Sanskrit, is Mandârava. The whole description of Heaven, or Paradise, bears the stamp of being taken, with more or less modification, from a non-Buddhistic source.

[3] There are different beliefs about the realm of the dead; the

15. Ay, many ko*t*is of years they may pass without ever having mentioned my name, the law, or my congregation[1]. That is the fruit of sinful deeds.

16. But when mild and gentle beings are born in this world of men, they immediately see me revealing the law, owing to their good works.

17. I never speak to them of the infinitude of my action. Therefore, I am, properly, existing since long[2], and yet declare: The *G*inas are rare (or precious).

18. Such is the glorious power of my wisdom that knows no limit, and the duration of my life is as long as an endless period; I have acquired it after previously following a due course.

19. Feel no doubt concerning it, O sages, and leave off all uncertainty: the word I here pronounce is really true; my word is never false.

20. For even as that physician skilled in devices, for the sake of his sons whose notions were perverted, said that he had died although he was still alive, and even as no sensible man would charge that physician with falsehood;

21. So am I the father of the world, the Self-

Brahma-world and Paradise are usually depicted as places of bliss, but Yama's kingdom is often represented as a kind of hell, though at other times the same King of righteousness is said to have gathered round him the blessed company of the pious departed.

[1] Elsewhere we find Vi*s*vanâtha, the Universal Lord, called Sangame*s*vara, the Lord of the gathering. Yama is Vaivasvata Sangamana *g*anânam, he of solar race, the gatherer of men, Rig-veda X, 14, 1.

[2] Tenâha sush*th*û ha *k*irasya bhomi. The phrase admits of being translated, 'therefore, truly, I am (repeatedly) born after a long time.'

born[1], the Healer[2], the Protector of all creatures. Knowing them to be perverted, infatuated, and ignorant I teach final rest, myself not being at rest.

22. What reason should I have to continually manifest myself? When men become unbelieving, unwise, ignorant, careless, fond of sensual pleasures, and from thoughtlessness run into misfortune,

23. Then I, who know the course of the world, declare: I am so and so[3], (and consider): How can I incline them to enlightenment? how can they become partakers of the Buddha-laws[4]?

---

[1] Lokapitâ Svayambhû*h*. The juxtaposition of these two words shows to an evidence that *S*âkyamuni is represented as Brahma, the uncreated Being, existing from eternity, the Father of the world, All-father.

[2] In a moral sense the Saviour, mythologically Apollo.

[3] I.e. I am so in reality, tathâtathâham. Burnouf's rendering, 'I am the Tathâgata,' points to a reading tathâgato 'ham, which comes to the same.

[4] Katha*m* nu bodhâya sanâmayeya (Sansk. sannâmayeya) katha buddhadharmâ*n*a bhaveyu lâbhina*h*.

CHAPTER XVI.

OF PIETY.

While this exposition of the duration of the Tathâgata's lifetime was being given, innumerable, countless creatures profited by it. Then the Lord addressed the Bodhisattva Mahâsattva Maitreya: While this exposition of the duration of the Tathâgata's lifetime was being given, A*g*ita, sixty-eight hundred thousand myriads of ko*t*is of Bodhisattvas, comparable to the sands of the Ganges[1], have acquired the faculty to acquiesce in the law that has no origin. A thousand times more Bodhisattvas Mahâsattvas have obtained Dhâra*n*î[2]; and other Bodhisattvas Mahâsattvas, equal to the dust atoms of one third of a macrocosm, have by hearing this Dharmaparyâya obtained the faculty of unhampered view. Other Bodhisattvas Mahâsattvas again, equal to the dust atoms of two-third parts of a macrocosm, have by hearing this Dharmaparyâya obtained the Dhâra*n*î that makes hundred thousand ko*t*is of revolutions.

[1] Ash*t*ashash*t*înâ*m* Gaṅgâ° Bodhisatvako*t*inayuta*s*atasahasrâ*n*â*m*. Burnouf connects ash*t*ashash*t*înâm with Gaṅgâ, and translates, 'soixante huit Ganges.' His version is justified by the analogy of other passages.

[2] Dhâra*n*î usually denotes a magic spell, a talisman. Here and there it interchanges with dhâra*n*â, support, the bearing in mind, attention. The synonymous rakshâ embraces the meanings of talisman and protection, support. It is not easy to decide what is intended in the text.

Again, other Bodhisattvas Mahâsattvas, equal to the dust atoms of a whole macrocosm, have by hearing this Dharmaparyâya moved forward the wheel that never rolls back. Some Bodhisattvas Mahâsattvas, equal to the dust atoms of a mean universe, have by hearing this Dharmaparyâya moved forward the wheel of spotless radiance. Other Bodhisattvas Mahâsattvas, equal to the dust atoms of a small universe, have by hearing this Dharmaparyâya come so far that they will reach supreme, perfect enlightenment after eight births. Other Bodhisattvas Mahâsattvas, equal to the dust atoms of four worlds of four continents[1], have by hearing this Dharmaparyâya become such as to require four births (more) before reaching supreme, perfect enlightenment. Other Bodhisattvas Mahâsattvas, equal to the dust atoms of three four-continental worlds, have by hearing this Dharmaparyâya become such as to require three births (more) before reaching supreme, perfect enlightenment. Other Bodhisattvas Mahâsattvas, equal to the dust atoms of two four-continental worlds, have by hearing this Dharmaparyâya become such as to require two births (more) before reaching supreme, perfect enlightenment. Other Bodhisattvas Mahâsattvas, equal to the dust atoms of one four-continental world, have by hearing this Dharmaparyâya become such as to require but one birth before reaching supreme, perfect enlightenment. Other Bodhisattvas Mahâsattvas, equal to the dust atoms of eight macrocosms consisting of three parts, have by hearing this Dharmaparyâya conceived the idea of supreme, perfect enlightenment[2].

[1] Or, perhaps, of one whole world of four continents.

[2] The number 8 being the half of 16, the number of kalâs of a

No sooner had the Lord given this exposition determining the duration and periods of the law, than there fell from the upper sky a great rain of Mandârava and great Mandârava flowers that covered and overwhelmed all the hundred thousand myriads of ko*t*is of Buddhas who were seated on their thrones at the foot of the jewel trees in hundred thousands of myriads of ko*t*is of worlds. It also covered and overwhelmed the Lord *S*âkyamuni, the Tathâgata, &c., and the Lord Prabhûtaratna, the Tathâgata, &c., the latter sitting fully extinct on his throne, as well as that entire host of Bodhisattvas and the four classes of the audience. A rain of celestial powder of sandal and agallochum trickled down from the sky, whilst higher up in the firmament the great drums resounded, without being struck, with a pleasant, sweet, and deep sound. Double pieces of fine heavenly cloth fell down by hundreds and thousands from the upper sky; necklaces, half-necklaces, pearl necklaces, gems, jewels, noble gems, and noble jewels were seen high in the firmament, hanging down from every side in all directions of space, while all around thousands of jewel censers, containing priceless, exquisite incense, were moving of their own accord. Bodhisattvas Mahâsattvas were seen holding above each Tathâgata, high aloft, a row of jewel umbrellas stretching as high as the Brahma-world. So acted the Bodhisattvas Mahâsattvas in respect to all the innumerable hundred

whole circle, it may be inferred that the description in the text alludes to the stars of that half of the sphere which is at the time below the horizon. Those stars then have reached Nirvâ*n*a, though not the immortal one.

thousands of myriads of kotis of Buddhas[1]. Severally they celebrated these Buddhas in appropriate stanzas, sacred hymns in praise of the Buddhas.

And on that occasion the Bodhisattva Mahâsattva Maitreya uttered the following stanzas:

1. Wonderful is the law which the Sugata has expounded, the law we never heard before; how great the majesty of the Leaders is, and how infinite the duration of their life!

2. And on hearing such a law imparted by the Sugata from face to face, thousands of kotis of creatures, the genuine sons of the Leader of the world, have been pervaded with gladness.

3. Some have reached the point of supreme enlightenment from whence there is no return, others are standing on the lower stage[2]; some have reached the standpoint of having an unhampered view, and others have obtained thousands of kotis of Dhâranîs[3].

4. There are others, (as) atoms[4], who have reached supreme Buddha-knowledge. Some, again, will after eight births become *G*inas seeing the infinite[5].

5. Among those who hear this law from the Master, some will obtain enlightenment and see the truth[6] after four births, others after three, others after two.

---

[1] The version followed by Burnouf is somewhat longer.

[2] Dhâranîye dharâyâm, which is ambiguous, because the latter may stand for adharâyâm. That dhâranî can denote bhûmi I infer from the phrase (bhûmi) lokadhârinî, Taitt. Âranyaka X, 1.

[3] The translation doubtful.

[4] Paramânu; the literal rendering is, others, extremely faint (or small).

[5] Cf. the phrase 'to see Nirvâna.'

[6] Evidently the same as 'seeing Nirvâna,' as appears from what is added and the analogy with the preceding stanza.

6. Some among them will become all-knowing[1] after one birth, in the next following existence[2]. Such will be the perfect result of learning the duration of life of the Chief.

7. Innumerable, countless as the atoms of the eight fields, are the ko*t*is of beings who by hearing this law have conceived the idea of superior enlightenment.

8. Such is the effect produced by the great Seer, when he reveals this Buddha-state that is endless and has no limit, which is as immense as the element of ether.

9. Many thousand ko*t*is of angels, Indras, and Brahma-angels, like the sands of the Ganges, have flocked hither from thousands of ko*t*is of distant fields and have poured a rain of Mandâravas.

10. They move in the sky like birds, and strew fragrant powder of sandal and agallochum, to cover ceremoniously the Chief of *G*inas withal.

11. High aloft tymbals without being struck emit sweet sounds; thousands of ko*t*is of white cloth whirl down upon the Chiefs.

12. Thousands of ko*t*is of jewel censers of costly incense move of their own accord on every side to honour the mighty[3] Lord of the world.

13. Innumerable wise Bodhisattvas hold myriads of ko*t*is of umbrellas, elevated and made of noble jewels, like chaplets[4], up to the Brahma-world.

14. The sons of Sugata, in their great joy, have

[1] Another term for seeing Nirvâ*n*a.

[2] These four descriptions of Bodhisattvas agree in the main with the four degrees of holiness, of Srotaâpanna, Sak*ri*dâgâmin, Anâgâmin, and Arhat.

[3] Tâyin.

[4] Utansakân (sic).

attached beautiful triumphal streamers at the top of the banner staffs[1] in honour of the Leaders whom they celebrate in thousands of stanzas.

15. Such a marvellous, extraordinary, prodigious, splendid[2] phenomenon, O Leader, is being displayed by all those beings who are gladdened by the exposition of the duration of life (of the Tathâgata).

16. Grand is the matter now (occurring) in the ten points of space, and (great) the sound raised by the Leaders; thousands of ko*t*is of living beings are refreshed and gifted with virtue for enlightenment.

Thereupon the Lord addressed the Bodhisattva Mahâsattva Maitreya: Those beings, A*g*ita, who during the exposition of this Dharmaparyâya in which the duration of the Tathâgata's life is revealed have entertained, were it but a single thought of trust, or have put belief in it, how great a merit are they to produce, be they young men and young ladies of good family? Listen then, and mind it well, how great the merit is they shall produce. Let us suppose the case, A*g*ita, that some young man or young lady of good family, desirous of supreme, perfect enlightenment, for eight hundred thousand myriads of ko*t*is of Æons practises the five perfections of virtue (Pâramitâs), to wit, perfect charity in alms, perfect morality, perfect forbearance, perfect energy, perfect meditation—perfect wisdom being excepted[3];

---

[1] Dhva*g*âgre; a marginal reading has dhva*g*â*m* *k*a (sic).

[2] Etâd*r*i*s*â*sk*arya vi*s*ish*t*am adbhutâ*h* (r. adbhuta*m*), vi*k*itra dar*s*ent' ima(m) adya Nâyaka.

[3] Virahitâ*h* pra*g*ñâpâramitâyâ(*h*). The five specified virtues are identical with those enumerated in Lalita-vistara, p. 38, and slightly different from those as found in the Pâli scriptures. Out of the five virtues, four, viz. *s*îla, kshânti, vîrya, dhyâna, answer to

let us, on the other hand, suppose the case, Agita, that a young man or young lady of good family, on hearing this Dharmaparyâya containing the exposition of the duration of the Tathâgata's life, conceives were it but a single thought of trust or puts belief in it; then that former accumulation of merit[1], that accumulation of good connected with the five perfections of virtue, (that accumulation) which has come to full accomplishment in eight hundred thousand myriads of kotis of Æons, does not equal one hundredth part of the accumulation of merit in the second case; it does not equal one thousandth part; it admits of no calculation, no counting, no reckoning, no comparison, no approximation, no secret teaching[2]. One who is possessed of such an accumulation of merit, Agita, be he a young man or a young lady of good family, will not miss supreme, perfect enlightenment; no, that is not possible.

---

dama, kshamâ, dhriti, dhî in Manu VI, 92, where vidyâ is the equivalent to the Pâramitâ of pragñâ.

[1] Punyâbhisamskâra, which may be said to be the common Buddhistic equivalent of karmâsaya, explained by Hindu scholastics to be the accumulation of moral merit and demerit. The term properly means 'one's moral disposition (at a given time as a necessary result of one's previous acts).' In a certain sense it may be contended that the sum of one's previous actions determines one's moral state at a given moment. As âsaya means disposition, character, and accumulation, we can understand how the Indian scholastics came to misunderstand the real purport of the word in karmâsaya. As to abhisamskâra, it properly means '(mental or moral) disposition, character, impression, conception.'

[2] Upanisâm api, upanishadam api na kshamate. Upanisâ is nothing else but the Prâkrit form of Sansk. upanishad. In Pâli it is explained by raho, mystery, secret lore, and kârana; the latter may mean 'mathematical operation.' See, however, the Editor's note on Sukhâvatî-vyûha, p. 31.

And on that occasion the Lord uttered the following stanzas:

17. Let a man who is seeking after this knowledge, superior Buddha-knowledge, undertake to practise in this world the five perfect virtues;

18. Let him, during eight thousand kotis of complete Æons, continue giving repeated alms to Buddhas and disciples;

19. Regaling Pratyekabuddhas and kotis of Bodhisattvas by giving meat, food and drink, clothing and lodging[1];

20. Let him build on earth refuges and monasteries of sandal-wood, and pleasant convent gardens provided with walks;

21. Let him after so bestowing gifts, various and diversified, during thousands of kotis of Æons, direct his mind to enlightenment[2];

22. Let him then, for the sake of Buddha-knowledge, keep unbroken the pure moral precepts which have been recommended by the perfect Buddhas and acknowledged by the wise;

23. Let him further develop the virtue of forbearance, be steady in the stage of meekness[3], be constant, of good memory, and patiently endure many censures;

24. Let him, moreover, for the sake of Buddha-

[1] These Pratyekabuddhas can hardly be other persons than hermits, and the Bodhisattvas must be the ministers of religion, who otherwise are called Panditas, and Vandyas, whence our Bonzes.

[2] I. e., if I rightly understand it, let him, after having lived in the world, retire from a busy life to take orders.

[3] I. e. of a monk under training.

knowledge, bear the contemptuous words of unbelievers who are rooted in pride;

25. Let him, always zealous, strenuous, studious, of good memory, without any other pre-occupation in his mind, practise meditation, during ko*t*is of Æons;

26. Let him, whether living in the forest or entering upon a vagrant life[1], go about, avoiding sloth and torpor[2], for ko*t*is of Æons;

27. Let him as a philosopher, a great philosopher[3] who finds his delight in meditation, in concentration of mind, pass eight thousand ko*t*is of Æons;

28. Let him energetically pursue enlightenment with the thought of his reaching all-knowingness, and so arrive at the highest degree of meditation;

29. Then the merit accruing to those who practise the virtues oft described, during thousands of ko*t*is of Æons,

30. (Is less than that of) a man or a woman who, on hearing the duration of my life, for a single moment believes in it; this merit is endless.

31. He who renouncing doubt, vacillation, and misgiving shall believe even for a short moment, shall obtain such a reward.

32. The Bodhisattvas also, who have practised those virtues during ko*t*is of Æons, will not be startled at hearing of this inconceivably long life of mine.

33. They will bow their heads (and think): 'May I also in future become such a one and release ko*t*is of living beings!

---

[1] *K*aṅkramam abhiruhya.

[2] Styânamiddhañ*k*a var*g*itvâ. Middha, well known from Buddhistic writings, is a would-be Sanskrit form; it ought to be m*ri*ddha, from Vedic m*ri*dhyati.

[3] I.e. a Yogin, a contemplative mystic.

34. 'As the Lord *S*âkyamuni, the Lion of the *S*âkya race, after he had occupied his seat on the terrace of enlightenment, raised his lion's roar;

35. 'So may I in future be sitting on the terrace of enlightenment, honoured by all mortals, to teach so long a life[1]!'

36. Those who are possessed of firmness of intention[2] and have learnt the principles, will understand the mystery[3] and feel no uncertainty[4].

Again, Agita, he who after hearing this Dharmaparyâya, which contains an exposition of the duration of the Tathâgata's life, apprehends it, penetrates and understands it, will produce a yet more immeasurable accumulation of merit conducive to Buddha-knowledge; unnecessary to add that he who hears such a Dharmaparyâya as this or makes others hear it; who keeps it in memory, reads, comprehends or makes others comprehend it; who writes or has it written, collects or has it collected into a volume, honours, respects, worships it with flowers, incense, perfumed garlands, ointments, powder, cloth, umbrellas, flags, streamers, (lighted) oil lamps, ghee lamps or lamps filled with scented oil, will produce a far greater accumulation of merit conducive to Buddha-knowledge.

And, Agita, as a test whether that young man or young lady of good family who hears this exposition

---

[1] It is difficult to say what difference there is between becoming Buddha or becoming Brahma, except in sound.

[2] Or strong application, the word used in the text being adhyosâya (Sansk. adhyavasâya).

[3] Sandhâbhâshya.

[4] The tenor of this stanza, and even the words, remind one of the *Sând*ilyavidyâ in *Kh*ândogya-upanishad III, 14, 4.

of the duration of the Tathâgata's life most decidedly believes in it may be deemed the following. They will behold me teaching the law[1] here on the G*ri*dhrakû*t*a[2], surrounded by a host of Bodhisattvas, attended by a host of Bodhisattvas, in the centre of the congregation of disciples. They will behold here my Buddha-field in the Saha-world, consisting of lapis lazuli and forming a level plain; forming a chequered board of eight compartments with gold threads; set off with jewel trees. They will behold the towers that the Bodhisattvas use as their abodes[3]. By this test, A*g*ita, one may know if a young man or young lady of good family has a most decided belief. Moreover, A*g*ita, I declare that a young man of good family who, after the complete extinction of the Tathâgata, shall not reject, but joyfully accept this Dharmaparyâya when hearing it, that such a young man of good family also is earnest in his belief; far more one who keeps it in memory or reads it. He who after collecting this Dharmaparyâya into a volume carries it on his shoulder[4] carries the Tathâgata on his shoulder. Such a young man or young lady of good family, A*g*ita, need make no Stûpas for me, nor monasteries; need not give to the congregation of monks medicaments for the

[1] And, pronouncing judgment.

[2] We have seen above that this is the true abode of the Dharmarâ*g*a.

[3] Kû*t*âgâraparibhogeshu Bodhisatvavâsa*m* vâ drakshyanti, properly, they will behold the dwelling of the Bodhisattvas in the towers which those Bodhisattvas have received for their use. About the technical meaning of kû*t*âgâra in Nepâl, see B. H. Hodgson, Essays, p. 49.

[4] I. e. holds it in high esteem and treats it with care.

sick or (other) requisites[1]. For, Agita, such a young man or young lady of good family has (spiritually) built for the worship of my relics Stûpas of seven precious substances reaching up to the Brahma-world in height, and with a circumference in proportion, with the umbrellas thereto belonging, with triumphal streamers, with tinkling bells and baskets; has shown manifold marks of respect to those Stûpas of relics with diverse celestial and earthly flowers, incense, perfumed garlands, ointments, powder, cloth, umbrellas, banners, flags, triumphal streamers, by various sweet, pleasant, clear-sounding tymbals and drums, by the tune, noise, sounds of musical instruments and castanets, by songs, nautch and dancing of different kinds, of many, innumerable kinds; has done those acts of worship during many, innumerable thousands of kotis of Æons. One who keeps in memory this Dharmaparyâya after my complete extinction, who reads, writes, promulgates it, Agita, shall also have built monasteries, large, spacious, extensive, made of red sandal-wood, with thirty-two pinnacles, eight stories, fit for a thousand monks, adorned with gardens and flowers, having walks furnished with lodgings, completely provided with meat, food and drink and medicaments for the sick, well equipped with all comforts. And those numerous, innumerable beings, say a hundred or a thousand or ten thousand or a koti or hundred kotis or thousand kotis or hundred thousand kotis or ten thousand times hundred thousand kotis, they

[1] This agrees with the teaching of the Vedânta that Brahma-knowledge is independent of good works; see e.g. Brahma-sûtra III, 4, 25.

must be considered to form the congregation of disciples seeing me from face to face, and must be considered as those whom I have fully blessed[1]. He who, after my complete extinction, shall keep this Dharmaparyâya, read, promulgate, or write it, he, I repeat, A*g*ita, need not build Stûpas of relics, nor worship the congregation; not necessary to tell, A*g*ita, that the young man or young lady of good family who, keeping this Dharmaparyâya, shall crown it by charity in alms, morality, forbearance, energy, meditation, or wisdom, will produce a much greater accumulation of merit; it is, in fact, immense, incalculable, infinite[2]. Just as the element of ether, A*g*ita, is boundless, to the east, south, west, north, beneath, above, and in the intermediate quarters, so immense and incalculable an accumulation of merit, conducive to Buddha-knowledge, will be produced by a young man or young lady of good family who shall keep, read, write, or cause to be written, this Dharmaparyâya. He will be zealous in worshipping the Tathâgata shrines; he will laud the disciples of the Tathâgata, praise the hundred thousands of myriads of ko*t*is of virtues of the Bodhisattvas Mahâsattvas, and expound them to others; he will be accomplished in forbearance, be moral, of good character[3], agreeable to live with, and tolerant, modest, not jealous of others, not wrathful, not vicious in mind, of good memory, strenuous and always busy, devoted to meditation in striving after the state of a Buddha, attaching great value to

[1] Paribhukta.

[2] The Vedântin does not deny the relative value of good works; see e. g. Brahma-sûtra III, 4, 26–27.

[3] Kalyâ*n*adharman.

abstract meditation, frequently engaging in abstract meditation, able in solving questions and in avoiding hundred thousands of myriads of kotis of questions. Any Bodhisattva Mahâsattva, Agita, who, after the Tathâgata's complete extinction, shall keep this Dharmaparyâya, will have the good qualities I have described. Such a young man or young lady of good family, Agita, must be considered to make for the terrace of enlightenment; that young man or young lady of good family steps towards the foot of the tree of enlightenment in order to reach enlightenment. And where that young man or young lady of good family, Agita, stands, sits, or walks, there one should make a shrine[1], dedicated to the Tathâgata, and the world, including the gods, should say: This is a Stûpa of relics of the Tathâgata.

And on that occasion the Lord uttered the following stanzas:

37. An immense mass of merit, as I have repeatedly mentioned, shall be his who, after the complete extinction of the Leader of men, shall keep this Sûtra.

38. He will have paid worship to me, and built Stûpas of relics, made of precious substances, variegated, beautiful, and splendid;

39. In height coming up to the Brahma-world, with rows of umbrellas, great in circumference[2], gorgeous, and decorated with triumphal streamers;

40. Resounding with the clear ring of bells, and decorated with silk bands, while jingles moved by

---

[1] One would rather expect, that place one should consider to be a shrine.

[2] Parinâhavantah. There is no word for Burnouf's 'proportionné' (anupûrva) in the text.

the wind form another ornament at (the shrines of) *G*ina relics[1]

41. He will have shown great honour to them by flowers, perfumes, and ointments; by music, clothes, and the repeated (sound of) tymbals.

42. He will have sweet musical instruments struck at those relics, and lamps with scented oil kept burning all around.

43. He who at the period of depravation shall keep and teach this Sûtra, he will have paid me such an infinitely varied worship.

44. He has built many ko*t*is of excellent monasteries of sandal-wood, with thirty-two pinnacles, and eight terraces high;

45. Provided with couches, with food hard and soft; furnished with excellent curtains, and having cells by thousands.

46. He has given hermitages and walks embellished by flower-gardens; many elegant objects[2] of various forms and variegated.

47. He has shown manifold worship to the host of disciples in my presence, he who, after my extinction, shall keep this Sûtra.

48. Let one be ever so good in disposition, much greater merit will he obtain who shall keep or write this Sûtra.

49. Let a man cause this to be written and

---

[1] *S*obhante *G*inadhâtushu. Burnouf gives a different translation of this passage: 'ces Stûpas, enfin, reçoivent leur éclat des reliques du Djina.'

[2] I am quite uncertain about the word in the text, u*kkh*adaka. It seems to be connected with the Pâli ussada, about which Childers, s. v., remarks that it probably means 'a protuberance.' Burnouf renders the word in our text by 'coussin.'

have it well put together in a volume; let him always worship the volume with flowers, garlands, ointments.

50. Let him constantly place near it a lamp filled with scented oil, along with full-blown lotuses and suitable[1] oblations of Michelia Champaka.

51. The man who pays such worship to the books will produce a mass of merit which is not to be measured.

52. Even as there is no measure of the element of ether, in none of the ten directions, so there is no measure of this mass of merit.

53. How much more will this be the case with one who is patient, meek, devoted, moral, studious, and addicted to meditation;

54. Who is not irascible, not treacherous, reverential towards the sanctuary, always humble towards monks, not conceited, nor neglectful;

55. Sensible and wise, not angry when he is asked a question; who, full of compassion for living beings, gives such instruction as suits them.

56. If there be such a man who (at the same time) keeps this Sûtra, he will possess a mass of merit that cannot be measured.

57. If one meets such a man as here described, a keeper of this Sûtra, one should do homage to him.

58. One should present him with divine flowers, cover him with divine clothes, and bow the head to salute his feet, in the conviction of his being a Tathâgata.

59. And at the sight of such a man one may

[1] Yuktai*h*. Burnouf must have read muktai*h*, for his translation has 'pearls.'

directly make the reflection that he is going towards the foot of the tree to arrive at superior, blessed enlightenment for the weal of all the world, including the gods.

60. And wherever such a sage is walking, standing, sitting, or lying down; wherever the hero pronounces were it but a single stanza from this Sûtra;

61. There one should build a Stûpa for the most high of men, a splendid, beautiful (Stûpa), dedicated to the Lord Buddha, the Chief, and then worship it in manifold ways.

62. That spot of the earth has been enjoyed by myself; there have I walked myself, and there have I been sitting; where that son of Buddha has stayed, there I am.

CHAPTER XVII.

INDICATION OF THE MERITORIOUSNESS OF JOYFUL ACCEPTANCE.

Thereupon the Bodhisattva Mahâsattva Maitreya said to the Lord: O Lord, one who, after hearing this Dharmaparyâya being preached, joyfully[1] accepts it, be that person a young man of good family or a young lady, how much merit, O Lord, will be produced by such a young man or young lady of good family?

And on that occasion the Bodhisattva Mahâsattva Maitreya uttered this stanza:

1. How great will be the merit of him who, after the extinction of the great Hero, shall hear this exalted Sûtra and joyfully accept it?

And the Lord said to the Bodhisattva Mahâsattva Maitreya: If any one, Agita, either a young man of good family or a young lady, after the complete extinction of the Tathâgata, hears the preaching of this Dharmaparyâya, let it be a monk or nun, a male or female lay devotee, a man of ripe understanding or a boy or girl; if the hearer joyfully accepts it, and then after the sermon rises up to go elsewhere, to a monastery, house, forest, street, village, town, or province, with the motive and express aim to expound the law such as he has understood, such as he has heard it, and according to the measure of his power,

[1] Or, gratefully.

to another person, his mother, father, kinsman, friend, acquaintance, or any other person; if the latter, after hearing, joyfully accepts, and, in consequence, communicates it to another; if the latter, after hearing, joyfully accepts, and communicates it to another; if this other, again, after hearing, joyfully accepts it, and so on in succession until a number of fifty is reached; then, A*g*ita, the fiftieth person to hear and joyfully accept the law so heard, let it be a young man of good family or a young lady, will have acquired an accumulation of merit connected with the joyful acceptance, A*g*ita, which I am going to indicate to thee. Listen, and take it well to heart; I will tell thee.

It is, A*g*ita, as if the creatures existing in the four hundred thousand Asaṅkhyeyas[1] of worlds, in any of the six states of existence, born from an egg, from a womb, from warm humidity, or from metamorphosis, whether they have a shape or have not, be they conscious or unconscious, neither conscious nor unconscious, footless, two-footed, four-footed, or many-footed, as many beings as are contained in the world of creatures,—(as if) all those had flocked together to one place. Further, suppose some man appears, a lover of virtue, a lover of good, who gives to that whole body the pleasures, sports, amusements, and enjoyments they desire, like, and relish. He gives to each of them all *G*ambudvîpa for his pleasures, sports, amusements, and enjoyments; gives bullion, gold, silver, gems, pearls, lapis lazuli, conches, stones (?), coral, carriages yoked with horses, with bullocks, with elephants; gives palaces and

[1] An incalculable great number.

towers. In this way, Agita, that master of munificence, that great master of munificence continues spending his gifts for fully eighty years. Then, Agita, that master of munificence, that great master of munificence reflects thus: All these beings have I allowed to sport and enjoy themselves, but now they are covered with wrinkles and grey-haired, old, decrepit, eighty years of age, and near the term of their life. Let me therefore initiate them in the discipline of the law revealed by the Tathâgata, and instruct them. Thereupon, Agita, the man exhorts all those beings, thereafter initiates them in the discipline of the law revealed by the Tathâgata, and makes them adopt it. Those beings learn the law from him, and in one moment, one instant, one bit of time, all become Srotaâpannas, obtain the fruit of the rank of Sakridâgâmin and of Anâgâmin, until they become Arhats, free from all imperfections, adepts in meditation, adepts in great meditation and in the meditation with eight emancipations. Now, what is thine opinion, Agita, will that master of munificence, that great master of munificence, on account of his doings, produce great merit, immense, incalculable merit? Whereupon the Bodhisattva Mahâsattva Maitreya said in reply to the Lord: Certainly, Lord; certainly, Sugata; that person, Lord, will already produce much merit on that account, because he gives to the beings all that is necessary for happiness; how much more then if he establishes them in Arhatship!

This said, the Lord spoke to the Bodhisattva Mahâsattva Maitreya as follows: I announce to thee, Agita, I declare to thee; (take) on one side the master of munificence, the great master of munificence, who produces merit by supplying all beings in the four hundred thousand Asaṅkhyeyas of worlds with all the necessaries for happiness and by establishing them in Arhatship; (take) on the other side the person who, ranking the fiftieth in the series of the oral tradition of the law, hears, were it but a single stanza, a single word, from this Dharmaparyâya and joyfully accepts it; if (we compare) the mass of merit connected with the joyful acceptance and the mass of merit connected with the charity of the master of munificence, the great master of munificence, then the greater merit will be his who, ranking the fiftieth in the series of the oral tradition of the law, after hearing were it but a single stanza, a single word, from this Dharmaparyâya, joyfully accepts it. Against this accumulation of merit, *Ag*ita, this accumulation of roots of goodness connected with that joyful acceptance, the former accumulation of merit connected with the charity of that master of munificence, that great master of munificence, and connected with the confirmation in Arhatship, does not fetch the $\frac{1}{100}$ part, not the $\frac{1}{100,000}$, not the $\frac{1}{10,000,000}$, not the $\frac{1}{1000,000,000}$, not the $\frac{1}{1000 \times 10,000,000}$, not the $\frac{1}{100,000 \times 10,000,000}$, not the $\frac{1}{100,000 \times 10,000 \times 10,000,000}$ part; it admits of no calculation, no counting, no reckoning, no comparison, no approximation, no secret teaching. So immense, incalculable, *Ag*ita, is the merit which a person, ranking the fiftieth in the series of the tradition of the law, produces by joyfully accepting, were it but a single stanza, a single word, from this Dharmaparyâya; how much more then (will) he (produce), *Ag*ita, who hears this Dharmaparyâya in my presence and then joyfully accepts it? I declare, *Ag*ita, that his accumulation of merit shall be even more immense, more incalculable.

And further, Agita, if a young man of good family or a young lady, with the design to hear this discourse on the law, goes from home to a monastery, and there hears this Dharmaparyâya for a single moment, either standing or sitting, then that person, merely by the mass of merit resulting from that action, will after the termination of his (present) life, and at the time of his second existence when he receives (another) body, become a possessor of carriages yoked with bullocks, horses, or elephants, of litters, vehicles yoked with bulls [1], and of celestial aerial cars. If further that same person at that preaching sits down, were it but a single moment, to hear this Dharmaparyâya, or persuades another to sit down or shares with him his seat, he will by the store of merit resulting from that action gain seats of Indra, seats of Brahma, thrones of a *K*akravartin. And, Agita, if some one, a young man of good family or a young lady, says to another person: Come, friend, and hear the Dharmaparyâya of the Lotus of the True Law, and if that other person owing to that exhortation is persuaded to listen, were it but a single moment, then the former will by virtue of that root of goodness, consisting in that exhortation, obtain the advantage of a connection with Bodhisattvas who have acquired Dhâra*n*î. He will become the reverse of dull, will get keen faculties, and have wisdom; in the course of a hundred thousand existences he will never have a fetid mouth, nor an offensive one; he will have no

[1] *Ri*shabhayânâ*n*âm.

diseases of the tongue, nor of the mouth; he will have no black teeth, no unequal, no yellow, no ill-ranged, no broken teeth, no teeth fallen out; his lips will not be pendulous, not turned inward, not gaping, not mutilated, not loathsome[1]; his nose will not be flat, nor wry; his face will not be long, nor wry, nor unpleasant. On the contrary, Agita, his tongue, teeth, and lips will be delicate and well-shaped; his nose long; his face perfectly round[2]; the eyebrows well-shaped; the forehead well-formed. He will receive a very complete organ of manhood. He will have the advantage that the Tathâgata renders sermons intelligible[3] to him and soon come in connection with Lords, Buddhas. Mark, Agita, how much good is produced by one's inciting were it but a single creature; how much more then by him who reverentially hears, reverentially reads, reverentially preaches, reverentially promulgates the law!

And on that occasion the Lord uttered the following stanzas:

2. Listen how great the merit is of one who, the fiftieth in the series (of tradition), hears a single stanza from this Sûtra and with placid mind joyfully adopts it.

3. Suppose there is a man in the habit of giving

---

[1] Burnouf has some terms wanting in my text; they have been added by a later hand in the margin, but the characters are indistinct.

[2] Pranîtamukhamandala; a marginal reading has prîna-mukha°.

[3] Tathâgatañ kâvavâdânubhâsakam pratilabhate. I am not sure of the real meaning of anubhâsaka; it may as well be 'suggesting.' Burnouf has, 'c'est de la bouche du Tathâgata qu'il recevra les avis et l'enseignement.'

alms to myriads of koṭis of beings, whom I have herebefore indicated by way of comparison [1]; all of them he satisfies during eighty years.

4. Then seeing that old age has approached for them, that their brow is wrinkled and their head grey (he thinks): Alas, how all beings come to decay! Let me therefore admonish them by (speaking of) the law.

5. He teaches them the law here on earth and points to the state of Nirvâṇa hereafter. 'All existences' (he says) 'are like a mirage; hasten to become disgusted with all existence.'

6. All creatures, by hearing the law from that charitable person, become at once Arhats, free from imperfections, and living their last life.

7. Much more merit than by that person will be acquired by him who through unbroken tradition shall hear were it but a single stanza and joyfully receive it. The mass of merit of the former is not even so much as a small particle of the latter's.

8. So great will be one's merit, endless, immeasurable, owing to one's hearing merely a single stanza, in regular tradition; how much more then if one hears from face to face!

9. And if somebody exhorts were it but a single creature and says: Go, hear the law, for this Sûtra is rare in many myriads of koṭis of Æons;

10. And if the creature so exhorted should hear the Sûtra even for a moment, hark what fruit is to result from that action. He shall never have a mouth disease;

[1] From this reference to the preceding prose we must gather that these stanzas are posterior to or coeval with the prose version.

11. His tongue is never sore; his teeth shall never fall out, never be black, yellow, unequal; his lips never become loathsome;

12. His face is not wry, nor lean, nor long; his nose not flat; it is well-shaped, as well as his forehead, teeth, lips, and round face.

13. His aspect is ever pleasant to men; his mouth is never fetid, it constantly emits a smell sweet as the lotus.

14. If some wise man, to hear this Sûtra, goes from his home to a monastery and there listen, were it but for a single moment, with a placid mind, hear what results from it.

15. His body is very fair; he drives with horse-carriages, that wise man, and is mounted on elevated carriages drawn by elephants and variegated with gems.

16. He possesses litters covered with ornaments and carried by numerous men. Such is the blessed fruit of his going to hear preaching.

17. Owing to the performance of that pious work he shall, when sitting in the assembly there, obtain seats of Indra, seats of Brahma, seats of kings[1].

---

[1] The purport of this passage seems to be that lay devotees who are regular in attending the sermon, besides receiving terrestrial blessings, will rank high as churchwardens and be entitled to conspicuous places apart in the chapel. The gist of the whole chapter, at any rate, is that it is highly meritorious to come to church.

CHAPTER XVIII.

THE ADVANTAGES OF A RELIGIOUS PREACHER[1].

The Lord then addressed the Bodhisattva Mahâsattva Satatasamitâbhiyukta (i.e. ever and constantly strenuous). Any one, young man of good family, who shall keep, read, teach, write this Dharmaparyâya or have it written, let that person be a young man of good family or a young lady[2], shall obtain eight hundred good qualities of the eye, twelve hundred of the ear, eight hundred of the nose, twelve hundred of the tongue, eight hundred of the body, twelve hundred of the mind[3]. By these many hundred good qualities the whole of the six organs shall be perfect, thoroughly perfect. By means of the natural, carnal eye derived from his parents being perfect, he shall see the whole triple universe,

---

[1] Dharmabhâ*n*akâ*n*ri*s*a*m*sâ*h*. The use of â*n*ri*s*a*m*sa, as a synonym to gu*n*a, is not limited to Buddhist writings, as we see from the inscription at Bassac in Camboja, st. 18. It is, of course, the Pâli ânisa*m*sa.

[2] The words 'or a young lady' are wanting in my MS., but Burnouf's text had them, and from the sequel it would seem that they have to be added. It is certainly remarkable that we find mention being made of female preachers, who may be compared with the brahmavâdinîs of ancient times, and, further up, with the wise women of the Teutons, the Velledas and Völvas, the Pythonissas of the Greeks, and the Valians of the Indian Archipelago.

[3] We may also render, of sight, hearing, smell, taste, touch, and thought.

outwardly and inwardly, with its mountains and woody thickets, down to the great hell Avîki and up to the extremity of existence. All that he shall see with his natural eye, as well as the creatures to be found in it, and he shall know the fruit of their works.

And on that occasion the Lord uttered the following stanzas:

1. Hear from me what good qualities shall belong to him who unhesitatingly and undismayed shall preach this Sûtra to the congregated assembly.

2. First, then, his eye (or, organ of vision) shall possess eight hundred good qualities by which it shall be correct, clear, and untroubled.

3. With the carnal eye derived from his parents he shall see the whole world from within and without.

4. He shall see the Meru and Sumeru, all the horizon and other mountains, as well as the seas.

5. He, the hero, sees all, downward to the Avîki and upward to the extremity of existence. Such is his carnal eye.

6. But he has not yet got the divine eye, it having not yet been produced[1] in him; such as here described is the range of his carnal eye.

Further, Satatasamitâbhiyukta, the young man of good family or the young lady[2] who proclaims this Dharmaparyâya and preaches it to others, is possessed of the twelve hundred good qualities of the ear. The various sounds that are uttered in the triple universe, downward to the great hell Avîki

[1] No *k*âpi *g*âyate. Burnouf's translation, 'il n'aura pas encore la science,' points to a reading, *g*ñâyate.

[2] This time the word is also found in my MS.

and upward to the extremity of existence, within and without, such as the sounds of horses [1], elephants, cows, peasants [2], goats, cars; the sounds of weeping and wailing; of horror, of conch-trumpets, bells, tymbals; of playing and singing; of camels, of tigers [3]; of women, men, boys, girls; of righteousness (piety) and unrighteousness (impiety); of pleasure and pain; of ignorant men and âryas; pleasant and unpleasant sounds; sounds of gods, Nâgas, goblins, Gandharvas, demons, Garudas, Kinnaras, great serpents, men, and beings not human; of monks, disciples, Pratyekabuddhas, Bodhisattvas, and Tathâgatas; as many sounds as are uttered in the triple world, within and without, all those he hears with his natural organ of hearing when perfect. Still he does not enjoy the divine ear, although he apprehends the sounds of those different creatures, understands, discerns the sounds of those different creatures, and when with his natural organ of hearing he hears the sounds of those creatures, his ear is not overpowered by any of those sounds. Such, Satatasamitâbhiyukta, is the organ of hearing that the Bodhisattva Mahâsattva [4] acquires; yet he does not possess the divine ear.

---

[1] Burnouf's version shows a few unimportant various readings.

[2] *Ganapadasabdâh*, rather strange between the others. I suppose that *ganapada* is corrupted from some word meaning a sheep, but I find no nearer approach to it than *gâlakinî*, a ewe; cf. st. 8 below.

[3] I follow Burnouf, who must have read vyâghra; my MS. has vâdya.

[4] This term, as it is here used, refers, so far as I can see, to the ministers of religion, the preachers. It is, however, just possible that we have to take it in the more general and original sense of any 'rational being,' for all the advantages enumerated belong to everybody who is not blind, not deaf, &c.

Thus spoke the Lord; thereafter he, the Sugata, the Master, added:

7. The organ of hearing of such a person becomes (or, is) cleared and perfect, though as yet it be natural; by it he perceives the various sounds, without any exception, in this world.

8. He perceives the sounds of elephants, horses, cars, cows, goats, and sheep; of noisy kettle-drums, tabours, lutes, flutes, Vallakî-lutes.

9. He can hear singing, lovely and sweet, and, at the same time, is constant enough not to allow himself to be beguiled by it; he perceives the sounds of ko*t*is of men, whatever and wherever they are speaking.

10. He, moreover, always hears the voice of gods and Nâgas; he hears the tunes, sweet and affecting, of song, as well as the voices of men and women, boys and girls.

11. He hears the cries of the denizens of mountains and glens; the tender notes[1] of Kalaviṅkas, cuckoos[2], peafowls[3], pheasants, and other birds.

12. He also (hears) the heart-rending cries of those who are suffering pains in the hells, and the yells uttered by the Spirits, vexed as they are by the difficulty to get food;

13. Likewise the different cries produced by the demons and the inhabitants of the ocean. All these

---

[1] Valgu*s*abda.

[2] Here we see that kalaviṅkas are distinguished from kokilas, cuckoos.

[3] The voice of the peafowl is proverbially unharmonious, but that is no reason why the poet should have omitted this item from his enumeration; such peculiarities give a relish to this kind of spiritual poetry.

sounds the preacher is able to hear from his place on earth, without being overpowered by them.

14. From where he is stationed here on the earth he also hears the different and multifarious sounds through which the inhabitants of the realm of brutes are conversing with each other.

15. He apprehends all the sounds, without any exception, whereby the numerous angels living in the Brahma-world, the Akanish*th*as and Âbhâsvaras[1], call one another.

16. He likewise always hears the sound which the monks on earth are raising when engaged in reading, and when preaching the law to congregations, after having taken orders under the command of the Sugatas.

17. And when the Bodhisattvas here on earth have a reading together and raise their voices in the general synods, he hears them severally.

18. The Bodhisattva who preaches this Sûtra shall, at one time, also hear the perfect law[2] that the Lord Buddha, the tamer of men[3], announces to the assemblies.

19. The numerous sounds produced by all beings in the triple world, in this field, within and without, (downward) to the Avî*k*i and upward to the extremity of existence, are heard by him.

20. (In short), he perceives the voices of all beings, his ear being open. Being in the possession of his six senses[4], he will discern the different sources (of sound), and that while his organ of hearing is the natural one;

---

[1] Two classes of angels of the Brahma-heaven.

[2] I. e. judgment. [3] I. e. in his quality of Dharmarâ*g*a.

[4] I. e. not being out of his wits.

21. The divine ear is not yet operating in him; his ear continues in its natural state. Such as here told are the good qualities belonging to the wise man who shall be a keeper of this Sûtra.

Further, Satatasamitâbhiyukta, the Bodhisattva Mahâsattva who keeps, proclaims, studies, writes this Dharmaparyâya becomes possessed of a perfect organ of smell with eight hundred good qualities. By means of that organ he smells the different smells that are found in the triple world, within and without, such as fetid smells, pleasant and unpleasant smells, the fragrance of diverse flowers, as the great-flowered jasmine, Arabian jasmine, Michelia Champaka, trumpet-flower; likewise the different scents of aquatic flowers, as the blue lotus, red lotus, white esculent water-lily and white lotus. He smells the odour of fruits and blossoms of various trees bearing fruits and blossoms, such as sandal, Xanthochymus, Tabernæmontana, agallochum[1]. The manifold hundred-thousand mixtures of perfumes he smells and discerns, without moving from his standing-place. He smells the diverse smells of creatures, as elephants, horses, cows, goats, beasts, as well as the smell issuing from the body of various living beings in the condition of brutes. He perceives the smells exhaled by the body of women and men, of boys and girls. He smells, even from a distance, the odour of grass, bushes, herbs, trees. He perceives those smells such as they really are, and is not surprised nor stunned by them. Staying on this very earth he smells the odour of gods and the

[1] There is something strange in enumerating these plants, after speaking of fruits.

fragrance of celestial flowers, such as Erythrina, Bauhinia, Mandârava and great Mandârava, Mañgûsha and great Mañgûsha. He smells the perfume of the divine powders of sandal and agallochum, as well as that of the hundred-thousands of mixtures of different divine flowers. He smells the odour exhaled by the body of the gods, such as Indra, the chief of the gods, and thereby knows whether (the god) is sporting, playing, and enjoying himself in his palace Vaigayanta or is speaking the law to the gods of paradise in the assembly-hall of the gods, Sudharmâ, or is resorting to the pleasure-park for sport[1]. He smells the odour proceeding from the body of the sundry other gods, as well as that proceeding from the girls and wives of the gods, from the youths and maidens amongst the gods, without being surprised or stunned by those smells. He likewise smells the odour exhaled by the bodies of all Devanikâyas, Brahmakâyikas, and Mahâbrahmas[2]. In the same manner he perceives the smells coming from disciples, Pratyekabuddhas, Bodhisattvas, and Tathâgatas. He smells the odour arising from the seats of the Tathâgatas and so discovers where those Tathâgatas, Arhats, &c. abide. And by none of all those different smells is his organ of smell hindered, impaired, or vexed; and, if required, he may give an account of those smells to others without his memory being impaired by it.

And on that occasion the Lord uttered the following stanzas:

22. His organ of smell is quite correct, and he

[1] The parallel passage in the poetical version, st. 41, is much less confused, and for that reason probably more original.

[2] Three classes of aerial beings, archangels.

perceives the manifold and various smells, good or bad, which exist in this world;

23. The fragrance of the great-flowered jasmine, Arabian jasmine, Xanthochymus, sandal, agallochum, of several blossoms and fruits.

24. He likewise perceives the smells exhaled by men, women, boys, and girls, at a considerable distance, and by the smell he knows where they are.

25. He recognises emperors, rulers of armies, governors of provinces, as well as royal princes and ministers, and all the ladies of the harem by their (peculiar) scent.

26. It is by the odour that the Bodhisattva discovers sundry jewels of things, such as are found on the earth and such as serve as jewels for women.

27. That Bodhisattva likewise knows by the odour the various kinds of ornament that women use for their body, robes, wreaths, and ointments.

28. The wise man who keeps this exalted Sûtra recognises, by the power of a good-smelling organ, a woman [1] standing, sitting, or lying; he discovers wanton sport and magic power [2].

29. He perceives at once where he stands, the fragrance of scented oils, and the different odours of flowers and fruits, and thereby knows from what source the odour proceeds.

30. The discriminating man recognises by the odour the numerous sandal-trees in full blossom in the glens of the mountains, as well as all creatures dwelling there.

31. All the beings living within the compass of

[1] Sthitâ*m* nishannâ*m* *s*ayitâ*m* tathaiva.

[2] Krî*d*âratim *ri*ddhibala*m* *k*a.

the horizon or dwelling in the depth of the sea or in the bosom of the earth the discriminating man knows how to distinguish from the (peculiar) smell.

32. He discerns the gods and demons, and the daughters of demons; he discovers the sports of demons and their luxury. Such, indeed, is the power of his organ of smell.

33. By the smell he tracks the abodes of the quadrupeds in the woods, lions, tigers, elephants, snakes, buffaloes, cows, gayals.

34. He infers from the odour, whether the child that women, languid from pregnancy, bear in the womb be a boy or a girl.

35. He can discern if a woman is big with a dead child[1]; he discerns if she is subject to throes[2], and, further, if a woman, the pains being removed, shall be delivered of a healthy boy.

36. He guesses the various designs of men, he smells (so to say) an air of design[3]; he finds out the odour of passionate, wicked, hypocritical, or quiet persons.

37. That Bodhisattva by the scent smells treasures hidden in the ground, money, gold, bullion, silver, chests, and metal pots[4].

38. Necklaces of two sorts, gems, pearls, nice priceless jewels he knows by the scent[5], as well as things priceless and brilliant in general.

39. That great man from his very place on earth

---

[1] Âpannasatvâ. [2] Vinâmadharmâ.

[3] Abhiprâyagandha.

[4] It need hardly be remarked that 'to smell' is here used in the same sense as in the English saying 'to smell a rat.'

[5] The word gandha also means 'some resemblance, faint likeness, an air.'

smells the flowers here above (in the sky) with the gods, such as Mandâravas, Ma*ñg*ûshakas, and those growing on the coral tree.

40. By the power of his organ of smell he, without leaving his stand on earth, perceives how and whose are the aerial cars, of lofty, low, and middling size, and other brilliant forms shooting[1] (through the firmament).

41. He likewise finds out the paradise, the gods (in the hall) of Sudharmâ and in the most glorious palace of Vai*g*ayanta[2], and the angels who there are diverting themselves.

42. He perceives, here on earth, an air of them; by the scent he knows the angels, and where each of them is acting, standing, listening, or walking.

43. That Bodhisattva tracks by the scent the houris who are decorated with many flowers, decked with wreaths and ornaments and in full attire; he knows wherever they are dallying or staying at the time.

44. By smell he apprehends the gods, Brahmas, and Brahmakâyas moving on aerial cars aloft, upwards to the extremity of existence; he knows whether they are absorbed in meditation[3] or have risen from it.

---

[1] *K*avanti, Sansk. *k*yavanti, altered by a later hand into bhavanti.

[2] A sculptured representation of Indra's palace of Vai*g*ayanta and the hall Sudharmâ is found on the bas reliefs of the Stûpa of Bharhut; see plate xvi in General Cunningham's splendid work on that Stûpa.

[3] The real meaning is, perhaps, to say that he knows whether those inhabitants of the empyreum are plunged in glimmer or disengaged from mist, &c.

45. He perceives the Âbhâsvara angels falling (and shooting) and appearing, even those that he never saw before. Such is the organ of smell of the Bodhisattva who keeps this Sûtra.

46. The Bodhisattva also recognises all monks under the rule of the Sugata, who are strenuously engaged in their walks and find their delight in their lessons and reading.

47. Intelligent as he is, he discerns those among the sons of *G*ina who are disciples and those who used to live at the foot of trees, and he knows that the monk so and so is staying in such and such a place.

48. The Bodhisattva knows by the odour whether other Bodhisattvas are of good memory, meditative, delighting in their lessons and reading, and assiduous in preaching to congregations [1].

49. In whatever point of space the Sugata, the great Seer, so benign and bounteous, reveals the law in the midst of the crowd of attending disciples, the Bodhisattva by the odour recognises him as the Lord of the universe.

50. Staying on earth, the Bodhisattva also perceives those beings who hear the law and rejoice at it, and the whole assembly of the *G*ina.

51. Such is the power of his organ of smell. Yet it is not the divine organ he possesses, but (the natural one) prior to the perfect, divine faculty of smell.

Further, Satatasamitâbhiyukta, the young man of good family or the young lady who keeps, teaches,

---

[1] Such Bodhisattvas may be said to stand in the odour of sanctity.

proclaims, writes this Dharmaparyâya shall have an organ of taste possessed of twelve hundred good faculties of the tongue. All flavours he takes on his tongue will yield a divine, exquisite relish. And he tastes in such a way that he is not to relish anything unpleasant; and even the unpleasant flavours that are taken on his tongue will yield[1] a divine relish. And whatever he shall preach in the assembly, the creatures will be satisfied by it; they will be content, thoroughly content, filled with delight. A sweet, tender, agreeable, deep voice goes out from him, an amiable voice which goes to the heart, at which those creatures will be ravished and charmed; and those to whom he preaches, after having heard his sweet voice, so tender and melodious, will, even (if they are) gods, be of opinion that they ought to go and see, venerate, and serve him[2]. And the angels and houris will be of opinion, &c. The Indras, Brahmas, and Brahmakâyikas will be of opinion, &c. The Nâgas and Nâga girls will be of opinion, &c. The demons and their girls will be of opinion, &c. The Garu*d*as and their girls will be of opinion, &c. The Kinnaras and their girls, the great serpents and their girls, the goblins and their girls, the imps and their girls will be of opinion that they ought to go and see, venerate, serve him, and hear his sermon, and all will show him honour, respect, esteem, worship, reverence, and veneration. Monks and nuns, male and female lay devotees will likewise be desirous of seeing him. Kings, royal princes, and grandees (or ministers) will also be

[1] Mokshyante, properly, 'will emit.'

[2] In the margin added *s*rava*n*âya, 'to hear.'

desirous of seeing him. Kings ruling armies and emperors possessed of the seven treasures[1], along with the princes royal, ministers, ladies of the harem, and their retinue will be desirous of seeing him and paying him their homage. So sweet will be the speech delivered by that preacher, so truthful and according to the teaching of the Tathâgata will be his words. Others also, Brahmans and laymen, citizens and peasants, will always and ever follow that preacher till the end of life. Even the disciples of the Tathâgata will be desirous of seeing him; likewise the Pratyekabuddhas and the Lords Buddhas. And wherever that young man of good family or young lady shall stay, there he (or she) will preach, the face turned to the Tathâgata, and he (or she) will be a worthy vessel of the Buddha-qualities. Such, so pleasant, so deep will be the voice of the law going out from him.

And on that occasion the Lord uttered the following stanzas:

52. His organ of taste is most excellent, and he will never relish anything of inferior flavour; the flavours are no sooner put on his tongue than they become divine and possessed of a divine taste[2].

53. He has a tender voice and delivers sweet words, pleasant to hear, agreeable, charming; in the

---

[1] The seven treasures or jewels of an emperor are the wheel, the elephant, the horse, the gem, the empress, the major domo (according to others, the retinue of householders), and the viceroy or marshal. See Spence Hardy, Manual of Buddhism, p. 127; Burnouf, Lotus, p. 580; Senart, Légende du Buddha, pp. 22–60; Lalita-vistara, pp. 15-19.

[2] Nikshiptamâtrâs *k*a bhavanti divyâ rasena divyena samarpitâs *k*a.

midst of the assembly he is used to speak with a melodious and deep voice.

54. And whosoever hears him when he is delivering a sermon with myriads of ko*t*is of examples, feels a great joy and shows him an immense veneration.

55. The gods, Nâgas, demons, and goblins always long to see him, and respectfully listen to his preaching. All those good qualities are his.

56. If he would, he might make his voice heard by the whole of this world; his voice is (so) fine, sweet, deep, tender, and winning.

57. The emperors on earth, along with their children and wives, go to him with the purpose of honouring him, and listen all the time to his sermon with joined hands.

58. He is constantly followed by goblins, crowds of Nâgas, Gandharvas, imps, male and female, who honour, respect, and worship him.

59. Brahma himself becomes his obedient servant; the gods Î*s*vara and Mahe*s*vara, as well as Indra and the numerous heavenly nymphs, approach him.

60. And the Buddhas, benign and merciful for the world, along with their disciples, hearing his voice, protect him by showing their face, and feel satisfaction in hearing him preaching.

Further, Satatasamitâbhiyukta, the Bodhisattva Mahâsattva who keeps, reads, promulgates, teaches, writes this Dharmaparyâya shall have the eight hundred good qualities of the body. It will be pure, and show a hue clear as the lapis lazuli; it will be pleasant to see for the creatures. On that perfect body he will see the whole triple universe; the beings who in the triple world disappear and appear, who are low or lofty, of good or of bad colour, in fortunate or in unfortunate condition, as well as the beings dwelling within the circular plane of the horizon and of the great horizon, on the chief mountains Meru and Sumeru, and the beings dwelling below in the Avî*k*i and upwards to the extremity of existence; all of them he will see on his own body. The disciples, Pratyekabuddhas, Bodhisattvas, and Tathâgatas dwelling in the triple universe, and the law taught by those Tathâgatas and the beings serving the Tathâgatas, he will see all of them on his own body, because he receives the proper body of all those beings, and that on account of the perfectness of his body.

And on that occasion the Lord uttered the following stanzas:

61. His body becomes thoroughly pure, clear as if consisting of lapis lazuli; he who keeps this sublime Sûtra is always a pleasant sight for (all) creatures.

62. As on the surface of a mirror an image is seen, so on his body this world. Being self-born, he sees no other beings[1]. Such is the perfectness of his body.

63. Indeed, all beings who are in this world, men, gods, demons, goblins, the inhabitants of hell, the spirits, and the brute creation are seen reflected on that body.

64. The aerial cars of the gods up to the extremity of existence, the rocks, the ridge of the

[1] This seems to mean that the thinking subject or thinking power only (svayambhû or brahma) has real existence, the objects being products from one's own mind. In so far it may be said that the thinking subject sees no other real beings.

horizon, the Himâlaya, Sumeru, and great Meru, all are seen on that body.

65. He also sees the Buddhas on his body, along with the disciples and other sons of Buddha; likewise the Bodhisattvas who lead a solitary life, and those who preach the law to congregations.

66. Such is the perfectness of his body, though he has not yet obtained a divine body; the natural property of his body is such.

Further, Satatasamitâbhiyukta, the Bodhisattva Mahâsattva who after the complete extinction of the Tathâgata keeps, teaches, writes, reads this Dharmaparyâya shall have a mental organ possessed of twelve hundred good qualities of intellect. By this perfect mental organ he will, even if he hears a single stanza, recognise its various meanings. By fully comprehending the stanza he will find in it the text to preach upon for a month, for four months, nay, for a whole year. And the sermon he preaches will not fade from his memory. The popular maxims of common life, whether sayings or counsels, he will know how to reconcile with the rules of the law. Whatever creatures of this triple universe are subject to the mundane whirl, in any of the six conditions of existence, he will know their thoughts, doings, and movements. He will know and discern their motions, purposes, and aims. Though he has not yet attained the state of an Ârya, his intellectual organ will be thoroughly perfect. And all he shall preach after having pondered on the interpretation of the law will be really true; he speaks what all Tathâgatas have spoken, all that has been declared in the Sûtras of former *G*inas.

And on that occasion the Lord uttered the following stanzas:

67. His mental organ is perfect, lucid, right, and untroubled. By it he finds out the various laws, low, high, and mean.

68. On hearing the contents of a single stanza, the wise man catches the manifold significations (hidden) in it, and he is able for a month, four months, or even a year to go on expounding both its conventional and its true sense.

69. And the beings living in this world, within or without, gods, men, demons, goblins, Nâgas, brutes,

70. The beings stationed in any of the six conditions of existence, all their thoughts the sage knows instantaneously. These are the advantages of keeping this Sûtra.

71. He also hears the holy sound of the law which the Buddha, marked with a hundred blessed signs, preaches all over the world, and he catches what the Buddha speaks.

72. He reflects much on the supreme law, and is in the wont of constantly dilating upon it; he is never hesitating. These are the advantages of keeping this Sûtra.

73. He knows the connections and knots[1]; he discerns in all laws contrarieties[2]; he knows the meaning and the interpretations, and expounds them according to his knowledge.

74. The Sûtra which since so long a time has been

---

[1] Sandhivisandhi, I am not sure of the real purport of these terms; Burnouf renders 'concordances et combinaisons.'

[2] Sarveshu dharmeshu vilakshanâni; the rendering is uncertain; Burnouf has, 'ne voit entre toutes les lois aucune différence.'

expounded by the ancient Masters of the world is the law which he, never flinching, is always preaching in the assembly.

75. Such is the mental organ of him who keeps or reads this Sûtra; he has not yet the knowledge of emancipation, but one that precedes it.

76. He who keeps this Sûtra of the Sugata stands on the stage of a master; he may preach to all creatures and is skilful in ko*t*is of interpretations.

CHAPTER XIX.

SADÂPARIBHÛTA.

The Lord then addressed the Bodhisattva Mahâsattva Mahâsthâmaprâpta. In a similar way, Mahâsthâmaprâpta, one may infer from what has been said that he who rejects such a Dharmaparyâya as this, who abuses monks, nuns, lay devotees male or female, keeping this Sûtra, insults them, treats them with false and harsh words, shall experience dire results, to such an extent as is impossible to express in words. But those that keep, read, comprehend, teach, amply expound it to others, shall experience happy results, such as I have already mentioned: they shall attain such a perfection of the eye, ear, nose, tongue, body, and mind as just described.

In the days of yore, Mahâsthâmaprâpta, at a past period, before incalculable Æons, nay, more than incalculable, immense, inconceivable, and even long before, there appeared in the world a Tathâgata, &c., named Bhîshmagar*g*itasvararâ*g*a, endowed with science and conduct, a Sugata, &c. &c., in the Æon Vinirbhoga, in the world Mahâsambhava. Now, Mahâsthâmaprâpta, that Lord Bhîshmagar*g*itasvararâ*g*a, the Tathâgata, &c., in that world Vinirbhoga, showed the law in the presence of the world, including gods, men, and demons; the law containing the four noble truths and starting from the chain of causes and effects, tending to overcome birth, decrepitude, sickness, death, sorrow, lamentation, woe, grief, despondency, and finally leading to Nirvâ*n*a, he showed to the disciples; the law connected with the six Perfections of virtue and terminating in the knowledge of the Omniscient, after the attainment of supreme, perfect enlightenment, he showed to the Bodhisattvas. The lifetime of that Lord Bhîshmagar*g*itasvararâ*g*a, the Tathâgata, &c., lasted forty hundred thousand myriads of ko*t*is of Æons equal to the sands of the river Ganges [1]. After his complete extinction his true law remained hundred thousands of myriads of ko*t*is of Æons equal to the atoms (contained) in *G*ambudvîpa, and the counterfeit of the true law continued hundred thousands of myriads of ko*t*is of Æons equal to the dust-atoms in the four continents. When the counterfeit of the true law of the Lord Bhîshmagar*g*itasvararâ*g*a, the Tathâgata, &c., after his complete extinction, had disappeared in the world Mahâsambhava, Mahâsthâmaprâpta, another Tathâgata Bhîshmagar*g*itasvararâ*g*a, Arhat, &c., appeared, endowed with science and conduct. So in succession, Mahâsthâmaprâpta, there arose in that world Mahâsambhava twenty hundred thousand myriads of ko*t*is of Tathâgatas, &c., called Bhîshmagar*g*itasvararâ*g*a. At the time, Mahâsthâmaprâpta, after the complete extinction of the first Tathâgata amongst all those of the name of Bhîshmagar*g*itasvararâ*g*a, Tathâgata, &c., endowed with science and conduct, &c. &c., when his true law had disappeared and the counterfeit of the true law was

[1] According to Burnouf: 'autant de centaines de mille de myriades de ko*t*is de Kalpas qu'il y a de grains de sable dans quarante Ganges.'

fading; when the reign (of the law) was being oppressed by proud monks, there was a monk, a Bodhisattva Mahâsattva, called Sadâparibhûta. For what reason, Mahâsthâmaprâpta, was that Bodhisattva Mahâsattva called Sadâparibhûta? It was, Mahâsthâmaprâpta, because that Bodhisattva Mahâsattva was in the habit of exclaiming to every monk or nun, male or female lay devotee, while approaching them: I do not contemn you, worthies. You deserve no contempt, for you all observe the course of duty of Bodhisattvas and are to become Tathâgatas, &c. In this way, Mahâsthâmaprâpta, that Bodhisattva Mahâsattva, when a monk, did not teach nor study; the only thing he did was, whenever he descried from afar a monk or nun, a male or female lay devotee, to approach them and exclaim: I do not contemn you, sisters[1]. You deserve no contempt, for you all observe the course of duty of Bodhisattvas and are to become Tathâgatas, &c. So, Mahâsthâmaprâpta, the Bodhisattva Mahâsattva at that time used to address every monk or nun, male or female devotee. But all were extremely irritated and angry at it, showed him their displeasure, abused and insulted him: Why does he, unasked, declare that he feels no contempt for us? Just by so doing he shows a contempt for us. He renders himself contemptible[2] by predicting our future destiny to supreme, perfect enlightenment; we do not care for what is not true. Many years, Mahâsthâmaprâpta, went on during which that

[1] It may seem strange that we find no other word than this, but the reading of the text cannot be challenged.

[2] Paribhûtam âtmâna*m* karoti, yad, &c. Burnouf must have followed a different reading.

Bodhisattva Mahâsattva was being abused, but he was not angry at anybody, nor felt malignity, and to those who, when he addressed them in the said manner, cast a clod or stick at him, he loudly exclaimed from afar: I do not contemn you. Those monks and nuns, male and female lay devotees, being always and ever addressed by him in that phrase gave him the (nick)name of Sadâparibhûta[1].

Under those circumstances, Mahâsthâmaprâpta, the Bodhisattva Mahâsattva Sadâparibhûta happened to hear this Dharmaparyâya of the Lotus of the True Law when the end of his life was impending, and the moment of dying drawing near. It was the Lord Bhîshmagar*g*itasvararâga, the Tathâgata, &c., who expounded this Dharmaparyâya in twenty times twenty hundred thousand myriads of ko*t*is of stanzas, which the Bodhisattva Mahâsattva Sadâparibhûta heard from a voice in the sky, when the time of his death was near at hand. On hearing that voice from the sky, without there appearing a person speaking, he grasped this Dharmaparyâya and obtained the perfections already mentioned: the perfection of sight, hearing, smell, taste, body, and mind. With the attainment of these perfections he at the same time made a vow to prolong his life for twenty hundred thousand myriads of ko*t*is of years, and promulgated this Dharmaparyâya of the Lotus of the True Law. And all those proud beings, monks, nuns, male and female lay devotees to whom he had said: I do not contemn you, and who had given him the name of Sadâparibhûta, became all his fol-

[1] I.e. both 'always contemned' (sadâ and paribhûta) and 'always not-contemned, never contemned' (sadâ and aparibhûta).

lowers to hear the law, after they had seen the power and strength of his sublime magic faculties, of his vow, of his readiness of wit, of his wisdom. All those and many hundred thousand myriads of ko*t*is of other beings were by him roused to supreme, perfect enlightenment.

Afterwards, Mahâsthâmaprâpta, that Bodhisattva Mahâsattva disappeared from that place and propitiated twenty hundred ko*t*is [1] of Tathâgatas, &c., all bearing the same name of *K*andraprabhâsvararâ*g*a, under all of whom he promulgated this Dharmaparyâya. By virtue of his previous root of goodness he, in course of time, propitiated twenty hundred thousand myriads of ko*t*is of Tathâgatas, &c., all bearing the name of Dundubhisvararâ*g*a, and under all he obtained this very Dharmaparyâya of the Lotus of the True Law and promulgated it to the four classes. By virtue of his previous root of goodness he again, in course of time, propitiated twenty hundred thousand myriads of ko*t*is of Tathâgatas, &c., all bearing the name of Meghasvararâ*g*a, and under all he obtained this very Dharmaparyâya of the Lotus of the True Law and promulgated it to the four classes. And under all of them he was possessed of the afore-mentioned perfectness of sight, hearing, smell, taste, body, and mind.

Now, Mahâsthâmaprâpta, that Bodhisattva Mahâsattva Sadâparibhûta, after having honoured, respected, esteemed, worshipped, venerated, revered so many hundred thousand myriads of ko*t*is of Tathâgatas, and after having acted in the same way towards

[1] From the sequel it appears that the text ought to have 'twenty hundred thousand myriads of ko*t*is.'

many hundred thousand myriads of ko*t*is of other Buddhas, obtained under all of them this very Dharmaparyâya of the Lotus of the True Law, and owing to his former root of goodness having come to full development, gained supreme, perfect enlightenment. Perhaps, Mahâsthâmaprâpta, thou wilt have some doubt, uncertainty, or misgiving, and think that he who at that time, at that juncture was the Bodhisattva Mahâsattva called Sadâparibhûta was one, and he who under the rule of that Lord Bhîshmagar*g*itasvararâ*g*a, the Tathâgata, &c., was generally called Sadâparibhûta by the four classes, by whom so many Tathâgatas were propitiated, was another. But thou shouldst not think so. For it is myself who at that time, at that juncture was the Bodhisattva Mahâsattva Sadâparibhûta. Had I not formerly grasped and kept this Dharmaparyâya, Mahâsthâmaprâpta, I should not so soon have arrived at supreme, perfect enlightenment. It is because I have kept, read, preached this Dharmaparyâya (derived) from the teaching of the ancient Tathâgatas, &c., Mahâsthâmaprâpta, that I have so soon arrived at supreme, perfect enlightenment. As to the hundreds of monks, nuns, male and female lay devotees, Mahâsthâmaprâpta, to whom under that Lord the Bodhisattva Mahâsattva Sadâparibhûta promulgated this Dharmaparyâya by saying: I do not contemn you; you all observe the course of duty of Bodhisattvas; you are to become Tathâgatas, &c., and in whom awoke a feeling of malignity towards that Bodhisattva, they in twenty hundred thousand myriads of ko*t*is of Æons never saw a Tathâgata, nor heard the call of the law, nor the call of the assembly, and for ten thousand Æons they suffered terrible pain in the great hell Avîki. Thereafter released from the ban, they by the instrumentality of that Bodhisattva Mahâsattva were all brought to full ripeness for supreme, perfect enlightenment. Perhaps, Mahâsthâmaprâpta, thou wilt have some doubt, uncertainty, or misgiving as to who at that time, at that juncture were the persons hooting and laughing at the Bodhisattva Mahâsattva. They are, in this very assembly, the five hundred Bodhisattvas headed by Bhadrapâla, the five hundred nuns following Simhakandrâ, the five hundred lay devotees[1] following Sugataketanâ, who all of them have been rendered inflexible in supreme, perfect enlightenment. So greatly useful it is to keep and preach this Dharmaparyâya, as it tends to result for Bodhisattvas Mahâsattvas in supreme, perfect enlightenment. Hence, Mahâsthâmaprâpta, the Bodhisattvas Mahâsattvas should, after the complete extinction of the Tathâgata, constantly keep, read, and promulgate this Dharmaparyâya.

And on that occasion the Lord uttered the following stanzas :

1. I remember a past period, when king Bhîshmasvara[2], the *G*ina, lived, very mighty, and revered by gods and men, the leader of men, gods, goblins, and giants.

2. At the time succeeding the complete extinction of that *G*ina, when the decay of the true law

---

[1] Upâsaka, the masculine ; this does not suit, but on the other hand it must be admitted that the omission of male devotees is not to be accounted for. Not unlikely some words have been left out by inadvertence, not only in the Cambridge MS., but also in the MSS. known to Burnouf. Cf., however, st. 9.

[2] Bhîshmasvaro râga gino yadâsi.

was far advanced, there was a monk, a Bodhisattva, called by the name of Sadâparibhûta.

3. Other monks and nuns who did not believe but in what they saw[1], he would approach (and say): I never am to contemn you, for you observe the course leading to supreme enlightenment.

4. It was his wont always to utter those words, which brought him but abuse and taunts from their part. At the time when his death was impending he heard this Sûtra.

5. The sage, then, did not expire; he resolved upon[2] a very long life, and promulgated this Sûtra under the rule of that leader.

6. And those many (persons) who only acknowledged the evidence of sensual perception[3] were by him brought to full ripeness for enlightenment. Then, disappearing from that place, he propitiated thousands of ko*t*is of Buddhas.

7. Owing to the successive good actions performed by him, and to his constantly promulgating this Sûtra, that son of *G*ina reached enlightenment. That Bodhisattva then is myself, *S*âkyamuni.

8. And those persons who only believed in perception by the senses[4], those monks, nuns, male and female lay devotees who by the sage were admonished of enlightenment,

9. And who have seen many ko*t*is of Buddhas,

---

[1] Upalambhad*r*ish*t*îna; I am not sure of the correctness of this translation; Burnouf renders it by 'qui ne voyaient que les objets extérieurs,' which comes pretty much to the same.

[2] Pratish*th*ihitvâ (Sansk. pratish*th*âya) *k*a sudîrgham âyu*h*, properly 'having stood still for a very long time of life.'

[3] Upalambhika.

[4] Aupalambhika.

are the monks here before me,—no less than five hundred,—nuns, and female lay devotees[1].

10. All of them have been by me brought to complete ripeness, and after my extinction they will all, full of wisdom, keep this Sûtra.

11. Not once in many, inconceivably many ko*t*is of Æons has such a Sûtra as this been heard. There are, indeed, hundreds of ko*t*is of Buddhas, but they do not elucidate this Sûtra.

12. Therefore let one who has heard this law exposed by the Self-born himself, and who has repeatedly propitiated him, promulgate this Sûtra after my extinction in this world.

[1] The text has upâsikâ*h*.

CHAPTER XX.

CONCEPTION OF THE TRANSCENDENT POWER OF THE TATHÂGATAS.

Thereupon those hundred thousands of myriads of ko*t*is of Bodhisattvas equal to the dust-atoms of a macrocosm, who had issued from the gaps of the earth, all stretched their joined hands towards the Lord, and said unto him: We, O Lord, will, after the complete extinction of the Tathâgata, promulgate this Dharmaparyâya everywhere (or on every occasion) in all Buddha-fields of the Lord, wherever (or whenever) the Lord shall be completely extinct[1]. We are anxious to obtain this sublime Dharmaparyâya, O Lord, in order to keep, read, publish, and write it.

Thereupon the hundred thousands of myriads of ko*t*is of Bodhisattvas, headed by Ma*ñg*u*s*rî; the monks, nuns, male and female lay devotees living in this world; the gods, Nâgas, goblins, Gandharvas, demons, Garu*d*as, Kinnaras, great serpents, men, and beings not human, and the many Bodhisattvas Mahâsattvas equal to the sands of the river Ganges, said unto the Lord: We also, O Lord, will promulgate this Dharmaparyâya after the complete extinction of the Tathâgata. While standing with an invisible body in the sky, O Lord, we will send

[1] Hence follows that Nirvâ*n*a is repeatedly entered into by the Lord.

forth a voice[1], and plant the roots of goodness of such creatures as have not (yet) planted roots of goodness.

Then the Lord addressed the Bodhisattva Mahâsattva Visishtakâritra, followed by a troop, a great troop, the master of a troop, who was the very first of those afore-mentioned Bodhisattvas Mahâsattvas followed by a troop, a great troop, masters of a troop: Very well, Visishtakâritra, very well; so you should do; it is for the sake of this Dharmaparyâya that the Tathâgata has brought you to ripeness.

Thereupon the Lord Sâkyamuni, the Tathâgata, &c., and the wholly extinct Lord Prabhûtaratna, the Tathâgata, &c., both seated on the throne in the centre of the Stûpa[2], commenced smiling to one another, and from their opened mouths stretched out their tongues, so that with their tongues they reached the Brahma-world, and from those two tongues issued many hundred thousand myriads of kotis of rays[3]. From each of those rays issued many hundred thousand myriads of kotis of Bodhisattvas, with gold-coloured bodies and possessed of the thirty-two characteristic signs of a great man, and seated on thrones consisting of the interior of lotuses. Those

[1] From this it appears that the abode of the monks &c. in the assembly of the Lord Sâkyamuni is in the sky, at least occasionally. Their attribute of 'an invisible body' shows them to be identical with the videhas, the incorporeal ones, i. e. the spirits of the blessed departed, Arhats, Muktas, Pitaras. The Pitaras form the assembly of Dharmarâga.

[2] Cf. Chapter XI.

[3] It is quite true that the moon as well as the sun is sahasrarasmi, possessed of thousand rays, but it is difficult to understand how the Bhagavat Prabhûtaratna can show his magic power in his state of extinction.

Bodhisattvas spread in all directions in hundred thousands of worlds, and while on every side stationed in the sky preached the law. Just as the Lord *S*âkyamuni, the Tathâgata, &c., produced a miracle of magic by his tongue, so, too, Prabhûtaratna, the Tathâgata, &c., and the other Tathâgatas, &c., who, having flocked from hundred thousands of myriads of ko*t*is of other worlds, were seated on thrones at the foot of jewel trees, by their tongues produced a miracle of magic.

The Lord *S*âkyamuni, the Tathâgata, &c., and all those Tathâgatas, &c., produced that magical effect during fully a thousand[1] years. After the lapse of that millennium those Tathâgatas, &c., pulled back their tongue, and all simultaneously, at the same moment, the same instant, made a great noise as of expectoration[2] and of snapping the fingers, by which sounds all the hundred thousands of myriads of ko*t*is of Buddha-fields in every direction of space were moved, removed, stirred, wholly stirred, tossed, tossed forward, tossed along, and all beings in all those Buddha-fields, gods, Nâgas, goblins, Gandharvas, demons, Garu*d*as, Kinnaras, great serpents, men, and beings not human beheld, by the power of the Buddha, from the place where they stood, this Saha-world. They beheld the hundred thousands of myriads of ko*t*is of Tathâgatas seated severally on their throne at the foot of a jewel tree, and the Lord *S*âkyamuni, the Tathâgata, &c., and the Lord Prabhûtaratna, the Tathâgata, &c., wholly extinct, sitting on the throne in the centre of the

---

[1] Burnouf has 'a hundred thousand.'

[2] Utkâ*s*ana, better °sana.

Stûpa of magnificent precious substances, along with the Lord *S*âkyamuni, the Tathâgata, &c.; they beheld, finally, those four classes of the audience. At this sight they felt struck with wonder, amazement, and rapture. And they heard a voice from the sky calling: Worthies, beyond a distance of an immense, incalculable number of hundred thousands of myriads of ko*t*is of worlds there is the world named Saha; there the Tathâgata called *S*âkyamuni, the Arhat, &c., is just now revealing to the Bodhisattvas Mahâsattvas the Dharmaparyâya of the Lotus of the True Law, a Sûtrânta of great extent, serving to instruct Bodhisattvas, and belonging in proper to all Buddhas. Ye accept it joyfully with all your heart, and do homage to the Lord *S*âkyamuni, the Tathâgata, &c., and the Lord Prabhûtaratna, the Tathâgata, &c.

On hearing such a voice from the sky all those beings exclaimed from the place where they stood, with joined hands: Homage to the Lord *S*âkyamuni, the Tathâgata. Then they threw towards the Saha-world various flowers, incense, fragrant wreaths, ointment, gold, cloth, umbrellas, flags, banners, and triumphal streamers, as well as ornaments, parures, necklaces, gems and jewels of all sorts, in order to worship the Lord *S*âkyamuni, the Tathâgata[1], and this Dharmaparyâya of the Lotus of the True Law. Those flowers, incense, &c., and those necklaces, &c., came down upon this Saha-world, where they formed a great canopy of flowers hanging in the sky above the Tathâgatas there sitting, as well as those in the hundred thousands of myriads of ko*t*is of other worlds.

[1] In Burnouf's translation we find added: and the Tathâgata Prabhûtaratna.

Thereupon the Lord addressed the Bodhisattvas Mahâsattvas headed by Visish*t*a*k*âritra: Inconceivable, young men of good family, is the power of the Tathâgatas, &c. In order to transmit this Dharmaparyâya, young men of good family, I might go on for hundred thousands of myriads of ko*t*is of Æons explaining the manifold virtues of this Dharmaparyâya through the different principles of the law, without reaching the end of those virtues. In this Dharmaparyâya I have succinctly taught all Buddha-laws (or Buddha-qualities), all the superiority, all the mystery, all the profound conditions of the Buddhas. Therefore, young men of good family, you should, after the complete extinction of the Tathâgata, with reverence keep, read, promulgate, cherish [1], worship it. And wherever on earth, young men of good family, this Dharmaparyâya shall be made known, read, written, meditated, expounded, studied or collected into a volume, be it in a monastery or at home, in the wilderness or in a town, at the foot of a tree or in a palace, in a building or in a cavern, on that spot one should erect a shrine in dedication to the Tathâgata. For such a spot must be regarded as a terrace of enlightenment; such a spot must be regarded as one where all Tathâgatas &c. have arrived at supreme, perfect enlightenment; on that spot have all Tathâgatas moved forward the wheel of the law; on that spot one may hold that all Tathâgatas have reached complete extinction.

And on that occasion the Lord uttered the following stanzas:

---

[1] Or develop; or meditate, bhâvayitavya. Burnouf seems to have read bhâshayitavya, for he translates it by 'expliquer.'

1. Inconceivable is the power to promote the weal of the world[1] possessed by those who, firmly established in transcendent knowledge, by means of their unlimited sight display their magic faculty in order to gladden all living beings on earth.

2. They extend their tongue over the whole world[2], darting thousands of beams to the astonishment of those to whom this effect of magic is displayed and who are making for supreme enlightenment.

3. The Buddhas made a noise of expectoration and of snapping the fingers, (and by it) called the attention of the whole world, of all parts of the world in the ten directions of space.

4. Those and other miraculous qualities they display in their benevolence and compassion (with the view) that the creatures, gladly excited at the time, may (also) keep the Sûtra after the complete extinction of the Sugata.

5. Even if I continued for thousands of ko*t*is of Æons speaking the praise of those sons of Sugata who shall keep this eminent Sûtra after the extinction of the Leader of the world,

6. I should not have terminated the enumeration of their qualities; inconceivable as the qualities of infinite space are the merits of those who constantly keep this holy Sûtra.

7. They behold me as well as these chiefs, and the Leader of the world now extinct; (they behold) all these numerous Bodhisattvas and the four classes.

8. Such a one now here[3] propitiates me and all

[1] Lokahitânudharmatâ. [2] Sarvalokam.

[3] Ten' ihâdya. The connection between this stanza and the next would have been clearer if the two stanzas had been transposed.

these leaders, as well as the extinct chief of *G*inas and the others in every quarter.

9. The future and past Buddhas stationed in the ten points of space will all be seen and worshipped by him who keeps this Sûtra.

10. He who keeps this Sûtra, the veritable law, will fathom the mystery of the highest man; will soon comprehend what truth it was that was arrived at on the terrace of enlightenment.

11. The quickness of his apprehension will be unlimited; like the wind he will nowhere meet impediments; he knows the purport and interpretation of the law, he who keeps this exalted Sûtra.

12. He will, after some reflection, always find out the connection of the Sûtras spoken by the leaders; even after the complete extinction of the leader he will grasp the real meaning of the Sûtras.

13. He resembles the moon and the sun; he illuminates all around him, and while roaming the earth in different directions he rouses many Bodhisattvas.

14. The wise Bodhisattvas who, after hearing the enumeration of such advantages, shall keep this Sûtra after my complete extinction will doubtless reach enlightenment.

CHAPTER XXI.

SPELLS.

Thereupon the Bodhisattva Mahâsattva Bhaishagyarâga rose from his seat, and having put his upper robe upon one shoulder and fixed the right knee upon the ground lifted his joined hands up to the Lord and said: How great, O Lord, is the pious merit which will be produced by a young man of good family or a young lady who keeps this Dharmaparyâya of the Lotus of the True Law, either in memory or in a book? Whereupon the Lord said to the Bodhisattva Mahâsattva Bhaishagyarâga: Suppose, Bhaishagyarâga, that some man of good family or a young lady honours, respects, reveres, worships hundred thousands of myriads of kotis of Tathâgatas equal to the sands of eighty Ganges rivers; dost thou think, Bhaishagyarâga, that such a young man or young lady of good family will on that account produce much pious merit? The Bodhisattva Bhaishagyarâga replied: Yes, Lord; yes, Sugata. The Lord said: I announce to thee, Bhaishagyarâga, I declare to thee: any young man or young lady of good family, Bhaishagyarâga, who shall keep, read, comprehend, and in practice follow, were it but a single stanza from this Dharmaparyâya of the Lotus of the True Law, that young man or young lady of good family, Bhaishagyarâga, will on that account produce far more pious merit.

Then the Bodhisattva Mahâsattva Bhaishagya-râga immediately said to the Lord: To those young men or young ladies of good family, O Lord, who keep this Dharmaparyâya of the Lotus of the True Law in their memory or in a book, we will give talismanic words [1] for guard, defence, and protection; such as, anye [2] manye mane mamane kitte karite same, samitâvi, sânte, mukte, muktatame, same avishame, samasame, gaye, kshaye, akshîne, sânte sanî, dhârani âlokabhâshe, pratyavekshani, nidhini, abhyantaravisishte, utkule mutkule, asade, parade, sukâṅkshî, asamasame, buddhavilokite, dharmaparîkshite, saṅghanirghoshani, nirghoshanî bhayâbhayasodhanî, mantre mantrâkshayate, rutakausalye, akshaye, akshavanatâya, vakule valoda, amanyatâya [3]. These words of charms and spells, O Lord, have been pronounced by reverend Buddhas (in number)

---

[1] Dhâranîpadâni.

[2] In giving these words I have followed the Camb. MS., even where the readings would seem to be incorrect.

[3] The list in Burnouf's translation seems in many respects more correct; it is as follows: anye manye, arau parau amane mamane kitte karite; same samitâ visânte, mukte muktatame same avisamasame, gaye kshaye akshaye akshîne sânte samite dhârani âlokabhâse pratyavekshani dhiru viviru abhyantaranivishte abhyantarapârisuddhi, utkule mukule arade parade sukâṅkshi asamasame buddhivilokite dharmaparîkshite pratyavekshani saṅghanirghoshani nirghoshani bhayavisodhani mantre mantrakshayate rutakausalya akshayavanatâ vakkulavaloka amanyatâye. All these words are, or ought to be, feminine words in the vocative. I take them to be epithets of the Great Mother, Nature or Earth, differently called Aditi, Pragñâ, Mâyâ, Bhavânî, Durgâ. Anyâ may be identified with the Vedic anyâ, inexhaustible, and synonymous with aditi. Most of the other terms may be explained as synonymous with pragñâ (e.g. pratyavekshanî), with nature (kshaye akshaye), with the earth (dhâranî).

equal to the sands of sixty-two Ganges rivers. All these Buddhas would be offended by any one who would attack such preachers, such keepers of the Sûtrânta.

The Lord expressed his approval to the Bodhisattva Mahâsattva Bhaisha*g*yarâ*g*a by saying: Very well, Bhaisha*g*yarâ*g*a, by those talismanic words being pronounced out of compassion for creatures, the common weal of creatures is promoted; their guard, defence, and protection is secured.

Thereupon the Bodhisattva Mahâsattva Pradânas*û*ra said unto the Lord: I also, O Lord, will, for the benefit of such preachers, give them talismanic words, that no one seeking for an occasion to surprise such preachers may find the occasion, be it a demon, giant, goblin, sorcerer, imp or ghost; that none of these when seeking and spying for an occasion to surprise may find the occasion. And then the Bodhisattva Mahâsattva Pradânas*û*ra instantly pronounced the following words of a spell: *g*vale mahâ*g*vale, ukke mukke, a*d*e a*d*âvati, t*rit*ye t*rit*yâvati, i*t*ini vi*t*ini *k*i*t*ini, t*ritt*i t*rit*yâvati svâhâ[1]. These talismanic words, O Lord, have been pronounced and approved by Tathâgatas, &c. (in number) equal to the sands of the river Ganges. All those Tathâgatas would be offended by any one who would attack such preachers.

[1] With Burnouf: *g*vale mahâ*g*vale ukke mukke ate atâvati n*ri*tye n*ri*tyâvati; i*tt*ini vi*tt*ini *k*i*tt*ini n*ri*tyâvati svâhâ. These terms are obviously names of the flame, mythologically called Agni's wife, the daughter of Daksha. As *S*iva may be identified with Agni, the feminine words again are epithets of Durgâ. *G*valâ and Mahâ*g*valâ are perfectly clear; ukkâ is the Prâkrit form of Sanskrit ulkâ.

Thereupon Vaisravana, one of the four rulers of the cardinal points, said unto the Lord: I also, O Lord, will pronounce talismanic words for the benefit and weal of those preachers, out of compassion to them, for their guard, defence, and protection: *atte natte vanatte anade, nâdi kunadi svâhâ*[1]. With these spells, O Lord, I shall guard those preachers over an extent of a hundred yoganas. Thus will those young men or young ladies of good family, who keep this Sûtrânta, be guarded, be safe.

At that meeting was present Virûdhaka, another of the four rulers of the cardinal points, sitting surrounded and attended by hundred thousands of myriads of kotis of Kumbhândas. He rose from his seat, put his upper robe upon one shoulder, lifted his joined hands up to the Lord, and spoke to him as follows: I also, O Lord, will pronounce talismanic words for the benefit of people at large, and to guard, defend, protect such preachers as are qualified, who keep the Sûtrânta as mentioned; viz. *agane gane gauri gandhâri kandâli mâtangi pukkasi sankule vrûsali svâhâ*[2]. These talismanic words, O Lord, have been pronounced by forty-two hundred thousand myriads of kotis of Buddhas. All those Buddhas would be offended by any one who would attack such preachers as are qualified.

Thereupon the giantesses called Lambâ, Vilambâ[3],

---

[1] Burnouf has atte hatte natte, &c.

[2] The list in Burnouf differs but slightly; a. g. g. gandhâri kândâli m. pukkasi s. vrûlasisi s. Vrûsalî or rather vrusalî must be the Sanskrit vrishalî. Gaurî, Kandâlikâ, Mâtangî are known from elsewhere as epithets of Durgâ; Pukkasî and Vrishalî denote nearly the same as Kandâlî and Mâtangî.

[3] With Burnouf, Pralambâ.

Kûtadantî, Pushpadantî, Makutadantî[1], Kesinî, Akalâ, Mâlâdhârî, Kuntî, Sarvasattvogahârî[2], and Hârîtî, all with their children and suite went up to the place where the Lord was, and with one voice said unto him: We also, O Lord, will afford guard, defence, and protection to such preachers as keep this Sûtrânta; we will afford them safety, that no one seeking for an occasion to surprise those preachers may find the occasion. And the giantesses all simultaneously and in a chorus gave to the Lord the following words of spells: iti me, iti me, iti me, iti me, iti me; nime nime nime nime nime; ruhe ruhe ruhe ruhe ruhe; stuhe stuhe stuhe stuhe stuhe, svâhâ. No one shall overpower and hurt such preachers; no goblin, giant, ghost, devil, imp, sorcerer, spectre, gnome; no spirit causing epilepsy, no sorcerer of goblin race, no sorcerer of not-human race, no sorcerer of human race; no sorcerer producing tertian ague, quartian ague, quotidian ague. Even if in his dreams he has visions of women, men, boys or girls, it shall be impossible that they hurt him.

And the giantesses simultaneously and in a chorus addressed the Lord with the following stanzas:

1. His head shall be split into seven pieces, like a sprout of Symplocos Racemosa, who after hearing this spell would attack a preacher.

2. He shall go the way of parricides and matricides, who would attack a preacher.

3. He shall go the way of oil-millers and sesamum-pounders, who would attack a preacher.

---

[1] Burnouf has Matutakandî.

[2] Burnouf better, Sarvasattvaugohârî.

4. He shall go the way of those who use false weights and measures, who would attack a preacher.

Thereafter the giantesses headed by Kuntî said unto the Lord: We also, O Lord, will afford protection to such preachers; we will procure them safety; we will protect them against assault and poison. Whereupon the Lord said to those giantesses: Very well, sisters, very well; you do well in affording guard, defence, and protection to those preachers, even to such who shall keep no more than the name of this Dharmaparyâya; how much more then to those who shall keep this Dharmaparyâya wholly and entirely, or who, possessing the text of it in a volume, honour it with flowers, incense, fragrant garlands, ointment, powder, cloth, flags, banners, lamps with sesamum oil, lamps with scented oil, lamps with *K*ampaka-scented oil, with Vârshika-scented oil, with lotus-scented oil, with jasmine-scented oil; who by such-like manifold hundred thousand manners of worshipping shall honour, respect, revere, venerate (this Sûtra), deserve to be guarded by thee and thy suite, Kuntî!

And while this chapter on spells was being expounded[1], sixty-eight thousand living beings received the faculty of acquiescence in the law that has no origin.

[1] The chapter was, properly speaking, not expounded at all; it simply contains a narrative with the speeches of different interlocutors. It may be observed that a poetical version is wanting.

CHAPTER XXII.

ANCIENT DEVOTION[1] OF BHAISHAGYARÂGA.

Thereupon the Bodhisattva Mahâsattva Nakshatrarâgasaṅkusumitâbhigña spoke to the Lord as follows: Wherefore, O Lord, does the Bodhisattva Bhaishagyarâga pursue his course[2] in this Saha-world, while he is fully aware of the many hundred thousands of myriads of kotis of difficulties he has to meet? Let the Lord, the Tathâgata, &c., deign to tell us any part of the course of duty of the Bodhisattva Mahâsattva Bhaishagyarâga, that by hearing it the gods, Nâgas, goblins, Gandharvas, demons, Garudas, Kinnaras, great serpents, men, and beings not human, as well as the Bodhisattvas Mahâsattvas from other worlds here present, and these great disciples here may be content, delighted, overjoyed.

And the Lord, out of regard to that request of the Bodhisattva Mahâsattva Nakshatrarâgasaṅkusumitâbhigña, told him the following: Of yore, young man of good family, at a past epoch, at a time (as many) Æons ago as there are grains of sand in the river Ganges, there appeared in the world a Tathâgata, &c., by the name of *K*andravimalasûryaprabhâsasrî[3], endowed with science and conduct, a

[1] Pûrvayoga; cf. foot-note, p. 153.

[2] Pravi*k*arati.

[3] I.e. moon-bright and illustrious by (or like) the radiance of the sun.

Sugata, &c. &c. Now that Tathâgata, &c., *K*andravimalasûryaprabhâsa*s*rî had a great assembly of eighty ko*t*is[1] of Bodhisattvas Mahâsattvas and an assembly of disciples equal to the sands of seventy-two Ganges rivers. His spiritual rule was exempt from the female sex, and his Buddha-field had no hell, no brute creation, no ghosts, no demons; it was level, neat, smooth as the palm of the hand. Its floor consisted of heavenly lapis lazuli, and it was adorned with trees of jewel and sandal-wood; inlaid with a multitude of jewels, and hung with long bands of silk, and scented by censors made of jewels. Under each jewel tree, at a distance not farther than a bow-shot, was made a small jewel-house[2], and on the top of those small jewel-houses stood a hundred ko*t*is of angels performing a concert of musical instruments and castanets, in order to honour the Lord *K*andravimalasûryaprabhâsa*s*rî, the Tathâgata, &c., while that Lord was extensively expounding this Dharmaparyâya of the Lotus of the True Law to the great disciples and Bodhisattvas, directing himself[3] to the Bodhisattva Mahâsattva Sarvasattvapriyadar*s*ana. Now, Nakshatrarâ*g*asaṅkusumitâbhi*gñ*a, the lifetime of that Lord *K*andravimalasûryaprabhâsa*s*rî, the Tathâgata, &c., lasted forty-two thousand Æons, and likewise that of the Bodhisattvas Mahâsattvas and great disciples. It was under the spiritual rule of that Lord that the Bodhisattva Mahâsattva Sarva-

[1] Thus Camb. MS.; Burnouf has eighty hundred thousand myriads of ko*t*is.

[2] Ratnadhâmaka. I am not certain of the correctness of my translation; Burnouf renders it by 'char fait de pierreries.'

[3] Sarvasatvapriyadar*s*ana*m*—adhish*th*âna*m* k*ri*tvâ; Burnouf has 'en commencant par le B. M. S.'

sattvapriyadarsana applied himself to his difficult course. He wandered twelve thousand years strenuously engaged in contemplation. After the expiration of those twelve thousand years he acquired the Samâdhi termed Sarvarûpasandarsana (i. e. the sight or display of all forms). No sooner had he acquired that Samâdhi than satisfied, glad, joyful, rejoicing, and delighted he made the following reflection: It is owing to this Dharmaparyâya of the Lotus of the True Law that I have acquired the Samâdhi of Sarvarûpasandarsana. Then he made another reflection: Let me do homage to the Lord *K*andravimalasûryaprabhâsasrî and this Dharmaparyâya of the Lotus of the True Law. No sooner had he entered upon such a meditation than a great rain of Mandârava and great Mandârava flowers fell from the upper sky. A cloud of Kâlânusârin sandal was formed, and a rain of Uragasâra sandal poured down. And the nature of those essences was so noble that one karsha of it was worth the whole Saha-world.

After a while, Nakshatrarâ*g*asaṅkusumitâbhi*gñ*a, the Bodhisattva Mahâsattva Sarvasattvapriyadarsana rose from that meditation with memory and full consciousness, and reflected thus: This display of magic power is not likely to honour the Lord and Tathâgata so much as the sacrifice of my own body will do[1]. Then the Bodhisattva Mahâsattva Sarvasattvapriyadarsana instantly began to eat Agallochum, Olibanum, and the resin of Boswellia Thurifera, and to drink oil of *K*ampaka[2]. So, Nakshatrarâ*g*asaṅkusumitâbhi*gñ*a,

---

[1] In the story of Sarvasattvapriyadarsana it is easy to recognise a Buddhist version of the myth of the Phœnix.

[2] In the Old English poem of the Phœnix, verse 192, we read that

the Bodhisattva Mahâsattva Sarvasattvapriyadarsana passed twelve years in always and constantly eating those fragrant substances and drinking oil of *K*ampaka. After the expiration of those twelve years the Bodhisattva Mahâsattva Sarvasattvapriyadarsana wrapped his body in divine garments, bathed[1] it in oil, made his (last) vow, and thereafter burnt his own body with the object to pay worship to the Tathâgata and this Dharmaparyâya of the Lotus of the True Law. Then, Nakshatrarâ*g*asañkusumitâbhi*g*ña, eighty worlds[2] equal to the sands of the river Ganges were brightened by the glare of the flames from the blazing body of the Bodhisattva Mahâsattva Sarvasattvapriyadarsana, and the eighty[3] Lords Buddhas[4] equal to the sands of the Ganges in those worlds all shouted their applause, (and exclaimed): Well done, well done, young man of good family, that is the real heroism which the Boddhisattvas Mahâsattvas should develop; that is the real worship of the Tathâgata, the real worship of the law. No worshipping with flowers, incense, fragrant wreaths, ointment, powder, cloth, umbrellas, flags, banners; no worshipping with material gifts or with Uragasâra sandal equals it. This, young man of good family,

---

the noble bird collects the sweetest herbs, blossoms, and perfumes; similarly verse 652. He feeds upon mildew, verse 260.

[1] The Phœnix bathes twelve times in the well before the sun's arrival, and as many times sips the cool water.

[2] According to the reading of the Camb. MS., asîtir Gañgâ°; Burnouf has 'sables de 80 Ganges,' which seems preferable.

[3] Here the same remark as in the preceding note.

[4] In the Old English poem, verse 355 seq., we read that hosts of birds flock together from all points of space 'to celebrate in song the hero and saint.' Further on, verse 590, the birds are identified with the released souls accompanying Christ.

is the sublimest gift, higher than the abandoning of royalty, the abandoning of beloved children and wife. Sacrificing one's own body, young man of good family, is the most distinguished, the chiefest, the best, the very best, the most sublime worship of the law. After pronouncing this speech, Nakshatrarâgasankusumitâbhigña, those Lords Buddhas were silent.

The body of Sarvasattvapriyadarsana continued blazing for twelve thousand years without ceasing to burn. After the expiration of those twelve thousand years the fire was extinguished. Then, Nakshatrarâgasankusumitâbhigña, the Bodhisattva Mahâsattva Sarvasattvapriyadarsana, having paid such worship to the Tathâgata, disappeared from that place, and (re)appeared under the (spiritual) reign of that very Lord Kandravimalasûryaprabhâsasrî, the Tathagata, &c., in the house of king Vimaladatta, by apparitional birth, and sitting cross-legged. Immediately after his appearance the Bodhisattva Mahâsattva Sarvasattvapriyadarsana addressed his father and mother in the following stanza:

1. This, O exalted king, is the walk in which I have acquired meditation; I have achieved a heroical feat, fulfilled a great vote by sacrificing my own dear body.

After uttering this stanza, Nakshatrarâgasankusumitâbhigña, the Bodhisattva Mahâsattva Sarvasattvapriyadarsana said to his father and mother: Even now, father and mother, the Lord Kandravimalasûryaprabhâsasrî, the Tathâgata, &c., is still living, existing, staying in the world, the Lord by worshipping whom I have obtained the spell of knowing all sounds[1] and this Dharmaparyâya of the Lotus of the True Law, consisting of eighty hundred thousand myriads of *k*otis of stanzas, of a hundred Niyutas[2], of Vivaras[3], of a hundred Vivaras, which I have heard from that Lord. Therefore, father and mother, I should like to go to that Lord and worship him again. Instantaneously, Nakshatrarâ*g*asaṅkusumitâbhi*gñ*a, the Bodhisattva Mahâsattva Sarvasattvapriyadar*s*ana rose seven tâlas[4] high into the sky and sat cross-legged on the top of a tower of seven precious substances. So he went up to the presence of that Lord, and having approached him humbly saluted him, circumambulated him seven times from left to right, stretched the joined hands towards the Lord, and after thus paying his homage addressed him with the following stanza:

2. O thou whose face is so spotless and bright; thou, king and sage! How thy lustre sparkles in all quarters! After having anciently paid thee homage, O Sugata, I now come again to behold thee, O Lord.

Having pronounced this stanza, the Bodhisattva Mahâsattva Sarvasattvapriyadar*s*ana said to the

---

[1] This comes rather unexpected; of the Phœnix in the Old English poem, verse 131, we read that 'the sound of the bird's song is sweeter and more beautiful than all other singer-craft, and more delicious than any other tune.'

[2] Equal to a thousand billions. The cyphers being noughts, the whole number = 1. Eighty is the number of intermediate kalpas in one Mahâkalpa or Great Æon, i. e. one day and night. The turn (paryâya) of the True Law is the regular revolution of the sun.

[3] Equal to a hundred thousand billions. As cyphers must be left out of account, all the numbers specified come to one.

[4] The height of a palm-tree, or a span.

Lord *K*andravimalasûryaprabhâsa*s*ri, the Tathâgata, &c.: Thou art then still alive, Lord? Whereon the Lord *K*andravimalasûryaprabhâsa*s*rî, the Tathâgata, &c., replied: The time of my final extinction, young man of good family, has arrived; the time of my death has arrived. Therefore, young man of good family, prepare my couch; I am going to enter complete extinction. Then, Nakshatrarâ*g*asankusumitâbhi*gñ*a, the Lord *K*andravimalasûryaprabhâsa*s*rî said to the Bodhisattva Mahâsattva Sarvasattvapriyadar*s*ana: I entrust to thee, young man of good family, my commandment (or mastership, rule); I entrust to thee these Bodhisattvas Mahâsattvas, these great disciples, this Buddha-enlightenment, this world, these jewel cars, these jewel trees, and these angels, my servitors. I entrust to thee also, young man of good family, my relics after my complete extinction. Thou shouldst pay a great worship to my relics, young man of good family, and also distribute them and build many thousands of Stûpas. And, Nakshatrarâ*g*asankusumitâbhi*gñ*a, after the Lord *K*andravimalasûryaprabhâsa*s*rî, the Tathâgata, &c., had given these instructions to the Bodhisattva Mahâsattva Sarvasattvapriyadar*s*ana he in the last watch of the night entered absolute final extinction[1]

Thereupon, Nakshatrarâ*g*asankusumitâbhi*gñ*a, the Bodhisattva Mahâsattva Sarvasattvapriyadar*s*ana, perceiving that the Lord *K*andravimalasûryaprabhâsa*s*rî, the Tathâgata, &c., had expired, made a pyre of Uragasâra sandal-wood and burnt the

[1] It is sufficiently clear that the Nirvâ*n*a of this Tathâgata is the end of a day of twenty-four hours, and that Sarvasattvapriyadar*s*ana is the new day.

body of the Tathâgata. When he saw that the body was burnt to ashes and the fire extinct, he took the bones[1] and wept, cried and lamented. After having wept, cried and lamented, Nakshatrarâgasankusumitâbhigña, the Bodhisattva Mahâsattva Sarvasattvapriyadarsana caused to be made eighty-four thousand urns of seven precious substances, deposed in them the bones of the Tathâgata, founded eighty-four thousand Stûpas[2], reaching in height to the Brahma-world, adorned with a row of umbrellas, and equipped with silk bands and bells. After founding those Stûpas he made the following reflection: I have paid honour to the Tathâgata-relics of the Lord *K*andravimalasûryaprabhâsasrî, but I will pay to those relics a yet loftier and most distinguished honour. Then, Nakshatrarâgasankusumitâbhigña, the Bodhisattva Mahâsattva Sarvasattvapriyadarsana addressed that entire assembly of Bodhisattvas, those great disciples, those gods, Nâgas, goblins, Gandharvas, demons, Garudas, Kinnaras, great serpents, men, and beings not human: Ye all, young men of good family, unani-

[1] In the Phœnix myth it is the bird himself that, after his resurrection, collects the relics; verses 269–272. Both versions come to the same, for the sun of to-day is essentially the same as yesterday's.

[2] Exactly the same number of monasteries was erected by Asoka, according to the Dîpavamsa VI, 96. The king was induced to build so many monasteries because there were eighty-four or, optionally, eighty-four thousand towns in India, a number precisely coinciding with that of the sections of the Law. Notwithstanding the difference in details, it may be assumed that there is some connection between the two tales, especially because Asoka was a namesake of Sarvasattvapriyadarsana, one of his epithets being Priyadarsana.

mously vow to pay worship to the relics of the Lord. Immediately after, Nakshatrarâ*g*asankusumitâbhi*gñ*a, the Bodhisattva Mahâsattva Sarvasattvapriyadar*s*ana, in presence of those eighty-four thousand Stûpas, burnt his own arm which was marked by the one hundred auspicious signs, and so paid worship to those Stûpas containing the relics of the Tathâgata, during seventy-two thousand years. And while paying worship, he educated countless hundred thousands of myriads of ko*t*is of disciples from that assembly, in consequence whereof all those Bodhisattvas acquired the Samâdhi termed Sarvarûpasandar*s*ana.

Then, Nakshatrarâ*g*asankusumitâbhi*gñ*a, the entire assembly of Bodhisattvas and all great disciples, seeing the Bodhisattva Mahâsattva Sarvasattvapriyadar*s*ana deprived of a limb, said, with tears in their eyes, weeping, crying, lamenting: The Bodhisattva Mahâsattva Sarvasattvapriyadar*s*ana, our master and instructor, is now deprived of a limb, deprived of one arm. But the Bodhisattva Mahâsattva Sarvasattvapriyadar*s*ana addressed those Bodhisattvas, great disciples, and angels in the following terms: Do not, young men of good family, weep, cry, lament at the sight of my being deprived of one arm. All the Lords Buddhas who be, exist, live in the endless, limitless worlds in every direction of space, have I taken to witness. Before their face have I pronounced a vow of truth, and by that truth, by that word of truth shall I, after the sacrifice of my own arm in honour of the Tathâgata, have a body of gold colour. By this truth, by this word of truth let this arm of mine become such as it was before, and let the great earth shake in six different ways, and let the angels in the sky pour down a rain of flowers. No sooner, Nakshatrarâgasaṅkusumitâbhigña, had the Bodhisattva Mahâsattva Sarvasattvapriyadarsana made that vow of truth, than the whole triple macrocosm was shaken in six different ways, and from the sky aloft fell a great rain of flowers. The arm of the Bodhisattva Mahâsattva Sarvasattvapriyadarsana became again as it was before, and that by the power of knowledge and by the power of pious merit belonging to that Bodhisattva Mahâsattva. Perhaps, Nakshatrarâgasaṅkusumitâbhigña, thou wilt have some doubt, uncertainty or misgiving, (and think) that the Bodhisattva Mahâsattva Sarvasattvapriyadarsana at that time, and that epoch, was another. But do not think so; for the Bodhisattva Mahâsattva Bhaishagyarâga here was at that time, and that epoch, the Bodhisattva Mahâsattva Sarvasattvapriyadarsana. So many hundred thousand myriads of kotis of difficult things, Nakshatrarâgasaṅkusumitâbhigña, and sacrifices [1] of his body does this Bodhisattva Mahâsattva Sarvasattvapriyadarsana accomplish. Now, Nakshatrarâgasaṅkusumitâbhigña, the young man or young lady of good family striving in the Bodhisattva vehicle towards the goal and longing for supreme, perfect enlightenment, who at the Tathâgata-shrines shall burn a great toe, a finger, a toe, or a whole limb, such a young man or young lady of good family, I assure thee, shall produce far more [2] pious merit, far more than results from giving up a king-

[1] Âtmabhâvaparityâgâms ka. The Phœnix in the poem, verse 364 seq., repeatedly, every thousand years, dies in the flames to arise anew from his ashes, and to be reborn.

[2] Bahutaram khalv api.

dom, sons, daughters, and wives, the whole triple world with its woods, oceans, mountains, springs, streams, tanks, wells, and gardens. And, Nakshatrarâ*g*asaṅkusumitâbhi*g*ña, the young man or young lady of good family, striving in the Bodhisattva-vehicle for the goal, who after filling with the seven precious substances this whole triple world should give it in alms to all Buddhas, Bodhisattvas, disciples, Pratyekabuddhas, that young man or young lady of good family, Nakshatrarâ*g*asankusumitâbhi*g*ña, does not produce so much pious merit as a young man or young lady of good family who shall keep, were it but a single verse from this Dharmaparyâya of the Lotus of the True Law. I positively declare that the accumulation of merit of the latter is greater than if a person, after filling the whole triple world with the seven precious substances, bestows it in alms on all Buddhas, Bodhisattvas, disciples, or Pratyekabuddhas.

Just as the great ocean, Nakshatrarâ*g*asaṅkusumitâbhi*g*ña, surpasses all springs, streams, and tanks, so, Nakshatrarâ*g*asaṅkusumitâbhi*g*ña, this Dharmaparyâya of the Lotus of the True Law surpasses all Sûtras spoken by the Tathâgata[1]. Just as the Sumeru, the king of mountains, Nakshatrarâ*g*asaṅkusumitâbhi*g*ña, all elevations at the cardinal points[2], horizon circles and great horizons[3], so,

[1] Or, the Tathâgatas. The same alternative in the sequel. All Sûtras in the world have their source in the Tathâgata, of course; just as all Vedas, Itihâsas, &c. are the breathing out, the uttering of the sentient principle, the âtman; *S*atapatha-Brâhma*n*a XIV, 5, 4, 10.

[2] Kâlaparvata, literally, 'time mountain,' because the points of rising and setting are called parvata, giri, &c., mountain in Sanskrit.

[3] The whole horizon is also an apparent elevation and therefore likewise called parvata, &c.

Nakshatrarâgasaṅkusumitâbhigña, this Dharmaparyâya of the Lotus of the True Law surpasses as a king all the Sûtrântas spoken by the Tathagâta. As the moon, Nakshatrarâgasaṅkusumitâbhigña, as a luminary, takes the first rank amongst the whole of the asterisms, so, Nakshatrarâgasaṅkusumitâbhigña, this Dharmaparyâya of the Lotus of the True Law ranks first amongst all Sûtrântas spoken by the Tathâgata, though it surpasses hundred thousands of myriads of kotis of moons. As the orb of the sun, Nakshatrarâgasaṅkusumitâbhigña, dispels gloomy darkness, so, Nakshatrarâgasaṅkusumitâbhigña, this Dharmapayâya of the Lotus of the True Law dispels all the gloomy darkness of unholy works. As Indra, Nakshatrarâgasaṅkusumitâbhigña, is the chief of the gods of paradise, so, Nakshatrarâgasaṅkusumitâbhigña, this Dharmaparyâya of the Lotus of the True Law is the chief of Sûtrântas spoken by the Tathâgata. As Brahma Sahâmpati, Nakshatrarâgasaṅkusumitâbhigña, is the king of all Brahmakâyika gods and exercises the function of a father in the Brahma world, so, Nakshatrarâgasaṅkusumitâbhigña, this Dharmaparyâya of the Lotus of the True Law exercises the function of a father to all beings, whether under training or past it, to all disciples, Pratyekabuddhas, and those who in the Bodhisattva-vehicle are striving for the goal. As the Srotaâpanna, Nakshatrarâgasaṅkusumitâbhigña, as well as the Sakridâgâmin, Anâgâmin, Arhat[1], and Pratyekabuddha, excels the ignorant people and the profanum vulgus, so, Nakshatrarâgasaṅkusumitâ-

[1] Terms denoting the four degrees of sanctification, answering to the Prathamakalpika, Madhubhûmika, Pragñâgyotis, and Atikrântabhâvanîya in the Yoga system; Yogasâstra III, 50, commentary.

bhi*g*ña, the Dharmaparyâya of the Lotus of the True Law must be held to excel and surpass all Sûtrântas spoken by the Tathâgata; and such as shall keep this king of Sûtras, Nakshatrarâ*g*asaṅkusumitâbhi*g*ña, must be held to surpass others (who do not). As a Bodhisattva is accounted superior to all disciples and Pratyekabuddhas, so, Nakshatrarâ*g*asaṅkusumitâbhi*g*ña, this Dharmaparyâya of the Lotus of the True Law is accounted superior to all Sûtrântas spoken by the Tathâgata. Even as the Tathâgata is the crowned king of the law[1] of all disciples, Pratyekabuddhas, and Bodhisattvas, so, Nakshatrarâ*g*asaṅkusumitâbhi*g*ña, this Dharmaparyâya is a Tathâgata in respect to those who in the vehicle of Bodhisattvas are striving to reach the goal. This Dharmaparyâya of the Lotus of the True Law, Nakshatrarâ*g*asaṅkusumitâbhi*g*ña, saves all beings from all fear, delivers them from all pains. It is like a tank for the thirsty, like a fire for those who suffer from cold, like a garment for the naked, like the caravan leader for the merchants, like a mother for her children, like a boat for those who ferry over, like a leech for the sick, like a lamp for those who are wrapt in darkness, like a jewel for those who want wealth, like the ocean for the rivers, like a torch for the dispelling of darkness. So, Nakshatrarâ*g*asaṅkusumitâbhi*g*ña, this Dharmaparyâya of the Lotus of the True Law delivers from all evils, extirpates all diseases, releases from the narrow bonds of the mundane whirl[2]. And he who shall hear this Dharmaparyâya of the Lotus of the True

[1] Dharmarâ*g*a*h* pa*tt*abaddha*h*, i. e. properly the legitimate crowned king.

[2] In other words, this Dharmaparyâya is Death or Nirvâ*n*a.

Law, who shall write it and cause it to be written, will produce an accumulation of pious merit the term of which is not to be arrived at even by Buddha-knowledge; so great is the accumulation of pious merit that will be produced by a young man of good family or a young lady who after teaching or learning it, writing it or having it collected into a volume, shall honour, respect, venerate, worship it with flowers, incense, fragrant garlands, ointment, powder, umbrellas, flags, banners, triumphal streamers, with music, with joining of hands, with lamps burning with ghee, scented oil, *K*ampaka oil, jasmine oil, trumpet-flower oil, Vârshikâ oil or double jasmine oil.

Great will be the pious merit, Nakshatrarâ*g*a-saṅkusumitâbhi*gñ*a, to be produced by a young man of good family or a young lady striving to reach the goal in the Bodhisattva-vehicle, who shall keep this chapter of the Ancient Devotion of Bhaisha*g*yarâ*g*a, who shall read and learn it. And, Nakshatrarâ*g*a, should a female, after hearing this Dharmaparyâya, grasp and keep it, then this existence will be her last existence as a woman. Any female, Nakshatra-râ*g*asaṅkusumitâbhi*gñ*a, who in the last five hundred years of the millennium shall hear and penetrate this chapter of the Ancient Devotion of Bhaisha-*g*yarâ*g*a, will after disappearing from earth be (re)born in the world Sukhâvatî, where the Lord Amitâyus[1], the Tathâgata, &c., dwells, exists, lives surrounded by a host of Bodhisattvas. There will he (who formerly was a female) appear seated on a throne consisting of the interior of a lotus; no affection, no hatred, no infatuation, no pride, no

[1] Another name of Amitâbha.

envy, no wrath, no malignity will vex him. With his birth he will also receive the five transcendent faculties, as well as the acquiescence in the eternal law, and, once in possession thereof, Nakshatrarâ*g*a-saṅkusumitâbhi*gñ*a, he as a Bodhisattva Mahâsattva will see Tathâgatas equal to the sands of seventy-two rivers Ganges[1]. So perfect will be his organ of sight that by means thereof he shall see those Lords Buddhas, which Lords Buddhas will applaud him (and say): Well done, well done, young man of good family, that after hearing this Dharmaparyâya of the Lotus of the True Law which has been promulgated by the spiritual proclamation of the Lord *S*âkyamuni, the Tathâgata, &c., thou hast studied, meditated, examined, minded it, and expounded it to other beings, other persons. This accumulation of thy pious merit, young man of good family, cannot be burnt by fire, nor swept away by water. Even a thousand Buddhas would not be able to determine this accumulation of thy pious merit, young man of good family. Thou hast subdued the opposition of the Evil One, young man of good family. Thou, young man of good family, hast victoriously emerged[2] from the battle of mundane existence, hast crushed the enemies annoying thee[3]. Thou, young man of good family, hast been superintended by thousands of Buddhas; thine equal, young man of good family, is not to be found in the world, including the gods[4], with the only exception of the

[1] Or, to seventy-two times the sands of the river Ganges.

[2] Uttîr*n*abhavasaṅgrâma.

[3] Mardita*s*atruka*nth*aka (sic; cf. Pâli ka*nth*aka).

[4] In the margin are added the words, also found in Burnouf's translation, 'including Mâras, Brahmans, and ascetics.'

Tathâgata; there is no other, be he disciple, Pratyekabuddha, or Bodhisattva, able to surpass thee in pious merit, knowledge, wisdom or meditation. Such a power of knowledge, Nakshatrarâ*g*asaṅkusumitâbhi*gñ*a, will be acquired by that Bodhisattva.

Any one, Nakshatrarâ*g*asaṅkusumitâbhi*gñ*a, who on hearing this chapter of the ancient devotion of Bhaisha*g*yarâ*g*a approves it, will emit from his mouth a breath sweet as of the lotus, and from his limbs a fragrance as of sandal-wood. Such temporal advantages as I have just now indicated will belong to him who approves this Dharmaparyâya. On that account then, Nakshatrarâ*g*asaṅkusumitâbhi*gñ*a, I transmit to thee this chapter of the Ancient Devotion of the Bodhisattva Mahâsattva Sarvasattvapriyadar*s*ana, that at the end of time, the last period, in the latter half of the millennium it may have course here in *G*ambudvîpa and not be lost; that neither Mâra the Fiend, nor the celestial beings called Mârakâyikas, Nâgas, goblins, imps may find the opportunity of hurting it. Therefore, Nakshatrarâ*g*asaṅkusumitâbhi*gñ*a, I bequeath this Dharmaparyâya; it is to be like a medicament for sick and suffering creatures in *G*ambudvîpa. No sickness shall overpower him who has heard this Dharmaparyâya, no decrepitude, no untimely death. Whenever a person striving to reach the goal in the vehicle of Bodhisattvas happens to see such a monk as keeps this Sûtrânta, then he should strew him with sandal-powder and blue lotuses, and reflect thus: This young man of good family is going to reach the terrace of enlightenment; he will spread the bundle of grass[1] on the terrace of enlightenment; he will put to flight the party of Mâra, blow the conch trumpet of the law, beat the drum of the law, cross the ocean of existence. Thus, Nakshatrarâgasankusumitâbhigña, should a young man of good family, striving to reach the goal in the vehicle of Bodhisattva, reflect when seeing a monk who keeps this Sûtra, and he will acquire such advantages as have been indicated by the Tathâgata.

While this chapter of the Ancient Devotion of Bhaishagyarâga was being expounded, eighty-four thousand Bodhisattvas attained the spell connected with skill in all sounds. And the Lord Prabhûtaratna, the Tathâgata, &c., intimated his approval (by saying): Well done, well done, Nakshatrarâgasankusumitâbhigña; thou hast done well in thus questioning the Tathâgata, who is endowed with such inconceivable qualities and properties.

[1] This is an allusion to the bundles of grass the Bodhisattva received from Svastika, the grass-cutter, when he was on his way to occupy his seat at the foot of the Bo tree; see Lalita-vistara, p. 357; Gâtaka I, p. 70 (English translation by Professor Rhys Davids, p. 95).

CHAPTER XXIII.

GADGADASVARA.

At that moment the Lord *S*âkyamuni, the Tathâgata, &c., darted a flash of light from the circle of hair between his eyebrows, one of the characteristic signs of a great man, by which flash of light hundred thousands of myriads of ko*t*is of Buddha-fields, equal to the sands of eighteen rivers Ganges, became illuminated. Beyond those Buddha-fields, equal, &c., is the world called Vairo*k*anara*s*mipratima*nd*ita (i.e. embellished by the rays of the sun). There dwells, lives, exists the Tathâgata named Kamaladalavimalanakshatrarâ*g*asaṅkusumitâbhi*gñ*a, who, surrounded and attended by a large and immense assembly of Bodhisattvas, preached the law. Immediately the ray of light flashing from the circle of hair between the eyebrows of the Lord *S*âkyamuni, the Tathâgata, &c., filled the world Vairo*k*anara*s*mipratima*nd*ita with a great lustre. In that world Vairo*k*anara*s*mipratima*nd*ita there was a Bodhisattva Mahâsattva called Gadgadasvara, who had planted roots of goodness, who had before seen similar luminous flashes emitted by many Tathâgatas, &c., and who had acquired many Samâdhis, such as the Samâdhi Dhva*g*âgrakeyûra (i. e. bracelet at the upper end of the banner staff), Saddharma-pu*nd*arîka (i.e. the Lotus of the True Law), Vimaladatta (i.e. given by Vimala), Nakshatrarâ*g*avikrî*d*ita (i.e. sport of the king of asterisms, the moon god), Anilambha[1], *G*ñânamudrâ (i.e. the seal of science), *K*andrapradîpa (i.e. moon-light[2]), Sarvarutakau*s*alya (i.e. skill in all sounds), Sarvapu*n*yasamu*kk*aya (i.e. compendium or collection of all piety), Prasâdavatî (i.e. the favourably-disposed lady), *Ri*ddhivikrî*d*ita (i.e. sport of magic), *G*ñânolkâ (i.e. torch of knowledge), Vyûharâ*g*a (i.e. king of expansions or speculations), Vimalaprabhâ (i.e. spotless lustre), Vimalagarbha (i.e. of spotless interior part), Apk*ri*tsna[3], Sûryâvarta (i.e. sun-turn); in short, he had acquired many hundred thousand myriads of ko*t*is of Samâdhis equal to the sands of the river Ganges. Now, the flash of light came down upon that Bodhisattva Mahâsattva Gadgadasvara. Then the Bodhisattva Mahâsattva Gadgadasvara rose from his seat, put his upper robe upon one shoulder, fixed his right knee on the ground, stretched his joined hands towards the Lord Buddha, and said to the Tathâgata Kamaladalavimalanakshatrarâ*g*asankusumitâbhi*g*ña: O Lord, I would resort to the Saha-world to see, salute, wait upon the Lord *S*âkyamuni, the Tathâgata, &c.; to see and salute Ma*ñg*u*s*rî, the prince royal; to see the Bodhisattvas Bhaisha*g*yarâ*g*a, Pradâna*s*ûra, Nakshatrarâ*g*asankusumitâbhi*g*ña, Vi*s*ish*t*a*k*âritra, Vyûharâ*g*a, Bhaisha*g*yarâ*g*asamudgata.

Then the Lord Kamaladalavimalanakshatrarâ*g*asankusumitâbhi*g*ña, the Tathâgata, &c., said to the Bodhisattva Mahâsattva Gadgadasvara: On coming to the Saha-world, young man of good family, thou

---

[1] Of uncertain meaning.

[2] Burnouf has read *K*andraprabha, moon-bright.

[3] I.e. belonging to the mystic rite, called Âpokasi*n*a in Pâli; for which I refer to Spence Hardy, Eastern Monachism, p. 252 seq.

must not conceive a low opinion of it. That world, young man of good family, has ups and downs, consists of earth, is replete with mountains of Kâla, filled with gutters[1]. The Lord *S*âkyamuni, the Tathâgata, &c., is short of stature[2], and so are the Bodhisattvas Mahâsattvas, whereas thou, young man of good family, hast got a body forty-two hundred thousand yo*g*anas[3] high, and myself have got a body sixty-eight hundred thousand yo*g*anas high. And, young man of good family, thou art lovely, handsome, of pleasant appearance, endowed with a full bloom of extremely fine colour, and abundantly blest with hundred thousands of holy signs. Therefore then, young man of good family, when you have come to the Saha-world, do not conceive a low opinion of the Tathâgata, nor of the Bodhisattvas, nor of that Buddha-field.

Thus addressed, the Bodhisattva Mahâsattva Gadgadasvara said to the Lord Kamaladalavimalanakshatrarâ*g*asaṅkusumitâbhi*gñ*a, the Tathâgata, &c.: I shall do, Lord, as the Lord commands; I shall go to that Saha-world by virtue of the Lord's resolution, of the Lord's power, of the Lord's might, of the Lord's disposal, of the Lord's foresight. Whereon the Bodhisattva Mahâsattva Gadgadasvara, without leaving that Buddha-field and without leaving his

---

[1] Gûtho*d*illa or gûtho*d*igalla; according to Burnouf the word means 'ordures;' cf. above, p. 142, and Pâli oligalla.

[2] Spence Hardy, Manual of Buddhism, p. 364: 'Buddha is sometimes said to be twelve cubits in height, and sometimes eighteen cubits.'

[3] That is considerably more than Râhu, the eclipse, was possessed of, his body being no more than forty-eight hundred yo*g*anas high; Spence Hardy, l.c.

seat, plunged into so deep a meditation that immediately after, on a sudden, there appeared before the Tathâgata on the Gridhrakûta-mountains in the Saha-world eighty-four hundred thousand myriads of kotis of lotuses on gold stalks with silver leaves and with cups of the hue of rosy lotuses and Butea Frondosa.

On seeing the appearance of this mass of lotuses the Bodhisattva Mahâsattva Mañgusrî, the prince royal, asked the Lord Sâkyamunî, the Tathâgata, &c.: By what cause and by whom, O Lord, have been produced these eighty-four hundred thousand myriads of kotis of lotuses on gold stalks with silver leaves and with cups of the hue of rosy lotuses and Butea Frondosa? Whereon the Lord replied to Mañgusrî, the prince royal: It is, Mañgusrî, the Bodhisattva Mahâsattva Gadgadasvara, who accompanied and attended by eighty-four hundred thousand myriads of kotis of Bodhisattvas arrives from the east, from the world Vairokanarasmipratimandita, the Buddha-field of the Lord Kamaladalavimalanakshatrarâgasankusumitâbhigña, the Tathâgata, &c., at this Saha-world to see, salute, wait upon me, and to hear this Dharmaparyâya of the Lotus of the True Law. Then Mañgusrî, the prince royal, said to the Lord: What mass of roots of goodness, O Lord, has that young man of good family collected, that he has deserved to obtain such a distinction? And what meditation is it, O Lord, that the Bodhisattva practises? Let us also learn that meditation, O Lord, and practise that meditation. And let us see that Bodhisattva, Lord; see how the colour, outward shape, character, figure, and behaviour of that Bodhisattva is. May the Lord deign to produce such a token that the Bodhisattva Mahâsattva be admonished by it to come to this Saha-world.

Then the Lord *S*âkyamuni, the Tathâgata, &c., said to the Lord Prabhûtaratna, the Tathâgata, &c., who was completely extinct: Produce such a token, Lord, that the Bodhisattva Mahâsattva Gadgadasvara be admonished by it to come to this Saha-world. And the Lord Prabhûtaratna, the Tathâgata, &c., who was completely extinct, instantly produced a token in order to admonish the Bodhisattva Mahâsattva Gadgadasvara (and said): Come, young man of good family, to this Saha-world; Ma*ñg*u*s*rî, the prince royal, will hail thy coming. And the Bodhisattva Mahâsattva Gadgadasvara, after humbly saluting the feet of the Lord Kamaladalavimalanakshatrarâ*g*asaṅkusumitâbhi*gñ*a, the Tathâgata, &c., and after three times circumambulating him from left to right, vanished from the world Vairo*k*anara*s*mipratima*nd*ita, along with eighty-four hundred thousand myriads of ko*t*is of Bodhisattvas who surrounded and followed him, and arrived at this Saha-world, among a stir of Buddha-fields, a rain of lotuses, a noise of hundred thousands of myriads of ko*t*is of musical instruments. His face showed eyes resembling blue lotuses, his body was gold-coloured, his person marked by a hundred thousand of holy signs; he sparkled with lustre, glowed with radiance, had limbs marked by the characteristic signs, and a body compact as Nârâya*n*a's. Mounted on a tower made of seven precious substances, he moved through the sky to a height of seven Tâlas[1], surrounded by a host of Bodhi-

[1] Or spans. There are seven regions of winds. Vâyu, the god of wind or air, is nearly akin to Indra and Vish*n*u.

sattvas, in the direction of this Saha-world, and approached the Gridhrakûta, the king of mountains. At his arrival, he alighted from the tower, and went, with a necklace of pearls worth a hundred thousands, to the place where the Lord was sitting. After humbly saluting the feet of the Lord, and circumambulating him seven times from left to right, he offered him the necklace of pearls in token of homage, whereafter he said to the Lord: The Lord Kamaladalavimalanakshatrarâgasankusumitâbhigña, the Tathâgata, &c., inquires after the Lord's health, welfare, and sprightliness; whether he feels free from affliction and at ease. That Lord has also charged me to ask: Is there something thou hast to suffer or allow[1]? the humours of the body are not in an unfavourable state? thy creatures are decent in manners, tractable, and easy to be healed? their bodies are clean? They are not too passionate, I hope, not too irascible, not too unwise in their doings? They are not jealous, Lord, not envious, not ungrateful to their father and mother, not impious, not heterodox, not unsubdued in mind, not unrestrained in sexual desires? Are the creatures able to resist the Evil One? Has the Lord Prabhûtaratna, the Tathâgata, &c., who is completely extinct, come to the Saha-world in order to hear the law, sitting in the centre of a Stûpa made of seven precious substances? And as to that, Lord Prabhûtaratna, the Tathâgata, &c., the Lord Kamaladalavimalanakshatrarâgasankusumitâbhigña, inquires: Is there some-

[1] Yâpanîya; it is a usual medical term applied to diseases which can be alleviated to a certain extent by means of palliatives, but can no longer be cured. It is manifest from the sequel that here also the term is derived from medical practice.

thing that the Lord Prabhûtaratna, &c., has to suffer or allow? Is the Lord Prabhûtaratna, &c., to stay long? We also, O Lord, are desirous of seeing the rudimentary frame[1] of that Lord Prabhûtaratna, the Tathâgata, &c. May the Lord therefore please to show us the rudimentary frame of the Lord Prabhûtaratna, the Tathâgata, &c.

Then the Lord *S*âkyamuni, the Tathâgata, &c., said to the Lord Prabhûtaratna, the Tathâgata, &c., who was completely extinct: Lord, the Bodhisattva Mahâsattva Gadgadasvara here wishes to see the Lord Prabhûtaratna, the Tathâgata, &c., who is completely extinct. Whereon the Lord Prabhûtaratna, the Tathâgata, &c., spoke to the Bodhisattva Mahâsattva Gadgadasvara in this strain: Well done, well done, young gentleman, that thou hast come hither in the desire to see the Lord *S*âkyamuni, the Tathâgata, &c.; to hear this Dharmaparyâya of the Lotus of the True Law, and see Ma*ñg*u*s*rî, the prince royal.

Subsequently the Bodhisattva Mahâsattva Padma*s*rî said to the Lord: What root of goodness has the Bodhisattva Mahâsattva Gadgadasvara formerly planted? And in presence of which Tathâgata? And the Lord *S*âkyamuni, the Tathâgata, &c., said to the Bodhisattva Mahâsattva Padma*s*rî: In the days of yore, young man of good family, at a past period[2] there appeared in the world a Tathâgata called Meghadundubhisvararâ*g*a (i.e. the king of the drum-sound of the clouds), perfectly enlightened, endowed with science and conduct, a Sugata, &c., in

---

[1] **Dhâtuvigraha**, the frame of the elementary parts, of the bone relics.

[2] In the margin is added the common phrase, 'at a time more incalculable than incalculable Æons.'

the world Sarvabuddhasandarsana (i. e. sight or display of all Buddhas), in the Æon Priyadarsana. To that Lord Meghadundubhisvararâga the Bodhisattva Mahâsattva Gadgadasvara paid homage by making resound hundred thousands of musical instruments during twelve thousand years. He presented to him also eighty-four thousand vessels of seven precious substances. Under the preaching[1] of the Tathâgata Meghadundubhisvararâga, young man of good family, has the Bodhisattva Mahâsattva Gadgadasvara obtained such a beauty as he now displays. Perhaps, young man of good family, thou hast some doubt, uncertainty or misgiving, (and thinkest) that at that time, that epoch, there was another Bodhisattva Mahâsattva called Gadgadasvara, who paid that homage to the Lord Meghadundubhisvararâga, the Tathâgata, and presented him the eighty-four thousand vessels. But, young man of good family, do not think so. For it was the very same Bodhisattva Mahâsattva Gadgadasvara, young man of good family, who paid that homage to the Lord Meghadundubhisvararâga, the Tathâgata, and presented to him the eighty-four thousand vessels. So, young man of good family, the Bodhisattva Mahâsattva Gadgadasvara has waited upon many Buddhas, has planted good roots under many Buddhas, and prepared the soil under each of them. And this Bodhisattva Mahâsattva Gadgadasvara had previously seen Lords Buddhas similar to the sands of the river Ganges. Dost thou see, Padmasrî, how the Bodhisattva Mahâsattva Gadgadasvara now looks? Padmasrî replied: I do, Lord; I do, Sugata. The Lord said: Now, Padmasrî, this Bodhisattva

[1] Pravakane.

Mahâsattva Gadgadasvara preaches this Dharmaparyâya of the Lotus of the True Law under many shapes he assumes; sometimes[1] under the shape of Brahma, sometimes under that of Indra, sometimes under that of *S*iva, sometimes under that of Kubera, sometimes under that of a sovereign, sometimes under that of a duke, sometimes under that of a chief merchant, sometimes under that of a citizen, sometimes under that of a villager, sometimes under that of a Brâhman[2]. Sometimes again the Bodhisattva Mahâsattva Gadgadasvara preaches this Dharmaparyâya of the Lotus of the True Law under a monk's shape, sometimes under a nun's, sometimes under a male lay devotee's, sometimes under a female lay devotee's, sometimes under that of a chief merchant's wife, sometimes under that of a citizen's wife, sometimes under a boy's, sometimes under a girl's shape. With so many variations in the manner to show himself[3], the Bodhisattva Mahâsattva Gadgadasvara preaches this Dharmaparyâya of the Lotus of the True Law to creatures. He has even assumed the shape of a goblin to preach this Dharmaparyâya to such as were to be converted by a goblin. To some he has preached this Dharmaparyâya of the Lotus of the True Law under the shape of a demon, to some under a Garu*d*a's, to some under a Kinnara's, to some under a great serpent's shape. Even to the beings in any of the wretched

[1] Or somewhere.

[2] From this one may infer that Gadgadasvara, i.e. he who has an interrupted sound, is Vâyu, πνεῦμα, inspiration personified. Materially, though not mythologically, Wind is identical with Rudra, Storm.

[3] Iyadbhî rûpasandar*s*aneryâpathai*h*.

states, in the hells, the brute creation, Yama's realm, the Bodhisattva Mahâsattva Gadgadasvara is a supporter. Even to the creatures in the gynæceums of this Saha-world has the Bodhisattva Mahâsattva Gadgadasvara, after metamorphosing himself into a woman, preached this Dharmaparyâya of the Lotus of the True Law. Verily, Padmasrî, the Bodhisattva Mahâsattva Gadgadasvara is the supporter of the creatures living in this Saha-world [1]. Under so many shapes, assumed at will, has the Bodhisattva Mahâsattva Gadgadasvara preached this Dharmaparyâya of the Lotus of the True Law to creatures. Yet, there is no diminution of wisdom, nor diminution of magic power in that good man [2]. So many, young man of good family, are the manifestations of knowledge by which this Bodhisattva Mahâsattva Gadgadasvara has made himself known in this Saha-world. In other worlds also, similar to the sands of the river Ganges, he preaches the law, under the shape of a Bodhisattva to such as must be converted by a Bodhisattva; under the shape of a disciple to such as must be converted by a disciple; under the shape of a Pratyekabuddha to such as must be con-

[1] Vâyu, prâna, breath of life, is the supporter of creatures.

[2] Satpurusha; the real meaning is 'the existing spirit;' air, breath, life, which shows itself in a diversity of forms. That living breath is not only the supporter of creatures, but also a constant admonisher of the transitoriness of life, who addresses his call to young and old, sages and fools, &c. The important mystic rite of inspiration and expiration is described by Spence Hardy, Eastern Monachism, p. 267; no less value is attached to prânâyâma in the Yoga system and in Indian mysticism in general; see e.g. Yogasâstra II, 49–51; Sarvadarsana-Sangraha, p. 175; the term prânâyâma not only denotes stopping of the breath, as the Dictionaries explain it, but also the regulation and measuring of the breath.

verted by a Pratyekabuddha; under the shape of a Tathâgata to such as must be converted by a Tathâgata. Nay, he will show to those who must be converted by a relic of the Tathâgata himself such a relic, and to those who must be converted by complete extinction he will show himself completely extinct[1]. Such is the powerful knowledge, Padma*s*rî, the Bodhisattva Mahâsattva is possessed of.

Thereafter the Bodhisattva Mahâsattva Padma*s*rî said to the Lord: The Bodhisattva Mahâsattva Gadgadasvara then has planted good roots, Lord. What meditation is it, Lord, whereby the Bodhisattva Mahâsattva Gadgadasvara, with unshaken firmness, has converted (or educated) so many creatures? Whereupon the Lord *S*âkyamuni, the Tathâgata, &c., replied to the Bodhisattva Mahâsattva Padma*s*rî: It is, young man of good family, the meditation termed Sarvarûpasandar*s*ana. By steadiness in it has the Bodhisattva Mahâsattva Gadgadasvara so immensely promoted the weal of creatures.

While this chapter of Gadgadasvara was being expounded[2], all the eighty-four hundred thousand myriads of ko*t*is of Bodhisattvas Mahâsattvas who, along with the Bodhisattva Mahâsattva Gadgadasvara, had come to the Saha-world, obtained the

---

[1] Gadgadasvara, being both inspiration and expiration, appears under the form of a dead corpse, and thereby converts fickle and thoughtless men.

[2] It need not be observed that the chapter was not expounded, the Buddha being one of the dramatis personæ, one of the interlocutors, but not the narrator. This confusion between epical and dramatical exposition is one of the most striking features of the Lotus. The Saddharma, the law of nature, may be said to have been expounded by the Tathâgata, not, however, the composition which bears that title.

meditation Sarvarûpasandarsana, and as to the number of Bodhisattvas Mahâsattvas of this Saha-world obtaining the meditation Sarvarûpasandarsana, it was beyond calculation.

Then the Bodhisattva Mahâsattva Gadgadasvara, after having paid great and ample worship to the Lord Sâkyamuni, the Tathâgata, &c., and at the Stûpa of relics of the Lord Prabhûtaratna, the Tathâgata, &c., again mounted the tower made of seven precious substances, among the stir of the fields, the rain of lotuses, the noise of hundred thousands of myriads of kotis of musical instruments[1], and with the eighty-four hundred thousand myriads of kotis of Bodhisattvas surrounding and following him, returned to his own Buddha-field. At his arrival there he said to the Lord Kamaladalavimalanakshatrarâgasankusumitâbhigña, the Tathâgata, &c.: O Lord, I have in the Saha-world promoted the weal of creatures; I have seen and saluted the Stûpa of relics of the Lord Prabhûtaratna, the Tathâgata, &c.; I have seen and saluted the Lord Sâkyamuni, the Tathâgata, &c.; I have seen Mañgusrî, the prince royal, as well as the Bodhisattva Bhaishagyarâga, who is possessed of mighty knowledge and impetuosity[2], and the Bodhisattva Mahâsattva Pradânasûra; and these eighty-four hundred thousand myriads of kotis of Bodhi-

[1] After a last effort the storm subsides.

[2] This quality stamps Bhaishagyarâga as Rudra; cf. Rig-veda II, 33, 7. He is essentially the same with Dhanvantari the physician, Arcitenens Apollo. He is, moreover, the same with Gadgadasvara, who is represented as breath of life. About the system of splitting up one natural phenomenon or abstraction into more beings, see p. 4, note.

sattvas Mahâsattvas have all obtained the meditation termed Sarvarûpasandarsana.

And while this relation of the going and coming of the Bodhisattva Mahâsattva Gadgadasvara was being delivered, forty-two thousand Bodhisattvas acquired the faculty of acquiescence in future things, and the Bodhisattva Mahâsattva Padmasrî acquired the meditation called the Lotus of the True Law.

CHAPTER XXIV.

CHAPTER CALLED THAT OF THE ALL-SIDED ONE, CONTAINING A DESCRIPTION OF THE TRANSFORMATIONS OF AVALOKITE*S*VARA[1].

Thereafter the Bodhisattva Mahâsattva Akshayamati rose from his seat, put his upper robe upon one shoulder, stretched his joined hands towards the Lord, and said: For what reason, O Lord, is the Bodhisattva Mahâsattva Avalokite*s*vara called Avalokite*s*vara? So he asked, and the Lord answered to the Bodhisattva Mahâsattva Akshayamati: All the hundred thousands of myriads of ko*t*is of creatures, young man of good family, who in this world are suffering troubles will, if they hear the name of the Bodhisattva Mahâsattva Avalokite*s*vara, be released from that mass of troubles. Those who shall keep the name of this Bodhisattva Mahâsattva Avalokite*s*vara, young man of good family, will, if they fall into a great mass of fire, be delivered therefrom by virtue of the lustre of the Bodhisattva Mahâsattva. In case, young man of good family, creatures, carried off by the current of rivers, should implore the Bodhisattva Mahâsattva Avalokite*s*vara, all rivers will afford them a ford. In case, young man of good family, many hundred thousand myriads of ko*t*is of creatures, sailing in a ship on the ocean,

[1] A translation of this chapter from the Chinese has been published by Rev. S. Beal in his Catena, pp. 389–396.

should see their bullion, gold, gems, pearls, lapis lazuli, conch shells, stones (?), corals, emeralds, Musâragalvas, read pearls (?), and other goods lost, and the ship by a vehement, untimely gale cast on the island of Giantesses[1], and if in that ship a single being implores Avalokitesvara, all will be saved from that island of Giantesses. For that reason, young man of good family, the Bodhisattva Mahâsattva Avalokitesvara is named Avalokitesvara[2].

If a man given up to capital punishment[3] implores Avalokitesvara, young man of good family, the swords of the executioners shall snap asunder[4] Further, young man of good family, if the whole triple chiliocosm were teeming with goblins and giants, they would by virtue of the name of the Bodhisattva Mahâsattva Avalokitesvara being pronounced lose the faculty of sight in their wicked designs[5] If some creature, young man of good

[1] In the Kâra*nd*a-vyûha, a work entirely devoted to the glorification of Avalokitesvara and his sublime achievements, the isle of the Giantesses is identified with Ceylon; see pp. 45 and 53 of that work (Calcutta edition), and the extract given by Burnouf, Introduction, pp. 221–227.

[2] Avalokita means 'beheld;' it is as such synonymous with d*ri*sh*t*a, seen, visible, and pratyaksha, visible, manifest, present. The Bodhisattva is everywhere present, and therefore implored in need and danger. If we take avalokita as a substantive in the neuter gender, the compound will mean 'the Lord of view, of regard,' with which one may compare *S*iva's epithet D*ri*sh*t*iguru, the Master of view.

[3] Vadhyotsish*t*a; I do not feel certain of the rendering of u*kkh*ish*t*a; perhaps we should translate it by 'a reprobate condemned to capital punishment.'

[4] Vadhyaghâtakânâ*m* tâni sastrâni (sic) vi*s*îryeyu*h*.

[5] It is well known that those children of darkness are unable to stand the sun's light.

family, shall be bound in wooden or iron manacles, chains or fetters, be he guilty or innocent, then those manacles, chains or fetters shall give way as soon as the name of the Bodhisattva Mahâsattva Avalokitesvara is pronounced. Such, young man of good family, is the power of the Bodhisattva Mahâsattva Avalokitesvara. If this whole triple chiliocosm, young man of good family, were teeming with knaves, enemies, and robbers armed with swords, and if a merchant leader of a caravan marched with a caravan rich in jewels; if then they perceived those robbers, knaves, and enemies armed with swords, and in their anxiety and fright thought themselves helpless; if, further, that leading merchant spoke to the caravan in this strain: Be not afraid, young gentlemen, be not frightened; invoke, all of you, with one voice the Bodhisattva Mahâsattva Avalokitesvara, the giver of safety; then you shall be delivered from this danger by which you are threatened at the hands of robbers and enemies; if then the whole caravan with one voice invoked Avalokitesvara with the words: Adoration, adoration be to the giver of safety, to Avalokitesvara Bodhisattva Mahâsattva! then, by the mere act of pronouncing that name, the caravan would be released from all danger. Such, young man of good family, is the power of the Bodhisattva Mahâsattva Avalokitesvara. In case creatures act under the impulse of impure passion, young man of good family, they will, after adoring the Bodhisattva Mahâsattva Avalokitesvara, be freed from passion. Those who act under the impulse of hatred will, after adoring the Bodhisattva Mahâsattva Avalokitesvara, be freed from hatred. Those who act under the impulse of infatuation will, after adoring the Bodhisattva Mahâsattva Avalokitesvara, be freed from infatuation. So mighty, young man of good family, is the Bodhisattva Mahâsattva Avalokitesvara. If a woman, desirous of male offspring, young man of good family, adores the Bodhisattva Avalokitesvara, she shall get a son, nice, handsome, and beautiful; one possessed of the characteristics of a male child, generally beloved and winning, who has planted good roots[1]. If a woman is desirous of getting a daughter, a nice, handsome, beautiful girl shall be born to her; one possessed of the (good) characteristics of a girl[2], generally beloved and winning, who has planted good roots. Such, young man of good family, is the power of the Bodhisattva Mahâsattva Avalokitesvara.

Those who adore the Bodhisattva Mahâsattva Avalokitesvara will derive from it an unfailing profit. Suppose, young man of good family, (on one hand) some one adoring the Bodhisattva Mahâsattva Avalokitesvara and cherishing his name; (on the other hand) another adoring a number of Lords Buddhas equal to sixty-two times the sands of the river Ganges[3], cherishing their names and worshipping so many Lords Buddhas during their stay, existence, and life, by giving robes, alms-bowls, couches, medicaments for the sick; how great is then in thine opinion, young man of good family, the accumulation of pious merit which that young gentleman or young lady will produce in consequence of it? So asked,

[1] We should rather say: in whom a good natural disposition is implanted.

[2] In the margin added paramayâ *s*ubhavar*n*apushkalatayâ, (and) of an egregiously blooming complexion.

[3] Dvâshash*t*înâ*m* Gaṅgâ°.

the Bodhisattva Mahâsattva Akshayamati said to the Lord: Great, O Lord, great, O Sugata, is the pious merit which that young gentleman or young lady will produce in consequence of it. The Lord proceeded: Now, young man of good family, the accumulation of pious merit produced by that young gentleman paying homage to so many Lords Buddhas, and the accumulation of pious merit produced by him who performs were it but a single act of adoration to the Bodhisattva Mahâsattva Avalokitesvara and cherishes his name, are equal. He who adores a number of Lords Buddhas equal to sixty-two times the sands of the river Ganges and cherishes their names, and he who adores the Bodhisattva Mahâsattva Avalokitesvara and cherishes his name, have an equal accumulation of pious merit[1]; both masses of pious merit are not easy to be destroyed even in hundred thousands of myriads of kotis of Æons. So immense, young man of good family, is the pious merit resulting from cherishing the name of the Bodhisattva Mahâsattva Avalokitesvara.

Again the Bodhisattva Mahâsattva Akshayamati said to the Lord: How, O Lord, is it that the Bodhisattva Mahâsattva Avalokitesvara frequents this Saha-world? And how does he preach the law? And which is the range of the skilfulness of the Bodhisattva Mahâsattva Avalokitesvara? So asked, the Lord replied to the Bodhisattva Mahâsattva Akshayamati: In some worlds, young man of good family, the Bodhisattva Mahâsattva Avalokitesvara preaches the law to creatures in the shape of a Buddha;

[1] Burnouf has followed a text of greater length.

in others he does so in the shape of a Bodhisattva. To some beings he shows the law in the shape of a Pratyekabuddha; to others he does so in the shape of a disciple; to others again under that of Brahma, Indra, or a Gandharva. To those who are to be converted by a goblin, he preaches the law assuming the shape of a goblin; to those who are to be converted by Îsvara, he preaches the law in the shape of Îsvara; to those who are to be converted by Mahesvara, he preaches assuming the shape of Mahesvara. To those who are to be converted by a *K*akravartin[1], he shows the law after assuming the shape of a *K*akravartin; to those who are to be converted by an imp, he shows the law under the shape of an imp; to those who are to be converted by Kubera, he shows the law by appearing in the shape of Kubera; to those who are to be converted by Senâpati[2], he preaches in the shape of Senâpati; to those who are to be converted by assuming a Brâhman[3], he preaches in the shape of a Brâhman; to those who are to be converted by Vagrapâ*n*i[4], he preaches in the shape of Vagrapâ*n*i[5]. With such inconceivable qualities, young man of good family, is the Bodhi-

[1] This term is ambiguous; it means both 'the mover of the wheel,' i.e. Vish*n*u, and 'an emperor.'

[2] Ambiguous; the word denotes both 'the commander-in-chief of the army of the gods, Skanda,' and 'a commander-in-chief in general.'

[3] The Brâhman may be B*r*ihaspati.

[4] Vagrapâ*n*i is the name of one of the Dhyânibuddhas, and of certain geniuses, and an epithet of Indra.

[5] The functions of Avalokitesvara, as it appears from these passages, agree with those of Gadgadasvara mentioned in the foregoing chapter. Both beings have many qualities in common, just as *S*iva and Vish*n*u have.

sattva Mahâsattva Avalokitesvara endowed[1]. Therefore then, young man of good family, honour the Bodhisattva Mahâsattva Avalokitesvara. The Bodhisattva Mahâsattva Avalokitesvara, young man of good family, affords safety to those who are in anxiety. On that account one calls him in this Saha-world Abhayandada (i. e. Giver of Safety).

Further, the Bodhisattva Mahâsattva Akshayamati said to the Lord: Shall we give a gift of piety, a decoration of piety, O Lord, to the Bodhisattva Mahâsattva Avalokitesvara? The Lord replied: Do so, if thou thinkest it opportune. Then the Bodhisattva Mahâsattva Akshayamati took from his neck a pearl necklace, worth a hundred thousand (gold pieces), and presented it to the Bodhisattva Mahâsattva Avalokitesvara as a decoration of piety, with the words: Receive from me this decoration of piety, good man. But he would not accept it. Then the Bodhisattva Mahâsattva Akshayamati said to the Bodhisattva Mahâsattva Avalokitesvara: Out of compassion to us, young man of good family, accept this pearl necklace. Then the Bodhisattva Mahâsattva Avalokitesvara accepted the pearl necklace from the Bodhisattva Mahâsattva Akshayamati, out of compassion to the Bodhisattva Mahâsattva Akshayamati and the four classes, and out of compassion to the gods, Nâgas, goblins, Gandharvas, demons, Garudas, Kinnaras, great serpents, men, and beings not human. Thereafter he divided (the necklace) into two parts, and offered one part to the Lord Sâkyamuni, and the other to the jewel Stûpa of the Lord Prabhûtaratna, the Tathâgata, &c., who had become completely extinct.

[1] Burnouf has followed another reading.

With such a faculty of transformation, young man of good family, the Bodhisattva Mahâsattva Avalokitesvara is moving in this Saha-world.

And on that occasion the Lord uttered the following stanzas:

1. *K*itradhva*g*a asked Akshayamati the following question: For what reason, son of *G*ina, is Avalokitesvara (so) called[1]?

2. And Akshayamati, that ocean of profound insight, after considering how the matter stood[2], spoke to *K*itradhva*g*a: Listen to the conduct of Avalokitesvara.

3. Hear from my indication how for numerous, inconceivable Æons he has accomplished his vote under many thousand ko*t*is of Buddhas.

4. Hearing, seeing, regularly and constantly thinking[3] will infallibly destroy all suffering, (mundane) existence, and grief of living beings here on earth.

5. If one be thrown into a pit of fire, by a wicked enemy with the object of killing him, he has but to think of Avalokitesvara, and the fire shall be quenched as if sprinkled with water.

6. If one happens to fall into the dreadful ocean, the abode of Nâgas, marine monsters, and demons, he has but to think of Avalokitesvara, and he shall never sink down in the king of waters[4].

---

[1] It will be observed that this poetical version here entirely differs from the preceding prose introduction. As to the name of *K*itradhva*g*a, I have not met with it elsewhere.

[2] Tâd*ri*s*a*tâ vilokiyâ.

[3] Of whom or what? is not expressed. From the sequel one might be tempted to infer that Avalokitesvara, or the exposition of his power, is the object of hearing, &c.

[4] Smarato (for smaratu), Avalokitesvara*m g*alarâ*g*e na kadâ*k*i sîdati.

7. If a man happens to be hurled down from the brink of the Meru, by some wicked person with the object of killing him, he has but to think of Avalokite*s*vara, and he shall, sunlike, stand firm in the sky[1].

8. If rocks of thunderstone and thunderbolts are thrown at a man's head to kill him, he has but to think of Avalokite*s*vara, and they shall not be able to hurt one hair of the body.

9. If a man be surrounded by a host of enemies armed with swords, who have the intention of killing him, he has but to think of Avalokite*s*vara, and they shall instantaneously become kind-hearted.

10. If a man, delivered to the power of the executioners, is already standing at the place of execution, he has but to think of Avalokite*s*vara, and their swords shall go to pieces.

11. If a person happens to be fettered in shackles of wood or iron, he has but to think of Avalokite*s*vara, and the bonds shall be speedily loosened.

12. Mighty spells, witchcraft, herbs, ghosts, and spectres, pernicious to life, revert thither whence they come, when one thinks of Avalokite*s*vara.

13. If a man is surrounded by goblins, Nâgas, demons, ghosts, or giants, who are in the habit of taking away bodily vigour, he has but to think of Avalokite*s*vara, and they shall not be able to hurt one hair of his body[2].

---

[1] Smarato Avalokite*s*varo (r. °ra*m*) sûryabhûta*m* (r. °to) va nabhe pratish*th*ati. I have taken the liberty of translating pratish*th*ati as if the text had pratitish*th*ati. The version of Beal has 'stand in space, fixed as the sun.'

[2] Here I have followed the marginal reading, which agrees with Burnouf's. The older text has instead of thirteen and fourteen but one stanza, the translation of which runs thus: 'If, &c., sur-

14. If a man is surrounded by fearful beasts with sharp teeth and claws, he has but to think of Avalokitesvara, and they shall quickly fly in all directions.

15. If a man is surrounded by snakes malicious and frightful on account of the flames and fires (they emit), he has but to think of Avalokitesvara, and they shall quickly lose their poison.

16. If a heavy thunderbolt shoots from a cloud pregnant with lightning and thunder, one has but to think of Avalokitesvara, and the fire of heaven shall quickly, instantaneously be quenched.

17. He (Avalokitesvara) with his powerful knowledge beholds all creatures who are beset with many hundreds of troubles and afflicted by many sorrows, and thereby is a saviour in the world, including the gods.

18. As he is thoroughly practised in the power of magic, and possessed of vast knowledge and skilfulness, he shows himself[1] in all directions and in all regions of the world.

19. Birth, decrepitude, and disease will come to an end for those who are in the wretched states of existence, in hell, in brute creation, in the kingdom of Yama, for all beings (in general[2]).

[Then Akshayamati in the joy of his heart uttered the following stanzas[3]:]

20. O thou whose eyes are clear, whose eyes are

rounded by Nâgas, marine monsters, demons, ghosts, or giants he has, &c., and they shall quickly fly in all directions.'

[1] Drisyate.

[2] We have to understand: in consequence of the conduct of the great Avalokitesvara.

[3] The words in brackets have been added in the margin by a later hand.

kind, distinguished by wisdom and knowledge, whose eyes are full of pity and benevolence; thou so lovely by thy beautiful face and beautiful eyes!

21. Pure one, whose shine is spotless bright, whose knowledge is free from darkness, thou shining as the sun, not to be beaten away, radiant as the blaze of fire, thou spreadest in thy flying course thy lustre in the world[1].

22. O thou who rejoicest in kindness having its source in compassion, thou great cloud of good qualities and of benevolent mind[2], thou quenchest the fire that vexes living beings, thou pourest out nectar, the rain of the law.

23. In quarrel[3], dispute, war, battle, in any great danger one has to think of Avalokite*s*vara, who shall quell the wicked troop of foes.

24. One should think of Avalokite*s*vara, whose sound is as the cloud's and the drum's, who thunders like a rain-cloud, possesses a good voice like Brahma, (a voice) going through the whole gamut of tones.

25. Think, O think with tranquil mood of Avalokite*s*vara, that pure being; he is a protector, a refuge, a recourse in death, disaster, and calamity.

26. He who possesses the perfection of all virtues, and beholds all beings with compassion and benevolence, he, an ocean of virtues, Virtue itself, he, Avalokite*s*vara, is worthy of adoration.

---

[1] Aparâhata anila*g*alaprabhâ (voc. case) prapatento *g*agatî viro*k*asi. For anila*g*ala I read anala*g*ala (Sansk. anala*g*vala). Cf. Kâra*nd*a-vyûha, p. 43: Athâryâvalokite*s*varo *g*valad ivâgnipi*nd*am âkâ*s*e 'ntarhita*h*.

[2] K*r*ipasa*m*bhûtamaitragar*g*itâ (voc.) *s*ubhagu*n*a maitrama*n*â mahâghanâ (voc.)

[3] Kalahe.

27. He, so compassionate for the world, shall once become a Buddha, destroying all dangers and sorrows[1]; I humbly bow to Avalokitesvara.

28. This universal Lord, chief of kings, who is a (rich) mine of monastic virtues, he, universally worshipped, has reached pure, supreme enlightenment, after plying his course (of duty) during many hundreds of Æons.

29. At one time standing to the right, at another to the left of the Chief Amitâbha, whom he is fanning, he, by dint of meditation, like a phantom, in all regions honours the *G*ina.

30. In the west, where the pure world Sukhâkara[2] is situated, there the Chief Amitâbha, the tamer of men[3], has his fixed abode.

31. There no women are to be found; there sexual intercourse is absolutely unknown; there the sons of *G*ina, on springing into existence by apparitional birth, are sitting in the undefiled cups of lotuses.

32. And the Chief Amitâbha himself is seated on a throne in the pure and nice cup of a lotus, and shines as the *S*âla-king[4].

---

[1] The present will make room for the future, life will end in death; the living Avalokitesvara will pass into the state of Buddha, al. Dharmarâ*g*a, i.e. Death, the great physician.

[2] I.e. procuring bliss or tranquillity; the more common name is Sukhâvatî. In Greek and Roman mythology we find the Insulae Fortunatae and the gardens of the Hesperidae lying in the same quarter.

[3] From this it appears that Amitâbha or Amitâyus is but another name of Yama, and just as Yama also governs the planet Saturn, it may be held that Amitâbha, as one of the five Dhyâni-Buddhas, among his other offices, is invested with the dignity of being the ruler of Saturn.

[4] I do not understand the meaning of this compound. In the

33. The Leader of the world, whose store of merit has been praised, has no equal in the triple world. O supreme of men, let us soon become like thee!

Thereupon the Bodhisattva Mahâsattva Dhara*n*indhara rose from his seat, put his upper robe upon one shoulder, fixed his right knee against the earth, stretched his joined hands towards the Lord and said: They must be possessed of not a few good roots, O Lord, who are to hear this chapter from the Dharmaparyâya about the Bodhisattva Mahâsattva Avalokite*s*vara and this miraculous power of transformation of the Bodhisattva Mahâsattva Avalokite*s*vara.

And while this chapter of the All-sided One was being expounded by the Lord, eighty-four thousand living beings from that assembly felt their minds drawn to that supreme and perfect enlightenment, with which nothing else can be compared[1].

next following chapter we shall meet with a Tathâgata named *S*âlendrarâ*g*a, i.e. king of the *S*âla-chiefs.

[1] Asamasama; Burnouf takes it as 'qui est égal à ce qui n'a pas d'égal.' The term also occurs Lalita-vistara, p. 114, l. 9.

CHAPTER XXV.

ANCIENT DEVOTION[1].

Thereupon the Lord addressed the entire assemblage of Bodhisattvas: Of yore, young men of good family, at a past epoch, incalculable, more than incalculable Æons ago, at that time there appeared in the world a Tathâgata named *G*aladharagar*g*itaghoshasusvaranakshatrarâ*g*asaṅkusumitâbhi*gñ*a, an Arhat, &c., endowed with science and conduct, &c. &c., in the Æon Priyadarsana, in the world Vairo*k*anaras*m*ipratima*nd*ita. Now, there was, young men of good family, under the spiritual rule of the Tathâgata *G*aladharagar*g*itaghoshasusvaranakshatrarâ*g*asaṅkusumitâbhi*gñ*a a king called *S*ubhavyûha. That king *S*ubhavyûha, young men of good family, had a wife called Vimaladattâ, and two sons, one called Vimalagarbha, the other Vimalanetra. These two boys, who possessed magical power and wisdom[2], applied themselves to the course of duty of Bodhisattvas, viz. to the perfect virtues (Pâramitâs) of almsgiving, morality, forbearance, energy, meditation, wisdom, and skilfulness; they were accomplished in benevolence, compassion, joyful sympathy and indifference, and in all the thirty-

---

[1] Pûrvayoga; rather, ancient history; cf. p. 153.

[2] In the margin sundry epithets have been added, which here are omitted.

seven constituents of true knowledge[1]. They had perfectly mastered the meditation Vimala (i.e. spotless), the meditation Nakshatrarâ*g*âditya[2], the meditation Vimalanirbhâsa, the meditation Vimalâbhâsa, the meditation Alankârasûra[3], the meditation Mahâte*g*ogarbha[4]. Now at that time, that period the said Lord preached the Dharmaparyâya of the Lotus of the True Law out of compassion for the beings then living and for the king *S*ubhavyûha. Then, young men of good family, the two young princes Vimalagarbha and Vimalanetra went to their mother, to whom they said, after stretching their joined hands: We should like to go, mother, to the Lord *G*aladharagar*g*itaghoshasusvaranakshatrarâ*g*asankusumitâbhi*g*ña, the Tathâgata, &c., and that, mother, because the Lord *G*aladharagar*g*itaghoshasusvaranakshatrarâ*g*asankusumitâbhi*g*ña, the Tathâgata, &c., expounds, in great extension, before the world, including the gods, the Dharmaparyâya of the Lotus of the True Law. We should like to hear it. Whereupon the queen Vimaladattâ said to the two young princes Vimalagarbha and Vimalanetra: Your father, young gentlemen, the king *S*ubhavyûha, favours the Brah-

---

[1] Bodhipakshika or Bodhapakshika (dharmâs). They form part of the 108 Dharmâlokamukhas in Lalita-vistara, p. 36, l. 17–p. 38, l. 6; an enumeration of them is found in Spence Hardy's Manual of Buddhism, p. 497.

[2] Burnouf's reading is Nakshatratârârâ*g*aditya, i.e. the Sun, king of stars and asterisms.

[3] So Burnouf; my MS. has Alankâra*s*ubha, i.e. splendid with ornaments.

[4] I.e. having great lustre in the interior, or womb of great lustre. Nirmalanirbhâsa may mean both 'spotless radiance' and 'having a spotless radiance;' Vimalâbhâsa, 'spotless shine,' or 'having a spotless shine.'

mans. Therefore you will not obtain the permission to go and see the Tathâgata. Then the two young princes Vimalagarbha and Vimalanetra, stretching their joined hands, said to their mother: Though born in a family that adheres to a false doctrine, we feel as sons to the king of the law. Then, young men of good family, the queen Vimaladattâ said to the young princes: Well, young gentlemen, out of compassion for your father, the king *S*ubhavyûha, display some miracle, that he may become favourably inclined to you, and on that account grant you the permission of going to the Lord *G*aladharagar*g*ita-ghoshasusvaranakshatrarâ*g*asaṅkusumitâbhi*gñ*a, the Tathâgata, &c.

Immediately the young princes Vimalagarbha and Vimalanetra rose into the atmosphere to a height of seven Tâl trees[1] and performed miracles such as are allowed by the Buddha, out of compassion for their father, the king *S*ubhavyûha. They prepared in the sky a couch and raised dust; there they also emitted from the lower part of their body a shower of rain, and from the upper part a mass of fire; then again they emitted from the upper part of their body a shower of rain, and from the lower part a mass of fire[2]. While in the firmament they became now big, then small; and now small, then big. Then they vanished from the sky to come up again from the earth and reappear in the air. Such, young men of good family, were the miracles produced by the

[1] Or seven spans, whatever may be meant by it.

[2] A similar miracle was performed by the Buddha, according to the traditions of the Southern Buddhists, when he had to show his superiority to the six heretical doctors; see Bigandet, Life of Gaudama, vol. i, p. 218.

magical power of the two young princes, whereby their father, the king *S*ubhavyûha, was converted. At the sight of the miracle produced by the magical power of the two young princes, the king *S*ubhavyûha was content, in high spirits, ravished, rejoiced, joyful, and happy, and, the joined hands raised, he said to the boys: Who is your master, young gentlemen? whose pupils are you? And the two young princes answered the king *S*ubhavyûha: There is, noble king, there exists and lives a Lord *G*aladharagar*g*itaghoshasusvaranakshatrarâ*g*asaṅkusumitâbhi*gñ*a, a Tathâgata, &c.; seated on the stool of law at the foot of the tree of enlightenment; he extensively reveals the Dharmaparyâya of the Lotus of the True Law to the world, including the gods. That Lord is our Master, O noble king; we are his pupils. Then, young gentlemen of good family, the king *S*ubhavyûha said to the young princes: I will see your Master, young gentlemen; I am to go myself to the presence of that Lord.

After the two young princes had descended from the sky, young gentlemen, they went to their mother and with joined hands stretched forward said to her: Mother, we have converted our father to supreme and perfect knowledge; we have performed the office of masters towards him; therefore let us go now; we wish to enter upon the ecclesiastical life in the face of the Lord. And on that occasion, young men of good family, the young princes Vimalagarbha and Vimalanetra addressed their mother in the following two stanzas:

1. Allow us, O mother, to go forth from home and to embrace the houseless life; ay, we will

become ascetics, for rare to be met with (or precious) is a Tathâgata.

2. As the blossom of the glomerated fig-tree, nay, more rare is the *G*ina. Let us depart; we will renounce the world; the favourable moment is precious (or not often to be met with).

Vimaladattâ said:

3. Now I grant you leave; go, my children, I give my consent. I myself will likewise renounce the world, for rare to be met with (or precious) is a Tathâgata.

Having uttered these stanzas, young men of good family, the two young princes said to their parents: Pray, father and mother, you also go together with us to the Lord *G*aladharagar*g*itaghoshasusvaranakshatrarâ*g*asankusumitâbhi*gñ*a, the Tathâgata, &c., in order to see, humbly salute and wait upon him, and to hear the law. For, father and mother, the appearance of a Buddha is rare to be met with as the blossom of the glomerated fig-tree, as the entering of the tortoise's neck into the hole of the yoke formed by the great ocean [1]. The appearance of Lords Buddhas, father and mother, is rare. Hence, father and mother, it is a happy lot we have been blessed with, to have been born at the time of such a prophet. Therefore, father and mother, give us leave; we would go and become ascetics in presence [2] of the Lord *G*aladharagar*g*itaghoshasusvaranakshatrarâ*g*asankusumitâbhi*gñ*a, the Tathâgata, &c., for the

[1] I am as unable to elucidate this comparison as Burnouf was. Not unlikely the mythological tortoise in its quality of supporter of the earth is alluded to.

[2] Sakâ*s*e; Burnouf has 'sous l'enseignement' (*s*âsane), which is the more usual phrase.

seeing of a Tathâgata is something rare. Such a king of the law is rarely met with; such a favourable occasion[1] is rarely met with.

Now at that juncture, young men of good family, the eighty-four thousand women of the harem of the king *S*ubhavyûha became worthy of being receptacles of this Dharmaparyâya of the Lotus of the True Law. The young prince Vimalanetra exercised himself in this Dharmaparyâya, whereas the young prince Vimalagarbha for many hundred thousand myriads of ko*t*is of Æons practised the meditation Sarvasattvapâpa*g*ahana[2], with the object that all beings should abandon all evils. And the mother of the two young princes, the queen Vimaladattâ, acknowledged the harmony between all Buddhas and all topics treated by them[3]. Then, young men of good family, the king *S*ubhavyûha, having been converted to the law of the Tathâgata by the instrumentality of the two young princes, having been initiated and brought to full maturity in it, along with all his relations and retinue; the queen Vimaladattâ with the whole crowd of women in her suite, and the two young princes, the sons of the king *S*ubhavyûha, accompanied by forty-two thousand living beings, along with the women of the harem and the ministers, went all together and unanimously to the Lord *G*aladharagar*g*itaghoshasusvaranakshatrarâ*g*asankusumitâbhi*gñ*a, the Tathâgatha, &c. On arriving at the place where the Lord was, they humbly saluted his

---

[1] Îd*r*i*s*î kshanasampad.

[2] I.e. means whereby (all) evils are abandoned by all creatures.

[3] Sarvabuddhasthânâni; in the margin added the word for 'secret.'

feet, circumambulated him three times from left to right and took their stand at some distance.

Then, young men of good family, the Lord *G*aladharagar*g*itaghoshasusvaranakshatrarâ*g*asaṅkusumitâbhi*gñ*a, the Tathâgata, &c., perceiving the king *S*ubhavyûha, who had arrived with his retinue, instructed, roused, excited, and comforted him with a sermon. And the king *S*ubhavyûha, young men of good family, after he had been well and duly instructed, roused, excited, and comforted by the sermon of the Lord, was so content, glad, ravished, joyful, rejoiced, and delighted, that he put his diadem on the head of his younger brother and established him in the government, whereafter he himself with his sons, kinsmen, and retinue, as well as the queen Vimaladattâ and her numerous train of women, the two young princes accompanied by forty-two [1] thousand living beings went all together and unanimously forth from home to embrace the houseless life, prompted as they were by their faith in the preaching of the Lord *G*aladharagar*g*itaghoshasusvaranakshatrarâ*g*asaṅkusumitâbhi*gñ*a, the Tathâgata, &c. Having become an ascetic, the king *S*ubhavyûha, with his retinue, remained for eighty-four thousand years applying himself to studying, meditating, and thoroughly penetrating this Dharmaparyâya of the Lotus of the True Law. At the end of those eighty-four thousand years, young men of good family, the king *S*ubhavyûha acquired the meditation termed Sarvagu*n*âlaṅkâravyûha [2]. No sooner had he ac-

[1] Burnouf has eighty-four, but this must be a faulty reading, because the number of forty-two agrees with that given above.

[2] I. e. collocation (or disposition) of the ornaments of all good qualities.

quired that meditation, than he rose seven Tâls up to the sky, and while staying in the air, young men of good family, the king *S*ubhavyûha said to the Lord *G*aladharagar*g*itaghoshasusvaranakshatrarâ*g*a-sankusumitâbhi*gñ*a, the Tathâgata, &c.: My two sons, O Lord, are my masters, since it is owing to the miracle produced by their magical power that I have been diverted from that great heap of false doctrines, been established in the command of the Lord, brought to full ripeness in it, introduced to it, and exhorted to see the Lord. They have acted as true friends to me, O Lord, those two young princes who as sons were born in my house, certainly to remind me of my former roots of goodness.

At these words the Lord *G*aladharagar*g*itaghoshasusvaranakshatrarâ*g*asankusumitâbhi*gñ*a, the Tathâgata, &c., spoke to the king *S*ubhavyûha: It is as thou sayest, noble king. Indeed, noble king, such young men or young ladies of good family as possess roots of goodness, will in any existence, state, descent, rebirth or place [1] easily find true friends, who with them shall perform the task of a master [2], who shall admonish, introduce, fully prepare them to obtain supreme and perfect enlightenment. It is an exalted position, noble king, the office of a true friend who rouses (another) to see the Tathâgata. Dost thou see these two young princes, noble king? I do, Lord; I do, Sugata, said the king. The Lord

[1] Bhavagati*k*yutyupapattyâyataneshu. Burnouf must have read bhagava*kk*yu° or something like it, for he translates: 'qui sont nés dans les lieux où se sont accomplies la naissance et la mort d'un Bienheureux.'

[2] I. e. of a teacher, *s*âst*ri*k*ri*tyena.

proceeded: Now, these two young gentlemen, noble king, will pay worship to sixty-five (times the number of) Tathâgatas, &c., equal to the sands of the Ganges; they will keep this Dharmaparyâya of the Lotus of the True Law, out of compassion for beings who hold false doctrines, and with the aim to produce in those beings an earnest striving after the right doctrine.

Thereupon, young men of good family, the king *S*ubhavyûha came down from the sky, and, having raised his joined hands, said to the Lord *G*aladharagar*g*itaghoshasusvaranakshatrarâ*g*asankusumitâbhi*gñ*a, the Tathâgata, &c.: Please, Lord, deign to tell me, what knowledge the Tathâgata is possessed of, so that the protuberance on his head is shining; that the Lord's eyes are so clear; that between his brows the Ûr*n*â (circle of hair) is shining, resembling in whiteness the moon; that in his mouth a row of equal and close-standing teeth is glittering; that the Lord has lips red as the Bimba and such beautiful eyes.

As the king *S*ubhavyûha, young men of good family, had celebrated the Lord *G*aladharagar*g*itaghoshasusvaranakshatrarâ*g*asankusumitâbhi*gñ*a, the Tathâgata, &c., by enumerating so many good qualities and hundred thousands of myriads of ko*t*is of other good qualities besides, he said to the Lord *G*aladharagar*g*itaghoshasusvaranakshatrarâ*g*asankusumitâbhi*gñ*a, the Tathâgata, &c.: It is wonderful, O Lord, how valuable the Tathâgata's teaching is, and with how many inconceivable virtues the religious discipline proclaimed by the Tathâgata is attended; how beneficial the moral precepts proclaimed by the Tathâgata are. From henceforward, O Lord, we will no more be slaves to our own mind; no more be slaves to false doctrine; no more slaves to rashness; no more slaves to the sinful thoughts arising in us. Being possessed of so many good qualities, O Lord, I do not wish to go away from the presence of the Lord[1].

After humbly saluting the feet of the Lord *G*aladharagar*g*itaghoshasusvaranakshatrarâ*g*asankusumitâbhi*gñ*a, the Tathâgata, &c., the king rose up to the sky and there stood. Thereupon the king *S*ubhavyûha and the queen Vimaladattâ from the sky, threw a pearl necklace worth a hundred thousand (gold pieces) upon the Lord; and that pearl necklace no sooner came down upon the head of the Lord than it assumed the shape of a tower with four columns, regular, well-constructed, and beautiful. On the summit of the tower appeared a couch covered with many hundred thousand pieces of fine cloth, and on the couch was seen the image of a Tathâgata sitting cross-legged. Then the following thought presented itself to the king *S*ubhavyûha: The Buddha-knowledge must be very powerful, and the Tathâgata endowed with inconceivable good qualities that this Tathâgata-image shows itself on the summit of the tower, (an image) so nice, beautiful, possessed of an extreme abundance of good colours. Then the Lord *G*aladharagar*g*itaghoshasusvaranakshatrarâ*g*asankusumitâbhi*gñ*a, the Tathâgata, &c., addressed the four classes

[1] Here I have followed Burnouf's reading; the Cambridge MS. has: ebhir aha*m* Bhagavann iyadbhir akusalair dharmai*h* samanvâgato ne*kkh*âmi Bhagavato 'ntika*m* (sic) upasa*m*kramitu*m*, i.e. being possessed of so many unholy qualities, O Lord, I do (or did) not wish to approach the Lord.

(and asked): Do you see, monks, the king *S*ubhavyûha who, standing in the sky, is emitting a lion's roar? They answered: We do, Lord. The Lord proceeded: This king *S*ubhavyûha, monks, after having become a monk under my rule shall become a Tathâgata in the world, by the name of *S*âlendrarâ*g*a[1], endowed with science and conduct, &c. &c., in the world Vistîr*n*avatî; his epoch shall be called Abhyudgatarâ*g*a. That Tathâgata *S*âlendrarâ*g*a, monks, the Arhat, &c., shall have an immense congregation of Bodhisattvas, an immense congregation of disciples. The said world Vistîr*n*avatî shall be level as the palm of the hand, and consist of lapis lazuli. So he shall be an inconceivably great Tathâgata, &c. Perhaps, young men of good family, you will have some doubt, uncertainty or misgiving (and think) that the king *S*ubhavyûha at that time, that juncture was another. But you must not think so; for it is the very same Bodhisattva Mahâsattva Padma*s*rî here present, who at that time, that juncture was the king *S*ubhavyûha. Perhaps, young men of good family, you will have some doubt, uncertainty or misgiving (and think) that the queen Vimaladattâ at that time, that juncture was another. But you must not think so; for it is the very same Bodhisattva Mahâsattva called Vairo*k*anara*s*mipratima*nd*itarâ*g*a[2], who at that time, that juncture was the queen Vimaladattâ, and who out of compassion for the king *S*ubhavyûha and the creatures had assumed

---

[1] Also written Sâlendrarâ*g*a. In the Calcutta edition of the Lalita-vistara, p. 201, l. 12, he occurs as Sârendrarâ*g*a, but Hodgson, Essays, p. 33, in a list drawn from the same work, has Sâlendrarâ*g*a.

[2] Burnouf's reading has dhva*g*a for râ*g*a.

the state of being the wife of king *S*ubhavyûha. Perhaps, young men of good family, you will have some doubt, uncertainty or misgiving (and think) that the two young princes were others. But you must not think so; for it was Bhaisha*g*yarâ*g*a and Bhaisha*g*yarâ*g*asamudgata, who at that time, that juncture were sons to the king *S*ubhavyûha. With such inconceivable qualities, young men of good family, were the Bodhisattvas Mahâsattvas Bhaisha*g*yarâ*g*a and Bhaisha*g*yarâ*g*asamudgata endowed, they, the two good men, having planted good roots under many hundred thousand myriads of ko*t*is of Buddhas. Those that shall cherish the name of these two good men shall all become worthy of receiving homage from the world, including the gods.

While this chapter on Ancient Devotion was being expounded, the spiritual insight of eighty-four thousand living beings in respect to the law was purified so as to become unclouded and spotless.

CHAPTER XXVI.

ENCOURAGEMENT[1] OF SAMANTABHADRA.

Thereupon the Bodhisattva Mahâsattva Samantabhadra, in the east, surrounded and followed by Bodhisattvas Mahâsattvas surpassing all calculation, amid the stirring of fields, a rain of lotuses, the playing of hundred thousands of myriads of ko*t*is of musical instruments, proceeded with the great pomp of a Bodhisattva, the great display of transformations proper to a Bodhisattva, the great magnificence of a Bodhisattva, the great power of a Bodhisattva, the great lustre of a glorious Bodhisattva, the great stately march of a Bodhisattva, the great miraculous display of a Bodhisattva, a great phantasmagorical sight of gods, Nâgas, goblins, Gandharvas, demons, Garu*d*as, Kinnaras, great serpents, men, and beings not human, who, produced by his magic, surrounded and followed him; Samantabhadra, then, the Bodhisattva, amid such inconceivable miracles worked by magic, arrived at this Saha-world. He went up to the place of the Lord on the G*ri*dhrakû*t*a, the king of mountains, and on approaching he humbly saluted the Lord's feet, made seven circumambulations from left to right, and said to the Lord: I have come hither, O Lord, from the field of the Lord Ratna-

[1] Utsâhana.

te*g*obhyudgata, the Tathâgata, &c., as I am aware, Lord, that here in the Saha-world is taught the Dharmaparyâya of the Lotus of the True Law, to hear which from the mouth of the Lord *S*âkyamuni I have come accompanied by these hundred thousands of Bodhisattvas Mahâsattvas. May the Lord deign to expound, in extension, this Dharmaparyâya of the Lotus of the True Law to these Bodhisattvas Mahâsattvas. So addressed, the Lord said to the Bodhisattva Mahâsattva Samantabhadra: These Bodhisattvas, young man of good family, are, indeed, quick of understanding, but this is the Dharmaparyâya of the Lotus of the True Law, that is to say, an unmixed truth[1]. The Bodhisattvas exclaimed: Indeed Lord; indeed, Sugata. Then in order to confirm, in the Dharmaparyâya of the Lotus of the True Law, the females[2] among the monks, nuns, and lay devotees assembled at the gathering, the Lord again spoke to the Bodhisattva Mahâsattva Samantabhadra: This Dharmaparyâya of the Lotus of the True Law, young man of good family, shall be entrusted to a female if she be possessed of four requisites, to wit: she shall stand under the superintendence of the Lords Buddhas; she shall have planted good roots[3]; she shall keep steadily to the mass of disci-

[1] Yad utâsambhinnatathatâ.

[2] Tâsâm. I am not able to discover the connection between this confirming of the females in the gathering, and the foregoing remark on the character of the Saddharma. The explanation is probably to be sought in the term asambhinna, unallayed, unmixed. The meaning of the passage may be that the Saddharmapu*nd*arîka, as a general rule, is fit for males only, but under certain conditions may be entrusted to females also.

[3] We would say: she must have a good antecedent behaviour.

plinary regulations; she shall, in order to save creatures, have the thoughts fixed on supreme and perfect enlightenment. These are the four requisites, young man of good family, a female must be possessed of, to whom this Dharmaparyâya of the Lotus of the True Law is to be entrusted.

Then the Bodhisattva Mahâsattva Samantabhadra said to the Lord: At the end of time, at the end of the period, in the second half of the millennium, I will protect the monks who keep this Sûtrânta; I will take care of their safety, avert blows[1], and destroy poison, so that no one laying snares for those preachers may surprise them, neither Mâra the Evil One, nor the sons of Mâra, the angels called Mârakâyikas, the daughters of Mâra, the followers of Mâra, and all other servitors to Mâra; that no gods, goblins, ghosts, imps, wizards, spectres laying snares for those preachers may surprise them. Incessantly and constantly, O Lord, will I protect such a preacher. And when a preacher who applies himself to this Dharmaparyâya shall take a walk, then, O Lord, will I mount a white elephant with six tusks, and with a train of Bodhisattvas betake myself to the place where that preacher is walking, in order to protect this Dharmaparyâya. And when that preacher, applying himself to this Dharmaparyâya, forgets, be it but a single word or syllable, then will I mount the white elephant with six tusks, show my face to that preacher, and repeat this entire Dharmaparyâya[2]. And when the preacher has

[1] Or punishment.

[2] Samantabhadra renders the same service to pious and studious preachers as the Buddha himself; see chapter X, especially stanzas 29–31. As to the elephant on which he is mounted, one knows

seen my proper body and heard from me this entire Dharmaparyâya, he, content, in high spirits, ravished, rejoiced, joyful, and delighted, will the more do his utmost to study this Dharmaparyâya, and immediately after beholding me he will acquire meditation and obtain spells, termed the talisman[1] of preservation, the talisman of hundred thousand ko*t*is, and the talisman of skill in all sounds.

Again, Lord, the monks, nuns, male or female lay devotees, who at the end of time, at the end of the period, in the second half of the millennium, shall study this Dharmaparyâya, when walking for three weeks, (or) twenty-one days, to them will I show my body, at the sight of which all beings rejoice. Mounted on that same white elephant with six tusks, and surrounded by a troop of Bodhisattvas, I shall on the twenty-first day betake myself to the place where the preachers are walking; there I shall rouse, excite, and stimulate them, and give them spells whereby those preachers shall become inviolable, so that no being, either human or not human, shall be able to surprise them, and no women able to beguile them. I will protect them, take care of their safety, avert blows[2], and destroy poison. I will, besides, O Lord, give those preachers words of talismanic spells, such as, Ada*nd*e da*nd*apati, da*nd*âvartani da*nd*akusale da*nd*asudhâri dhâri sudhârapati, buddhapa*s*yani dhâra*n*i, âvartani sa*m*vartani saṅghaparîkshite saṅghanirghâtani dharmaparîkshite sarva-

that the Bodhisattva entered the womb of his mother Mâyâ Devî in the shape of an elephant with six tusks; see Lalita-vistara, p. 63. According to the description of the elephant, it must, originally, be a name of lightning.

[1] Âvarta.

[2] Or punishment.

sattvarutakausalyânugate simhavikrîdite[1]. The Bodhisattva Mahâsattva, whose organ of hearing is struck by these talismanic words, Lord, shall be aware that the Bodhisattva Mahâsattva Samantabhadra is their ruling power[2].

Further, Lord, the Bodhisattvas Mahâsattvas to whom this Dharmaparyâya of the Lotus of the True Law shall be entrusted, as long as it continues having course in Gambudvîpa, those preachers, Lord, should take this view: It is owing to the power and grandeur of the Bodhisattva Mahâsattva Samantabhadra that this Dharmaparyâya has been entrusted to us. Those creatures who shall write and keep this Sûtra, O Lord, are to partake of the course of duty of the Bodhisattva Mahâsattva Samantabhadra; they will belong to those who have planted good roots under many Buddhas, O Lord, and whose heads are caressed by the hands of the Tathâgata. Those who shall write and keep this Sûtra, O Lord, will afford me pleasure. Those who shall write this Sûtra, O Lord, and comprehend it, shall, when they disappear from this world, after having written it, be reborn in the company of the

[1] In Burnouf's translation we find added: anuvarte vartani vartâli svâhâ. All terms are, or ought to be, vocatives of feminine words in the singular. Pati, as in Pâli pagâpati, Buddhistic Sansk. pragâpatî, interchanges with the ending vatî; not only in pragâvatî (e.g. in Lalita-vistara), but in some of the words occurring in the spell; so for dandapati the Tibetan text has dandâvati. As Siva in Mahâbhârata XII, 10361 is represented as the personified Danda, we may hold that all the names above belong to Siva's female counterpart, Durgâ. The epithet of Simhavikrîditâ is but a variation of Simhikâ, one of the names of Dâkshâyanî or Durgâ in her quality of mother to Râhu. Cf. the remarks on the spells in chap. XXI.

[2] As the presiding deity of lightning he is also the lord of flame, of Svâhâ, identified with Dâkshâyanî-Durgâ.

gods of paradise, and at that birth shall eighty-four thousand heavenly nymphs immediately come near them. Adorned with a high crown, they shall as angels dwell amongst those nymphs. Such is the mass of merit resulting from writing this Dharmaparyâya; how much greater will be the mass of merit reaped by those who recite, study, meditate, remember it! Therefore, young men of good family[1], one ought to honour this Dharmaparyâya of the Lotus of the True Law, and write it with the utmost attention. He who writes it with undistracted attention shall be supported by the hands of a thousand Buddhas, and at the moment of his death he shall see another thousand of Buddhas from face to face. He shall not sink down into a state of wretchedness, and after disappearing from this world he shall enter the company of the Tushita-gods, where the Bodhisattva Mahâsattva Maitreya is residing, and where, marked by the thirty-two sublime characteristics, surrounded by a host of Bodhisattvas, and waited upon by hundred thousands of myriads of ko*t*is of heavenly nymphs he is preaching the law. Therefore, then, young men of good family, a wise young man or young lady of good family should respectfully write this Dharmaparyâya of the Lotus of the True Law, respectfully recite it, respectfully study it, respectfully treasure it up in his (or her) mind. By writing, reciting, studying this Dharmaparyâya, and by treasuring it up in one's mind, young men of good family, one is to acquire innumerable good qualities. Hence a wise young man or young lady of good

[1] Burnouf's reading has, O Lord. The reading of the Cambridge MS. is no mere mistake, for we find it repeated in the sequel.

family ought to keep this Dharmaparyâya of the Lotus of the True Law. I myself, O Lord, will superintend this Dharmaparyâya, that through my superintendence it may here spread in *G*ambudvîpa.

Then the Lord *S*âkyamuni, the Tathâgata, &c., expressed his approval to the Bodhisattva Mahâsattva Samantabhadra: Very well, very well, Samantabhadra. It is happy that thou art so well disposed to promote the weal and happiness of the people at large, out of compassion for the people, for the benefit, weal, and happiness of the great body of men; that thou art endowed with such inconceivable qualities, with a mind so full of compassion, with intentions so inconceivably kind, so that of thine own accord thou wilt take those preachers under thy protection. The young men of good family who shall cherish the name of the Bodhisattva Mahâsattva Samantabhadra may be convinced that they have seen *S*âkyamuni, the Tathâgata, &c.; that they have heard this Dharmaparyâya of the Lotus of the True Law from the Lord *S*âkyamuni; that they have paid homage to the Tathâgata *S*âkyamuni; that they have applauded the preaching of the Tathâgata *S*âkyamuni. They will have joyfully accepted this Dharmaparyâya; the Tathâgata *S*âkyamuni will have laid his hand upon their head, and they will have decked the Lord *S*âkyamuni with their robes. Those young men or young ladies of good family, Samantabhadra, must be held to have accepted the command of the Tathâgata[1]. They

[1] If I rightly understand these cautious and veiled words, the meaning is that such persons, though no Buddhists, must be held in equal esteem as if they were. The persons alluded to are, not unlikely, *S*aiva monks or devotees, who, if leading a pious life, have

will have no pleasure in worldly philosophy[1]; no persons fondly addicted to poetry will please them; no dancers, athletes, vendors of meat, mutton butchers, poulterers, pork butchers, or profligates will please them. After having heard, written, kept, or read such Sûtrântas as this, they will find no delight in those persons. They must be held to be possessed of natural righteousness[2]; they will be right-minded from themselves, possess a power to do good of their own accord, and make an agreeable impression on others. Such will be the monks who keep this Sûtrânta. No passionate attachment will hinder them, no hatred, no infatuation, no jealousy, no envy, no hypocrisy, no pride, no conceitedness, no mendaciousness. Those preachers, Samantabhadra, will be content with what they receive. He, Samantabhadra, who at the end of time, at the end of the period, in the second half of the millennium, sees a monk keeping this Dharmaparyâya of the Lotus of the True Law, must think thus: This young man of good family will reach the terrace of enlightenment; this young man will conquer the troop of the

for protector or patron Samantabhadra, who, as we have seen above, is the lord of Svâhâ or Dâkshâyanî, consequently Siva-Kâla.

[1] Na Lokâyate rukir bhavishyati. The Lokâyatikas are the Indian Epicureans.

[2] Svabhâvadharmasamanvâgatâh, which may also be rendered by, possessed of the religion of Svabhâva (Nature). This I think to be the recondite and real meaning of the term, whether it alludes to the Svâbhâvika sect of Buddhism or to materialistic schools among the Saivas. Though the philosophical tenets of all Svâbhâvikas are identical with those of the Lokâyatikas, their opinions on morals are exactly the reverse. Hence it may have been deemed necessary to inculcate on devotees of more or less strong ascetic habits the precept that they should have no intercourse with the immoral vulgar materialists.

wicked Mâra[1], move forward the wheel of the law, strike the drum of the law, blow the conch trumpet of the law, spread the rain of the law, and ascend the royal throne of the law. The monks who at the end of time, at the end of the period, in the second half of the millennium, keep this Dharmaparyâya, will not be covetous, nor greedy of robes or vehicles[2]. Those preachers will be honest, and possessed of three emancipations; they will refrain from worldly business. Such persons as lead into error monks who know this Sûtrânta, shall be born blind; and such as openly defame them, shall have a spotted body in this very world. Those who scoff and hoot at the monks who copy this Sûtrânta, shall have the teeth broken and separated far from each other; disgusting lips, a flat nose, contorted hands and feet, squinting eyes; a putrid body, a body covered with stinking boils, eruptions, scabs, and itch. If one speaks an unkind word, true or not true, to such writers, readers, and keepers of this Sûtrânta, it must be considered a very heinous sin. Therefore then, Samantabhadra, people should, even from afar, rise from their seats before the monks who keep this Dharmaparyâya and show them the same reverence as to the Tathâgata.

While this chapter of the Encouragement of Samantabhadra was being expounded, hundred thousands of ko*t*is of Bodhisattvas Mahâsattvas, equal to the sands of the river Ganges, acquired the talismanic spell Âvarta.

---

[1] Mârakali*k*akram.

[2] Yâna; Burnouf has read pâna, drink. It is, indeed, generally impossible to distinguish between pa and ya in the Nepalese MSS.

CHAPTER XXVII.

THE PERIOD[1].

Thereupon the Lord Sâkyamuni, the Tathâgata, &c., rose from his pulpit, collected the Bodhisattvas, took their right hands with his own right hand, which had become strong by the exercise of magic, and spoke on that occasion as follows: Into your hands, young men of good family, I transfer and transmit, entrust and deposit this supreme and perfect enlightenment arrived at by me after hundred thousands of myriads of kotis of incalculable Æons. Ye, young men of good family, do your best that it may grow and spread.

A second time, a third time the Lord spoke to the host of Bodhisattvas after taking them by the right hands: Into your hands, young men of good family, I transfer and transmit, entrust and deposit this supreme and perfect enlightenment arrived at by me after hundred thousands of myriads of kotis of incalculable Æons. Receive it, young men of good family, keep, read, fathom, teach, promulgate, and preach it to all beings. I am not avaricious, young men of good family, nor narrow-minded; I am confident and willing to impart Buddha-knowledge, to impart the knowledge of the Tathâgata, the knowledge of the Self-born. I am a bountiful giver, young

[1] Dharmaparyâya, properly, the period of the law.

men of good family, and ye, young men of good family, follow my example; imitate me in liberally showing this knowledge of the Tathâgata, and in skilfulness, and preach this Dharmaparyâya to the young men and young ladies of good family who successively shall gather round you. And as to unbelieving persons, rouse them to accept this law. By so doing, young men of good family, you will acquit your debt to the Tathâgatas.

So addressed by the Lord *S*âkyamuni, the Tathâgata, &c., the Bodhisattvas filled with delight and joy, and with a feeling of great respect they lowered, bent, and bowed their body towards the Lord, and, the head inclined and the joined hands stretched out, they spoke in one voice to the Lord *S*âkyamuni, the Tathâgata, &c., the following words: We shall do, O Lord, what the Tathâgata commands; we shall fulfil the command of all Tathâgatas. Let the Lord be at ease as to this, and perfectly quiet. A second time, a third time the entire host of Bodhisattvas spoke in one voice the same words: Let the Lord be at ease as to this, and perfectly quiet. We shall do, O Lord, what the Tathâgata commands us; we shall fulfil the command of all Tathâgatas.

Thereupon the Lord *S*âkyamuni, the Tathâgata, &c., dismissed all those Tathâgatas, &c., who had come to the gathering from other worlds, and wished them a happy existence, with the words: May the Tathâgatas, &c., live happy. Then he restored the Stûpa of precious substances of the Lord Prabhûtaratna, the Tathâgata, &c., to its place, and wished him also a happy existence.

Thus spoke the Lord. The incalculable, innumerable Tathâgatas, &c., who had come from other worlds and were sitting on their thrones at the foot of jewel trees, as well as Prabhûtaratna, the Tathâgata, &c., and the whole host of Bodhisattvas headed by Visishtakâritra, the innumerable, incalculable Bodhisattvas Mahâsattvas who had issued from the gaps of the earth, the great disciples, the four classes, the world, including gods, men, demons, and Gandharvas, in ecstasy applauded the words of the Lord.

INDEX.

Transliteration of Oriental Alphabets adopted for the Translations of the Sacred Books of the East.

Consonants.	Missionary Alphabet. I Class.	II Class.	III Class.	Sanskrit.	Zend.	Pehlevi.	Persian.	Arabic.	Hebrew.	Chinese.
Gutturales.										
1 Tenuis	k	...	...	क	𐬐	[illegible]	ک	ک	כ	k
2 „ aspirata	kh	...	...	ख	𐬑	[illegible]	...	...	ח	kh
3 Media	g	...	...	ग	𐬔	[illegible]	گ	...	ג	...
4 „ aspirata	gh	...	...	घ	𐬖	[illegible]	...	...	ג	...
5 Gutturo-labialis	q	...	...	...	...	...	ق	ق	ק	...
6 Nasalis	ṅ (ng)	...	...	ङ	{ 𐬧 (ng) / 𐬣 (N) }	...	...	...	...	...
7 Spiritus asper	h	...	...	ह	𐬵 (𐬒 hv)	[illegible]	ه	ه	ה	h, hs
8 „ lenis	ʼ	...	...	...	...	...	ا	ا	א	...
9 „ asper faucalis	ʽh	...	...	...	...	...	ح	ح	ח	...
10 „ lenis faucalis	ʼh	...	...	...	...	...	ع	ع	ע	...
11 „ asper fricatus	...	ʽ*h*	...	...	...	...	خ	خ	ח	...
12 „ lenis fricatus	...	ʼ*h*	...	...	...	...	...	...	...	...
Gutturales modificatae (palatales, &c.)										
13 Tenuis	...	*k*	...	च	𐬗	[illegible]	چ	...	...	*k*
14 „ aspirata	...	*kh*	...	छ	...	...	...	...	...	*kh*
15 Media	...	*g*	...	ज	𐬘	[illegible]	ج	ج	...	...
16 „ aspirata	...	*gh*	...	झ	...	...	غ	غ	...	...
17 „ Nasalis	...	*ñ*	...	ञ	...	...	...	...	...	...

CONSONANTS (*continued*).	MISSIONARY ALPHABET. I Class.	II Class.	III Class.	Sanskrit.	Zend.	Pehlevi.	Persian.	Arabic.	Hebrew.	Chinese.
18 Semivocalis	y	...	...	य	𐬌𐬌 ; 𐬫 init.	[illegible]	ي	ي	י	y
19 Spiritus asper	...	(ŷ)	...	...	...	...	...	...	...	...
20 „ lenis	...	(y̓)	...	...	...	...	...	...	...	...
21 „ asper assibilatus	...	*s*	...	श	𐬱	[illegible]	ش	ش	...	...
22 „ lenis assibilatus	...	*z*	...	...	𐬲	[illegible]	ژ	...	...	*z*
Dentales.										
23 Tenuis	t	...	...	त	𐬙	[illegible]	ت	ت	תּ	t
24 „ aspirata	th	...	...	थ	𐬚	...	...	...	ת	th
25 „ assibilata	...	...	TH	...	...	...	ث	ث	...	...
26 Media	d	...	...	द	𐬛	[illegible]	د	د	דּ	...
27 „ aspirata	dh	...	...	ध	𐬜	...	...	...	ד	...
28 „ assibilata	...	...	DH	...	...	...	ذ	ذ	...	...
29 Nasalis	n	...	...	न	𐬥	[illegible]	ن	ن	נ	n
30 Semivocalis	l	...	...	ल	...	[illegible]	ل	ل	ל	l
31 „ mollis 1	...	*l*	...	ळ	...	...	...	...	...	...
32 „ mollis 2	...	...	L	...	...	...	...	...	...	...
33 Spiritus asper 1	s	...	...	स	𐬯	[illegible]	س (ث)	س	שׂ	s
34 „ asper 2	...	...	s (ʃ)	...	...	...	...	...	ס	...
35 „ lenis	z	...	...	...	𐬰	[illegible]	ز (ذ)	ز	ז	z
36 „ asperrimus 1	...	...	z (ʒ)	...	...	...	ص	ص	צ	ʒ, ʒh
37 „ asperrimus 2	...	...	ẓ (ʒ̣)	...	...	...	ض	...	...	...

Dentales modificatae (linguales, &c.)										
38 Tenuis	...	*t*	...	ट	...	...	ط	ط	ט	...
39 „ aspirata	...	*th*	...	ठ	...	...	ظ	ظ	...	...
40 Media	...	*d*	...	ड	[illegible]	[illegible]	...	...	...	...
41 „ aspirata	...	*dh*	...	ढ	...	...	...	ض	...	...
42 Nasalis	...	*n*	...	ण	[illegible]	...	...	...	...	...
43 Semivocalis	r	...	...	र	𐬭	[illegible]	ر	ر	ר	...
44 „ fricata	...	*r*	...	...	...	...	...	...	...	*r*
45 „ diacritica	...	...	R	...	...	...	...	...	...	...
46 Spiritus asper	sh	...	...	ष	[illegible]	[illegible]	...	...	...	'sh
47 „ lenis	zh	...	...	...	...	...	...	...	...	...
Labiales.										
48 Tenuis	p	...	...	प	𐬞	[illegible]	پ	...	פּ	p
49 „ aspirata	ph	...	...	फ	...	...	...	...	פ	ph
50 Media	b	...	...	ब	𐬠	[illegible]	ب	ب	בּ	...
51 „ aspirata	bh	...	...	भ	...	...	...	...	ב	...
52 Tenuissima	...	*p*	...	...	...	...	...	...	...	...
53 Nasalis	m	...	...	म	𐬨	[illegible]	م	م	מ	m
54 Semivocalis	w	...	...	...	𐬎𐬎	...	...	...	...	w
55 „ aspirata	hw	...	...	...	...	...	...	...	...	...
56 Spiritus asper	f	...	...	...	𐬟	[illegible]	ف	ف	...	f
57 „ lenis	v	...	...	व	»	[illegible]	و	و	ו	...
58 Anusvâra	...	*m*	...	अं	[illegible]	...	...	...	...	...
59 Visarga	...	*h*	...	अः	...	...	...	...	...	...

VOWELS.	MISSIONARY ALPHABET. I Class.	II Class.	III Class.	Sanskrit.	Zend.	Pehlevi.	Persian.	Arabic.	Hebrew.	Chinese.
1 Neutralis	o	. . .	. . . .	. . .	. . . .	. . .	. . .	. . .	ְ	ă
2 Laryngo-palatalis	ĕ	. . .	. . . .	. . .	. . . .	. . .	. . .	. . .	. . .	. . .
3 „ labialis	ŏ	. . .	. . . .	. . .	. . . .	𐭠 fin.	. . .	. . .	. . .	. . .
4 Gutturalis brevis	a	. . .	. . . .	अ	𐬀	𐭠 init.	َ	َ	ַ	a
5 „ longa	â	(*a*)	. . . .	आ	𐬁	𐭠	ـَا	ـَا	ָ	â
6 Palatalis brevis	i	. . .	. . . .	इ	𐬌	. . .	ِ	ِ	ִ	i
7 „ longa	î	(*i*)	. . . .	ई	𐬍	𐭩	ـِي	ـِي	ִי	î
8 Dentalis brevis	*li*	. . .	. . . .	ऌ	. . . .	. . .	. . .	. . .	. . .	. . .
9 „ longa	*lî*	. . .	. . . .	ॡ	. . . .	. . .	. . .	. . .	. . .	. . .
10 Lingualis brevis	*ri*	. . .	. . . .	ऋ	. . . .	. . .	. . .	. . .	. . .	. . .
11 „ longa	*rî*	. . .	. . . .	ॠ	. . . .	. . .	. . .	. . .	. . .	. . .
12 Labialis brevis	u	. . .	. . . .	उ	𐬎	. . .	ُ	ُ	ֻ	u
13 „ longa	û	(*u*)	. . . .	ऊ	𐬏	𐭥	ـُو	ـُو	וּ	û
14 Gutturo-palatalis brevis . . .	e	. . .	. . . .	. . .	𐬈(e) 𐬉(*e*)	. . .	. . .	. . .	ֶ	e
15 „ longa . . .	ê (ai)	(*e*)	. . . .	ए	𐬊, 𐬛	𐭩	ـَيْ	ـَيْ	ֵ	ê
16 Diphthongus gutturo-palatalis	âi	(*ai*)	. . . .	ऐ	. . . .	. . .	. . .	. . .	. . .	âi
17 „ „	ei (ĕi)	. . .	. . . .	. . .	. . . .	. . .	. . .	. . .	. . .	ei, êi
18 „ „	oi (ŏu)	. . .	. . . .	. . .	. . . .	. . .	. . .	. . .	. . .	. . .
19 Gutturo-labialis brevis	o	. . .	. . . .	. . .	𐬊	. . .	. . .	. . .	ָ	o
20 „ longa	ô (au)	(*o*)	. . . .	ओ	𐬋	𐭥	. . .	. . .	וֹ	. . .
21 Diphthongus gutturo-labialis	âu	(*au*)	. . . .	औ	𐬈𐬎 (*au*)	. . .	ـَوْ	ـَوْ	. . .	âu
22 „ „	eu (ĕu)	. . .	. . . .	. . .	. . . .	. . .	. . .	. . .	. . .	. . .
23 „ „	ou (ŏu)	. . .	. . . .	. . .	. . . .	. . .	. . .	. . .	. . .	. . .
24 Gutturalis fracta	ä	. . .	. . . .	. . .	. . . .	. . .	. . .	. . .	. . .	. . .
25 Palatalis fracta	ï	. . .	. . . .	. . .	. . . .	. . .	. . .	. . .	. . .	. . .
26 Labialis fracta	ü	. . .	. . . .	. . .	. . . .	. . .	. . .	. . .	. . .	ü
27 Gutturo-labialis fracta	ö	. . .	. . . .	. . .	. . . .	. . .	. . .	. . .	. . .	. . .

April, 1884.

Clarendon Press, Oxford

A SELECTION OF

BOOKS

PUBLISHED FOR THE UNIVERSITY BY

HENRY FROWDE,

AT THE OXFORD UNIVERSITY PRESS WAREHOUSE,

AMEN CORNER, LONDON.

ALSO TO BE HAD AT THE

CLARENDON PRESS DEPOSITORY, OXFORD.

[*Every book is bound in cloth, unless otherwise described.*]

LEXICONS, GRAMMARS, &c.

(See also Clarendon Press Series, pp. 14, 18, 21, 24, 25.)

ANGLO-SAXON.—*An Anglo-Saxon Dictionary*, based on the MS. Collections of the late Joseph Bosworth, D.D., Professor of Anglo-Saxon, Oxford. Edited and enlarged by Prof. T. N. Toller, M.A. (To be completed in four parts.) Parts I and II. 1882. 4to. 15*s*. each.

CHINESE.—*A Handbook of the Chinese Language*. Parts I and II, Grammar and Chrestomathy. By James Summers. 1863. 8vo. half bound. 1*l*. 8*s*.

ENGLISH.—*A New English Dictionary, on Historical Principles:* founded mainly on the materials collected by the Philological Society. Edited by James A. H. Murray, LL.D., President of the Philological Society; with the assistance of many Scholars and men of Science. Part I. A—ANT (pp. xvi, 352). Imperial 4to. 12*s*. 6*d*.

—— *An Etymological Dictionary of the English Language*, arranged on an Historical Basis. By W. W. Skeat, M.A. 1882. 4to. 2*l*. 4*s*.

—— *A Concise Etymological Dictionary of the English Language*. By W. W. Skeat, M.A. 1882. Crown 8vo. 5*s*. 6*d*.

GREEK.—*A Greek-English Lexicon*, by Henry George Liddell, D.D., and Robert Scott, D.D. Seventh Edition, Revised and Augmented throughout. 1883. 4to. 1*l*. 16*s*.

GREEK.—*A Greek-English Lexicon*, abridged from Liddell and Scott's 4to. edition, chiefly for the use of Schools. Twentieth Edition. Carefully Revised throughout. 1883. Square 12mo. 7*s*. 6*d*.

—— *A copious Greek-English Vocabulary*, compiled from the best authorities. 1850. 24mo. 3*s*.

—— *A Practical Introduction to Greek Accentuation*, by H. W. Chandler, M.A. Second Edition. 1881. 8vo. 10*s*. 6*d*.

HEBREW.—*The Book of Hebrew Roots*, by Abu 'l-Walîd Marwân ibn Janâh, otherwise called Rabbî Yônâh. Now first edited, with an Appendix, by Ad. Neubauer. 1875. 4to. 2*l*. 7*s*. 6*d*.

—— *A Treatise on the use of the Tenses in Hebrew*. By S. R. Driver, M.A. Second Edition, Revised and Enlarged. 1881. Extra fcap. 8vo. 7*s*. 6*d*.

—— *Hebrew Accentuation of Psalms, Proverbs, and Job*. By William Wickes, D.D. 1881. Demy 8vo. stiff covers, 5*s*.

ICELANDIC.—*An Icelandic-English Dictionary*, based on the MS. collections of the late Richard Cleasby. Enlarged and completed by G. Vigfússon, M.A. With an Introduction, and Life of Richard Cleasby, by G. Webbe Dasent, D.C.L. 1874. 4to. 3*l*. 7*s*.

—— *A List of English Words the Etymology of which is illustrated by comparison with Icelandic*. Prepared in the form of an APPENDIX to the above. By W. W. Skeat, M.A. 1876. stitched, 2*s*.

—— *An Icelandic Prose Reader*, with Notes, Grammar and Glossary, by Dr. Gudbrand Vigfússon and F. York Powell, M.A. 1879. Extra fcap. 8vo. 10*s*. 6*d*.

LATIN.—*A Latin Dictionary*, founded on Andrews' edition of Freund's Latin Dictionary, revised, enlarged, and in great part rewritten by Charlton T. Lewis, Ph.D., and Charles Short, LL.D. 1879. 4to. 1*l*. 5*s*.

SANSKRIT.—*A Practical Grammar of the Sanskrit Language*, arranged with reference to the Classical Languages of Europe, for the use of English Students, by Monier Williams, M.A. Fourth Edition, 1877. 8vo. 15*s*.

—— *A Sanskrit-English Dictionary*, Etymologically and Philologically arranged, with special reference to Greek, Latin, German, Anglo-Saxon, English, and other cognate Indo-European Languages. By Monier Williams, M.A. 1872. 4to. 4*l*. 14*s*. 6*d*.

—— *Nalopákhyánam*. Story of Nala, an Episode of the Mahá-Bhárata: the Sanskrit text, with a copious Vocabulary, and an improved version of Dean Milman's Translation, by Monier Williams, M.A. Second Edition, Revised and Improved. 1879. 8vo. 15*s*.

—— *Sakuntalā*. A Sanskrit Drama, in Seven Acts. Edited by Monier Williams, M.A. Second Edition, 1876. 8vo. 21*s*.

SYRIAC.—*Thesaurus Syriacus:* collegerunt Quatremère, Bernstein, Lorsbach, Arnoldi, Field: edidit R. Payne Smith, S.T.P. Fasc. I-VI. 1868-83. sm. fol. each, 1*l*. 1*s*. Vol. I, containing Fasc. I-V, sm. fol. 5*l*. 5*s*.

GREEK CLASSICS, &c.

Aristophanes: A Complete Concordance to the Comedies and Fragments. By Henry Dunbar, M.D. 4to. 1*l.* 1*s.*

Aristotle: The Politics, translated into English, with Introduction, Marginal Analysis, Notes, and Indices, by B. Jowett, M.A. Medium 8vo. *Nearly ready.*

Heracliti Ephesii Reliquiae. Recensuit I. Bywater, M.A. Appendicis loco additae sunt Diogenis Laertii Vita Heracliti, Particulae Hippocratei De Diaeta Libri Primi, Epistolae Heracliteae. 1877. 8vo. 6*s.*

Homer: A Complete Concordance to the Odyssey and Hymns of Homer; to which is added a Concordance to the Parallel Passages in the Iliad, Odyssey, and Hymns. By Henry Dunbar, M.D. 1880. 4to. 1*l.* 1*s.*

—— *Scholia Graeca in Iliadem.* Edited by Professor W. Dindorf, after a new collation of the Venetian MSS. by D. B. Monro, M.A., Fellow of Oriel College.

Vols. I. II. 1875. 8vo. 24*s.*
Vol. III. IV. 1877. 8vo. 26*s.*

—— *Scholia Graeca in Odysseam.* Edidit Guil. Dindorfius Tomi II. 1855. 8vo. 15*s.* 6*d.*

Plato: Apology, with a revised Text and English Notes, and a Digest of Platonic Idioms, by James Riddell, M.A. 1878. 8vo. 8*s.* 6*d.*

—— *Philebus*, with a revised Text and English Notes, by Edward Poste, M.A. 1860. 8vo. 7*s.* 6*d.*

—— *Sophistes and Politicus*, with a revised Text and English Notes, by L. Campbell, M.A. 1867. 8vo. 18*s.*

—— *Theaetetus*, with a revised Text and English Notes, by L. Campbell, M.A. Second Edition. 8vo. 10*s.* 6*d.*

—— *The Dialogues*, translated into English, with Analyses and Introductions, by B. Jowett, M.A. A new Edition in 5 volumes, medium 8vo. 1875. 3*l.* 10*s.*

—— *The Republic*, translated into English, with an Analysis and Introduction, by B. Jowett, M.A. Medium 8vo. 12*s.* 6*d.*

—— *Index to.* Compiled for the Second Edition of Professor Jowett's Translation of the Dialogues. By Evelyn Abbott, M.A. 1875. 8vo. paper covers, 2*s.* 6*d.*

Thucydides: Translated into English, with Introduction, Marginal Analysis, Notes, and Indices. By B. Jowett, M.A. 2 vols. 1881. Medium 8vo. 1*l.* 12*s.*

THE HOLY SCRIPTURES, &c.

ENGLISH.—*The Holy Bible in the earliest English Versions*, made from the Latin Vulgate by John Wycliffe and his followers: edited by the Rev. J. Forshall and Sir F. Madden. 4 vols. 1850. Royal 4to. 3*l*. 3*s*.

[**Also reprinted from the above, with Introduction and Glossary by W. W. Skeat, M.A.**

—— *The Books of Job, Psalms, Proverbs, Ecclesiastes, and the Song of Solomon:* according to the Wycliffite Version made by Nicholas de Hereford, about A.D. 1381, and Revised by John Purvey, about A.D. 1388. Extra fcap. 8vo. 3*s*. 6*d*.

—— *The New Testament in English*, according to the Version by John Wycliffe, about A.D. 1380, and Revised by John Purvey, about A.D. 1388. Extra fcap. 8vo. 6*s*.]

—— *The Holy Bible:* an exact reprint, page for page, of the Authorised Version published in the year 1611. Demy 4to. half bound, 1*l*. 1*s*.

GOTHIC.—*The Gospel of St. Mark in Gothic*, according to the translation made by Wulfila in the Fourth Century. Edited with a Grammatical Introduction and Glossarial Index by W. W. Skeat, M.A. Extra fcap. 8vo. 4*s*.

GREEK.—*Vetus Testamentum* ex Versione Septuaginta Interpretum secundum exemplar Vaticanum Romae editum. Accedit potior varietas Codicis Alexandrini. Tomi III. Editio Altera. 18mo. 18*s*.

—— *Origenis Hexaplorum* quae supersunt; sive, Veterum Interpretum Graecorum in totum Vetus Testamentum Fragmenta. Edidit Fridericus Field, A.M. 2 vols. 1875. 4to. 5*l*. 5*s*.

—— *The Book of Wisdom:* the Greek Text, the Latin Vulgate, and the Authorised English Version; with an Introduction, Critical Apparatus, and a Commentary. By William J. Deane, M.A. Small 4to. 12*s*. 6*d*.

—— *Novum Testamentum Graece*. Antiquissimorum Codicum Textus in ordine parallelo dispositi. Accedit collatio Codicis Sinaitici. Edidit E. H. Hansell, S.T.B. Tomi III. 1864. 8vo. half morocco, 2*l*. 12*s*. 6*d*.

—— *Novum Testamentum Graece*. Accedunt parallela S. Scripturae loca, necnon vetus capitulorum notatio et canones Eusebii. Edidit Carolus Lloyd, S.T.P.R. 18mo. 3*s*.

The same on writing paper, with large margin, 10*s*.

—— *Novum Testamentum Graece* juxta Exemplar Millianum. 18mo. 2*s*. 6*d*.

The same on writing paper, with large margin, 9*s*.

GREEK.—*Evangelia Sacra Graece.* Fcap. 8vo. limp, 1*s.* 6*d.*

—— *The Greek Testament*, with the Readings adopted by the Revisers of the Authorised Version:—

(1) Pica type. Second Edition, with Marginal References. Demy 8vo. 10*s.* 6*d.*

(2) Long Primer type. Fcap. 8vo. 4*s.* 6*d.*

(3) The same, on writing paper, with wide margin, 15*s.*

—— *The Parallel New Testament*, Greek and English; being the Authorised Version, 1611; the Revised Version, 1881; and the Greek Text followed in the Revised Version. 8vo. 12*s.* 6*d.*

The Revised Version is the joint property of the Universities of Oxford and Cambridge.

—— *Canon Muratorianus:* the earliest Catalogue of the Books of the New Testament. Edited with Notes and a Facsimile of the MS. in the Ambrosian Library at Milan, by S. P. Tregelles, LL.D. 1867. 4to. 10*s.* 6*d.*

—— *Outlines of Textual Criticism applied to the New Testament.* By C. E. Hammond, M.A. Third Edition. Extra fcap. 8vo. 3*s.* 6*d.*

HEBREW, etc.—*The Psalms in Hebrew without points.* 1879. Crown 8vo. 3*s.* 6*d.*

—— *A Commentary on the Book of Proverbs.* Attributed to Abraham Ibn Ezra. Edited from a MS. in the Bodleian Library by S. R. Driver, M.A. Crown 8vo. paper covers, 3*s.* 6*d.*

—— *The Book of Tobit.* A Chaldee Text, from a unique MS. in the Bodleian Library; with other Rabbinical Texts, English Translations, and the Itala. Edited by Ad. Neubauer, M.A. 1878. Crown 8vo. 6*s.*

—— *Horae Hebraicae et Talmudicae*, a J. Lightfoot. A new Edition, by R. Gandell, M.A. 4 vols. 1859. 8vo. 1*l.* 1*s.*

LATIN.—*Libri Psalmorum* Versio antiqua Latina, cum Paraphrasi Anglo-Saxonica. Edidit B. Thorpe, F.A.S. 1835. 8vo. 10*s.* 6*d.*

—— *Old-Latin Biblical Texts: No. I.* The Gospel according to St. Matthew from the St. Germain MS. (g_1). Edited with Introduction and Appendices by John Wordsworth, M.A. Small 4to., stiff covers, 6*s.*

OLD-FRENCH.—*Libri Psalmorum* Versio antiqua Gallica e Cod. MS. in Bibl. Bodleiana adservato, una cum Versione Metrica aliisque Monumentis pervetustis. Nunc primum descripsit et edidit Franciscus Michel, Phil. Doct. 1860. 8vo. 10*s.* 6*d.*

FATHERS OF THE CHURCH, &c.

St. Athanasius: Historical Writings, according to the Benedictine Text. With an Introduction by William Bright, D.D. 1881. Crown 8vo. 10*s*. 6*d*.

—— *Orations against the Arians.* With an Account of his Life by William Bright, D.D. 1873. Crown 8vo. 9*s*.

St. Augustine: Select Anti-Pelagian Treatises, and the Acts of the Second Council of Orange. With an Introduction by William Bright, D.D. Crown 8vo. 9*s*.

Canons of the First Four General Councils of Nicaea, Constantinople, Ephesus, and Chalcedon. 1877. Crown 8vo. 2*s*. 6*d*.

—— *Notes on the Canons of the First Four General Councils.* By William Bright, D.D. 1882. Crown 8vo. 5*s*. 6*d*.

Cyrilli Archiepiscopi Alexandrini in XII Prophetas. Edidit P. E. Pusey, A.M. Tomi II. 1868. 8vo. cloth, 2*l*. 2*s*.

—— *in D. Joannis Evangelium.* Accedunt Fragmenta varia necnon Tractatus ad Tiberium Diaconum duo. Edidit post Aubertum P. E. Pusey, A.M. Tomi III. 1872. 8vo. 2*l*. 5*s*.

—— *Commentarii in Lucae Evangelium* quae supersunt Syriace. E MSS. apud Mus. Britan. edidit R. Payne Smith, A.M. 1858. 4to. 1*l*. 2*s*.

—— Translated by R. Payne Smith, M.A. 2 vols. 1859. 8vo. 14*s*.

Ephraemi Syri, Rabulae Episcopi Edesseni, Balaei, aliorumque Opera Selecta. E Codd. Syriacis MSS. in Museo Britannico et Bibliotheca Bodleiana asservatis primus edidit J. J. Overbeck. 1865. 8vo. 1*l*. 1*s*.

Eusebius' Ecclesiastical History, according to the text of Burton, with an Introduction by William Bright, D.D. 1881. Crown 8vo. 8*s*. 6*d*.

Irenaeus: The Third Book of St. Irenaeus, Bishop of Lyons, against Heresies. With short Notes and a Glossary by H. Deane, B.D. 1874. Crown 8vo. 5*s*. 6*d*.

Patrum Apostolicorum, S. Clementis Romani, S. Ignatii, S. Polycarpi, quae supersunt. Edidit Guil. Jacobson, S.T.P.R. Tomi II. Fourth Edition, 1863. 8vo. 1*l*. 1*s*.

Socrates' Ecclesiastical History, according to the Text of Hussey, with an Introduction by William Bright, D.D. 1878. Crown 8vo. 7*s*. 6*d*.

ECCLESIASTICAL HISTORY, BIOGRAPHY, &c.

Ancient Liturgy of the Church of England, according to the uses of Sarum, York, Hereford, and Bangor, and the Roman Liturgy arranged in parallel columns, with preface and notes. By William Maskell, M.A. Third Edition. 1882. 8vo. 15*s.*

Baedae Historia Ecclesiastica. Edited, with English Notes, by G. H. Moberly, M.A. 1881. Crown 8vo. 10*s.* 6*d.*

Bright (W.). Chapters of Early English Church History. 1878. 8vo. 12*s.*

Burnet's History of the Reformation of the Church of England. A new Edition. Carefully revised, and the Records collated with the originals, by N. Pocock, M.A. 7 vols. 1865. 8vo. *Price reduced to* 1*l.* 10*s.*

Councils and Ecclesiastical Documents relating to Great Britain and Ireland. Edited, after Spelman and Wilkins, by A. W. Haddan, B.D., and W. Stubbs, M.A. Vols. I. and III. 1869–71. Medium 8vo. each 1*l.* 1*s.*

Vol. II. Part I. 1873. Medium 8vo. 10*s.* 6*d.*

Vol. II. Part II. 1878. Church of Ireland; Memorials of St. Patrick. Stiff covers, 3*s.* 6*d.*

Hammond (C. E.). Liturgies, Eastern and Western. Edited, with Introduction, Notes, and a Liturgical Glossary. 1878. Crown 8vo. 10*s.* 6*d.*

An Appendix to the above. 1879. Crown 8vo. paper covers, 1*s.* 6*d.*

John, Bishop of Ephesus. The Third Part of his Ecclesiastical History. [In Syriac.] Now first edited by William Cureton, M.A. 1853. 4to. 1*l.* 12*s.*

—— Translated by R. Payne Smith, M.A. 1860. 8vo. 10*s.*

Leofric Missal, The, as used in the Cathedral of Exeter during the Episcopate of its first Bishop, A.D. 1050–1072; together with some Account of the Red Book of Derby, the Missal of Robert of Jumièges, and a few other early MS. Service Books of the English Church. Edited, with Introduction and Notes, by F. E. Warren, B.D. 4to. half morocco, 35*s.*

Monumenta Ritualia Ecclesiae Anglicanae. The occasional Offices of the Church of England according to the old use of Salisbury, the Prymer in English, and other prayers and forms, with dissertations and notes. By William Maskell, M.A. Second Edition. 1882. 3 vols. 8vo. 2*l.* 10*s.*

Records of the Reformation. The Divorce, 1527–1533. Mostly now for the first time printed from MSS. in the British Museum and other libraries. Collected and arranged by N. Pocock, M.A. 1870. 2 vols. 8vo. 1*l.* 16*s.*

Shirley (*W. W.*). *Some Account of the Church in the Apostolic Age.* Second Edition, 1874. fcap. 8vo. 3*s.* 6*d.*

Stubbs (*W.*). *Registrum Sacrum Anglicanum.* An attempt to exhibit the course of Episcopal Succession in England. 1858. Small 4to. 8*s.* 6*d.*

Warren (*F. E.*). *Liturgy and Ritual of the Celtic Church.* 1881. 8vo. 14*s.*

ENGLISH THEOLOGY.

Butler's Works, with an Index to the Analogy. 2 vols. 1874. 8vo. 11*s.*

Also separately,

Sermons, 5*s.* 6*d.* *Analogy of Religion*, 5*s.* 6*d.*

Greswell's Harmonia Evangelica. Fifth Edition. 8vo. 1855. 9*s.* 6*d.*

Heurtley's Harmonia Symbolica: Creeds of the Western Church. 1858. 8vo. 6*s.* 6*d.*

Homilies appointed to be read in Churches. Edited by J. Griffiths, M.A. 1859. 8vo. 7*s.* 6*d.*

Hooker's Works, with his life by Walton, arranged by John Keble, M.A. Sixth Edition, 1874. 3 vols. 8vo. 1*l.* 11*s.* 6*d.*

—— the text as arranged by John Keble, M.A. 2 vols. 1875. 8vo. 11*s.*

Jewel's Works. Edited by R. W. Jelf, D.D. 8 vols. 1848. 8vo. 1*l.* 10*s.*

Pearson's Exposition of the Creed. Revised and corrected by E. Burton, D.D. Sixth Edition, 1877. 8vo. 10*s.* 6*d.*

Waterland's Review of the Doctrine of the Eucharist, with a Preface by the present Bishop of London. 1880. Crown 8vo. 6*s.* 6*d.*

—— *Works*, with Life, by Bp. Van Mildert. A new Edition, with copious Indexes. 6 vols. 1856. 8vo. 2*l.* 11*s.*

Wheatly's Illustration of the Book of Common Prayer. A new Edition, 1846. 8vo. 5*s.*

Wyclif. A Catalogue of the Original Works of John Wyclif, by W. W. Shirley, D.D. 1865. 8vo. 3*s.* 6*d.*

—— *Select English Works.* By T. Arnold, M.A. 3 vols. 1869–1871. 8vo. *Price reduced to* 1*l.* 1*s.*

—— *Trialogus.* With the Supplement now first edited. By Gotthard Lechler. 1869. 8vo. *Price reduced to* 7*s.*

HISTORICAL AND DOCUMENTARY WORKS.

British Barrows, a Record of the Examination of Sepulchral Mounds in various parts of England. By William Greenwell, M.A., F.S.A. Together with Description of Figures of Skulls, General Remarks on Prehistoric Crania, and an Appendix by George Rolleston, M.D., F.R.S. 1877. Medium 8vo. 25*s.*

Britton. A Treatise upon the Common Law of England, composed by order of King Edward I. The French Text carefully revised, with an English Translation, Introduction, and Notes, by F. M. Nichols, M.A. 2 vols. 1865. Royal 8vo. 1*l.* 16*s.*

Clarendon's (Edw. Earl of) History of the Rebellion and Civil Wars in England. 7 vols. 1839. 18mo. 1*l.* 1*s.*

Clarendon's (Edw. Earl of) History of the Rebellion and Civil Wars in England. Also his Life, written by himself, in which is included a Continuation of his History of the Grand Rebellion. With copious Indexes. In one volume, royal 8vo. 1842. 1*l.* 2*s.*

Clinton's Epitome of the Fasti Hellenici. 1851. 8vo. 6*s.* 6*d.*

—— *Epitome of the Fasti Romani.* 1854. 8vo. 7*s.*

Corpvs Poeticvm Boreale. The Poetry of the Old Northern Tongue, from the Earliest Times to the Thirteenth Century. Edited, classified, and translated, with Introduction, Excursus, and Notes, by Gudbrand Vigfússon, M.A., and F. York Powell, M.A. 2 vols. 1883. 8vo. 42*s.*

Freeman (E. A.). History of the Norman Conquest of England; its Causes and Results. In Six Volumes. 8vo. 5*l.* 9*s.* 6*d.*

Vols. I–II together, 3rd edition, 1877. 1*l.* 16*s.*
Vol. III, 2nd edition, 1874. 1*l.* 1*s.*
Vol. IV, 2nd edition, 1875. 1*l.* 1*s.*
Vol. V, 1876. 1*l.* 1*s.*
Vol. VI. Index. 1879. 8vo. 10*s.* 6*d.*

Freeman (E. A.). The Reign of William Rufus and the Accession of Henry the First. 2 vols. 8vo. 1*l.* 16*s.*

Gascoigne's Theological Dictionary ("Liber Veritatum"): Selected Passages, illustrating the condition of Church and State, 1403–1458. With an Introduction by James E. Thorold Rogers, M.P. Small 4to. 10*s.* 6*d.*

Magna Carta, a careful Reprint. Edited by W. Stubbs, M.A. 1879. 4to. stitched, 1*s.*

Passio et Miracula Beati Olaui. Edited from a Twelfth-Century MS. in the Library of Corpus Christi College, Oxford, with an Introduction and Notes, by Frederick Metcalfe, M.A. Small 4to. stiff covers, 6*s.*

Protests of the Lords, including those which have been expunged, from 1624 to 1874; with Historical Introductions. Edited by James E. Thorold Rogers, M.A. 1875. 3 vols. 8vo. 2*l*. 2*s*.

Rogers (J. E. T.). History of Agriculture and Prices in England, A.D. 1259–1793.

Vols. I and II (1259–1400). 1866. 8vo. 2*l*. 2*s*.

Vols. III and IV (1401–1582). 1882. 8vo. 2*l* 10*s*.

Sturlunga Saga, including the Islendinga Saga of Lawman Sturla Thordsson and other works. Edited by Dr. Gudbrand Vigfússon. In 2 vols. 1878. 8vo. 2*l*. 2*s*.

Two of the Saxon Chronicles parallel, with Supplementary Extracts from the Others. Edited, with Introduction, Notes, and a Glossarial Index, by J. Earle, M.A. 1865. 8vo. 16*s*.

Statutes made for the University of Oxford, and for the Colleges and Halls therein, by the University of Oxford Commissioners. 1882. 8vo. 12*s*. 6*d*.

Also separately,

Statutes made for the University. 2*s*.

—— *the Colleges*. 1*s*. each.

Statuta Universitatis Oxoniensis. 1883. 8vo. 5*s*.

The Student's Handbook to the University and Colleges of Oxford. Seventh Edition. 1883. Extra fcap. 8vo. 2*s*. 6*d*.

MATHEMATICS, PHYSICAL SCIENCE, &c.

Acland (H. W., M.D., F.R.S.). Synopsis of the Pathological Series in the Oxford Museum. 1867. 8vo. 2*s*. 6*d*.

Astronomical Observations made at the University Observatory, Oxford, under the direction of C. Pritchard, M.A. No. 1. 1878. Royal 8vo. paper covers, 3*s*. 6*d*.

Müller (J.). On certain Variations in the Vocal Organs of the Passeres that have hitherto escaped notice. Translated by F. J. Bell, B.A., and edited with an Appendix, by A. H. Garrod, M.A., F.R.S. With Plates. 1878. 4to. paper covers, 7*s*. 6*d*.

Phillips (John, M.A., F.R.S.). Geology of Oxford and the Valley of the Thames. 1871. 8vo. 21*s*.

—— *Vesuvius*. 1869. Crown 8vo. 10*s*. 6*d*.

Price (Bartholomew, M.A., F.R.S.). Treatise on Infinitesimal Calculus.

Vol. I. Differential Calculus. Second Edition. 8vo. 14*s*. 6*d*.

Vol. II. Integral Calculus, Calculus of Variations, and Differential Equations. Second Edition, 1865. 8vo. 18*s*.

Vol. III. Statics, including Attractions; Dynamics of a Material Particle. Second Edition, 1868. 8vo. 16*s*.

Vol. IV. Dynamics of Material Systems; together with a chapter on Theoretical Dynamics, by W. F. Donkin, M.A., F.R.S. 1862. 8vo. 16*s*.

Rigaud's Correspondence of Scientific Men of the 17th Century, with Table of Contents by A. de Morgan, and Index by the Rev. J. Rigaud, M.A. 2 vols. 1841–1862. 8vo. 18*s*. 6*d*.

Sachs' Text-Book of Botany, Morphological and Physiological. A New Edition. Translated by S. H. Vines, M.A. 1882. Royal 8vo., half morocco, 1*l*. 11*s*. 6*d*.

Westwood (J. O., M.A., F.R.S.). Thesaurus Entomologicus Hopeianus, or a Description of the rarest Insects in the Collection given to the University by the Rev. William Hope. With 40 Plates. 1874. Small folio, half morocco, 7*l*. 10*s*.

The Sacred Books of the East.

TRANSLATED BY VARIOUS ORIENTAL SCHOLARS, AND EDITED BY F. MAX MÜLLER.

[Demy 8vo. cloth.]

Vol. I. The Upanishads. Translated by F. Max Müller. Part I. The *Kh*ândogya-upanishad, The Talavakâra-upanishad, The Aitareya-âra*n*yaka, The Kaushîtaki-brâhma*n*a-upanishad, and The Vâ*g*asaneyi-sa*m*hitâ-upanishad. 10*s*. 6*d*.

Vol. II. The Sacred Laws of the Âryas, as taught in the Schools of Âpastamba, Gautama, Vâsish*th*a, and Baudhâyana. Translated by Prof. Georg Bühler. Part I. Âpastamba and Gautama. 10*s*. 6*d*.

Vol. III. The Sacred Books of China. The Texts of Confucianism. Translated by James Legge. Part I. The Shû King, The Religious portions of the Shih King, and The Hsiâo King. 12*s*. 6*d*.

Vol. IV. The Zend-Avesta. Translated by James Darmesteter. Part I. The Vendîdâd. 10*s*. 6*d*.

Vol. V. The Pahlavi Texts. Translated by E. W. West. Part I. The Bundahis, Bahman Yast, and Shâyast lâ-shâyast. 12*s*. 6*d*.

Vols. VI and IX. The Qur'ân. Parts I and II. Translated by E. H. Palmer. 21*s*.

Vol. VII. The Institutes of Vishnu. Translated by Julius Jolly. 10*s*. 6*d*.

Vol. VIII. The Bhagavadgîtâ, with The Sanatsugâtîya, and The Anugîtâ. Translated by Kâshinâth Trimbak Telang. 10*s*. 6*d*.

Vol. X. The Dhammapada, translated from Pâli by F. Max Müller; and The Sutta-Nipâta, translated from Pâli by V. Fausböll; being Canonical Books of the Buddhists. 10*s*. 6*d*.

Vol. XI. Buddhist Suttas. Translated from Pâli by T. W. Rhys Davids. 1. The Mahâparinibbâna Suttanta; 2. The Dhamma-kakka-ppavattana Sutta; 3. The Tevigga Suttanta; 4. The Akankheyya Sutta; 5. The Ketokhila Sutta; 6. The Mahâ-sudassana Suttanta; 7. The Sabbâsava Sutta. 10*s*. 6*d*.

Vol. XII. The Satapatha-Brâhmana, according to the Text of the Mâdhyandina School. Translated by Julius Eggeling. Part I. Books I and II. 12*s*. 6*d*.

Vol. XIII. Vinaya Texts. Translated from the Pâli by T. W. Rhys Davids and Hermann Oldenberg. Part I. The Pâtimokkha. The Mahâvagga, I-IV. 10*s*. 6*d*.

Vol. XIV. The Sacred Laws of the Âryas, as taught in the Schools of Âpastamba, Gautama, Vâsishtha and Baudhâyana. Translated by Georg Bühler. Part II. Vasishtha and Baudhâyana. 10*s*. 6*d*.

Vol. XV. The Upanishads. Translated by F. Max Müller. Part II. The Katha-upanishad, The Mundaka-upanishad, The Taittirîyaka-upanishad, The Brihadâranyaka-upanishad, The Svetasvatara-upanishad, The Prasña-upanishad, and The Maitrâyana-Brâhmana-upanishad. 10*s*. 6*d*.

Vol. XVI. The Sacred Books of China. The Texts of Confucianism. Translated by James Legge. Part II. The Yî King. 10*s*. 6*d*.

Vol. XVII. Vinaya Texts. Translated from the Pâli by T. W. Rhys Davids and Hermann Oldenberg. Part II. The Mahâvagga, V-X. The Kullavagga, I-III. 10*s*. 6*d*.

Vol. XVIII. Pahlavi Texts. Translated by E. W. West. Part II. The Dâdistân-î Dînîk and The Epistles of Mânûskîhar. 12*s*. 6*d*.

Vol. XIX. The Fo-sho-hing-tsan-king. A Life of Buddha by Asvaghosha Bodhisattva, translated from Sanskrit into Chinese by Dharmaraksha, A.D. 420, and from Chinese into English by Samuel Beal. 10*s*. 6*d*.

Vol. XXI. The Saddharma-pu*nd*arîka, or the Lotus of the True Law. Translated by H. Kern. 12*s*. 6*d*.

Vol. XXIII. The Zend-Avesta. Part II. The Sîrôzahs, Ya*s*ts, and Nyâyi*s*. Translated by James Darmesteter. 10*s*. 6*d*.

The following Volumes are in the Press:—

Vol. XX. Vinaya Texts. Translated from the Pâli by T. W. Rhys Davids and Hermann Oldenberg. Part III. The *K*ullavagga, I–IV.

Vol. XXII. The Â*k*ârâṅga Sûtra. Translated by H. Jacobi.

Vol. XXIV. Pahlavi Texts. Translated by E. W. West. Part III. Dînâ-î Maînôg-î Khîrad, Shikand-gu-mânî, and Sad-dar.

Second Series.

Vol. XXV. Manu. Translated by GEORG BÜHLER. Part I.

Vol. XXVI. Manu. Translated by GEORG BÜHLER. Part II.

Anecdota Oxoniensia:

[Small 4to.]

Classical Series. I. i. *The English Manuscripts of the Nicomachean Ethics*, described in relation to Bekker's Manuscripts and other Sources. By J. A. Stewart, M.A. 3*s*. 6*d*.

—— I. ii. *Nonius Marcellus*, de Compendiosa Doctrina, Harleian MS. 2719. Collated by J. H. Onions, M.A. 3*s*. 6*d*.

—— I. iii. *Aristotle's Physics*. Book VII. Collation of various MSS.; with an Introduction by R. Shute, M.A. 2*s*.

—— I. iv. *Bentley's Plautine Emendations*. From his copy of Gronovius. By E. A. Sonnenschein, M.A. 2*s*. 6*d*.

Semitic Series. I. i. *Commentary on Ezra and Nehemiah.* By Rabbi Saadiah. Edited by H. J. Mathews, M.A. 3*s*. 6*d*.

Aryan Series. I. i. *Buddhist Texts from Japan*. Edited by F. Max Müller, M.A. 3*s*. 6*d*.

—— I. ii. *Sukhâvatî-Vyûha*. Description of Sukhâvatî, the Land of Bliss. Edited by F. Max Müller, M.A., and Bunyiu Nanjio. 7*s*. 6*d*.

Mediaeval and Modern Series. I. i. *Sinonoma Bartholomei;* A Glossary from a Fourteenth-Century MS. in the Library of Pembroke College, Oxford. Edited by J. L. G. Mowat, M.A. 3*s*. 6*d*.

—— I. iii. *The Saltair Na Rann*. A Collection of Early Middle Irish Poems. Edited from a MS. in the Bodleian Library by Whitley Stokes, LL.D. 7*s*. 6*d*.

Clarendon Press Series

I. ENGLISH.

A First Reading Book. By Marie Eichens of Berlin; and edited by Anne J. Clough. Extra fcap. 8vo. stiff covers, 4*d.*

Oxford Reading Book, Part I. For Little Children. Extra fcap. 8vo. stiff covers, 6*d.*

Oxford Reading Book, Part II. For Junior Classes. Extra fcap. 8vo. stiff covers, 6*d.*

An Elementary English Grammar and Exercise Book. By O. W. Tancock, M.A. Second Edition. Extra fcap. 8vo. 1*s.* 6*d.*

An English Grammar and Reading Book, for Lower Forms in Classical Schools. By O. W. Tancock, M.A. Fourth Edition. Extra fcap. 8vo. 3*s.* 6*d.*

Typical Selections from the best English Writers, with Introductory Notices. Second Edition. In Two Volumes. Extra fcap. 8vo. 3*s.* 6*d.* each.

Vol. I. Latimer to Berkeley. Vol. II. Pope to Macaulay.

Shairp (J. C., LL.D.). Aspects of Poetry; being Lectures delivered at Oxford. Crown 8vo. 10*s.* 6*d.*

A Book for the Beginner in Anglo-Saxon. By John Earle, M.A. Second Edition. Extra fcap. 8vo. 2*s.* 6*d.*

An Anglo-Saxon Reader. In Prose and Verse. With Grammatical Introduction, Notes, and Glossary. By Henry Sweet, M.A. Fourth Edition, Revised and Enlarged. Extra fcap. 8vo. 8*s.* 6*d.*

An Anglo-Saxon Primer, with Grammar, Notes, and Glossary. By the same Author. Extra fcap. 8vo. 2*s.* 6*d.*

The Philology of the English Tongue. By J. Earle, M.A. Third Edition. Extra fcap. 8vo. 7*s.* 6*d.*

A Handbook of Phonetics, including a Popular Exposition of the Principles of Spelling Reform. By Henry Sweet, M.A. Extra fcap. 8vo. 4*s.* 6*d.*

The Ormulum; with the Notes and Glossary of Dr. R. M. White. Edited by R. Holt, M.A. 1878. 2 vols. Extra fcap. 8vo. 21*s.*

English Plant Names from the Tenth to the Fifteenth Century. By J. Earle, M.A. Small fcap. 8vo. 5*s*.

Specimens of Early English. A New and Revised Edition. With Introduction, Notes, and Glossarial Index. By R. Morris, LL.D., and W. W. Skeat, M.A.

Part I. From Old English Homilies to King Horn (A.D. 1150 to A.D. 1300). Extra fcap. 8vo. 9*s*.

Part II. From Robert of Gloucester to Gower (A.D. 1298 to A.D. 1393). Second Edition. Extra fcap. 8vo. 7*s*. 6*d*.

Specimens of English Literature, from the 'Ploughmans Crede' to the 'Shepheardes Calender' (A.D. 1394 to A.D. 1579). With Introduction, Notes, and Glossarial Index. By W. W. Skeat, M.A. Extra fcap. 8vo. 7*s*. 6*d*.

The Vision of William concerning Piers the Plowman, by William Langland. Edited, with Notes, by W. W. Skeat, M.A. Third Edition. Extra fcap. 8vo. 4*s*. 6*d*.

Chaucer. I. *The Prologue to the Canterbury Tales;* the Knightes Tale; The Nonne Prestes Tale. Edited by R. Morris, Editor of Specimens of Early English, &c., &c. Fifty-first Thousand. Extra fcap. 8vo. 2*s*. 6*d*.

—— II. *The Prioresses Tale; Sir Thopas;* The Monkes Tale; The Clerkes Tale; The Squieres Tale, &c. Edited by W. W. Skeat, M.A. Second Edition. Extra fcap. 8vo. 4*s*. 6*d*.

—— III. *The Tale of the man of Lawe;* The Pardoneres Tale; The Second Nonnes Tale; The Chanouns Yemannes Tale. By the same Editor. Second Edition. Extra fcap. 8vo. 4*s*. 6*d*.

Spenser's Faery Queene. Books I and II. Designed chiefly for the use of Schools. With Introduction, Notes, and Glossary. By G. W. Kitchin, M.A.

Book I. Tenth Edition. Extra fcap. 8vo. 2*s*. 6*d*.

Book II. Sixth Edition. Extra fcap. 8vo. 2*s*. 6*d*.

Hooker. Ecclesiastical Polity, Book I. Edited by R. W. Church, M.A. Second Edition. Extra fcap. 8vo. 2*s*.

Marlowe and Greene. Marlowe's Tragical History of Dr. Faustus, and *Greene's Honourable History of Friar Bacon and Friar Bungay.* Edited by A. W. Ward, M.A. 1878. Extra fcap. 8vo. 5*s*. 6*d*.

Marlowe. Edward II. With Introduction, Notes, &c. By O. W. Tancock, M.A. Extra fcap. 8vo. 3*s*.

Shakespeare. Select Plays. Edited by W. G. Clark, M.A., and W. Aldis Wright, M.A. Extra fcap. 8vo. stiff covers.

I. The Merchant of Venice. 1*s.*
II. Richard the Second. 1*s.* 6*d.*
III. Macbeth. 1*s.* 6*d.*
IV. Hamlet. 2*s.*

—— Edited by W. Aldis Wright, M.A. Extra fcap. 8vo. stiff covers.

V. The Tempest. 1*s.* 6*d.*
VI. As You Like It. 1*s.* 6*d.*
VII. Julius Cæsar. 2*s.*
VIII. Richard the Third. 2*s.* 6*d.*
IX. King Lear. 1*s.* 6*d.*
X. A Midsummer Night's Dream. 1*s.* 6*d.*
XI. Coriolanus. 2*s.* 6*d.*
XII. Henry the Fifth. 2*s.*
XIII. Twelfth Night. *In the Press.*

Bacon. I. *Advancement of Learning.* Edited by W. Aldis Wright, M.A. Second Edition. Extra fcap. 8vo. 4*s.* 6*d.*

—— II. *The Essays.* With Introduction and Notes. By J. R. Thursfield, M.A. *In Preparation.*

Milton. I. *Areopagitica.* With Introduction and Notes. By J. W. Hales, M.A. Third Edition. Extra fcap. 8vo. 3*s.*

—— II. *Poems.* Edited by R. C. Browne, M.A. 2 vols. Fifth Edition. Extra fcap. 8vo. 6*s.* 6*d.*

Sold separately, Vol. I. 4*s.*; Vol. II. 3*s.*

In paper covers:—

Lycidas, 3*d.* L'Allegro, 3*d.* Il Penseroso, 4*d.* Comus, 6*d.* Samson Agonistes, 6*d.*

—— III. *Samson Agonistes.* Edited with Introduction and Notes by John Churton Collins. Extra fcap. 8vo. stiff covers, 1*s.*

Bunyan. I. *The Pilgrim's Progress, Grace Abounding, Relation of the Imprisonment of Mr. John Bunyan.* Edited, with Biographical Introduction and Notes, by E. Venables, M.A. 1879. Extra fcap. 8vo. 5*s.*

—— II. *Holy War, &c.* Edited by E. Venables, M.A. In the Press.

Dryden. Select Poems. Stanzas on the Death of Oliver Cromwell; Astræa Redux; Annus Mirabilis; Absalom and Achitophel; Religio Laici; The Hind and the Panther. Edited by W. D. Christie, M.A. Second Edition. Extra fcap. 8vo. 3*s*. 6*d*.

Locke's Conduct of the Understanding. Edited, with Introduction, Notes, &c., by T. Fowler, M.A. Second Edition. Extra fcap. 8vo. 2*s*.

Addison. Selections from Papers in the Spectator. With Notes. By T. Arnold, M.A. Extra fcap. 8vo. 4*s*. 6*d*.

Pope. With Introduction and Notes. By Mark Pattison, B.D.

—— I. *Essay on Man.* Sixth Edition. Extra fcap. 8vo. 1*s*. 6*d*.

—— II. *Satires and Epistles.* Second Edition. Extra fcap. 8vo. 2*s*.

Parnell. The Hermit. Paper covers, 2*d*.

Johnson. I. *Rasselas; Lives of Pope and Dryden.* Edited by Alfred Milnes, B.A. (London). Extra fcap. 8vo. 4*s*. 6*d*.

—— II. *Vanity of Human Wishes.* With Notes, by E. J. Payne, M.A. Paper covers, 4*d*.

Gray. Elegy and Ode on Eton College. Paper covers, 2*d*.

Goldsmith. The Deserted Village. Paper covers, 2*d*.

Cowper. Edited, with Life, Introductions, and Notes, by H. T. Griffith, B.A.

—— I. *The Didactic Poems of* 1782, with Selections from the Minor Pieces, A.D. 1779–1783. Extra fcap. 8vo. 3*s*.

—— II. *The Task, with Tirocinium,* and Selections from the Minor Poems, A.D. 1784–1799. Second Edition. Extra fcap. 8vo. 3*s*.

Burke. Select Works. Edited, with Introduction and Notes, by E. J. Payne, M.A.

—— I. *Thoughts on the Present Discontents; the two Speeches on America.* Second Edition. Extra fcap. 8vo. 4*s*. 6*d*.

—— II. *Reflections on the French Revolution.* Second Edition. Extra fcap. 8vo. 5*s*.

—— III. *Four Letters on the Proposals for Peace with the Regicide Directory of France.* Second Edition. Extra fcap. 8vo. 5*s*.

Keats. Hyperion, Book I. With Notes by W. T. Arnold, B.A. Paper covers, 4*d.*

Scott. Lay of the Last Minstrel. Introduction and Canto I, with Preface and Notes by W. Minto, M.A. Paper covers, 6*d.*

II. LATIN.

An Elementary Latin Grammar. By John B. Allen, M.A. Third Edition, Revised and Corrected. Extra fcap. 8vo. 2*s.* 6*d.*

A First Latin Exercise Book. By the same Author. Fourth Edition. Extra fcap. 8vo. 2*s.* 6*d.*

A Second Latin Exercise Book. By the same Author. *In the Press.*

Reddenda Minora, or Easy Passages for Unseen Translation for the use of Lower Forms. Composed and selected by C. S. Jerram, M.A. Extra fcap. 1*s.* 6*d.*

Anglice Reddenda, or Easy Extracts, Latin and Greek, for Unseen Translation. By C. S. Jerram, M.A. Third Edition, Revised and Enlarged. Extra fcap. 8vo. 2*s.* 6*d.*

Passages for Translation into Latin. For the use of Passmen and others. Selected by J. Y. Sargent, M.A. Fifth Edition. Extra fcap. 8vo. 2*s.* 6*d.*

First Latin Reader. By T. J. Nunns, M.A. Third Edition. Extra fcap. 8vo. 2*s.*

Caesar. The Commentaries (for Schools). With Notes and Maps. By Charles E. Moberly, M.A.

Part I. *The Gallic War.* Second Edition. Extra fcap. 8vo. 4*s.* 6*d.*

Part II. *The Civil War.* Extra fcap. 8vo. 3*s.* 6*d.*

The Civil War. Book I. Second Edition. Extra fcap. 8vo. 2*s.*

Cicero. Selection of interesting and descriptive passages. With Notes. By Henry Walford, M.A. In three Parts. Extra fcap. 8vo. 4*s.* 6*d.* Each Part separately, limp, 1*s.* 6*d.*

Part I. Anecdotes from Grecian and Roman History. Third Edition.

Part II. Omens and Dreams: Beauties of Nature. Third Edition.

Part III. Rome's Rule of her Provinces. Third Edition.

—— *De Amicitia* and *De Senectute.* With Notes. By W. Heslop, M.A. *In the Press.*

Cicero. *Selected Letters* (for Schools). With Notes. By the late C. E. Prichard, M.A., and E. R. Bernard, M.A. Second Edition. Extra fcap. 8vo. 3*s.*

—— *Select Orations* (for Schools). In Verrem I. De Imperio Gn. Pompeii. Pro Archia. Philippica IX. With Notes. By J. R. King, M.A. Second Edition. Extra fcap. 8vo. 2*s.* 6*d.*

Cornelius Nepos. With Notes. By Oscar Browning, M.A. Second Edition. Extra fcap. 8vo. 2*s.* 6*d.*

Livy. *Selections* (for Schools). With Notes and Maps. By H. Lee-Warner, M.A. Extra fcap. 8vo. In Parts, limp, each 1*s.* 6*d.*

Part I. The Caudine Disaster.
Part II. Hannibal's Campaign in Italy.
Part III. The Macedonian War.

Livy. Books V–VII. With Introduction and Notes. By A. R. Cluer, B.A. Extra fcap. 8vo. 3*s.* 6*d.*

Ovid. Selections for the use of Schools. With Introductions and Notes, and an Appendix on the Roman Calendar. By W. Ramsay, M.A. Edited by G. G. Ramsay, M.A. Second Edition. Extra fcap. 8vo. 5*s.* 6*d.*

Pliny. *Selected Letters* (for Schools). With Notes. By the late C. E. Prichard, M.A., and E. R. Bernard, M.A. Second Edition. Extra fcap. 8vo. 3*s.*

Catulli Veronensis Liber. Iterum recognovit, apparatum criticum prolegomena appendices addidit, Robinson Ellis, A.M. 1878. Demy 8vo. 16*s.*

—— *A Commentary on Catullus.* By Robinson Ellis, M.A. 1876. Demy 8vo. 16*s.*

—— *Veronensis Carmina Selecta,* secundum recognitionem Robinson Ellis, A.M. Extra fcap. 8vo. 3*s.* 6*d.*

Cicero de Oratore. With Introduction and Notes. By A. S. Wilkins, M.A.

Book I. 1879. 8vo. 6*s.* Book II. 1881. 8vo. 5*s.*

—— *Philippic Orations.* With Notes. By J. R. King, M.A. Second Edition. 1879. 8vo. 10*s.* 6*d.*

—— *Select Letters.* With English Introductions, Notes, and Appendices. By Albert Watson, M.A. Third Edition. 1881. Demy 8vo. 18*s.*

Cicero. Select Letters. Text. By the same Editor. Second Edition. Extra fcap. 8vo. 4*s.*

Cicero pro Cluentio. With Introduction and Notes. By W. Ramsay, M.A. Edited by G. G. Ramsay, M.A. Second Edition. Extra fcap. 8vo. 3*s.* 6*d.*

Horace. With a Commentary. Volume I. The Odes, Carmen Seculare, and Epodes. By Edward C. Wickham, M.A. Second Edition. 1877. Demy 8vo. 12*s.*

—— A reprint of the above, in a size suitable for the use of Schools. Extra fcap. 8vo. 5*s.* 6*d.*

Livy, Book I. With Introduction, Historical Examination, and Notes. By J. R. Seeley, M.A. Second Edition. 1881. 8vo. 6*s.*

Ovid. P. Ovidii Nasonis Ibis. Ex Novis Codicibus edidit, Scholia Vetera Commentarium cum Prolegomenis Appendice Indice addidit, R. Ellis, A.M. Demy 8vo. 10*s.* 6*d.*

Persius. The Satires. With a Translation and Commentary. By John Conington, M.A. Edited by Henry Nettleship, M.A. Second Edition. 1874. 8vo. 7*s.* 6*d.*

Plautus. The Trinummus. With Notes and Introductions. Intended for the Higher Forms of Public Schools. By C. E. Freeman, M.A., and A. Sloman, M.A. Extra fcap. 8vo. 3*s.*

Sallust. With Introduction and Notes. By W. W. Capes, M.A. *In the Press.*

Tacitus. The Annals. Books I–VI. Edited, with Introduction and Notes, by H. Furneaux, M.A. 8vo. 18*s.*

Vergil: Suggestions Introductory to a Study of the Aeneid. By H. Nettleship, M.A. 8vo. sewed, 1*s.* 6*d.*

Vergil, Ancient Lives of. With an Essay on the Poems of Vergil, in connection with his Life and Times. By H. Nettleship, M.A. 8vo. sewed, 2*s.*

Virgil. With Introduction and Notes. By T. L. Papillon, M.A. Two vols. crown 8vo. 10*s.* 6*d.*

Nettleship (H., M.A.). The Roman Satura: its original form in connection with its literary development. 8vo. sewed, 1*s.*

Papillon (T. L., M.A.). A Manual of Comparative Philology. Third Edition, Revised and Corrected. 1882. Crown 8vo. 6*s.*

Pinder (North, M.A.). Selections from the less known Latin Poets. 1869. Demy 8vo. 15*s.*

Sellar (W. Y., M.A.). Roman Poets of the Augustan Age. VIRGIL. By William Young Sellar, M.A., Professor of Humanity in the University of Edinburgh. New Edition. 1883. Crown 8vo. 9*s*.

—— *Roman Poets of the Republic.* New Edition, Revised and Enlarged. 1881. 8vo. 14*s*.

Wordsworth (J., M.A.). Fragments and Specimens of Early Latin. With Introductions and Notes. 1874. 8vo. 18*s*.

III. GREEK.

A Greek Primer, for the use of beginners in that Language. By the Right Rev. Charles Wordsworth, D.C.L. Seventh Edition. Extra fcap. 8vo. 1*s*. 6*d*.

Graecae Grammaticae Rudimenta in usum Scholarum. Auctore Carolo Wordsworth, D.C.L. Twentieth Edition, 1882. 12mo. 4*s*.

A Greek-English Lexicon, abridged from Liddell and Scott's 4to. edition, chiefly for the use of Schools. Nineteenth Edition. Carefully revised throughout. 1881. Square 12mo. 12*s*. 6*d*.

Greek Verbs, Irregular and Defective; their forms, meaning, and quantity; embracing all the Tenses used by Greek writers, with references to the passages in which they are found. By W. Veitch. Fourth Edition. Crown 8vo. 10*s*. 6*d*.

The Elements of Greek Accentuation (for Schools): abridged from his larger work by H. W. Chandler, M.A. Extra fcap. 8vo. 2*s*. 6*d*.

A SERIES OF GRADUATED GREEK READERS:—

First Greek Reader. By W. G. Rushbrooke, M.L. Second Edition. Extra fcap. 8vo. 2*s*. 6*d*.

Second Greek Reader. By A. M. Bell, M.A. Extra fcap. 8vo. 3*s*. 6*d*.

Fourth Greek Reader; being Specimens of Greek Dialects. With Introductions and Notes. By W. W. Merry, M.A. Extra fcap. 8vo. 4*s*. 6*d*.

Fifth Greek Reader. Part I. Selections from Greek Epic and Dramatic Poetry, with Introductions and Notes. By Evelyn Abbott, M.A. Extra fcap. 8vo. 4*s*. 6*d*.

Part II. By the same Editor. In Preparation.

The Golden Treasury of Ancient Greek Poetry: being a Collection of the finest passages in the Greek Classic Poets, with Introductory Notices and Notes. By R. S. Wright, M.A. Extra fcap. 8vo. 8*s*. 6*d*.

A Golden Treasury of Greek Prose, being a Collection of the finest passages in the principal Greek Prose Writers, with Introductory Notices and Notes. By R. S. Wright, M.A., and J. E. L. Shadwell, M.A. Extra fcap. 8vo. 4*s*. 6*d*.

Aeschylus. Prometheus Bound (for Schools). With Introduction and Notes, by A. O. Prickard, M.A. Second Edition. Extra fcap. 8vo. 2*s*.

—— *Agamemnon*. With Introduction and Notes, by Arthur Sidgwick, M.A. Extra fcap. 8vo. 3*s*.

—— *Choephoroe*. With Introduction and Notes by the same Editor. Preparing.

Aristophanes. In Single Plays. Edited, with English Notes, Introductions, &c., by W. W. Merry, M.A. Extra fcap. 8vo.

I. The Clouds, Second Edition, 2*s*.
II. The Acharnians, 2*s*.
III. The Frogs, 2*s*.

Other Plays will follow.

Cebes. Tabula. With Introduction and Notes. By C. S. Jerram, M.A. Extra fcap. 8vo. 2*s*. 6*d*.

Euripides. Alcestis (for Schools). By C. S. Jerram, M.A. Extra fcap. 8vo. 2*s*. 6*d*.

—— *Helena*. Edited, with Introduction, Notes, and Critical Appendix, for Upper and Middle Forms. By C. S. Jerram, M.A. Extra fcap. 8vo. 3*s*.

Herodotus, Selections from. Edited, with Introduction, Notes, and a Map, by W. W. Merry, M.A. Extra fcap. 8vo. 2*s*. 6*d*.

Homer. Odyssey, Books I–XII (for Schools). By W. W. Merry, M.A. Twenty-seventh Thousand. Extra fcap. 8vo. 4*s*. 6*d*.

Book II, separately, 1*s*. 6*d*.

—— *Odyssey*, Books XIII–XXIV (for Schools). By the same Editor. Second Edition. Extra fcap. 8vo. 5*s*.

—— *Iliad*, Book I (for Schools). By D. B. Monro, M.A. Second Edition. Extra fcap. 8vo. 2*s*.

—— *Iliad*, Books I–XII (for Schools). By D. B. Monro, M.A. *Nearly ready*.

—— *Iliad*, Books VI and XXI. With Introduction and Notes. By Herbert Hailstone, M.A. Extra fcap. 8vo. 1*s*. 6*d*. each.

Lucian. Vera Historia (for Schools). By C. S. Jerram, M.A. Second Edition. Extra fcap. 8vo. 1*s*. 6*d*.

Plato. Selections (for Schools). Edited, with Notes, by J. Purves, M.A. Extra fcap. 8vo. 6*s*. 6*d*.

Sophocles. In Single Plays, with English Notes, &c. By Lewis Campbell, M.A., and Evelyn Abbott, M.A. Extra fcap. 8vo. limp.

Oedipus Tyrannus, Philoctetes. New and Revised Edition, 2*s*. each.
Oedipus Coloneus, Antigone, 1*s*. 9*d*. each.
Ajax, Electra, Trachiniae, 2*s*. each.

—— *Oedipus Rex:* Dindorf's Text, with Notes by the present Bishop of St. David's. Ext. fcap. 8vo. limp, 1*s*. 6*d*.

Theocritus (for Schools). With Notes. By H. Kynaston, M.A. (late Snow). Third Edition. Extra fcap. 8vo. 4*s*. 6*d*.

Xenophon. Easy Selections. (for Junior Classes). With a Vocabulary, Notes, and Map. By J. S. Phillpotts, B.C.L., and C. S. Jerram, M.A. Third Edition. Extra fcap. 8vo. 3*s*. 6*d*.

—— *Selections* (for Schools). With Notes and Maps. By J. S. Phillpotts, B.C.L. Fourth Edition. Extra fcap. 8vo. 3*s*. 6*d*.

—— *Anabasis*, Book II. With Notes and Map. By C. S. Jerram, M.A. Extra fcap. 8vo. 2*s*.

—— *Cyropaedia*, Books IV and V. With Introduction and Notes by C. Bigg, D.D. Extra fcap. 8vo. 2*s*. 6*d*.

Aristotle's Politics. By W. L. Newman, M.A. [*In preparation.*]

Aristotelian Studies. I. On the Structure of the Seventh Book of the Nicomachean Ethics. By J. C. Wilson, M.A. 1879. Medium 8vo. stiff, 5*s*.

Demosthenes and Aeschines. The Orations of Demosthenes and Æschines on the Crown. With Introductory Essays and Notes. By G. A. Simcox, M.A., and W. H. Simcox, M.A. 1872. 8vo. 12*s*.

Geldart (*E. M., B.A.*). *The Modern Greek Language* in its relation to Ancient Greek. Extra fcap. 8vo. 4*s*. 6*d*.

Hicks (*E. L., M.A.*). *A Manual of Greek Historical Inscriptions.* Demy 8vo. 10*s*. 6*d*.